Commentary on True and False Religion

ZWINGLI

Edited by
Samuel Macauley Jackson
and
Clarence Nevin Heller

The Labyrinth Press
Durham, North Carolina 27701
1981

Library of Congress Cataloging in Publication Data

Zwingli, Ulrich, 1484–1531.
Commentary on true and false religion.

Translation of: De vera et falsa religione commentarius.
Reprint. Originally published: The Latin works and the correspondence of Huldreich Zwingli, v. 3, issued under title: The Latin works of Huldreich Zwingli. Philadelphia: Heidelberg Press, 1929.
Includes index.
1. Theology, Doctrinal—Early works to 1800.
I. Jackson, Samuel Macauley, 1851–1912. II. Heller, Clarence Nevin. III. Title.
BT70.Z8713 1981 2308.42 81-8272

ISBN 0-939464-00-4
Printed in the United States of America

PREFACE

THE earliest truly comprehensive treatise on Protestant theology is here presented in English for the first time. To be sure, Melanchthon's famous *Loci Theologici* of 1521 antedates by four years Zwingli's *De Vera et Falsa Religione,* but it does not deal with the full-orbed Protestant faith, emphasizing rather special points then in controversy. A venerated teacher of mine, the late Professor Wilhelm Herrmann of Marburg, once declared that he could predict most of the arguments that would be employed in a new book on systematic divinity by merely analyzing the sequence of topics in its table of contents. By this test, Melanchthon is seen to have been influenced by the sequence used by St. Paul in the Epistle to the Romans;[1] whereas Zwingli presents an original and far more comprehensive plan of arrangement[2] and, therefore, justifies the claim that among Protestant system-builders he is the pioneer.

Zwingli's reply to his critic, Jerome Emser, which is called for short the *Antibolon* (1524), also finds a place in this present volume, for Zwingli quotes it frequently and at length in his *True and False Religion.*

The Latin text here followed is that of the third volume of the critical edition: *Huldreich Zwinglis Sämtliche Werke unter Mitwirkung des Zwingli-Vereins in Zürich herausgegeben von Emil Egli, Georg Finsler und Walther Köhler* (Leipzig, 1914). Since the Great War the publication of this series has been resumed by the firm of Heinsius in Leipzig.

Translations of both these treatises were prepared nearly a generation ago for the late Professor Samuel Macauley Jackson,

[1]See Philippi Melanthonis Opera quae Supersunt Omnia, ed. H. E. Bindseil, vol. XXI (Brunsvigae, 1854) p. 82, also p. 74.

[2]Egli, Finsler and Köhler, III, 912.

D.D., LL.D., of New York University. The *True and False Religion* was translated by Henry Preble, Esq., of New York, a classical philologian. To make his version conform more closely to the dialect of theologians, it was later reviewed by the Reverend Charles Tupper Baillie, B.D., now pastor of the Second Presbyterian Church, Bloomington, Illinois. The *Reply to Emser* was translated by Professor George William Gilmore, M.A., of New York. Both translations have now been carefully revised and annotated by Clarence Nevin Heller, Litt.D., Librarian of the Theological Seminary of the Reformed Church in the United States at Lancaster, Pennsylvania.

At the suggestion of several members of the American Society of Church History, each tract is preceded by an historical, analytical, and interpretative introduction prepared by the Reverend George W. Richards, D.D., LL.D., D.Th., President and Professor of Church History in the Seminary at Lancaster. Dr. Richards has used certain material from the German prefaces in the Egli and Finsler edition, as specifically authorized in a letter of its editors printed in facsimile in the first volume of the present series. It is hoped that these introductions will enable students to understand Zwingli more readily and will win fresh appreciation of his importance in the evolution of Protestant thought.

The present volume is the third of a series of five or six projected by Dr. Jackson, author of the well-known biography of Zwingli (1901). In a circular signed on March 29, 1912, a few months before his death, Dr. Jackson directed that "in case his own editorial labors should be interfered with by invalidism or death, the work will be brought to completion under the supervision of the American Society of Church History and under the immediate direction of the Secretary of this Society, the Rev. Professor William Walker Rockwell." The Society duly accepted this project, but had no money to appropriate for the purpose.

As stated in the Preface to Volume II, the Reverend James I. Good, D.D., was for many years most active in making financial preparations to insure publication. Since Dr. Good's death, which occurred at Philadelphia on January 21, 1924, there has been reprinted from the *Papers of the American Soci-*

ety of Church History (second series, volume VIII, 1928) the memorial address by Dr. Richards, which appraises his services to the cause of church history in the United States.

Dr. Good was chairman of a committee appointed by the General Synod of the Reformed Church in the United States on the publication of the Latin works of Zwingli in translation. The first volume appeared in 1912; the second in 1922. Some of the funds which make possible the publication of the present volume were procured from private individuals and some by appropriations of denominations belonging to the Western Section of the Alliance of Reformed Churches holding the Presbyterian System (see volume II, page vi).

After Dr. Good's death, Dr. George W. Richards, of the Theological Seminary of the Reformed Church in the United States at Lancaster, Pennsylvania, served as chairman of the committee. The funds held by Dr. Good were paid to him by the administrator of the estate. To supplement that money, the General Synod of the Reformed Church in the United States, meeting at Philadelphia, Pennsylvania, in 1926, appropriated six hundred dollars for the publication of the present volume.

The projected fourth volume will contain Zwingli's writings on the Eucharist, to be edited by Professor Robert Hastings Nichols, Ph.D., D.D., of the Auburn Theological Seminary. In the opinion of the undersigned, it is not fair to Dr. Nichols to ask him actually to begin the arduous labor of revising and editing Mr. Preble's translations until money is raised to guarantee their publication As Eucharistic doctrines held a central place in sixteenth century discussions, the fourth volume—an important aid to understanding the Protestant Reformation—will be a large one.

To complete the publication of the Latin Works will require a fifth volume. The slow progress of the critical edition of Egli, Finsler and Köhler makes it difficult to give as yet a list of all that it should include. Many parts of it are on hand in Mr. Preble's translations.

The extensive and valuable correspondence of Zwingli has also been translated on the basis of the old edition of Schuler and Schulthess. This should be revised in accordance with the critical text of Egli, Finsler, and Köhler and printed, probably as a sixth and concluding volume.

May the public-spirited labors of Drs. Jackson, Good, and Richards be rewarded before long by the completion of the project of making available in English, the language spoken by the largest linguistic group of Protestants, the Latin works of a valiant Protestant pioneer.

William Walker Rockwell.

New York, April 27, 1929.

CONTENTS

The Works of Huldreich Zwingli

I

Commentary on True and False Religion

INTRODUCTION
BY
GEORGE WARREN RICHARDS

IN the Preface and the Address to the Reader, Zwingli tells how he came to write the Commentary. "Many men in Italy and more in France, learned and devout," urged him "to write out in Latin his religious views for them." The request probably was made when Farel, Anton du Blet, and other men from Lyons came to Zurich in the spring of 1524. He shrank in "modesty" from such an undertaking, but "the high standing and importunity" of the men constrained him to yield to their wishes. He was prevented, however, by "various occupations" from beginning the task before the latter part of the year 1524. In a letter to Zwingli, dated October 7, 1524, Anton Papilio assumes that the former had undertaken to write a book, entitled, *De vera et falsa religione commentarius.* Having put his hand to the pen, he toiled incessantly, "sweating night and day for three and a half months"—a comparatively short time for so weighty a treatise. He regrets the fact that he was "so hurried all along, that I often hardly had a chance to reread what I had written, much less to correct or embellish it." The author was now in the "forty-second year of his age."

The book came from the press at the end of March, 1525. Zwingli sent a copy to Vadian (March 31) and one to Christoph Schappeler at Memmingen. Ludwig Sigwyn, of Swabia, is known to have had a copy by August 23, 1525; it was probably a gift from the author. Thus the new publication served to propagate Zwinglian doctrine in South Germany. A German edition of 608 octavo pages, translated by Leo Jude, was published in 1526 by Froschauer at Zurich. Professor Walther Köhler, of the University of Zurich, translated part of the Commentary into German and incorporated it in his work, entitled, *Ulrich Zwingli, eine Auswahl aus seinen Schriften,* Zurich, 1918.

Zwingli selected the name "commentary" for his book, because "commentaries, if I rightly understand the word," he says, "are means of communicating with friends, just as a letter is, save that commentaries are fuller and freer. . . . Since, therefore, I wanted to communicate with the most learned men of France on the subject of religion, I determined to send them a commentary." He apologized, also, for his haste in writing the book and excused his neglect to revise the manuscript for the reason that a commentary did not require the same accuracy of composition "as an oration or a book that had been held back eight years." The phrase, "true and false religion," does not refer, as one would today expect, to the Christian religion in distinction from the pagan religions; but, to use his own words, to "true and false religion as displayed by Christians." The "true religion" is that which is drawn from "the true fountains of the word of God"; the "false religion" is "superstition" taken from the traditions and opinions of men. The one is the religion of the Reformers; the other of the Catholic Church. He considers the two kinds of religion at the same time because "we get a clearer idea by comparing together things that are different than by portraying the one in elaborate detail and keeping the other out of sight." He describes his method of procedure as follows: "I shall speak first of 'true religion,' then of 'false'; not in separate and distinct books, but in distinct sections." The purpose of the treatise is to show the difference and conflict between the true religion of the Bible and the false religion of tradition and reason.

The author dedicated his book "to Francis, the most Christian King of France, the first of his name." The dedication is not a little surprising, because Zwingli vigorously opposed the party in the Swiss Confederacy playing French politics and boldly denounced the mercenary service of Swiss soldiers in the French army. He addressed the French King, however, wholly for religious reasons: "I have written especially for the good of France and, therefore, nothing could be more proper than to dedicate my production to her king."

He had reasonable hopes of winning the king's favor for the evangelical cause. Zwingli had entered into friendly relations, either through personal visits or through letters and theological writings, with prominent men in France. Among these were Glarean and a circle of kindred spirits in Paris, Faber Stapulensis, Lambert of Avignon, Anemond de Coct, and Anton du Blet. These men were humanists and most of them biblical reformers. The King himself was friendly to the new learning, and his sister, Margaret of Navarre, was a patron and protector of the reform party. It was, therefore, not beyond the range of probability for France to be won for the Reformation.

He gives three reasons for his address to the King of France. First, "this Commentary most Christian ought to be dedicated to none but the Most Christian King"; second, the people of France have from ancient times been reputed faithful to religion; to whom, therefore, could a "Commentary on True and False Religion" be more appropriately dedicated; third, Germany owes it to her neighbor, France, to share with her the light of truth which has recently been given her.

His hopes of winning Francis I. to his cause were not realized. For the king lent neither ear nor heart to the evangelical doctrine, but permitted his religious policy to be determined by political considerations. The theologians of the Sorbonne, to whom Zwingli repeatedly refers in biting phrases, made short work of the Commentary by putting it on the Index. France remained a Catholic land.

The author evidently planned a complete survey of Christian doctrine—the first and only systematic presentation of his theology. Professor Walther Köhler considers it Zwingli's "most mature and comprehensive work, containing a whole system of doctrine—a dogmatic and an ethics." The two books comparable with it are Melancthon's *Loci Communes,* 1521, and Calvin's *Institutio Christianae Religionis,* 1536.

The purpose of Melancthon was not to present a complete system of Christian doctrine, rather a brief exposition of the way of salvation based upon the Epistle to the Romans and a guide to the intelligent reader of the Bible. Calvin, following the lead of Zwingli's Commentary, prepared a more extended exposition of the true doctrine, which largely superseded the Commentary and became the foremost exposition of the faith published in the sixteenth century. It also was addressed to the *"Most Potent and Illustrious Monarch, Francis the Most Christian King of the Franks."*

The material of the Commentary is divided into twenty-nine sections. In the first eleven the author defines the term religion; its two factors, God and man; the person and work of Christ; the gospel and repentance. He adds, to the exposition of these points, sections nine, ten, and eleven in the form of *loci* on the law and on sin. This completes his presentation of the essentials of Christianity; it is the positive and definitive part of the treatise.

The remaining eighteen sections are loosely connected and are more polemical in tone. Zwingli criticises the Catholic doctrine of the Keys, the Church, and the Sacraments. Under each head he defines the biblical view in distinction from that of the Roman Church. He enters upon a detailed discussion of the sacraments of baptism, the eucharist, confession, and matrimony. He adds sections on vows, invocation of saints, merit, prayer, purgatory, government, and closes somewhat abruptly with two points—one on offences and another on statues and images. In a brief epilogue he sets forth in a concise way the Christian gospel in relation to the religious development of humanity.

The author omits scarcely any important point in Christian doctrine. Whatever is lacking or inadequately developed in the Commentary, he adds in two later tracts—the one, "On Original Sin, to Urbanus Rhegius"; and the other, "Of the Provi-

See vol. II: 1-32; 128-234

dence of God." The work is not an organic whole in the sense that every part is genetically related to every other and that all the parts are united by a single unifying principle—a garment of one cloth. The author wrote too hurriedly to produce a book of that kind. Yet the Commentary is the major writing of Zwingli; the next to it in significance is his *Auslegung der Schlussreden,* 1523. The Lutherans of Germany, however, valued his tracts on the Lord's Supper more highly than the Commentary.

SECTIONS 1-11

Religion defined

Zwingli, like Cicero in his *De Natura Deorum,* derives the term "religion" from the Latin verb, "relegere." "Because the religious," he says, "carefully consider and, as it were, peruse (relegerent) all the things that pertain to the worship of the gods." In its Christian usage, as Zwingli also takes it, the term "embraces the whole piety of Christians: namely, faith, life, laws, worship, sacraments."

Two factors are involved in religion in general: God, who is reached out toward, and man, who reaches out toward Him. To understand religion we must know both God and man. In the discussion of these two factors Zwingli does not take his material from the history of religions or the psychology of religion, as a modern philosopher of religion would do, but he confines himself almost wholly to the Bible for his knowledge of God and of man. For, apart from revelation, man cannot by natural reason or human effort of any kind know God. He may discern "that God *is,*" but he cannot know *"what* God is." The heathen recognized the existence of God, "though in widely different ways." "Some," says Zwingli, "have made Him many, others have made Him fewer, and a very few have made Him one." The knowledge of the philosophers, also, is obtained through revelation. According to Paul (Romans 1:19), "That which is known of God is manifest in them; for God manifested it to them." He manifested Himself through natural agency, which is "the constant and uninterrupted operation of God, His disposition of all things." Even the intellect, by which we can in a measure know God, comes from Him "who worketh all in all." In this way nature and the

GOD

spirit of man confirm the truth of biblical revelation. The natural knowledge of God is also a revelation "through the things He has made." Zwingli does not make the distinction in principle between the Christian's and the philosopher's knowledge of God.

The "pious" believe in the one true God, not because they have natural endowments superior to those of the "impious," nor because they read or hear the word of Scripture, but through "the power and grace of Him in whom we believe." In other words, "they are taught this of God." That the Christian believes that God exists, and that he has faith in Him, is a work of God alone. For the knowledge of "what God is," of his being in distinction from his mere existence, Zwingli depends wholly upon "the divine oracles." He desires "to learn out of His own mouth what God is." So wide is the difference between God and man, that man can know what God is "as little as a beetle can know what man is." Therefore man must "be taught by God Himself" (I Cor. 2: 11).

He leaves room, however, for his favorite philosophers—Plato, Seneca, and Cicero—whom he concedes to have "uttered certain truths on this subject." But whatever is true of what they said, they received from God, who scattered "seeds of knowledge of Himself" even among the heathen. Of "the theologians," who confuse divine revelation and "the inventions of philosophers," he speaks in terms of contempt. They "are puffed up with human wisdom and have corrupted what they received pure." They are full of the "arrogance of the flesh" and have held "such views as they liked about God."

Zwingli is equally opposed to rationalism and semi-rationalism. He is a supernaturalist and an irrationalist. He renounces reason as a source of knowledge of God and he denounces the compromising theologians who seek to know God partly through reason and partly through revelation. Theoretically, at least, he is a pure biblicist. By explaining his theory of knowledge in a prefatory section, he paves the way for his exposition of the revealed doctrine and never loses sight of the contrast between the truth of God as revealed in the Bible and "the dreams and lies" about God taken from human reason. He is, however, far more uncompromising in his biblicism when he meets the Catholic theologians than when he greets the ancient philosophers.

In the first part of his discussion of the being of God, he is betrayed by the natural bent of his mind into a philosophical and empirical treatment of the doctrine of providence and of the goodness of God, without appeal to biblical texts. Only at the end of his argument, he turns for support of his conclusions to the Bible. He defines the character of God in five points, using Jehovah's words to Moses, "I am that I am" (Ex. 3:13), as the source of his material. In reality he turns philosopher and reasons about the divine attributes, supporting his conclusions by an occasional text from the Bible. First, he declares that God is absolute and pure being, "from whom all things are," since they "could not possibly exist for a moment unless God existed." He "sustains all things, governs all things" (Isa. 4:12). Second, "This being is alone good, true, right, just, holy." Third, He is "perfect, efficient, and consummating power," who continually "so keeps, directs, and governs everything, that in all things made or done no fault can intervene able either to impede its power or to defeat its purpose." Four, God as motive power and life of all things "is not only a sort of stuff," but conscious intellect and will—in other words, "wisdom and foresight"; so that "nothing is unknown to Him, nothing is disobedient to Him." Five, God is not only absolute wisdom and controlling providence, but He is, also, perfect goodness and benevolence, who is unceasingly bountiful to those whom He created for no other purpose than to enjoy His bounty.

Thus he begins his argument with God as absolute being, the source of all being, and concludes with the idea that He is the absolute Good, the source of all good. The Absolute is the Holy and Righteous One of the Bible.

Zwingli may be charged with pantheism and determinism. Some of his statements have a pantheistic tone; as, for example, "He is the being of all things." Yet he was in reality a Christian theist, saved from pantheism by the sharp contrast he drew between the Creator and the creature—a distinction which was "the master light of all his seeing."

One cannot so easily absolve him from the charge of

determinism. He says more than once that God is life and motion of all things and permits no fortuitous occurrences, not even the free initiative of men. The God of providence becomes also the God of unconditional predestination. This is close to determinism, not of the impersonal naturalistic, but of the personal, spiritual kind. Zwingli was forced to take this position by the emphasis of his opponents upon human ability or freedom, which was the necessary presupposition of works having saving efficacy, such as sacrifices, fasting, alms, and meritorious performances of all sorts. But when he steered clear of the Scylla of righteousness by dint of human effort, he was borne by the currents uncomfortably close to the Charybdis of salvation by divine necessity. Predestination is the inevitable outcome of his assumption that God is the only active cause operative in all His creatures. Yet in this way he finds sufficient warrant for ascribing the cause and glory of salvation to God alone, and not in part to the self-achieved righteousness of man. To do him full justice one must always read the philosophical conclusions of Zwingli in connection with his biblical doctrines. "No man," he says, "can reproach me with having based my teachings about the knowledge of God upon human persuasions." In the same paragraph he adds: "I have shown without reserve that it is not through human power that we come to the knowledge and worship of God," for that "is not of him that willeth, nor of him that runneth, but of God that hath mercy" (Romans 9:16).

He concludes his section on God by asking the question: "What does such a discussion avail?" The godless cast it to the winds; the devout do not need it. For they know God through experience and not through argument or reason. God graciously manifests Himself in their hearts and begets faith in them. This statement clearly shows Zwingli's theory of the way of knowing God. Philosopher though he was and naturally inclined to convince others of the truth by logical argument, he always acknowledged in the end the limitations of the human reason and bowed in submission to the authority of divine revelation and devout living, which man cannot attain by effort but must ultimately receive through faith.

In his discussion of man, the second factor of religion,

Zwingli assumes that man can no more know man than he can know God. "The knowledge of God," he says, "is denied to our understanding because of its feebleness and His glory and splendor, but the knowledge of man because of his boldness and readiness in lying and dissembling." As "the cuttlefish hides himself in his own blackness," so does man conceal himself "in thick clouds of hypocrisy." The author, accordingly, does not confer with flesh and blood, that is, with science and history, for his doctrine of man, but turns directly to the sacred oracles. For "under no other teacher or guide than God alone will it ever be granted to see the secrets of the human heart." Faith, however, he considers as indispensable for knowing man as for knowing God. "For unless faith be present," he says, "so that a man believes that every word that proceedeth from the mouth of God is true, he will be as far from knowing himself as is the distance between spirit and flesh."

He begins the discussion of the nature and character of man with the fall and the consequent sinful state of man. Man was tempted by the devil, whom Zwingli puts in place of the serpent, and was lured by his wife to disobey God's command. The impulse to yield to temptation was man's *philautia* (self-love), which was the tap-root of his fatal desire to be like God and to know good and evil. The immediate result of his sin was death, not the death of the body but of the soul. This amounted to nothing less than the complete perversion of his moral nature—"to love himself more than God, more than any one; this at last is to be dead, this is the death that is sin, this is the character of corrupted fallen man."

Zwingli was a radical pessimist in his estimate of man's condition after the fall; his was the pessimism which underlies Paul's doctrine of redemption. His conception of sin as disease (morbus, Bresten) does not minimize his pessimistic idea of the natural man. He declares relentless war against the semi-Pelagianism of Rome and against the optimism of Erasmus expounded in his recently published *De libero arbitrio.*

His theory of salvation was the direct outcome of his doctrine of depravity. "To become a devout Christian," he says, "one must despair of oneself and cleave to God only." He conceded no saving value to human efforts: trust in them in any form ended in the total perversion of religion. In a passage that sears and blisters, he pillories his adversaries, saying of them: "Your distinguished theologians and hypocrites of animal appetite, not knowing this [that man is altogether bad], are satisfied—to quote but one of their views belonging to false religion—to grant that man's heart is prone to evil; at the same time attributing to him unimpaired power of choice, so as to be able freely to stretch out his hand towards anything he chooses. This is nothing else than trying to weave a rope of sand or to make an angel out of Belial." This doctrine of the unimpaired power of choice was, in Zwingli's opinion, the fontal source of all the ills of the Catholic Church. For it made room for saving merit in man, the creature, and to that extent detracted from the honor that belongs solely and wholly to God the Creator.

RELIGION

After a prolonged analysis and definition of the two factors of religion, he proceeds to consider the relation of God and man in religion, not without repetition of ideas in the preceding sections. He keeps close to the Bible and, without further ado, he traces the beginning of religion to God's call of Adam hiding in the garden. "Religion took its rise when God called runaway man back to him . . . O wonderful and unspeakable graciousness of the heavenly Father!" Here he is in accord with Melancthon, who, also, found, in the third chapter of Genesis, the sin, repentance, and justification of Adam.

He presupposes two conditions as fundamental in his idea of religion: God's initiative and man's response to divine grace. The "nakedness of Adam" symbolizes the utter helplessness and hopelessness of man. Instead of venturing to return to God he flees from Him. Zwingli asks the "theologians," Catholic and humanist, whom he has always before him: "Does it seem as if Adam would ever have come back of his own motion to ask for grace?" He himself answers the question: "You will certainly admit that he would not have returned, if the Lord had not followed him in his flight." He prods them still more, saying, "Why, then, will you not admit that the acquired faith (*fides acquisita*) about which you talk so much is a fiction?" He is convinced that his feet are planted on a rock when he cites the words of Jesus: "For no man is able to come to me unless the Father draw him."

Man's extremity, however, is God's opportunity. "He judged more kindly than the guilt deserved" and received back into favor "this traitorous deserter." Without the initiative of divine grace there would have been no religion. To put it in a negative form in Zwingli's own words: "Suppose God abandons Adam, he will never come back to Him from whom he has fled." Hence the general principle: "Suppose God abandons man; he will never seek Him by whom he was created."

The second condition of religion is that man responds to God's call and accepts the proferred grace. Man cries out of the depths of despair—a despondency that is born of God's revelation of man to himself. In the light of the divine word he sees his own sin and misery, so that "he utterly despairs of himself." Then only does God freely manifest His bountiful grace, which is irresistible and cannot be taken from him. For a man whom God calls "is forced to respond whether he will or not."

The effect of God's grace is "the clinging of man to God," the "constant adhesion to Him with unshaken trust in Him as the only Good." But Zwingli's strong ethical bent would not suffer man merely to cling to God and in a mystic way enjoy His grace. True religion includes "an eagerness to live according to the will of God." "Christians therefore will anxiously and unceasingly pore over, study, and consider the ways in which they can please Him and deserve well of Him." The way of serving God is to be found in His word alone—to which "we shall add nothing" and from which "we take away nothing." But "they only can understand the word of God who are born of the Spirit or are drawn of Him."

After he has defined the human side of religion, he directs a winged, piercing shaft at the "impious." "It is, therefore, madness and utter impiety to put enactments and decrees of certain men or councils upon an equality with the word of God." To trust in any other than God's word is *falsa religio*; "to hang upon the utterances of God alone" is *vera religio*.

Zwingli never fails to combine grace and law in the Christian life. In opposition to Erasmus and all forms of humanism, he emphasizes man's total disability and the sole sufficiency of divine grace. In the face of Rome he puts emphasis upon law and obedience—but law as revealed in the Bible and obedience motived by loyalty to Him who saves. He escapes bald heteronomy and servile submission to authority by blending, in the religious life, the divine favor of forgiveness, the revelation of the Scriptures, and the enlightening and compelling spirit of God in the soul. Man obeys the will of God, accordingly, without coercion of law through the free volition of love. This is the vital principle of Reformed ethics and the heart of Reformed piety.

THE CHRISTIAN RELIGION

So far Zwingli has discussed religion and its two factors—God and man—without special reference to Christ; yet he has no thought of religion save as it is revealed in the Scriptures. Its essential content is the immediate relation between God and man, growing out of faith in God's grace and expressing itself in paternal and filial piety, which might be described as a sort of prophetic monotheism. He fails to show how this relation is realized through Christ and His atoning death. In his interpretation of religion he is theocentric rather than Christocentric. He does not approach God through Christ but Christ through God, as we may infer from his own words: "The knowledge of God precedes the knowledge of Christ."

He formulates the fundamental thesis of the section on the Christian religion as follows: "Christ is the certainty and pledge of the grace of God" (*certitudo et pignus gratiae Dei*). This Wernle* terms the basal idea of the Zwinglian theology. What he hitherto assumed he now explains by showing Christ's part in God's redemptive work. His treatment of Christ is wholly controlled by soteriological motives.

The author finds the rational ground for the assurance of divine grace in the Anselmic theory of satisfaction. For once he agrees with the "theologians" who say that "God's justice must be satisfied." But he is quick to denounce the scholastic assertion, "*facere quod in se est*" (that man is to do what is in him), as a shallow and false estimate of human nature, rendering the satisfaction of Christ superfluous. Those who teach this doctrine "do not know either the righteousness of

***Der evangelische Glaube nach den Hauptschriften der Reformatoren*, vol. 2, "Zwingli" (Tübingen, 1919) p. 171.

God or the actual unrighteousness of man." God alone therefore can provide satisfaction; and He has done so through His incarnate Son. In a single paragraph Zwingli concisely summarizes the way of salvation. "God enlightens us," he says, "so that we may know ourselves. When this happens we are driven to despair. We flee for refuge to His mercy, but justice frightens us. His eternal wisdom finds a way by which to satisfy His justice—a thing wholly denied to ourselves—and at the same time to enable us, relying on His mercy, to enjoy Him. He sends His Son to satisfy His justice for us, and to be the indubitable pledge of salvation; but on condition that we become new creatures and that we walk having put on Christ. The whole life of the Christian, therefore, is repentance. For when do we not sin?" The last clause is almost identical with the first of the Ninety-five Theses of Luther.

In an unusually significant, though rather incidental, passage, Zwingli assures us that God did not require the satisfaction of divine justice to protect Himself against "the adversary," the Devil, or because the Potter was not free to make out of the clay whatever vessel He chose. It was the purpose of God "that by this example of justice He might remove drowsiness and sloth from us and show us what sort of being He was—just, good, merciful." Zwingli also warns the reader not to inquire too boldly into the counsel of God, but to rest satisfied with the words, "It so pleased Him." In other words, Zwingli intimates that Christ's atoning work had effect upon God, and, by way of example, deeply influenced man. The atoning death of Christ, therefore, had value not only for God but also for man—a distinctly Zwinglian idea. Christ was clothed in flesh (*carne indutus*), not merely to satisfy the justice of God so that in mercy He might redeem men; but, also, that "the divine majesty in coming into contact with the earthly world would not be too terrifying; or, conversely, to beget hope in men, when in Christ, the Almighty Son of God, they see a brother." This "unheard-of and extraordinary fact" was conceived by God only with the beginning of human misery (*ab exordio humanae miseriae proposita praeceptaque est*). Zwingli finds the first evidence of God's redemptive purpose in Genesis 3: 15—clearly an infralapsarian point of view.

The incarnation of Christ was foretold in prophecies, types, and symbols throughout the Old Testament. It was accomplished through birth from the Virgin, who remained ever virgin, so that Christ would be sinless and holy, since the sacrificial victim had to be free from blemish. Following Paul's idea of the first and second Adam, Zwingli draws a contrast between the two in ten theses, in order to show how the ills brought upon men by the sin of the first Adam were healed by the righteousness of the second Adam.

The life and doctrines of the historical Jesus are considered under three aspects: 1. His birth in a stable, His boyhood, and His subjection to His parents, to prove the poverty, humility, and humanity of the Savior; 2. the miracles and benevolent work as evidence of His divine mission and authority; 3. the passion, following in detail the record in the Gospels, showing how He triumphed over death and hell, through His death, His descent into hell, His resurrection, and His glorification. "All this I have briefly narrated . . . in order to make clear to every beholder the righteousness of Christ by which He healed the wound of Adam."

Of the character of Jesus, His teaching in parables and in the Sermon on the Mount, the quality and beauty of His life, he makes no mention; nor does he say what Christ meant for him in his own heart and struggle for life, as friend, companion, comforter, and co-worker. Zwingli writes as a theologian and defines Jesus the Savior in the language of dogma. To do him full justice we must listen to him as a preacher in the Grossmünster, when he thrills his hearers with the call of the Savior: "Come unto me, all ye that labor and are heavy-laden, and I will give you rest."

THE GOSPEL

The result of the redemptive work of Christ is set forth in the section on the Gospel, which opens with the words: "Christ suffered all these things for us." Gospel is the good news "that sins are remitted in the name of Christ." He defines what it is, what it does, and how it is to be received. The word itself means "good tidings." In Mark 16: 15-16, we are told what the gospel does—"it is a thing which saves believers." In Luke 24: 45-47, we are told what the gospel is—"that repentance and remission of sins should be preached in his name unto all nations." "No heart ever received tidings more glad." But gospel becomes "glad tidings" only to those who despair of themselves, which comes from a knowledge of ourselves in the light of God. "The divine Spirit alone enables man to know himself." Through a knowledge of his sins man is brought to repentance and finds refuge in divine grace. "For when our consciences are laboring amid narrows and cliffs of despair, what tidings more joyful can be brought us than that there is at hand a redeemer who will bring us forth into a large place, and a deliverer and leader who can do all things, for he is God." The gospel includes more than the offer of forgiveness; it "teaches us to embrace not only grace but a new life." He sounds the ethical note: "Our lives and characters must be changed; for to be a Christian is nothing less than to be a new man and a new creature." Zwingli reiterates his conviction that moral living is the fruit of divine grace, though divine grace does not depend on moral endeavor.

REPENTANCE

Although in the section on the gospel repentance was discussed, Zwingli devotes a whole chapter to its further consideration. He calls attention to the wide difference between evangelical repentance and Catholic penance under priestly directions. The latter he regards as a mere caricature of the former. The evangelical Christian has deeper insight into his sin and misery, at least theoretically, than the average Roman Catholic. When men despair of themselves they can not be satisfied with works of merit but are driven to find refuge in Christ's merits alone. Repentance does not cleanse men of their sins but it is a safeguard against lapsing into the sins of which they repent. Even though "men constantly sin through the weakness of the flesh, their sins are not imputed unto them, because of their faith." God requires that men bring forth fruits worthy of repentance. It does not suffice that we are baptized or that we say: Lord, Lord; but we must do the will of the Father. Zwingli has little or no understanding of sacramental mysticism; he transforms everything into ethical living. "All the writings of the apostles are filled with this idea, namely, that the Christian religion is nothing else than a firm hope in God through Jesus Christ and a blameless life wrought after the pattern of Christ as far as he giveth us." On the basis of Scripture Zwingli proclaims the paradox that men are saved only through Christ and yet a good life is demanded of those who are saved.

Zwingli concludes the first part of his exposition of the essential elements of "true religion" with two brief chapters on The Law and Sin.

THE LAW

Law is defined "as nothing else than the eternal will of God." The term does not include civil laws, "which have to do with the outer man" and which "change with the exigencies of the times," or ceremonial laws, which were "abolished by Christ." The divine law, to which he refers, has to do "with the inner man" and is "eternal." It is written by God "into the heart of man." Through the law men are to come to a knowledge of sin; but it also serves to point the way of life. It is not abolished by Christ, though He is the end of the law. In Him it is fulfilled through love: love is the fulfilment of the whole law. "They, therefore, who serve under Christ are bound to do that which love orders; what love does not order or what does not proceed from love either is not enjoined or is not profitable."

SIN

Zwingli is alone among the three great reformers in making the distinction between man's sinful nature and his actual sins. He distinguishes between inborn sin (called *morbus* in Latin, *Bresten* is Swiss German), which comes from Adam, and actual sins, which are voluntary transgressions of the law of God. "Sin that is transgression is born of sin that is disease." Inborn sin, the old man, the flesh, are synonymous terms. The primary motive of sinful man is philautia, self-love, which impels us to flee virtue and to pursue lusts, and to resist and to strive against the law of nature—"love thy neighbor as thyself." Men left to themselves would consume and destroy one another, unless God had hedged in man's selfish desires by the restraint of the natural law: "What thou wouldst that man do unto thee, do thou unto others."

We are freed from law for the breaking of which we are under condemnation. We are not freed from it in the sense that we are not bound to observe it, for it is unchangeable and eternal. We are freed only through love, "for he that loves does all things freely." He adds: "God, therefore, has put in our hearts a fire by which to kindle love of Him in place of love of ourselves." When this love burns in us we shall do all things not by compulsion but freely and cheerfully. Thus we are freed from law because we spontaneously obey it. We are free from law when we are in Christ Jesus: for us there is then no condemnation. We are sons, and therefore not under law but under grace.

Experience, however, proves that even those who are in Christ continue to sin. The life of the Christian, as appears in Romans VII, is a continual conflict between the law of sin and the law of the spirit of life. It leads men to cry out in despair: "Who will deliver me from this body of flesh?" Zwingli found solace in Paul's triumphal cry: "Thanks be unto God who giveth us the victory through Jesus Christ our Lord." "By these words," he says, "I think the very perplexing problem with which we are struggling is cleared up, viz., how it happens that a blamelessness is demanded which we can not possibly offer, and yet Christ is the efficient guarantee for the sins of all." This is one of the glaring paradoxes of the Christian life. Another follows close on the first: "Man therefore is ever dead, as is shown by his works; at the same time he ever lives, as is perceived by the anguish of his soul." So long as man has faith he never ceases to lament his unhappy proneness to sin; only when faith dies out does he become indifferent and callous to sin and the fear of God.

THE SIN AGAINST THE HOLY GHOST

This form of unbelief (*infidelitatum et incredulitatum*) is the unpardonable sin against the Holy Ghost. Unbelief is "the sin unto death." The author defines it at length: "It is, therefore, lack of faith alone, which we call infidelity or disbelief, that is never forgiven; for it never lays hold of or worships God, never fears Him, never regulates itself according to His will, never avoids sin not to offend Him."

SECTIONS 12-29

In the last eighteen sections Zwingli expounds the more practical aspects of the way of salvation—the keys, the government and discipline of the church, the meaning and administration of the sacraments, marriage, vows, invocation of saints, prayer, purgatory, magistrates, statues and images. In each section he contrasts the view of true religion with that of false religion—the one held by the Reformers, the other by the Roman Catholics. In some of the sections, as for example, that on the sacraments, he also distinguishes his own view and that of his associates from the teaching of the Lutherans and the Anabaptists.

THE KEYS

The office of the keys is power to loose and to bind as defined and conferred in John 20: 22-23: "Receive ye the Holy Spirit: whose soever sins ye forgive, they are forgiven unto them; whose soever sins ye retain, they are retained." In the author's words, "to loose is nothing else than to raise to sure hope the heart that is despairing of salvation; to bind is to abandon the obstinate heart." "To abandon" is explained by the words of Jesus: "And whosoever shall not receive you, nor hear your words as ye go forth out of that house or that city, shake off the dust of your feet." Again he says: "The keys are what sets free the captive conscience." The conscience is freed and the soul is comforted "when, under the illumination of the Holy Spirit, we understand the mystery of Christ and trust in Him." This illumination takes place when "the apostles preach repentance and remission of sin in His name, and those who hear and believe in His name are freed from their sins and consoled in their hearts." When the apostles were given authority to "preach the gospel," they received the office of the keys. "Here then are the keys which Christ committed to the apostles, by which they unlocked the gates of Heaven—they preached the gospel."

In the face of the papists he vigorously denies that the power of the keys is the right to lord it over the flock or to exploit it for one's own pleasure or profit. "Away, therefore, and away quickly, with these counterfeit keys of the Popes from the church of the faithful! For nothing is sought by them but dominion over the conscience, and when this has been acquired it opens the way for greed to the treasure of all."

Without mentioning the name of Luther, Zwingli refutes, also, the Lutheran conception of the keys, namely, that their efficacy is in the word of God, while the priest is only the instrument through which the word operates. Zwingli traces the power of the keys not primarily to the external word or to faith, but to the illumination of the Holy Spirit by which the word becomes active in faith. "We may be taught by the word, through human mediators, but our conscience can never find peace through human absolution unless the spirit of God opens the word in our hearts." Wernle says: "Luther did not differ widely from Zwingli, but the latter made the difference to appear wider than it actually was."

To whom has the power of the keys been given? The author demolishes the claims of the Romanists, who say that Christ gave the keys to Peter and his successors, according to the words in Matthew 16: 19: "I will give unto thee the keys of the kingdom of heaven, etc." These words, Zwingli argues, apply not to Peter alone but to the Twelve, "who all believed and confessed that Jesus was the Christ." Peter did not lay claims to primacy, for he calls himself a "fellow-elder." The office was not conferred upon a single person, not even upon a council of officers whom God ordained to exercise government and discipline; but "Christ promised the keys to all who, on being asked, recognized that He is the Son of God." The power of the keys is not exercised by an official act, reserved for the ordained priest alone; it is a function of the community of believers. "The word of God, then," says Zwingli, "by which we learn to know ourselves and are taught to trust in God, is the keys by which the ministers of the word set us free; for they that, taught by it, put all their trust in God are henceforth free indeed." Referring to the keys, he says at another place, "that they are the faith by which the gospel is believed, that is, by which we trust in the righteousness and merit of the Son of God, and utterly deny and cast ourselves aside."

The author summarizes his conclusion in the following words: "It is therefore established that it is by faith and not by absolution, as they call the made-up formula of papal authority, nor by any sacrament whatever that the inward man can be made secure. For faith alone knows how much trust it has in God through Christ."

THE CHURCH

He bitterly denounces the "human presumption" which for sinister reasons has "distorted the name church as well as the thing itself so as to make it apply to some few persons only." Reference is here made to "the popes" or to "a few bishops or rather mumblers." Turn "from the error of making out the popes to be the Church." "Nowhere in all Holy Writ" is there ground for such an assumption.

The church, in the true sense of the word, "is a company, an assemblage, the whole people, the whole crowd gathered together."

For further exposition of this topic he refers the reader to his reply to Emser, "that thoroughly impious and corrupt person."[1] That tract, with an introduction, forms the concluding portion of this volume.

THE SACRAMENTS

Zwingli refutes three interpretations of the sacraments in general. He modestly acknowledges his opponents, save Emser and Eck, for whom he has nothing but contempt, as "great men," and expresses regret that he is constrained to differ from them.

The first view, obviously that of the Catholics, resolves the sacraments into "something great and holy which by its own power (*vi sua*) can free the conscience from sin." Zwingli attributes this power to God, who alone can free the conscience. "How could water, fire, oil, milk, salt, and such crude things make their way to the mind?" If such access to the inner man is not possible for these material elements, then "God alone can forgive sin and cleanse the mind." They are wrong, then, "by the whole width of heaven who think that the sacraments have any cleansing power." Here, as always, he will not permit the Creator and the Spirit to be bound by the creature and by material agencies. The word of God and the faith of man—these are the only means and conditions for the purification of the consciences of men.

The second view is that of Luther and his followers. They agree with Zwingli in rejecting the Catholic theory, and Zwingli agrees with them when they define a sacrament as a "symbol of a sacred thing" (*sacrae rei signum*). He cannot, however, concur with Luther in the claim that "when you perform the sacrament outwardly a purification is certainly performed inwardly." In other words, he denies that the sacraments are "signs which, when they are performed, make a

[1]In the discussion of the sacraments, he stigmatizes Emser and Eck as "pests to the teaching of Christ" (p. 179).

man sure about what is performed within him." Such assurance cannot be given by material means "though one were deluged with the whole Jordan," nor "by a sacred formula" though it were "repeated a thousand times." We become new men and receive the benefits of Christ "by the action of the Holy Spirit." According to the Scriptures the Spirit was given sometimes before the sacramental act, as in the case of Cornelius, and sometimes after it, as in the case of the disciples of Apollos. It is clear, therefore, that "when the sacraments are applied to man, the thing signified by them does not necessarily at once take place within them." This again involves Zwingli's basal idea of the manner of the Spirit's operation. For, if the foregoing statement were true, "the liberty of the divine Spirit, which distributes itself to individuals as it will, that is, to whom it will, when it will, where it will, would be bound. For, if it were compelled to act within when we employ the signs externally, it would be absolutely bound by the signs."

The blessing symbolized by the sacraments is appropriated by faith in Christ, which is not effected by a sacramental transaction. "A man, therefore, feels faith within, in his heart; for it is born only when a man begins to despair of himself, and to see that he must trust in God alone." We are "freed from sin when the mind trusts itself unwaveringly to the death of Christ and finds rest there."

The third view is that of the Anabaptists. In the words of the author: "They see clearly that the sacraments can not purify, nor that the operation of the divine Spirit is such a slave to the sacraments that, when they are performed, it is compelled at the same time to operate within." That is, the Anabaptists accept neither the Roman Catholic nor the Lutheran view. They teach that "the sacraments are signs which make a man sure of the thing that has been accomplished within him" before the sacraments are administered. For example, they will baptize only those who give evidence of regeneration and faith before the baptismal act. Zwingli refutes this theory with a single question: "Why does one need baptism who already, through faith in God, is sure of the forgiveness of his sins?" Faith that requires a ceremonial to certify it is not true faith. And if the recipient of baptism does not beforehand have true faith, his baptism is meaningless. The only reason for baptism in the case of true believers is that it is enjoined in the New Testament. At best it was a sealing, not a saving ordinance: a sign of fellowship in the congregation of the converted and awakened Christians and of separation from the world and the world church. Both they and Zwingli took the sacramental value from baptism.

Zwingli briefly defines his own view of the sacraments by saying that they "are signs and ceremonials . . . by which a man proves to the church that he aims to be, or is, a soldier of Christ and which informs the whole church rather than yourself of your faith." They have declarative value only, not purifying power as the Catholics claim; nor do they declare aught to the recipient, as in the Anabaptists' view, but to the whole church they make known, in a solemn way, that the recipient either is or aims to be a soldier of Christ, and that he has faith in his heart, "relying on the mercy of God unwaveringly and firmly and single-heartedly."

In the last paragraph of his analysis of Zwingli's section on the sacraments in the Commentary, Wernle says:

"One can scarcely overestimate the significance of that which is new in Zwingli's doctrine of the sacraments, though Erasmus was his forerunner . . . He radically abolished their unique religious value, their significance in the way of salvation, and permitted only a political value to remain. He considers that they have nothing to do with the salvation which God, through Christ, freely gives us and through the Spirit works in our souls. On the contrary, they belong to the theocracy[1] as pledges and testimonials of the duty or of the covenant of the people of God. A clear conception, without any remnants obscuring the clearness, by which with a single stride we go from the mysterious dawn of antique mysteries and superstitions into the broad daylight of the modern age. The sacred

[1]Zwingli thought of the Church as a theocracy somewhat like that of the Old Testament—the whole community (city or state) ruled by the word of God. Baptism, *e. g.*, was man's initiation into the theocracy, analogous to circumcision, which was the sign of admission into the Old Testament theocracy. This is something wholly different from the New Testament view of baptism.

nimbus has disappeared and only the ethical duties of the Christian remain."[2]

Of the seven sacraments of the Catholic Church Zwingli accepts two "and no more, Baptism and the Lord's Supper." The other five he regards as "rather ceremonials." He excludes them as sacraments because "they were not instituted by God to help us initiate anything in the Church."

BAPTISM

Zwingli finds no difference, so far as the nature, effect, and purpose are concerned, between the baptism of John and that of Jesus. He concedes a "slight difference" in "procedure or form." The sameness is proved by the fact that Christ received the baptism of John and "made no change in it either in his own case or that of his apostles." The end of both baptisms was "that we might come forth new men and might model our lives according to the teaching which each proclaimed." The baptism of John required a new life and hope in Christ, and so did the baptism of Jesus. The author had small regard for the outward form of baptism: "John's dipping effected nothing" and "Christ's dipping effected nothing." This act was a mere ceremony pointing to the "real thing" —the baptism of the Holy Spirit.

Even the Spirit's baptism is assumed to be twofold: First, "the baptism by which all are flooded within, who trust in Christ." This kind of baptism "is so necessary that no one can be saved without it." Second, "the external baptism of the Holy Spirit, just as there is the baptism of water." This was the baptism on the day of Pentecost, when the apostles and disciples spoke in foreign tongues—"a sign to others rather than to themselves." This "latter baptism is not necessary," nor does it often recur in the church.

Zwingli does not agree with the Anabaptists when they refuse to baptize children. They claim that neither the baptized nor the unbaptized infants are under condemnation: they are not under the law. The promise is that only they who believe and are baptized shall be saved. Since infants are not capable of faith and yet are not under damnation, all infants are in a state of salvation. Zwingli claimed, however, that the children

[2]*Zwingli,* p. 204.

of Christians are God's own, no less than those of the Israelites were God's own; and therefore the former are eligible to baptism as the latter were to circumcision. "If, then, the children of Christians are no less God's than those of the Israelites, who would forbid their being baptized according to the words of Peter?" It is generally felt by scholars that by so simple an argument and conclusion he did not prove the necessity of infant baptism.

Zwingli concludes his brief discussion of baptism of infants with the promise of publishing a treatise on the subject after he finished the Commentary.[1]

THE LORD'S SUPPER

The Lord's Supper was the cardinal issue in the Reformation, and when Zwingli wrote the *Commentary* controversy was reaching its height, on the one side with the Roman Catholics, on the other, with the Lutherans and the Anabaptists. The author for good reasons devotes most space and care to the exposition of this subject. He acknowledges, also, that he has advanced beyond the view he set forth two years before in the 18th article of the *Sixty-seven Conclusions* (1523).[2]

The Greeks called this service εὐχαριστία, thanksgiving; Paul speaks of it as *communicatio,* communion. Zwingli accordingly defines the Lord's Supper as "the thanksgiving and common rejoicing of those who declare the death of Christ, that is, trumpet, praise, confess, and exalt his name above all others." He reminds us that the reverse of *communicatio* is *excommunicatio,* exclusion from the fellowship of believers who put their trust in Christ alone.

He bases his own exposition of the Lord's Supper upon John 6:26sq.; and with his interpretation of the words of Jesus he refutes the views of his opponents—the Roman Catho-

[1]The preface of the tract *Von der Taufe von der Wiedertaufe und von der Kindertaufe,* was dated May 27, 1525. The *Commentary* was in press, March, 1525.

[2]In the Conclusions and their Explanation, Zwingli ascribed a twofold purpose to the Lord's Supper: a remembrance of the sacrifice of Christ and an assurance for the weak that Christ has redeemed them. In the Commentary he omits the second purpose and resolves the Eucharist wholly into a memorial of the death of Christ. See Finsler-Köhler-Rüegg, *Ulric Zwingli; eine Auswahl aus seinen Schriften,* chapters 8-9; also, Wernle, *Zwingli,* p. 210.

lics, the Anabaptists, and the Lutherans.

In answer to the Roman Catholic theory of "sacramental eating," he says: "They are wrong who think that in this chapter (John 6) Christ is saying something about sacramental food." He heaps words of biting irony (*salsa ironia*) upon the contemporary theologians who distort, to the abuse of the sacrament, everything they have drawn from this passage (John 6) and lean toward Berengar and the Catholic scholastics. Berengar in his first recantation (1059) affirmed that "after consecration the corporeal and essential body and blood of Christ are present." They are handled by the priest, "broken and torn by the teeth of the faithful." This opinion Zwingli regards as "opposed by all sense and reason and understanding and by faith itself." Innumerable people eat and drink sacramentally the body and blood of Christ, and yet they are not in God nor is God in them "save as he is in an elephant or a flea. To abide in Christ means to cling in love to God, with the same love He gave himself for us, and this is only possible through faith." He says further: "Observe what a monstrosity of speech this is: 'I believe that I eat the sensible and bodily flesh.' For if it is bodily, there is no need of faith, for it is perceived by the senses; and things perceived by sense have no need of faith, for by sense they are perceived to be perfectly sure."

Zwingli refuses to accept the modification of the views in the confession of Berengar offered by those who say: "We eat, indeed, the true and bodily flesh of Christ but spiritually (sed spiritualiter)." These persons fail to see that the two statements cannot stand: "It is body" and "it is eaten spiritually." "To eat the fleshly body spiritually" amounts to making "body" into spirit, and this is not possible, philosophy bearing witness. Zwingli, however, does not deny one the right to speak of spiritual eating (de spirituale manducatione). So we may infer from his own words: "Meanwhile I leave every one free to hold what view he will of spiritual manducation, provided he rests on Christ's dicta and not his own; until he has weighed what I am going to bring forward about the words of Christ." He himself can conceive of no other spiritual eating than what he describes as follows: "We eat spiritually, when through the grace of God we come to Christ"; or "To eat spiritually the body of Christ is nothing more than to put your trust in Christ."

In his own interpretation of Christ's words in John 6, he makes "bread" equivalent to "gospel" and "eat" to "believe." Augustine, also, identified *edere* (to eat) with *credere* (to believe). Zwingli goes a step further and makes "faith" equivalent to food when he says: "This food then of which Christ speaks is faith." In place of "sacramental" food he puts "spiritual" food; and the eating of it is "that we believe in Christ." "He that eateth of this bread, *me,* to wit, that is, that believes on me, hath eternal life." True to his idea of the close relation between faith and life, he sounds an ethical note in the Lord's Supper. "So, surely," he says, "they, also, that eat me, that is, that believe on me, will fashion themselves to my pattern. Ye will in vain pretend that ye believe unless ye also change your life." Wernle says: "Both together, the memorial of the death of Christ and the showing forth (Bezeugung) of brotherly fellowship, constitute the distinctive character of Zwingli's doctrine of the Lord's Supper. His favorite text in answer to all theories of a carnal presence (that is, *Christus realiter, corporaliter, aut essentialiter*) was John 6:63: "The flesh profiteth nothing"—"It is the spirit that giveth life." Yet he conceded that the flesh profiteth something *as an offering* (*caesa*) but not as food (*ambesa*). "The flesh profiteth by being slain but not by being eaten; slain it has saved us from the slaughter but eaten it profiteth absolutely nothing." He is our salvation *non esus sed caesus,* that is, not eaten but crucified. Against the theory of a visible and tangible presence in the elements he quotes John 1:18: "No man hath seen God at any time, etc." His last appeal always is to "that indestructible adamant (*infractus ille adamas*): "The flesh profiteth nothing." He says of it: "It stands uninjured however you beat upon it, and all opposing weapons are shattered without even making a dent upon it."

Carlstadt, originally a colleague of Luther in the University of Wittenberg, proposed a new interpretation of the words: "This is my body." He made the pronoun "this" (τοῦτο or *hoc*) refer to the body of Jesus and not to the bread which he broke and gave to his disciples. The passage would read thus: "This (body) is my body." Zwingli commends this interpretation not because it is right but because those who hold it see clearly that Jesus did not regard the bread in his hand as bodily flesh. But in escaping "the Charybdis of bodily flesh he was driven into the Scylla" of an awkward and untenable interpretation. In an argument of some length Zwingli shows that Carlstadt's exegesis is not correct.

He then proceeds, in the remaining part of this chapter, to prove that the true theory of the Lord's Supper is not based on the meaning of the pronoun "this" but upon the verb "is" (est). The verb "is" means, in the formula used by Jesus, "signifies."

At great length he argues this point. He cites numerous passages from the Old Testament and the New in which clearly "is" means "signifies." See Genesis 41: 26; Luke 8: 11; Matthew 13: 38. He points out that other words in the Scriptures are used not literally but symbolically. See Matthew 21: 42; Galatians 5: 7; John 10, etc.

He supports his own interpretation by appeal to Wycliffe and the Waldensians. He calls to witness the church fathers, especially Origen and Augustine. "We see by these words that Origen held the view that the essential thing in this sacrament is the faith by which we believe that Christ made sacrifice for us, for this is the food of the soul." He represents Augustine as teaching that "we do not in any other way eat Christ than through faith, trusting in him as the sure pledge of our salvation."

The protest against the symbolical interpretation of the word "is" (est) came from Luther. He feared that if one would not take the words of the Bible in their literal sense, the way would be opened for reading all sorts of human opinions and imaginations into the word of God, and that the outcome would be either fanaticism or rationalism. Zwingli put this protest in his own words as follows: "I hear some people burst forth indignantly, 'If we are to force any word we please, thus to signify anything we please, nothing in the Holy Scripture will retain its integrity, for license will be given to the impious to twist everything into anything you like'."

This objection, which has weight, did not deter Zwingli from reaching the conclusion after careful study of all the evidence, in words as follows: "This word 'is', then, is in my judgment used for 'signifies'; yet it is not my judgment but that of eternal God." He is ready to forego all arguments based on analogous passages in the Bible and quotations from the fathers, and to stake his whole theory upon the words, "The flesh profiteth nothing."

Zwingli expresses regret that he is compelled to differ from men whom he highly respects, and he assures the reader that he did not rashly reach his conclusion. He says: "I secretly considered this matter with various learned men for several years, because I was unwilling to spread among the crowd thoughtlessly anything that might give rise to some great commotion."

Zwingli was not the first one to explain the Lord's Supper as a symbolical transaction commemorating the death of Christ. Others before him held similar views. Yet his interpretation was epoch-making because he was first among the Reformers who expounded a conception of the Lord's Supper that was free from every remnant of superstition and was accepted by Protestants in Switzerland and in other European lands. At the same time he preserved the seriousness, dignity, and solemnity of its celebration—an invaluable part of Christian worship. He took from it the sacramental value which was ascribed to it in the Catholic Church and was implied in the Greek term "mysterion." He does not regard it as a sacrament either in the Catholic sense or in the sense of Greek or Oriental mysteries. It is a Christian celebration of Christ's redemptive death analogous to the celebration of a decisive victory through which a people has won civil freedom. It is a thanksgiving of the congregation of believers to their Lord and Redeemer for something He has done for them; at the same time it is a pledge of renewed loyalty and obedience to Him. It is also a "holy sacramental act of initiation" by which we are "united into the one army and peculiar people of God."[1]

The question arises, whether or not this theory adequately explains the original purpose of the Lord's Supper and the legitimate experience of those who have participated in it. It

[1]*Reply to Emser. See* below, p. 394.

is now generally conceded that in the celebration of the Eucharist by the early Christians, those who took part in it found elements more realistic and with deeper religious values than are contained in Zwingli's theory of it. He finds no place for the central idea of a living personal fellowship between the glorified Christ and His disciples upon earth. He resolves it wholly into a solemn service commemorating an historical redemptive act which of course has significance for believers to the end of time. The distant historical fact is central; not the present living fellowship of the Lord and His people.

Calvin felt this defect in Zwingli's theory. On that account he was for years in closer sympathy with the Lutherans, especially those of the Melancthonian type in South Germany, than with the Zwinglians. The fact, also, that in the course of a generation Calvin's view of the Lord's Supper prevailed even in German Switzerland seems to indicate that Zwingli's theory came to be regarded as one-sided and unsatisfactory.

Zwingli, however, will always be considered the forerunner of all modern Christians to whom the idea of mystery in the Lord's Supper in a realistic and sacramental sense is offensive and who profess to worship God in spirit and in truth, that is, with an enlightened mind unhampered by baseless superstitions. For these men Zwingli will remain the Reformer of the Sixteenth Century who, in his thinking, approached most nearly to that of the modern man.[1]

MARRIAG

Marriage is not to be regarded as a sacrament. Zwingli is willing, however, since "sacrament" has come into use, and that he may not appear "obstreperous," that the term be applied to marriage as long as its meaning is properly defined. The reason why marriage was made a sacrament is found in an erroneous translation of the Greek word *mysterion* (Ephes. 5: 32) into the Latin word *sacramentum*. The word *arcanum* would have been more accurate. Zwingli, however, would prefer, in the interest of clarity and veracity, that marriage be not counted a sacrament. For it is "not made any more holy or any clearer by being called a sacrament, but darker and less clear." Sacraments are "initiations" and nothing else, while "marriage is a compact existing between two persons only." It

[1]Wernle, *Zwingli*, pp. 217-218.

is an appropriate symbol of the fellowship between Christ and the Church; to make more of it is to obscure rather than to clarify its meaning.

In Section 21 the author returns to the subject of marriage in relation to the celibate priesthood. Since marriage is an honorable estate according to the Scripture (Heb. 13: 4), "why should priests be forbidden to marry?" Not only does the word of God sanction it but the experience of the church with its priesthood requires it. Zwingli contends that celibacy does not work for chastity but for shameful unchastity among the clergy. "These, therefore, who forbid wives to ministers of the word build up with words to tear down with deeds." It was common knowledge that priests, in spite of their vows, lived in concubinage and were fathers of families. In the interest of the word of God as well as of purity and integrity of living, he pleads for the right of clerical marriage.

CONFESSION

Confession, in its true sense, is a private transaction between the soul and God. The mediation of a priest is not necessary. "As, therefore, it is God alone who remits sins and puts the heart at rest, so to Him alone ought we to ascribe the healing of our wounds, to Him alone display them to be healed." Those, however, who are weak in the faith and sincerely distressed may consult with the minister of the word and ask counsel, and he will direct them to God and His saving and comforting grace. "Auricular confession, then, is nothing but a consultation in which we receive from him whom God has appointed to the end that we may seek the law from his lips." "Nonsense and sheer trumpery therefore are the promises of the Papalists concerning the Keys."

The following elements are parts of true confession: 1. To praise and give thanks to the Lord; 2. To trust the Lord; 3. To acknowledge that of which you are accused; 4. To inform our neighbor or a learned scholar of our secret guilt in order that he may join us in asking forgiveness of the Heavenly Father. Zwingli admonishes the reader to confess frequently to the Lord, to begin a new life frequently; and, "if there is anything not clear, let him go frequently to a wise scholar who looks not at the pocket but at the conscience."

Confirmation

Confirmation was introduced into the Church when the

baptism of infants became common. He acknowledges that at first only dying infants were baptized. That practice, however, was based upon a false assumption, namely, "that next after baptism faith washes away sin." Before long salvation was denied infants dying without baptism. Zwingli does not offer an explanation of the true significance of confirmation, nor does he propose a modification of the rite so that it may be continued in the Church at present.

Extreme Unction

Extreme unction is "a human office of kindness." It is an imitation of the apostolic practice of anointing the sick (Mk. 6:13). James, also, admonishes the elders of the church to anoint the sick with oil (5:14). Zwingli favors the continuance of the practice: "if occasion demands or the sickness allows, the older persons should rub the sick man, anoint him, and pray God to heal him."

Ordination

The idea that ordination "impresses upon the soul a special character (character indelebilis) is a human invention." Neither the rite nor the Catholic interpretation of it can be based upon the apostolic custom of the laying on of hands (Acts 4:30; I Tim. 4:14). "That was an external sign by which they marked those upon whom the gift of tongues was about to descend or those whom they were going to send out to the ministry of the word." It had no sacramental value.

The episcopate is nothing more than the ministry of the word. "He, therefore, that administers the word is a bishop; and he who does not is no more a bishop than a man is a mayor or a judge who does not fill the office." The ministry of the word, accordingly, is not an order but a function; and he who does not perform the function cannot claim the office.

Vows

Zwingli's pet aversions are the vow-bound monks, against whom he offers the following scathing indictment: "They promise chastity, but are content with having promised; poverty, though the King himself is in greater need than they; obedience which is manifest disobedience to God and foreign to all Christian love. Therefore they betray Christ who bind themselves by these vows." "This kind of life has been sown by the enemy, that is, Satan, like tares among the wheat of the Lord."

The vows are contrary to the Scripture and to the nature

of man. They work unchastity, self-indulgence, and disobedience—the very opposite of the virtues which they are intended to cultivate. Continence is a gift of God, and no one has a right to pledge to God what is not in his power to give. "Those to whom it is not given" (Matt. 19:11) ought to follow the counsel of Paul, who says: "It is better to marry than to burn" (I Cor. 7:9). Furthermore, celibacy dishonors marriage and the family. It deprives the state of useful citizens and it disregards God's ordinance requiring that men beget and rear children. Monks evade this command. "But how?" he asks. "They go awhoring more shamelessly than dogs."

Their pretended poverty is deception and fraud. For in reality they enjoy greater riches and more luxuries than many a wealthy citizen, without sharing the cares of wealth or the burdens of the government. They pay no taxes; they do not attend to business; "they look out for no one but themselves." Though they are supposed to be poor monks, they enjoy all the delicacies of food in season. They clothe themselves "with skin and wool and furs so that they sometimes have to sweat in spite of themselves. In summer their robes are so open to the breeze, they lay aside so completely all heavy clothing, that you might think they could live on air."

In no other section of the Commentary does the author write with more fascinating style, more stinging satire, more cogent argument. Wernle describes it as "a brilliant and terrible arraignment of the vow-bound monks."

INVOCATION OF SAINTS

The author directs the reader to the discussion of the subject in his books of the two years preceding the Commentary. They are: *Archeteles* (1522); *Sixty-seven Conclusions* (1523); *Refutation of the Canon of the Mass* (1523). In this section he inserts *verbatim* what he wrote in the *Reply to Emser*. He also refers to a book on *Invocation of Saints* (1523) by Clichtove, Bishop of Chartres, France. However, he disclaims having read it carefully, partly for want of time and partly on account of the puerility of its contents. He speaks of the author as "a theologian taking the Sacred Writings in hand like a donkey running a solemn ceremony."

His own view of the invocation of saints is tersely expressed in the following sentence: "We 'worship' them rightly when we all cling firmly to that God to whom they also in their lifetime clung and taught others to cling." . . . "Faith needs no protecting patron; it knows only one God."

MERIT

Zwingli bases his opposition to works of merit on his theory of divine providence and its correlate, predestination. He assumes that God determines everything and that man of himself is capable of nothing. "Since all things are done of His activity how are we to have any merit?" The so-called good works, to which merit is ascribed, are inventions of men—"shams, snares, traps to extort money." Works that are actually good are the "fruit of faith"; therefore "they are of God, not ours." "Why then do we ask a return for things that are not ours?"

At the close of this section he attacks the ceremonies of the Church which often are closely related to works of merit. Jesus Himself rejected them when He said: "In vain do they worship me, teaching the doctrines and precepts of men" (Matt. 15:9). The prophets, Isaiah, Jeremiah, Ezekiel, Amos, long before Jesus, denounced them. Zwingli contrasts the worship of God by obedience to His will in daily living and by the observance of the ritual and ceremonials of the Catholic order. Zwingli stressed the former to such an extent that he permitted, in his form of worship, as little as possible of the sensuous element. He considered the sermon as the principal part of worship, even as preaching was central in the work of Jesus. "Our ceremonies ought to be none other than those that Christ used; for by this is God glorified, that is, when we are zealously devoted to truth and guilelessness and are more ready to expose ourselves for the brethren than to trample upon them in our own interest. This is to worship the Father in spirit and in truth."

PRAYER

Two abuses of prayer are denounced—prayer as "matter of gain" and prayer as a work of merit. True prayer is "the conversation which as a result of faith you have with God as with a father and a most safe and sure helper." It is adoration, "the lifting up of the heart to God." It must be offered in the spirit of the petition, "Thy will be done." No one can pray for another unless he loves him and seeks his good; not because he is paid for it. "Thus all hired praying—psalms, chants, masses, vigils—fall to the ground, for what we do without love profiteth nothing." To the priests, who say they pray for persons who, on account of their work, have no time to pray and who in turn "pay only sufficient for our maintenance," he replies: "Go ye also, therefore, sometime and till their fields, and let those who have hitherto labored hard while ye were idle refresh themselves in your snug nests."

The implication of prayers for hire is that they have merit before God for which He will show us His favor. "The devotion of the heart has dared to sell itself as merit." It is thus brought on a level with other works of merit. He grows impatient with such a prostitution of the most sacred act of the soul. "Who could ever impute it to you as a good work that you often come to Him to ask now for money, now for clothing or food, or counsel or aid? Since, then, our praying to God is nothing but a begging of aid in some matter, why do we impute it to ourselves as a work of merit?"

He encourages public and common prayer, such as was held "in the early times." Each church is "to have its own custom" as far as the form of prayer is concerned. "For the same thing is not adapted to all, but everything . . . should proceed from the same piety." Zwingli is especially concerned about having "the collects," that is, the prayers, "plainly pronounced," so that they may be understood by the congregation, that "all may pray together following the words of him who is leading." The language spoken by the people, instead of the Latin in vogue in the services of the Catholic Church, was to be used in public worship.

PURGATORY

Zwingli delivers a staggering blow, as it were, between the eyes of the doctrine of Purgatory, in the first sentence: "Holy Scripture knows nothing of the fire of Purgatory in the sense used by the theologians, but the mind of man knows it well, for by means of this false notion of the fire of Purgatory such wealth has been heaped up that the riches of Croesus and the Hyborboreans and the gems of India are cheap in comparison."

A somewhat plausible reason has been given for the invention of this pernicious doctrine. It served to keep those "who go hence" and "who are not utterly bad" from going straight into Hell, and those "who are not wholly good" from going directly into heaven. Even this argument for Purgatory the author considers a device of the human reason.

In this matter "we should follow what God says within us," and not the dictates of reason. He shows at length that the doctrine is nowhere affirmed in the Scriptures. "How is it, then, that we believe in such vapid and suspicious nonsense?" Those who have discovered "that they who trust in Christ are the sons of God and do not come into judgment" will not "be held captive by such foolish lies."

He takes up the classic passages in the New Testament (Matt. 5:25; 18:34; 12:32; I Cor. 3:13) upon which the Catholic tradition of Purgatory is based and clearly proves that they have no bearing upon the doctrine. It contravenes the all-sufficient grace of God, by which alone we are saved; for, "if we are compelled to endure the fire of Purgatory to satisfy the righteousness of God, as these people say, the righteousness of Christ will profit nothing." Furthermore, it denies the assurance that "through Him alone is access to the Father." In conclusion he admonishes the reader "to give up this most empty fiction," so to live here "that when death draws nigh we shall rejoice to depart and to be with Christ."

MAGISTRACY

Zwingli controverts the Anabaptist theory of civil magistracy and the claims to ecclesiastical magistracy of bishops and popes.

The Anabaptists made two denials: 1. Christians have no need of a magistrate; 2. A Christian ought not to serve as a magistrate.

As to the first point, the Anabaptists held that "the church of Christ ought to be so blameless as to have absolutely no need of magistrates; for Christians do not quarrel but yield. They do not carry their wrong to court, but if smitten upon one cheek turn the other also." What have they who are ruled by love to do with law? They are above law and above politics. Zwingli retorts by saying that it is on account of the behavior of the people who say that we need no magistrate that we must have one. True, while the Anabaptists conceded that "magistrates were necessary under the old law," they insisted that "these external things do not apply to us." This the author does not admit; law and magistrates, in his view, are necessary, also, in the Christian dispensation; if Christians were blameless and perfect, the magistracy would not be necessary: "but that will be in the other world."

The Anabaptists, in vindication of their own theory and practice, were quick to appeal to the words of Peter: "We must obey God rather than men" (Acts 5: 29). Zwingli has little confidence in their sincerity and warns them against using this text "as an excuse for irregularity."

When they were told that in the New Testament Christians are admonished to obey the "powers that be," they argued that the admonition applied only to the time when the state was pagan and godless and, therefore, it was impossible for Christians to put into practice their ideas of civil magistracy. Now, however, that is, in the sixteenth century, being free from ancient tyranny, they ought to establish a communal order without the coercion of laws and penalties. Only men of the world, not Christians, need civil rulers.

Zwingli's view of the state contradicted this specious argument of his opponents. He found a basis for it in the word of God, in the character of Christians, and in human experience generally. As long as Christians are not perfect—and perfection is not attainable in this world—the regulations and restraints of law are indispensable. In all circumstances the state and the Christian life are inseparable; instead of excluding each other, they are necessary to each other.

The duties of the citizen and the Christian are largely the same in form, if not in principle and motive. The state requires that "one serve the common weal, not one's own; that dangers be shared by citizens, and fortunes, also, if necessity arises; that no one exercise a selfish prudence; that no one exalt himself; that no one stir up strife." All these duties and modes of conduct are included in the law of love which controls the Christian community professing the sovereignty of God through Jesus Christ. Christians are to seek one another's interests, not their own. They are to be mutually sympathetic and helpful, weeping with them that weep and rejoicing with them that rejoice; they are "to put all their fortunes in their girdles to render aid whenever occasion requires."

The difference between the state and the kingdom of God

is in the motives of conduct. The citizen is coerced by law, the Christian lives and walks in the Spirit, fulfilling the law in love. The spirit of Christ furnishes that which the state most needs. "The state becomes strong and holy only in case good hearts are united with good laws."

The denial of the right of a Christian to serve as a magistrate, Zwingli calls a "mad theory." There is nothing in the Bible to forbid it and much reason to prove that only the Christian is fit to be a magistrate. History tells us that "devout men have been magistrates and have ruled so that peace prevailed among men and the righteousness of God was magnified." It is impious rulers "who will heap up riches by means right or wrong, will climb to renown over the dead bodies of their own; the pious ruler will share all things with those over whom he rules and will prefer the safety and peace of people to renown."

Incidentally, the author discusses, also, the arrogant claims to magistracy of bishops and popes in the church. They have no authority, as individuals or as officers, to exercise discipline and to excommunicate members of the church. "The power of the church by which the shameless sinner is shut out from communion is not that of magistrates, as the bishops have thus far exercised it; it belongs to the whole church, not to certain persons who have despotically arrogated supreme authority to themselves." If one says: "Cannot the Pope cast out of the church?" Zwingli without hesitation replies: "I say that he cannot; that belongs to the church alone." He heartily endorses the exercise of strict discipline in the evangelical way. "We must see to it that the true rod of discipline be restored to the church of Christ."

Offence

In this section Zwingli explains the principles which controlled him in his reform. He tried, as far as possible, in making changes in doctrine, worship, and ways of living, not to give offence either to "the weak" or to "the contumacious." An offence is "action that combines offence with contempt." He feels constrained to write on this subject on account of those who were easily offended, even when there was no cause for it, and those who rashly and rudely abolished things that deserved to be set aside, and thus gave unnecessary offence to the weaker brethren. Zwingli had no sympathy with image-breakers and idol-stormers; nor would he permit himself to be deterred from necessary reforms by the plaintive cries of hypersensitive souls.

Offences are given in teaching new doctrine and in putting away "externals" such as ceremonies and rules of conduct. As to teaching, one is to be courageous, true to the word of God, and yet one ought to have "regard to timeliness." He cites the way of Paul, "who boasts that in the beginning he fed the Corinthians with milk" (I Cor. 3: 2). "Of external things some have to do with eating, some with the regulation of life, and some seem to have to do with salvation, though they really amount to nothing." As far as eating is concerned, Zwingli claims that the word of God forbids no foods, not even part of the time. Laws in regard to eating "have been made a stumbling-block of offence by the huckster business of the high priest of Rome." Yet in abrogating these man-made rules one must have regard for one's neighbor, that is, for the "weak, or the contumacious, or the pious." You must spare a man as long as he is weak, and extend to him a helping hand and teach him the truth of Scripture, so that he may become enlightened and may eat without distinction of foods or seasons. One should even spare the "contumacious"; for "we should not for the sake of liberty as to foods act so as to render the gospel hateful." He concedes, however, that there is a limit to the sparing of the "contumacious." There "are always wanton persons who have the audacity lightly to misinterpret any act or motive whatsoever." As for the "pious" brethren, they will never take offence no matter what you eat, so long as you observe moderation.

Probably the primary cause of offence was the marrying of priests and monks, who were bound by vows of celibacy. Zwingli is an ardent advocate of the right of priests to marry; if for no other reason than to prevent fornication and adultery. For few men, even though they have taken vows, have the gift of continence, and therefore they ought to marry. On this matter, however, the people ought to be taught the truth in the word of God, so that they will not be needlessly offended by such marriages. "But until men are enlightened on the subject one must have regard for their conscience and beware of giving offence." Zwingli acknowledges that in marrying men have acted rashly and seem to have "demonstrated their Christianity by nothing else than their marriage." They created disturbance far more than they prevented it.

Zwingli's way of reforming the church and introducing changes in doctrine and ceremonies is by education. "Let nothing be done in the heat of passion." Show the people what the practices really mean and what saving value they have, if they have any. Things of this sort are "anointings, sprinklings, benedictions, etc." When properly taught the people will recognize "these external things as signs with which we do something for our neighbor rather than for ourselves"; and they will discover that they "have been brought in by device of man in the same way as forbidden foods."

In answer to the question "when these things ought to be abolished," he presents two tests: 1. When one does these things in fidelity to his Lord and not for his own sake; 2. When one deals in love with his fellow men and is concerned about making righteousness prevail. Let the people be first taught the truth and that "they be upright in things pertaining to God and they will immediately see all these objectionable things fall away."

Statues and Images

Zwingli did not intend to write anything for the Commentary on this subject. He had planned a tract, in German, on Statues and Images to be written as soon as his time permitted. In response to the request of "some of the brethren" he added to the Commentary a brief discussion of the main points at issue.

He makes a sharp distinction between images used as objects of worship and images as works of art. The former use, or abuse, of them he cannot tolerate. It is contrary to the word of God in the Old and New Testaments. But he goes further and argues that, if the Scriptures were silent about images, the spirit of love would admonish men to apply to the needs of the poor what is spent on the making and worship of images. He finds no ground for the contention that men are taught by images and "influenced to piety." Christ nowhere "taught this method of teaching, and He certainly would not have omitted it if He had foreseen that it would be profitable." We ought rather "to be taught by the word of God and not by sculpture wrought by the artist's hand." There are those who avow that "images are not worshipped but those whose images they are." He replies that "none of the heathen was ever so stupid as to worship their images of stone, bronze, and wood for what they were in themselves; they reverenced in these their Joves and Apollos."

After all the arguments favorable to images are heard, he concludes that images are not permissible in worship, for two reasons: 1. Worship of idols is expressly forbidden in the Old and New Testaments; 2. No art can or should represent the divine nature.

As works of art images are much to be desired and have great value. "No one is a greater admirer than I of paintings and statuary." They adorned the mercy seat in the tabernacle and were placed in Solomon's temple; and there they were inoffensive and harmless. Zwingli did not countenance disturbing painted images in windows of churches provided they were put there for the sake of decoration and not for worship.

In the removal of images he advocates the same mode of procedure that he proposed in the preceding section on Offence: "Teaching should come first and the abolition of the images follow without disturbance; and love will teach all things in all cases."

EPILOGUE

Zwingli announces that his purpose in the concluding section is "to gather the substance of all that I have said into a short epilogue." Wernle considers this part of the Commentary one of the author's "most original contributions." He combines in brief compass elements of a history and a philosophy of religion. He traces the development of religion from the primitive to the Christian man. In his point of view and method of procedure he is not so far removed from modern historians, which is an evidence both of the breadth and of the maturity of his thinking.

He assumes that man in his earliest stage was on a level with the animal. That which separated him from, and lifted him above, the brute was religion. "There is no difference between the life of man and that of the beasts if you take away the knowledge of God." That man might rise above his original condition, might become more than an animal, God revealed Himself to man. Even when man "had fallen into forgetfulness of God," He did not permit him "to perish with the beasts," but He "called him back," that "he might live forever with Him." He cites the succeeding crises in the history of man as recorded in the Bible, in each of which God in mercy approached man and gave him promises of redemption.

There were two revelations of God, each with the same end in view, namely, to benefit men. The first is the general revelation through nature to all men, and the second is the special revelation to the Chosen People which is recorded in the Bible. In this way He showed Himself as a loving Father to one race; yet He was nowhere lacking to others, "that the whole world might recognize that He is the one and the only one who can do all things, by whom all things exist, by whom all things are governed." Zwingli reiterates here his favorite theory of revelation, namely, that the external revelation through nature or through His word cannot be understood "unless God Himself draws the heart to Himself so that it shall recognize that He is its God and shall receive the law as good" (John 6: 44). In view of God's manifestation of Himself "from the foundation of the world," we ought to do two things: 1. "Firmly believe that He whom we confess as our God is God, the Source and Father of all things"; 2. "We should know ourselves; for when we have not knowledge of ourselves we accept no law."

The benefit that comes to men through His providence is twofold: "To live here blamelessly and, when the course of this life has been finished, to enjoy eternal bliss with Him."

In revealing Himself to man He kindled aspirations in his heart which reach beyond the animal and beyond his sensuous nature. God precipitated a struggle in the inner life of man. His "soul strives to fashion itself upon the pattern of Him towards whom it is hastening, who is holiness, purity, light, rest, refreshment, and all blessedness together." In the striving of the soul to rise upward, it is held back by the body, "which by its nature scorns what the soul greatly values." Hence there is a constant battle between the flesh and the spirit. To save man from despair, "God so manifests Himself to him that he can safely trust His mercy." God revealed Himself in Christ "to strengthen the hopes of all that they should see clearly that nothing can be refused, now that the Son is given for mortals."

The Christian life consists in faith in redemption through Christ and the obligation of the redeemed to live according to His example. "We ought, then, to be as eagerly bent upon a change of life as we trust in redemption through Him." Observe, again, how closely Zwingli relates the religious and the moral life.

His final definition of a Christian is as follows: "A Christian, therefore, is a man who trusts in the one and only God; who relies upon His mercy through His Son Christ, God of God; who models himself upon His example; who dies daily; who daily renounces himself; who is intent upon this one thing, not to do anything that will offend his God." Luther resolves Christian life into faith and love; Zwingli into "faith and blamelessness"; in this respect the two Reformers are not widely apart.

He takes a last fling at the Roman Catholic system, mostly an invention of men. "We have substituted a vicar for Christ and in our folly have decreed that he is to be listened to in place of God, etc." And in all these things God takes no delight; "why do we find it so hard to change from useless trifles to those true and solid things, righteousness, faith, mercy, in which Christ comprehended all religion?"

He bids farewell to the reader in these words: "So, then, good reader, receive this Commentary, so hurriedly written and printed in three months and a half that, as you see, it stands clumsy indeed but zealous for the truth and holiness; consider it calmly and take it in good part." "All that I have said, I have said to the glory of God and for the benefit of the Commonwealth of Christ and the good of the conscience."

"Thanks be to God!"

Lancaster, Pa., January, 1929.

COMMENTARY ON TRUE AND FALSE RELIGION

(March, 1525)

[DE VE | RA ET FALSA RELIGIONE | Huldrychi Zuinglij Com- | mentarius. | *Indicem capitum totius operis inue- | nies in fine libri.* TIGVRI | *in aedibus Christopheri Fro- | schouer. Anno* M. D. XXV. | *Mense Martio.* | *Venite ad me omnes qui laboratis & one | rati estis, & ego requiem vobis | praestabo. Matt 11.* | 456 octavo pages, of which pages 18-452 are numbered 2-446. The numbers jump from 320 to 331. Page 1, Title; pages 2-15, Dedication; pages 15-16, To the reader; pages 17-452, Text; pages 453-454, Errata; page 455, Index; page 456, Froschauer's printer's device.

Another edition was printed in 1525, entitled: DE VERA | ET FALSA RELI- | GIONE, HULDRYCHI | Zuinglij Commentarius. | *Matth. XI.* | *Venite ad me omnes qui laboratis & onerati | estis, & ego requiem vobis praestabo.* | Then Froschouer's printer's device. | TIGVRI EX OFFICINA | FROSCHOVIANA. | At the end of the dedication to Francis I. signed: *Ex Tiguro, Anno* M. D. XXV. | 456 octavo pages, of which pages 17-453 are numbered 1-437; pages 453-454, Index; pages 455-456 blank. Printed in *Opera Zwinglii,* tom. II, fol. 158b-242b; Schuler and Schultess ed., vol. 3, pp. 147-325; Egli-Finsler ed., vol. 3, pp. 628-912.

A German edition, translated by Leo Jud and published by Froschauer in 1526 has the title: *Von warem und falschem Glouben Commentarius, dz ist, underrichtung, Huldyrch Zwinglins. Vertütschet durch Leonem Jud . . . Getruckt zü Zürich by Christoffel Froschouer,* M. D. XXVI . . . —608 octavo pages, of which pages 29-605 are numbered by leaves. On pages 26-28 is Leo Jud's dedication to Wilhelm von Zell. For the chapter on the Eucharist Jud used a translation by three unknown persons, of which three editions were published by Froschauer in 1525.

A partial modern German translation by Walter Köhler is in *Ulrich Zwingli: Eine Auswahl aus seinen Schriften,* Zurich, 1918, pp. 484-608.

The following English translation, made by Mr. Henry Preble, was revised by the editor.]

To the most Christian King of France, Francis, the first of that name, grace and peace from the Lord. Huldreich Zwingli.

WE all know, most illustrious King, what an impertinence it is for one of the crowd to venture to address one of the great leaders in the Christian world, as in these days we see not a few doing, who under color of a Christian profession persist in obtruding upon men of eminence in ways the very effrontery of which shows that they have not a particle of Christian spirit. For the Christian spirit causes no annoyance, so far is it from asserting itself in a forward or disrespectful manner. Yet we know, too, how outrageous and utterly unworthy of him it is for a prince to be so arrogant and swollen with pride as to suffer none to approach him except those few whom he has chosen out of all mankind to advise him and to attend him upon every possible occasion. For what else is this than to surround the prince with a barrier which it is unlawful to overleap, and, indeed, in the nature of a crime to imagine oneself across? Who would not call such a prince the most wretched of men, as being the slave of those very persons who to all appearance are his slaves? Not that it is not the sacred duty of a king or a prince to hear good counsel, to reverence the old, to honor the prudent, and to have a high regard for the wise; but that often —such is human life—those who are honored overmuch by princes for some unquestionably real and extraordinary merit, as soon as they see they have completely won the confidence of their prince, straightway degenerate, and take advantage of him for their own ends. This result we see at many courts.

Pardon my language. The laws and customs of the Kings of the French are so little known to me that I am wholly ignorant regarding the men by whom Your Highness is hedged about. There are, to be sure, not a few princes who are surrounded by such a crowd of greedy courtiers that, if an audience were granted, you could much more quickly get what you desire from a thousand kings than work your way through their serried ranks. They are like the sleepless dragon that, according to the tales of the poets, guarded the golden fleece. Such are in these days certain bishops in mitre and purple, who so encompass the most powerful kings that it would be strange how the kings can endure the continual sight of them or the bishops never leave, were it not that the latter take very great care to let no knowledge reach the kings that might betray their artifices.

Since, however, Your Highness is proclaimed by all to be too clever to be hampered in this fashion, and too affable and kind to frighten any one away, I have put my trust in your kindness, not in my own boldness, and have determined to dedicate to you this Commentary, such as it is. This I do for many reasons:

First, you, who rule over the French, boast not without reason of the title "Most Christian,"* and as, in spite of all the haters of Christ, I think this Commentary most Christian, it surely ought to be dedicated to none but the Most Christian King. Second, the peoples of France have from ancient times been reputed faithful to religion; to whom,† therefore, could a "Commentary on True and False Religion" have been more appropriately dedicated. Finally, now that Germany, which has very great intercourse with France, has begun to open its eyes to the light of truth, I have thought that on neighborly principles France is entitled to this healing lotion, by which the light is being restored. For, alas! we were for a long time so crushed under the dark machinations of covetous men that we had to endure all things, as the people of Israel did the Egyptian bondage. But the Author of all things had regard for the affliction of our hearts as He had for their troubles, and brought forth the light of His word, whereby we can determine the identity and the character of the things that have hitherto so banefully imposed upon us. Heavenly Providence has this special attribute, that it gives early warning, rising up in the night, like the householder [cf. Lk. 13: 25], and speaking seasonably to us the things needful by the mouth of His servants the prophets [cf. Jer. 25: 4]. Yet, when we listen not to the warning, He sometimes suffers us to be vexed for a long while by those trials into which we have fallen through our disobedience. Witness the long line of ages from Adam to Christ, which hardly sufficed to allow salvation at last to shine upon man, because he had not listened to the loving warning not to eat of the forbidden fruit [cf. Gen. 2: 17]. Witness the three captivities, the Egyptian, the Babylonian, and the Roman,

*Cf. vol. 1, p. 274.
†Plural.

which last God has so prolonged to these days that the Jews have rightly given up all hope. Witness the folly of our own selves, whom Christ, the apostles, and countless others with such solicitude have warned not to believe the false prophets who would show us Christ, *i. e.,* the Anointed and Savior, far otherwise than he and his have done [cf. Mt. 24: 24; II Cor. 11: 4]; but all in vain. For we have taken unto us strange gods, far more absurd than any heathen nations ever had. What heathen nation ever worshipped as God a man destined to die tomorrow, or rather today, as we worship the Roman pontiff? Nor can we deny it. We have called him "God upon earth,"* and have worshipped a man with far more honorable worship than God. For when have emperors and kings prostrated themselves to the earth to adore the Most High God? It was enough to bend the knee. Except a certain few, who kissed or embraced the feet of Christ? But who is here admitted to an audience unless he has first licked the boots of this god? Because of our sins, therefore, we failed to understand this abominable idolatry, and that for a long time [cf. Rom. 1: 24 f.]. And now, when at last it has pleased the Eternal Goodness to free poor mortals from such disaster by restoring His word, as I have said, who does not see how disgracefully we have been deceived about this clear light? Nay, who does not wonder that men endowed with minds and senses could have been so stupidly deceived? Thus, I say, does the kind providence of God give early warning; but when we disobey or disregard His voice, He who was just before a Father becomes an Avenger, and pursues us with disaster that continues until in the enemy's land we recognize our fault; and then, as soon as we have confessed our fault, He restores us to our former favor. Therefore those who are at all wise ought frequently to review their lives, and these, if very bad, ought to be changed; and unless this is done they may be sure that punishment awaits them before the bar. If, on the other hand, one fashions oneself daily upon the pattern of Christ, one should hope all things, for it is just as unlikely that

*So Pope Adrian II was addressed by a speaker at the Fifth Lateran Council, Fourth Session (1512). See Mansi, *Sacrorum Concilium Collectio*, vol. 32 (Paris, 1902), p. 762, and Williston Walker, *The Reformation* (New York, 1900), p. 7.

God would neglect any of the things He has made as it would be strange and unheard of for a mother to forget the child she had borne in her womb and nursed [cf. Isa. 49: 15]. Since, therefore, He never rests, never slumbers [cf. Ps. 121: 3 f.], we must never be careless or asleep, but, as soon as He speaks, instantly spring up and say with Samuel, "Speak, Lord, for thy servant heareth."

Let us, therefore, Most Illustrious King, raise our eyes for a little while and look around to see whether, in view of the foully disordered state of this order we call the world, we cannot from the very magnitude of the disease comprehend how necessary a remedy was. For if that was most clearly needed, no less clearly, as we shall see, did Divine Providence in due season provide the means of cure; for He never loiters, never fails. I will not speak here of the pontiffs, though, as they have always shamelessly arrogated the first place unto themselves, so shall they be the first to be smitten. For this reason, and because they are sufficiently exposed in my Commentary, I will pass them by, and direct attention to the kings and princes.

You see then, Most Christian King, how almost all princes rage and in their folly commit sin, just as did the Trojans and the Greeks, the former following a youth* lost in the madness of his love, the later seeking to recover a harlot.† Do we not perceive the surging tide of folly of nations and kings? Do we not see the poor subjects smitten for the sins of their kings? Does not greed confound all things, bringing under its spell all that it turns its poisonous gaze upon, even though it gets it not within its hold, so that nothing is safe and secure from its power? It casts its eye upon another's province or kingdom, puts all its forces into the field, and does not sound a retreat till it either utterly perishes itself or utterly destroys that which it covets; for no seizure of others' possessions has ever taken place without the destruction of one side or the other. But, since princes ought above all things to beware of wrong, and since wars so rashly begun cannot be carried through without wrong, and since the princes themselves are usually the originators of wars, who does not see that it is necessary for the

*Paris, the son of Priam.

†Helen, the wife of Menelaos, king of Sparta.

Lord to place the lamp of His word at last in the very midst of us, that even the crowd may distinguish whether the conduct of their greedy princes is straight or crooked, just or unjust?

Now I will direct attention to the great mass of humble Christian folk. Do you see how depressed they are? And do you see that they have plenty of reason to be so? In the first place, consider, I pray you, how many and how heavy are the extortions, tributes, and taxes with which they are oppressed, that over their bodies and entire possessions greedy princes may force their way to glory and riches, and do it so lightly that even dread Hannibal seems to have held one elephant* of more account than these hold companies of men. Though they destroy many thousands, that is reckoned as nothing, provided they attain what they desire. And what am I to say of the twofold oppression they endure? It is not enough that all their goods are in the power of the kings; what the kings have left them must be exposed to the cunning of the most abandoned of men. The wolf is among us—for I will not call "pastor" or "bishop" him whom not even the name of wolf can worthily characterize. The monks are among us, some so rich that they outdo the richest in arrogance and folly, some so shameless and insolent in begging that they extort through injustice what pity refused, though in accumulated wealth they are but little inferior to the richest. For whence have they the wherewithal to pay so many thousands for one red hat?† The nuns are among us likewise, tearing and mangling and treading under foot the poor people of Christ in such fashion that, as far as the body is concerned, it is better, it seems, to live under an impious king than under a Christian one who suffers the people entrusted to him by the Lord to be so impiously plucked to pieces. I cannot help speaking out freely here what I think, Most Christian King. What madness was it—for it cannot have been piety—that caused kings to allow monasteries of idle men to be created within their boundaries? If a band of robbers had built a stronghold or two, would they not have been crushed and dispersed by whole armies? Though,

*When Hannibal left Carthage in the spring of 218 B. C., he took with him 37 elephants. Of these only one reached Italy.

†The "cappa magna" or Cardinal's hat.

for all that, their plundering would be not without risk, since they would have to fear the hand of the avenger. But now, when so many monasteries of robbers plundering unmolested have so long been flourishing everywhere, as if in a paradise of all delights and debauchery, and when it is no secret how they claim all men's goods as their own (for both princes and kinglets have experience how their own revenues are beginning to fall off through the greed of these fellows), how is it that no one considers the people thus cruelly oppressed? It is surely because all men are given over to greed, according to the word of the prophet [Amos 9: 1].* When they ought, in some measure at least, to alleviate the evil, they cry "Peace, peace!"† but only in their own interest and not that of the people of Christ. Do we, then, imagine, that the Heavenly Father is fast asleep in the face of these troubles of His people? He sees and judges. Consider, also, that the people sometimes suffer these cruel hardships deservedly. For all are so filled with greed that no man more shamelessly cheats, deceives, and oppresses his neighbor than one Christian another. None is more hopelessly given over to fornication and adultery, and to enduring or perpetrating every form of lewdness. And our arrogance and luxury of dress are so great that all who in times past were notorious for these vices are surpassed. Our drunkenness is such that it outdoes all the tales of all the ages. Therefore doth the Lord visit so many ills upon His people, to bring them back into the way.

Since, then, to come back to the beginning, we are compelled to admit that the whole world is so corrupt, wicked, and shameless that it absolutely must be reformed, and since we know that the Heavenly Father never fails, but constantly warns or smites; and also, since we see that He has sent His word to heal this old sore and to snatch us from destruction, who will not lift up his head at the voice of the Lord? Who can fail to see that the day of the Lord is at hand?—not that last day on which the Lord will judge the whole world, but the day on which He is to correct the present condition of things.

*Zwingli has in mind the reading of the Latin Vulgate: Avarita enim in capite omnium.

†Alluding to such passages as Micah 3: 5, 11; Jer. 6: 14, etc.

"The lion will roar," saith the prophet [Amos 3:8], "who will not fear? The Lord God hath spoken; who will not prophesy?" The Most High, I say, has put forth His voice; who, then, will not say, "I will hear what the Lord God hath to say to me"? His Gospel, which to our loss has long been hid, even though the letter of it was not hidden, He has now brought back again, as Deuteronomy once to the Jews [cf. II Kings 22:8], to cleanse the foul of sin. He nowhere fails us, provided we do not fail ourselves. He never suffers the world to be very bad with impunity, but ever warns us to mend our ways in time, before He has prepared His rod. They, therefore, that change their lives set free their souls; they that fail to do so are miserably destroyed, as Sodom [cf. Gen. 19:24f.] and Nineveh [cf. Jonah 3:4ff.] prove. Wherefore we, too, must look to this one point only, how we may transform our lives from very bad to very good. Else shall we suffer such disaster that we shall be forced to lament with the prophet [Jer. 9:1]: "Who will give my head water," that we may be filled with weeping for the calamity that hath fallen upon us? The word of God has never been disregarded with impunity. Since, therefore, we now both see and hear that the true word of the true God is thriving, we shall by no means disregard it with impunity. Suppose some one says: "It is not the word of God that these fellows preach. Certainly, if it were the word of God, I would receive it gladly." Let us not be moved a jot thereby, for the very wickedness of the whole world cries out for correction. When, therefore, at such a time we hear a new word, it cannot be the word of any other than God, who warns us every time we persist in our wickedness, and chastises us if we refuse to hear. From our crimes, therefore, we can infer that God is forced to send His word and rod. There is also another sure test, by which we see clearly that this word that has come forth at this particular time is the word of God. I say nothing for the moment of the imposture of certain persons who under the cover of the word study their own interest or glory. Enough has been said already of the corruption of the world, which no one denies. Since, therefore, any man can easily see that this word which we preach today is diametrically opposed to the vices in which we abound, it cannot be denied that it is the word of God. For this reason, Illustrious King, when I, too, saw that our world is overflowing with the most iniquitous wars and the fiercest battles, and is defiled and unsettled with rapine, assault, theft, robbery, I, too, put my hand to the plough [cf. Lk. 9:62] and raised my voice so loudly that greedy Rome and the idol* worshipped there did hear, even though its hide is very thick. Hence condemnations, execrations, and excommunications on the part of those theologians who prophesy for hire [cf. Mic. 3:11] and worship the belly as their only God [cf. Phil. 3:19], which have forced me and not a few others much against our will to maintain our cause with pen as well as tongue. When, therefore, many men in Italy and more in your France, men so learned and pious that modesty almost made me refuse what they begged of me—for what can you do with a man who says, "These are the pillars [Gal. 2:9], and you shall write out your religious views for them"?—when, I say, the best men on all sides, having caught a whisper of my name, were so insistent upon my publishing a pamphlet to bear witness to my own religious views, their high standing and importunity overcame my modesty, and I did my best to comply. May Your Illustrious Highness, therefore, Most Christian King, graciously accept this work, such as it is, dedicated to you. That most holy and learned man, Hilary,‡ a native of your France, once wrote to all the brethren and bishops of Germany. May it be possible for us sometime to boast of having made a suitable return! In saying this, of course, I am not referring to this crude little pamphlet of mine, but to other writings of learned and pious men in Germany. But listen, pray, Most Kindly King; you have in your kingdom that body of theologians of the Sorbonne,† which no man can paint as it deserves. They know not tongues, yet

*Sc. the Pope.

‡Hilary of Poitiers addressed his epistle *De Synodis* (358 A. D.) to the bishops of Germany, France, and Britain.

†Though in the 15th century men from the Sorbonne had demanded a reformation of the Church (Pierre d'Ailly, Nicolas de Clamengis, Jean Charlier de Gerson), in the 16th century the spirit of the institution was altogether different. During the years 1517-1534, the doctors of the Sorbonne condemned writings of Luther, Erasmus, and Melanchthon. Zwingli probably has these in mind.

they not only scorn but persecute us, habitually using their own tongues to curse with the sharpness of a serpent's fangs. The things we have got from the Sacred Writings they pronounce impious, heretical, and blasphemous, though I see no kind of teaching more blasphemous against God than that which they follow. Philosophy has been forbidden in the schools of Christ [cf. Col. 2: 8], but these people have made it the arbiter of the heavenly word, and that, indeed, a philosophy which they have drawn from the last dregs of the pool; for, my life on it! they deal with not one idea—not a single one, I say—that is worthy of Aristotle. So barbarous is all that they teach, so lifeless, that you would sooner think they were telling dreams than expounding philosophy. Bid this class of men, I say, by every thing divine or human, act Harpocrates* a bit, lest, while you suffer them with impunity to blab out against Christ whatever comes into their heads, you find yourself incurring His displeasure. Then, as to myself, warn them, if they care to read and refute me, not to try to do it without the help of the truly sacred Scriptures. If they once accomplish that, they will gain a brother [cf. Mt. 18: 15]; if not, I shall not care a straw for all their croakings. You have also another class of learned men, whose skill is in heavenly, not in human, things, and who yet have everything that is of importance to the latter, namely, skill in tongues, simplicity of character, and holiness of life. This class do you cherish, and hold nothing so valuable as these men; nor only keep them about yourself, save a few to confer with you upon sacred things, but assign them posts through the length and breadth of your kingdom in which to fix not upon pillars but in men's hearts the new commands of Christ. Then you will see your kingdom, torn as it has been with long warfare,‡ straightway blooming again; arrogance, vain show, luxury, lust, debauchery, and all sins falling away; righteousness, faith, and mercy putting forth new shoots. And never suffer yourself to be drawn into the notion into which a certain man tried to draw your illustrious mother,† of opposing the teachings of

*The god of silence.

‡A reference to the war between Francis I and Charles V, 1521-1526.

†Louise of Savoy. At her court and with Francis I, the French Chan-

the Gospel on the ground that it is a disturber of the peace because in Germany everything is in confusion and no one listens to the commands of the princes and everything is altogether upset. For they that talk thus serve not God but their own bellies [cf. Phil. 3: 19]. For this is how it is with the Gospel: It has come down from heaven, and cannot return thither void [cf. Isa. 55: 11], with its work unaccomplished. Therefore it cannot but be that wherever it is preached it is accepted of many. Since, therefore, the world consists of the good and just, and of the wicked and worthless, it comes to pass that the less of a hypocrite a man is the more readily he yields to the gospel, whether he be one of the good or one of the bad. For publicans and sinners often have preceded certain nice little saints in the Kingdom of God. And, indeed, those who are very bad and see that some of their own kind have gone over to Christ pretend that they, too, have gone over, with the view of getting themselves supported in idleness. For the pious vigorously assist needy brethren; indeed, unless they do so they are not pious. Where the government, therefore, obstructs the free course of the heavenly word, the best men turn away from the government and have regard to everything that can preserve the heavenly teaching. Even though it be very hard to do this, they yet do it, because they are unwilling to lose the soul's treasure when it has been found. It is on this account, perhaps, that in some places in Germany dangerous dissensions are taking place,* the government having attempted to prohibit the preaching of the word. But believe me, Illustrious King, wherever the government does not attempt to curb the word, there the best men are on the side of the government; and then the hypocrites and gluttons, who after the fashion of the devil transform themselves into angels of light [cf. II Cor. 11:14], are easily rendered harmless. This is reckoning the gain. If it is reward that any one chooses to look for, he will find, by reading the book through, how much relief can accrue to kings and nations if we

cellor Antoine Duprat and the Constable Anne de Montmorency worked against the introduction of evangelical doctrine. Both had great influence upon Francis I.

*A reference to the earlier stages of the Peasants' War of 1524-1525.

determine to correct our ways according to the word of the gospel.

Now I pray for the safety of Your Highness and of all your subjects. The kingdom is the Lord's [cf. Mt. 6:13]. Do not, then, act so as to destroy His word in His own kingdom. Take in good part this bold way of addressing you. I have written especially for the good of France; therefore nothing could be more proper than to dedicate my production to her king, that it might in no way be misconstrued. Zurich, 1525.

To the Reader

I had given a promise, gentle reader, about a year ago, to many learned and pious men on the other side of the Alps, some of whom had had much conversation with me on many matters of faith, that I would write out in Latin my views on the Christian religion. Various occupations prevented me for some time from fulfilling the promise. However, now that the penalty for the pledge is due, my plighted word has compelled me to toil so hard for three and a half months night and day that instead of "Commentary" I might just as well, after the example of Gellius, have called my work "Nights"; as, no doubt, my enemies will gladly do, though for a different reason. But I have chosen to name it "Commentary" for this reason, because commentaries, if I rightly understand the word, are a means of communicating (commentantur) with friends, just as a letter is, except that commentaries are fuller and freer. Since, therefore, I wanted to communicate with the most learned men of France on the subject of the Christian religion, having no other way, I determined to send them a Commentary. I have been so hurried all along, that I have often hardly had a chance to reread what I had written, much less to correct or embellish it. But it doesn't matter: it is a commentary, not an oration or a book that has been "held back eight years."* Do not, good reader, condemn offhand the things that may seem to displease you, but see whether what I say is in harmony with simple faith or not.

*Horace *Ars poetica,* 388f.: nonumque prematur in annum, membranis intus positis.

Farewell, and if you see that I am wrong anywhere, pray Christ that I, too, may finally see it; if, on the other hand, you perceive misty remnants of old error, again pray that He who is the light will take away all darkness, that we may all together see that which is true. Amen.

LIST OF TOPICS TREATED IN THIS WORK:*

HULDREICH ZWINGLI'S

COMMENTARY ON TRUE AND FALSE RELIGION

Essaying to write on true and false religion as displayed by Christians, I am faced at the very start with the danger of being judged presumptuous. For I know that there will immediately rise up those who will say that I have not duly considered my capabilities nor weighed the burden. Would that they had minds so wise, and so pure a faith, as to receive my words of explanation with a kindness equal to the composure with which I bear their hasty judgment! What, pray, can anyone more easily expound than the religion which he has in his heart of God and to God? Have there not always been persons who have differed in their religious views and who have

*In the first edition this list is at the end of the book.

been religious in different ways? Certainly there have been those who thought it not worth while to have God in their knowledge, Rom. 1: 28,* and, on the contrary, those who did think it worthwhile. Hence disagreement in regard to religion. For into those who counted nothing of greater value than, according to the word of the prophet, Jer. 9: 24, to understand and know God, the heavenly Spirit entered with such ample inspiration that they recognized only "the Lord who exerciseth loving-kindness, justice, and righteousness." But they that, on the other hand, were wise in their own conceit, or mighty, or rich, determined about God as seemed good to themselves; yet, in order not to be esteemed impious, served Him with such worship as pleased themselves, not with that in which He delights. Thus it has gradually come about that many of us have embraced only such a religion as the deceitfulness of human wisdom has ventured to invent and spread abroad; and this is so far from deserving to be called "religion" that it ought more properly to be dubbed "hypocrisy, impiety, and superstition." It is, therefore, perfectly easy for me to write on true and false religion as displayed by Christians, and to render an account, as it were, of my faith, since I have drunk it in not from the stagnant pools of human wisdom, but from the living water of the divine Spirit, which is the word of God. Accordingly I care nothing for these critics, for it is not wares of my own that I am displaying, but the goods of the Lord that I offer, which, according to the word of the prophet [Isa. 55: 1], one may dispense without money and without price. If any man scorn them, let him scorn; if he make onslaught upon them, he will accomplish no more than the giants of story.

The Word Religion

Cicero, in the second book of his De Natura Deorum,†

*When Zwingli wrote, the text of the Bible had not yet been divided into verses. In this translation the verse numbers have been added.

†Cicero *De natura deorum,* II, 72. Qui omnia, quae ad cultum deorum pertinerent, diligenter retractarent et tamquam relegerent, religiosi dicti sunt ex relegendo, ut elegantes ex eligendo, itemque ex diligendo diligentes, etc.

thinks that the word "religion" was derived from the verb "relegere," because the religious carefully considered and, as it were, perused (relegerent) all the things that pertain to the worship of the gods. This meaning of the word will suit us, too; for I take "religion" in that sense which embraces the whole piety of Christians: namely, faith, life, laws, worship, sacraments. And when I distinguish religion from superstition by adding the words "true" and "false," I do it for this purpose: that, having set before you religion drawn from the true fountains of the word of God, I may offer you superstition also in another cup, as it were, not for anyone to drink of but for him to pour out and shatter. For it is usually the case that we get a clearer idea by comparing together things that are different and contrary than by portraying the one in elaborate detail and keeping the other out of sight; for some men's minds are so slow or so feeble that they either take in nothing except just what you put before them, or, from fear of princes, dare not speak out what they have taken in. I will speak plainly. There are many who, hearing that Christ's words [Luke 22:26], "But ye shall not be so," namely, exercising lordship, were said of those whom we call "ecclesiastics," are yet so unthinking that, when they see a bishop pursuing a course different from what Christ directed, they never say to themselves, "This, surely, is contrary to God's command." Others, again, are so timid that, though they see, they yet dare not proclaim that the thing is wicked. It will, therefore, be worth while, after we have spoken of real and true religion, next to treat of false religion also, that we may not, while constantly engaged in the earnest discussion of true religion, in fact prove irreligious, impious, and unbelieving. For this, we see plainly, is what is happening at this time, when we see that not only certan bishops but also several princes are making laws of this kind: "I want the gospel preached, but according to the letter, without any explanations or comparisons whatever." Doubtless they have observed that, as I have said, there are many who ponder nothing of their own motion, but if you give them a chance to think, take it and see the difference between religion and superstition—which is likely to bring no small damage to these gentry afterwards. Hence it happens that many hear the word of faith, but are nothing but bundles of superstition. What else is such a proceeding than setting uncracked nuts before little children? Being unable to reach the meat, they lick the shell, till finally in disgust they throw away shell and meat and all.

This then shall be the order of procedure in this work: I shall speak first of "true religion," then of "false," not in separate and distinct books, but in distinct sections.

[2]. Between Whom Religion Subsists

Now, since religion involves two factors, one that towards which religion reaches out, and one that which by means of religion reaches out towards the other, our next task must be to speak of each of these. That is, since it is God towards whom religion reaches out and man who by means of religion reaches out toward Him, religion cannot be duly treated of without first of all discerning God and knowing man.

[3]. God*

What God is is perhaps above human understanding, but not *that* God is. For many of the wise have got so far as to have no doubt of the existence of God, though there have been some who attributed divinity to many beings—through their limited understanding, no doubt, which did not venture to attribute to one and only one being the great power and majesty that they saw must belong to divinity. There were, however, men who perceived the μικρολογία ["mean conception"] these philosophers had of God, and saw that the existence of God was less certain if divinity were attributed to many than if to one only. Therefore (whether through divine or human agency I will not now consider, as I will discuss that point presently), they arrived at the opinion that there is one and only one God, though such is the sluggishness and carelessness of the human intellect that they did not think it of any great importance to hold fast to this recognition of God, but, content to have recognized the fact and satisfied with them-

*Cf. Zwingli's *On the providence of God,* in vol. 2 of this series, pp. 128-234.

selves for this, they scorned to live according to His will. And this we see the general body of Christian scholars doing even now, zealously disputing about the word and the true worship of God, but in fact not becoming one whit better men. The foundation on which they all build is what Paul wrote in Rom. 1, 19: "That which is known of God is manifest in them; for God manifested it unto them." Here I will treat in passing what I held back above. We here see plainly that that knowledge of God which we credit to some natural agency is really from God. "For God," Paul says, "manifested it." And what else is natural agency than the constant and uninterrupted operation of God, His disposition of all things? And whence, pray, comes our intellect but from Him, who "worketh all things in all" [I Cor. 12: 6]? Now Paul in this passage conformed somewhat to the usage of the Gentiles in speaking of God, not because he holds the view that our knowledge of God proceeds from human reason, but because this was the view of the Gentiles, between whom and the Jews he is here acting as mediator. Hence he carefully adds, "God manifested it unto them." Following his example, I have begun with the questions of God's existence and nature, in order that I may be more easily understood by those who have derived their knowledge of God from man rather than from God. Now I come back to Paul's words, that "the knowledge of God was manifest even in the Gentiles, for God manifested it unto them. For the invisible things of him," he says, "are clearly seen, being understood by the things that were made from the foundation of the world, even his power and Godhead; so that they are without excuse, because they indeed knew God, but glorified him not as God, neither were thankful; nay rather became vain in their reasonings, and their foolish heart was darkened. And though in their own judgment they were wise, they became fools, and changed the glory of the uncorruptible God for the likeness of an image not merely of mortal man, but even of birds and four-footed beasts, and creeping things, etc." Therefore, that God exists was generally acknowledged among all the heathen, but in widely different ways. Some came to the recognition of one God but did not worship Him as they ought; though of these there were very few. Others, seeing clearly a might and power grander than that of man, recognized that this was God. They did not, however, regard it as the one only Power, but turned to themselves for a conception of what kind of being God was. So they, first of all, divided Him into many, because they were incapable of comprehending His infinite power; and presently they clothed these many with different forms according to their own imaginations. Hence the worship of idols and spirits, who cunningly made themselves such as poor mortals in their poor wisdom had installed as gods and distinguished with various forms. Thus I think it is clearly apparent that nearly all the heathen have agreed in acknowledging that God exists, though some have made Him many, others have made Him fewer, and a very few have made Him one. Yet from slowness of mind and confidence in their own wisdom they have disregarded Him, have held such views of Him as pleased them, and likewise have worshipped Him as they chose. On this subject not only our people but also the philosophers* have written lengthy volumes.

Now the faithful (for this is the generally accepted term for believers or pious persons, or worshippers of the true God) are by virtue of this one thing faithful, because they believe in one only true and omnipotent God and have faith in Him only. Furthermore, how it comes about that the pious hold this view of God, and do not, after the fashion of the heathen, make just any unknown power God, is easy for a pious man to explain: It comes about through the power and grace of Him in whom we believe; for as far as the nature and endowment of man are concerned, there is no difference between the pious man and the impious. Accordingly, in the realm of error in regard to gods, anything that could happen to one man could happen to any other, unless there were some higher power to call and attach to itself the human heart, which has no natural aversion to those who are most completely in error. Here, then, the first traces of faith and piety disclose themselves. It is not the fact, as most men have thought, that the faithful become faithful because they hear Moses say [Gen. 1:1], "In the beginning God created the heaven and the earth"; for those are numberless who hear this but do not believe the

*The heathen philosophers.

world was made according to the Mosaic tradition. So also those who hear the Lord Himself speak, and see Him do miracles, are not all straightway pious; for both in early times and in Christ's time there were men who were so far from turning to God because they saw or heard, that none raged more violently not only against the pious but against piety itself. Since, therefore, it is clear that whoever upon hearing the words, "In the beginning God created the heaven and the earth," immediately believes that the world is the work of God does not come to this through the power of the words or of our intellect (for if the words could effect this, all would be made pious; and if our intellect could, no one who heard would be impious), it is manifest that the faithful believe that God exists, and that the world is His work, etc., just because they are taught this by God. It is of God alone, therefore, that you believe that God exists and that you have faith in Him.

Furthermore, *what* God is, we have just as little knowledge of from ourselves as a beetle has of what man is. Nay, this infinite and eternal divine is much farther separated from man than man is from the beetle, because a comparison between any kinds of created things can more properly be made than between any created thing and the Creator, and all perishable things are nearer and more closely related to each other than to the eternal and unbounded divine, however much you may find in them a likeness and footprints, as they say,* of that divine. Since, then, we can in no way attain of our own effort to a knowledge of what God is—for if, according to Solomon's words, Eccles. 1: 13-18, all things (he is speaking of things under the sun) are so difficult that man cannot unfold them, what presumption it would be to try to explain what God is!—and since Isaiah, 45: 15, in solemn warning says, "Verily thou art a God that hidest thyself," it must be admitted that only by God Himself can we be taught what He is. For, according to the view of Paul, I Cor. 2: 11, as no one "knoweth the things of a man, save the spirit of the man, which is the man himself, even so all are ignorant of the things of God save the Spirit Himself of God." We may well call it the rash boldness of a Lucifer or a Prometheus if any one

*Cf. Rom. 4: 12; II Cor. 12: 18; I Pet. 2:21.

presumes to know from any other source what God is than from the Spirit Himself of God.

All, therefore, is sham and false religion that the theologians have adduced from philosophy as to what God is. If certain men have uttered certain truths on this subject, it has been from the mouth of God, who has scattered even among the heathen some seeds of the knowledge of Himself, though sparingly and darkly; otherwise they would not be true. But we, to whom God Himself has spoken through His Son and through the Holy Spirit, are to seek these things not from those who were puffed up with human wisdom, and consequently corrupted what they received pure, but from the divine oracles. For when men began to disregard these, they fell into all that is fleshly, *i. e.,* into the inventions of philosophy, took to believing these, and, relying upon them, not only held such views as they liked about God, but forced others to hold the same. And this, though none of them would have permitted any one to hold such view of himself as that other, whoever he was, wished. Such is the arrogance of the flesh that gave itself out as theology. We wish to learn out of His own mouth what God is, lest we become corrupt and do abominable works. Psalm 14.

When Moses asked the Lord, Exod. 3:13, to declare His name unto him, in order that he might be in a better position to deal with the Children of Israel, the Lord said unto him, "I AM THAT I AM." In these words God disclosed Himself wholly; for it is just as if He had said, "I am he who am of myself, who am by my own effort, who am absolute being, who 'am' par excellence." And this meaning He immediately brings out by adding, "This shalt thou say unto the children of Israel, He that is hath sent me unto you." By these words He indicated that He alone is the being (esse) of all things; for unless you take it in this way, that "He that is" is, and alone is, the being of all things, the Lord would not have distinguished Himself from other things that have being, which, though they have being from Him and through Him, yet still have being; and consequently God would be regarded as having evaded the question of Moses, rather than as having answered it. For suppose that neither Moses nor the Children of Israel understood the words "He that is" to mean anything different from what we mean when we say of anything that it is, what else do you suppose could have been understood both by Moses and by the Children of Israel than, "Some one hath sent me unto you"? And what would there have been great or remarkable or worthy of faith in that? It is plain, therefore, that by the words, I AM THAT I AM, and "He that is hath sent me unto you," Moses understood Him who is of His own nature, and who so is as to be the being of all things; and that the Children of Israel understood the same words in the same sense. For they never could have been persuaded by somebody thus casually announced to go away, leaving Egypt behind them, and to follow one whom they knew not. The same thing becomes still plainer when we examine the etymon of the supreme name of God, which the Jews pronounce as "Adonai," to be sure, in reading, in spite of the fact that the signs, *i. e.*, the letters, by no means form that word. Not that the Hebrews cannot read it according to the value of the letters, but because they think the name ineffable on account of its sanctity. For this name is derived from the word for being; or perhaps the word which to them signifies being is derived from this name. For "Hih" [היה] signifies "was" to them, and "Ihuh" [יהוה] is the four-lettered supreme name of God, which still remains ineffable among the Jews.* When, therefore, Moses heard the aforesaid words of God, he straightway understood that He that is, and from whom all things are, was speaking to him. And this the Lord manifested to him still more clearly, when further He bade him begin before the elders of Israel thus [Exod. 3:16]: "The Lord God of your fathers appeared unto me, etc.," now plainly calling Himself "Lord" from His power and majesty, as He had just before from His being called Himself "I AM," and "He that is." By all this I wish to make this point only, that the first thing in acquiring knowledge of God is to know that He is he who is by nature, who Himself is, and who receives being from none other. From this we afterwards are easily brought to see clearly that

*In the first sermon which Zwingli preached at Berne, there is a very similar treatment of the word [יהוה]. See the Egli-Finsler-Köhler edition of Zwingli's Works, vol. VI, No. 116.

all things are from God, and that nothing we can see can have being from itself, but must have its being and existence from another, from this source and fountain of being, namely, God. He shall be, then, the only God who has His being from Himself, and who bestows being upon all, and so bestows it that they could not possibly exist a moment unless God existed, who is being and life unto all, sustains all things, governs all things. This Isaiah, 40: 12, has beautifully indicated, saying: "Who hath measured the waters in the hollow of his hand, and weighed heaven with his palm? Who hath poised with three fingers the bulk of the earth, and weighed the mountains in scales, and the hills in a balance, etc.?"

This "Being" is as really good as it is being. For as it exists alone and of itself, so it is alone good, true, right, just, holy; for it is of itself good, true, right, etc. This is again clear from His own words, Gen. 1: 31, "And God saw everything that he had made, and, behold, it was very good." If, therefore, such a countless brood of created things was very good, in the sense that singly and collectively they were good, it is clear that their author must be good, and in such a way good as to have his goodness from no other but his own self, and to be not only the force and essence of all things that are, but the source and fountain of all good. And this Christ expresses a little more plainly, Luke 18: 19, saying: "None is good, save one, that is, God." If, now, all the things which He has made are exceeding good even in His own judgment, and nevertheless none is good save God alone, it follows that all the things which are are in Him and through Him. For since all the things which are are good, and yet God alone is good, all the things which are are God; *i. e.,* the reason they exist is because God exists and is their essence. This Paul expressed thus, Rom. 11: 36, "For of him, and through him, and in him,* are all things."

This good, therefore, is not a thing idle or inert, so as to lie torpid and motionless, moving neither itself nor other things; for we saw above that it is the essence and constitution of all things. What does this mean but that through it and in

*In ipso: the reading of the Latin Vulgate. English versions follow the Greek original, εἰς αὐτόν. See Zwingli's comment, *ante,* vol. 2, p. 148.

it all things are contained and live and move [cf. Acts 17: 28]? Indeed, it is called by the philosophers ἐντελέχεια καὶ ἐνέργεια *i. e.*, the perfect, efficient, and consummating power, which, since it is perfect, will never cease, never rest, never waver, but continually so keep, direct, and govern everything that in all things made or done no fault can intervene able either to impede its power or to defeat its purpose. And this, again, is made manifest by His own word, for at the beginning of the story of creation you find [Gen. 1: 3]: "And God said, Let there be light: and there was light." See how light when called not only was immediately at hand, but in obedience to the command of its Creator appeared from nothing. For so great is His power that, when He calls things that are not, they obey like those that are [cf. Rom. 4: 17], even if they first have to be born of nothing. And a little after He says: "Let the earth bring forth the green herb and such as yields seed, and the fruit tree bearing fruit after its kind, whose seed is in itself, upon the earth: and it was so." See how here the crude earth at the first word of command from its Creator put on a glad aspect! For when the waters had retired to their own depths and the earth had appeared in its own place, it was bare and unsightly to look upon. God was unwilling, therefore, that its bareness should be exposed to the eyes of mortals, and bade it straightway clothe itself with grass and adorn itself by producing trees, that to all the different kinds of animals, as they forthwith came into existence, it might be able to offer a shelter according to the nature of each. And not this only, but, that there might never be a scarcity of food, He conferred upon the grass and the trees the power of producing seed, so that when they had given us for the exigencies of winter all that they had, they might presently with the returning spring gird themselves again for the same task, and so on alternately without end. When we see this going on every year in unchanging course, do we not recognize the measureless power and wisdom of the Creator, and His care and grace towards His work? For He not only spoke and it was so, commanded and the things He desired were created, but He also fed what He had created. Why, He forgot not even the raven's young [Job 38: 41; Ps. 147: 9;

Lk. 12: 24]. Since, therefore, all that moves or lives lives and moves because it has being (for unless it had being it could not move or live, and in that it has being has it in God and through God), it may be most clearly inferred that, as God is being and existence to all things, so He is the life and motion of all things that live and move. And this is beautifully shown by Paul, Acts 17: 28, when after a somewhat extended discourse he sums up by saying: "For in him we live, and move, and have our being; as certain even of your own poets* have said, For we are also his offspring." We see here in passing how the Apostle quotes from profane writers, not by any means using them as authorities, but, when the heavenly Spirit has willed to say anything through their mouths, showing where we may find this, so that we may not have to dig over all their filth in the search for one or two pearls. I come back to the subject. It is clear from this, therefore, that just as all things have being and existence in God and through God, so all things live and move in Him and through Him. This He Himself shows also by the mouth of His servant Moses, saying, Deut. 30: 20, "For he is thy life, and the length of thy days."

Again, He is not the life and motion of all things in such a way that either He Himself blindly puts breath or motion into them, or they which breathe and move ask blindly of Him life or motion. How could things that could not even exist unless they existed from Him ask of Him, or how ask before they existed? It is evident, therefore, that God not only is a sort of stuff, as it were, from which all things have being and motion and life, but is at the same time such wisdom, knowledge, and foresight that nothing is hidden from Him, nothing unknown to Him, nothing beyond His reach, nothing disobedient to Him. Hence not even the mosquito has its sharp sting and musical hum without God's wisdom, knowledge, and foresight. His wisdom, then, knows all things even before they exist, His knowledge comprehends all things, His foresight regulates all things. For that thing which is God would not be the supreme good unless it were at the same time supreme wisdom and foresight. For if there were anything which could be hidden from God, His wisdom and knowledge

*Aratus *Phaenomena* 5, and Cleanthes *Hymn to Zeus* 5.

would be ineffectual to that extent, and if any thing were regulated by other providence than His, then divine providence would be inert and defective in this particular, and accordingly would not be supreme nor absolute; for in as far as it failed to act it would be imperfect. But this is so far from being true of God that nothing is so at variance with His nature and character as imperfection. For that which is imperfect is not God; and, on the other hand, that alone is God which is perfect, *i. e.,* absolute, and which lacks nothing, but has everything that befits the supreme good. I am not speaking here of perfection as the theologians usually speak. Nothing, therefore, can escape God, nothing defeat or alter His purpose and ordering; and when we with more temerity than faith demand of Him a reason for His acts or designs, asking why He made the flea, the gadfly, the wasp, and the hornet, things that are a plague to man and beast, we simply display a vain and useless feminine curiosity. As if, indeed, the human mind could comprehend divine wisdom, and as if, when one or two things become known, many more would not emerge, insisting upon being known just like the first! No mind but the infinite and immeasurable mind can hold the knowledge of all these things, while one as narrow as is the human mind simply makes vain labor for itself by such inquisitiveness; as Solomon reminds us in Ecclesiastes, Chap. 1. In contemplating divine wisdom and providence poor mortals will, therefore, have to do as each does in his own sphere. Different persons have different utensils and implements adapted to their activities, and they desire the use of some to be disclosed to all, that of others to remain unknown to all, though not unknown to themselves; for they know how and for what purpose they are going to use them at the proper time. So, let us contemplate with reverence what God has wished disclosed to us. But what He has hidden, let us not impudently desire to touch, lest it be taken indignantly away from us, and punishment be inflicted upon us for our rashness, as was done to Prometheus* of story. For the dwelling of God is large, the heaven is His abode and the earth His

*Because Prometheus brought fire from heaven to men he was chained to a rock and his liver torn by an eagle.

footstool [cf. Isa. 66:1]; and the contents are so vast and various that one who desires to know them all should rather be overwhelmed with despair than entertain the hope of comprehending them all. If you set yourself to examine one grape leaf closely and completely, you will fail. It has a stem running through the middle to the apex, and from this aortas, or principal veins, that branch out and extend to particular areas, and from these the so-called mesial or mesenteric veins, minute ducts that run out to every last particle of the blade, properly distributing the sap—just such complexity as you will find when you consider man as a whole or the entire universe. Yet the workmanship in this little leaf will force you to give up before you have learned it all. See how all human wisdom, in fact, seems to amount to nothing, and is forced to confess its ignorance and lack of knowledge; but neither ignorant nor lacking in knowledge is the divine wisdom and foresight, by which all things are rightly done and regulated.

Now it is time to bring forward the witness of the word itself to everything that has been said so far about the wisdom and providence of God.

Solomon, Prov. 8:22-36, has a fine description in praise of wisdom, commending it first for its antiquity, in that it was with the Lord Himself before He began to create the universe; and then because afterwards through it the poles of the world were hung in place, and all things put together. And Jeremiah, 51:15, says: "He hath made the earth by his power, he hath prepared the world by his wisdom, and stretched out the heavens by his understanding." But none speaks more delightfully than David in Psalm 104. He portrays both the wisdom and the providence of God so that you see God as Creator balancing the mountains in His mighty hand, putting each in its place, drawing out the valleys between and the cool streams in the valleys, spreading out the fields, thrusting back the turbulent sea into its own depths, that there may be no confusion from its unruliness, then assigning settlers to each region and adding provision abundantly.

Now I will hasten on to the witness of the New Testament, content with the more striking passages just cited, because the whole Scripture of the Old Testament views everything as done by the providence of God. Hence the frequent appearing of angels, the many utterances of God Himself, and in time of urgent necessity the miracles. Hence the watchful care and guardianship of God over individual men dwelling among the wicked, such as Noah, Abraham, Lot, and others. Hence the sending of prophets to give warning of what was to come, and the terrible chastenings sent upon those who did not heed their warnings, the frequent victories at the hands of the Lord, if they had been obedient, the frequent defeats and disasters if disobedient.

Christ warns us distinctly, Matt. 6:25-34, not to be troubled even about the things that pertain to the body, since we can be sure that in these matters God's providence exercises care over us, from the fact that He provides so bountifully for the birds of the air, and clothes the lilies of the field so sumptuously that Solomon's gorgeous robes of state and all his adornments are mean in comparison. How much more will He give all these things to us, who are of much more value in His sight! Why, He says in Chapter 5:36, that it is not in our power to make one hair of our own heads white if it is black, or black if it is white. And that even the hair of our heads, a thing of so little account that it can be taken away without any loss, is His care, Luke also testifies, 12:7: "Even the very hairs of your head are all numbered." See how wide is the care of the heavenly providence, and how sure: "are all numbered," He says. What will the advocates of free will say here? Will they argue that there is a trope here? But that is just what I maintain, that the words are used τροπικῶς ["tropically"]. Must we, then, wait for them to expound the trope? Not in the least, for a child can explain the meaning of this trope: namely, that God exercises constant care over even those things that in our judgment seem hardly worthy of human care. Or is it a hyperbole? "When I feed the birds and clothe the flowers, shall I forget you? Are ye not of much more value in my sight?" [Mt. 6:25-34.] But of this more when I come by and by to speak of free will. In Matt. 10:29, Christ says: "Are not two sparrows sold for a penny? and not one of them shall fall on the ground without your Father." Here no one may fairly plead a hyperbole. It is plainly an argument from the less to the greater, in which the first term must be absolutely true; otherwise the conclusion will not hold. Christ, then, means this: "Since not one of the sparrows bought for a penny falls to the ground even by accident without the Heavenly Father, how much more will you, who are of so much value in His eyes, nowhere perish without His so ordering?" This, then, will be absolutely true, that God is the author even of things which to us seem to happen accidentally. Christ seemed to the sisters of Lazarus not to know that their brother was sick [cf. Jn. 11: 3]; but after it was told Him, He made it plain in a word whether God could fail to know anything and whether anything could happen without His care and purpose and ordinance. For he said: "This sickness is not unto death, but for the glory of God, that the Son of God may be glorified thereby." You see whence this sickness came? From God, surely; for He was going to use it for the glory of His Son. Christ answered his disciples in the same fashion, John 9: 3, when they asked for whose sin it came about that a man who was there was born blind: "Neither did this man sin," He said, "nor his parents: but that the work of God should be made manifest in him."

I will be content with these citations now, meaning to treat this topic, as I said, more fully elsewhere. Do you, good reader, remember these meanwhile, that you may not be bored to death with repetition. For the whole business of predestination, free will, and merit rests upon this matter of providence.

Now it would be vain, fruitless, and useless to mortals, if this supreme good, God, were wise for Himself alone, as is said; were goodness, life, motion, knowledge, foresight for Himself alone. For in that case He would not differ at all from mortals, whose natural characteristic is to sing for themselves, to look out for their own interests, and to wish themselves better off than others. It must be, therefore, that this supreme good, which is God, is by its nature kind and bountiful, not with that bounty with which we like to seem bountiful, looking for a return or for glory, but with a bounty that causes Him to desire the profit of those to whom He gives, with only this one thing in view, that He may belong to those things which were made by Him; for He desires to impart Himself freely.

For, as He is the fountain-source of all things (for no one before he existed had any claim to be born of Him), so also is He unceasingly bountiful to those whom He begot with this one purpose, that they might enjoy His bounty. In a word, this good differs from other things that seem good in this, that they do not spend themselves ἀμισθωτί, *i. e.*, gratuitously, being mean and poor; whereas this, on the contrary, neither would nor could be spent except gratuitously. Again, things that are good merely in outward appearance desire to be sparing of themselves; for they can satisfy only a very few, being of narrow and slender compass. But this good is so exuberantly abundant that it is more than sufficient for the needs of all; for it is limitless and loves to impart itself. For it cannot enjoy others, for they are beneath it; and unless they enjoy it, from which they have their being, they in no wise can exist.

Now follow the testimonies to the preceding.

The whole company of created things testifies to this view. For if God had not willed that His works should enjoy Him, He never would have called them forth from nothing; for God does not enjoy them. For what purpose, then, did He create them? That they might enjoy their Creator.

In Genesis 15:1, the Lord thus speaks to Abraham: "Fear not, Abraham: I am thy shield, and thy exceeding great reward." What, pray, is it to be shield and reward, or prize, or good, which thou mayest enjoy, rich and abundant beyond what thou canst imagine, but to be God? Furthermore, that He thus of His own accord discloses Himself, to whom is this not a proof that He loves to impart Himself?

Isaiah, 45:1, proves clearly enough that all things are done by the providence and bounty of God, when he represents Him as talking to Cyrus. Cyrus did not know God, but God knew Cyrus, for He showered upon him victories, riches, and whole kingdoms so bountifully that the East and the West ought of right to have seen that He who gave all these things so lavishly was the one true God. After a long admonition the Lord speaks thus to him [Isa. 45:21-22] (not to write down the whole speech): "Tell ye, and come, and consult together. Who hath declared this from the beginning? From that time I have foretold this." (See the providence which exercises care even over the impious.) "Have not I the Lord, and there is no God else beside me? A just God and a Saviour, there is none beside me. Be converted to me, and be ye saved, all ye ends of the earth: for I am God, and there is no other, etc." See the bounty with which He of His own accord invites to Himself all the ends of the earth. See also the certainty that He is the only one who dispenses all things justly, is the only Savior, and there is no God beside Him.

In the same way He displays his kindness, Isa. 55: 1, when He calls to Himself all who desire or need heavenly wisdom and help, thus: "All ye that thirst, come to the waters, and ye that have no money, make haste, buy, and eat." See how He encourages them not only to hasten, but also to drink generously.

Now from the Old Covenant enough testimony has been adduced; for what is the whole gist of it but the showing that God is the only one who saves, who looks out for us, who desires that all things be asked from Him? "I, even I, am he that blotteth out thy transgressions for mine own sake," Isa. 43: 25. "The earth is full of the mercy of the Lord," Psalms 33: 5; and [Ps. 145: 15], "Thou givest them their meat in due season;" and [Ps. 145: 16], "Thou openest thy hand, and fillest with blessing every living creature." And Joel, 2: 27, "Ye shall know that I am in the midst of Isræl." And what is it to be in the midst of Isræl but to be among them in such a way that it is not necessary to ask His aid as from one afar off, but as from Him alone who dwells among them in familiar and affable fashion like one of themselves? For, being in the midst means this, that there is no haughtiness for anyone to dread.

From the New Testament, what other testimony shall I bring forward than Jesus Christ, the Son of God and the Virgin, who is himself the Testament? For when we were by nature children of wrath, Eph. 2: 1-7, we were restored to favor by God, who is very rich in mercy, through his Son Jesus Christ. God also appointed him a propitiator, Rom. 3: 25, that they that have faith in his blood may be accounted holy and spotless before the Father. He, then, is our propitiation, therefore also our covenant and testament, which God has made with us. He is Himself the propitiator also, for through

Him we have access to God, I John 2:1; Heb. 10:19; Eph. 2:18.

Furthermore, whatever Christ is to us, He is by the bountiful gift of God; for we have not of ourselves merited that He should offer His Son for our life. If it had been possible for life to be given for our merits, there would have been no need of Christ. If there had been no need of Him, why should the Father clothe Him with flesh? The work of God is not idle, nor vain, nor superfluous, but the Son of God came into this world that we might have life and that we might have it most abundantly. Christ Himself, to reveal Himself wholly to us, cries, Matt. 11:28, "Come unto me, all ye that labor and are heavy laden, and I will give you rest." What, good God, is it to be bountiful and generous, if this is not? We all teem with evils outside and inside, to such an extent that we are weighed down under them as under a vast load. The Son of God sees this woe and calls us all to Him. And that no one's consciousness of guilt may prevent him from thinking that he may go to Him, He says distinctly, "all, both ye that labor and ye that are heavy laden" [Mt. 11:28]; for He had come to save sinners and to do it without recompense. This the divine prophets had foretold many ages before, especially Jeremiah, who says, 31:33-34, that it will come to pass that we shall all know the Lord on account of His bounty, with which He will be so indulgent to our sins that He will remember them and reproach us with them no more. What generosity more clear and striking could be shown us? John 13:13 declares that He is rightly called Lord and Master who yet condescended to wash His disciples' feet, and to wipe them with a towel. What else than most devoted bounty is this? In Rom. 8:32 Paul says that God "spared not His own Son, but delivered him up for us all," and immediately argues in this way: "How shall he not also with him freely give us all things?" By this he certainly means: Can anyone offer anything greater for a friend or brother than his only son? Now, God delivered up His Son for us. Could He have proved more clearly the bounteousness of His mercy to us? Will He who freely gave His Son be able to deny us anything? How can it be that, having given His Son, he will not with him give all things? For all things in heaven and on earth are less than the Son. For this purpose, then, He delivered up His Son for us, that we, seeing that what was highest as well in heaven as on earth had been made ours, might be sure that nothing could be denied us. For He who has given His Son has given His all. For the Father hath nothing which the Son also hath not. This will, perhaps, be enough to show the untaught that as God is the fountain-source of all good, so He is bountiful and by no means niggardly or inexorable, but is so lavish and prodigal of Himself for the benefit of those who enjoy Him that He delights to be taken, and held, and possessed by all. And He is, accordingly, so ever ready to help that He always runs to our assistance and never lags. Hence some of the Greeks think* that the word θεός, "God," is derived from θέειν ["to run"], because He runs to us everywhere, and is everywhere present to aid.

But why should I treat at greater length of the knowledge of God, when the very words that I have quoted from His own mouth have no more value with the impious man than so-called gift goods? Anyone who casts these pearls before those swine will find he has been feeding the wind. On the other hand, the pious have in their own hearts too good and intimate a knowledge of God to get any increase of it from these words of mine. For to them God is everything—being, life, light, strength, treasure, sufficiency of all things, a veritable storehouse of blessings. Having experienced this, holy men of God have from the creation of the world called God by various names, as one may see all through both Testaments, naming Him Lord or God, Life, Existence, Father, the Mighty, Light, All-powerful, All-sufficient. Yet all these names they have given Him from the faith within them, because, namely, they felt in their hearts as to God that He was their strength, life, being, father, etc. And from that faith with which they credited to Him strength, life, etc., they afterwards gave Him the names Enduring Power, Lord, Life, Strength. It must be admitted, therefore, that what I have said thus far about knowledge of God is idle unless faith be added. Hence no man can reproach me with having based my teaching about the knowledge of God

*Cf. Plato *Kratylos*, 397 C; Macrobius *Saturnal.* I, 23. 3. Zwingli again notes this etymology in his *Reply to Emser;* see below, p. 388.

upon human persuasions. For, in the first place, I have relied upon the divine utterances only; and, in the second place, I have shown without reserve that it is not through human power that we come to the knowledge and worship of God, for that "is not of him that willeth, nor of him that runneth, but of God that hath mercy" [Rom. 9:16]. It is He who grants that the works of His Hand recognize Him only as true God, Lord, Savior, Helper, Strength, Life, Light, Father, the heaped-up measure of all good things, generous, kind, well-wishing, eager to impart Himself freely (for all that is what I understand by this word "God"). For unless we feel in this way in regard to Him, we shall never have faith in Him alone, never have recourse to Him alone, never love Him with all our heart and with all our strength. So much for the knowledge of God.

[4]. Man

To know man is as toilsome as to catch a cuttlefish, for as the latter hides himself in his own blackness in order not to be caught, so does man, as soon as he sees one is after him, stir up such sudden and thick clouds of hypocrisy that no Lynceus, no Argus, can discover him. Not only that biting critic Momus* complained of this, but the divine herald of the Gospel, Paul, understood it so well that in I Cor. 2:11 he speaks on this wise: "For who among men knoweth the things of a man, save the spirit of the man, which is in him?" Though he says this only for the purpose of illustration, he really holds it as established that the human heart hides its purposes with such zeal and so many wiles that no one can have knowledge of them but itself; for unless this were his view, he could not logically draw the conclusion he is trying to prove in the passage. And Jeremiah says of this fleer from the light and this wiggler of ours, chap. 17:9, "The heart of man is wicked and unsearchable. Who can know it? I, the Lord, who search the heart and try the reins."

From this testimony it becomes manifest that man cannot be known by man. He has such recklessness in lying, such readiness in pretending and concealing, that when you think

*The spirit of censoriousness.

you have caught him somewhere, you find he has long since slipped away elsewhere. If you say, "The prophet bears witness openly that the human heart is wicked" [cf. Jer. 17:9], he immediately crawls out with the explanation that "wicked" is put here for "inclined to wickedness," and that it is not asserted of all men; looking the while to this, that, if he can convince you that some are strangers to all wickedness, he shall himself be counted among these, for the very reason that he so stoutly defends the glory and innocence of an honest heart.

Since, then, it is such an unattainable thing to penetrate into the recesses of the human heart, we shall doubtless have to give up the hope of a knowledge of it. So be it, then! May everyone learn to know himself—by another in no wise is one known—although the defenses of self-love are so strong that very few persons, if any at all, break through to a knowledge of their own selves.

Under no other teacher or guide than God alone, the builder of man, will it ever be granted to see the secrets of the human heart. For as He created man, so He knows all the headwaters of his cunning and the source whence they come. All of which Jeremiah signified by the words [17:9]: "Who can know it?" doubtless not supposing that any one would venture to avouch that he had knowledge of it, except the God who fashioned it. Hence, at once, he adds: "I, the Lord, who search the heart and try the reins."

From the Lord God, therefore, the Creator of man, is the knowledge of man to be sought, no less than the knowledge of Himself, though for different reasons. The knowledge of God is denied to our understanding because of its feebleness and His glory and splendor, but the knowledge of man, because of his boldness and readiness in lying and dissembling, as has been said.

The Heavenly Builder formed man in His own image, and, having formed him, placed him in a garden abounding in all delights, nor only as a denizen of it, but as proprietor and lord; but on this condition, that he might eat of everything that grew there except of the tree of the knowledge of good and evil. This tree's fruit he was not to touch or taste, and if he did so he was to die an instant death, Gen. 2:17. The

Devil envied man this happy condition, and persuaded Adam's spouse that it was from fear for His dominion that God had forbidden them that tree, the very name of which showed that as soon as they had eaten of its fruit they would become like gods, *i. e.,* would know good and evil. The unhappy woman believed his high promises, plucked the fruit, ate, and then with faithful intent gave to her husband. He, being without knowledge or experience of snares and feminine indiscretion, obeyed (for what could he refuse to his wife?), and did what no husband would have declined to do to please his wife. But see how evils burst suddenly upon us from quarters whence they are least feared. Our first parent, having hoped through the knowledge of good and evil to become a god, learned nothing but his own disgrace and found everlasting death. For thus God spake unto him, "In the day that thou eatest thereof thou shalt surely die." But it is easier for heaven and earth to pass away than for any word of God [Mt. 24: 35]. Therefore, as He had foretold that man should die, man died when he had plunged his teeth into the fatal fruit.

But it is necessary to consider what sort of death Adam died after he ate the fruit of the forbidden tree.

First, then, it is evident that he did not immediately die a natural death when he ate this food, for he lived many ages afterwards. Next, it is evident that in due time the fatal day came, for no other reason than that he had once transgressed the law: "Through sin came death," Rom. 5: 12. For he would have lived in happiness forever, if he had refrained from eating the unhappy apple. It is evident, in the third place, that Adam did besides die a death of some kind as soon as he put to his mouth his reckless hand laden with the fatal fruit. For the word of God says: "In the day that thou eatest, thou shalt surely die." Death, therefore, ensued in the same moment in which he ate. But bodily death did not immediately ensue; it was, therefore, the death of the soul that instantly ensued. For the death of the body was born of sin, as has been said, whence also it followed the death of the soul. This is clearly put in Rom. 5: 12: "As by one man sin entered into the world, and death by sin; and so death passed upon all men, for that all have sinned." The death, therefore, by which Adam so suddenly perished was sin; and this death is as much more destructive than bodily death as the cause is greater than the effect. For the death that is sin is the parent of bodily death.

Now we must see what the death that is sin is, or what its character is.

We infer the character of everything we see from the inward urge by which it is impelled to the pursuit and acquisition of what it desires. Thus we call a man avaricious who for the sake of pelf ploughs the sea, though he fears its dangers.* We must, therefore, take pains to observe just what it was that Adam showed his character by seeking. He was going to be equal with the gods, and if he succeeded he would know by the exercise of his own faculties what good and evil were. This, then, is the bait that he craved and by which he was taken: to be a God and himself to know what good was, what evil was. But whence could this craving have originated except from love of self? For we all wish things to be better for us than for others. Φιλαυτία, therefore, *i. e.*, love of self, was the cause of Adam listening to the evil counsel of his wife. Man is, then, by nature a lover of self; not by the nature with which he had been made and endowed by God, but by that which he acquired, when, not content with the lot that God had given him, he desired in his heart to become skilled in good and evil, yea, to become equal with God. Since, therefore, man has become guilty of self-love, and has been convicted of that offense, it is manifest that the death that is sin, as far as its character is concerned, consists in man's unceasingly loving himself, pleasing himself, trusting in himself, crediting everything to himself, thinking he sees what is straight and what is crooked, and believing that what he approves all ought to approve, even his Creator. For he was caught αὐτοφόρῳ, in the very act, of trying to make himself a God knowing good and evil, without the knowledge of his Creator. His viciousness, therefore, his inborn character, his defect of nature (and what is that but death?) cannot be denied.

But it is better to prove the matter by the testimony of the mouth of God than by arguments, even though these are

*Cf. Horace, Car. I, 1, 13f. . . . ut trabe Cypria Myrtoum pavidus nauta secet mare.

founded upon the word of God. For this Proteus of ours, with whom we are dealing, evades, denies, lies, unless you convict him by witnesses. For he is shameless and reckless, puts on any shape [cf. II Cor. 11: 14], makes all sorts of promises and all sorts of threats, to prevent your dragging him out into the light. Therefore, God says, Gen. 6: 3, "My Spirit shall not abide in man forever, because he is flesh." God here gives man up as a degenerate, because he has become wholly flesh. And this He also testified to before, when He pushed him out of the nest as an intruder, and stationed a guard at the gates of Paradise to prevent him from returning, Gen. 3: 24. But if man is wholly flesh, what, pray, does he meditate but the things of the flesh [cf. Rom. 8: 5]? And if this is all he meditates, what other part does he play than that of an enemy of God? For the spirit lusts against the flesh, and the flesh against the spirit; "for these are contrary the one to the other" [Gal. 5: 17]. See how plain it begins to be that man, in so far as he is man, and in so far as he thinks and acts in accordance with his own character, thinks and does nothing but what is of the flesh, of the enemies of God, of the adversaries of the Spirit. In the same passage we read [Gen. 6: 5f.]: "And God saw that the wickedness of man was great in the earth, and that every imagination of the thoughts of his heart was only evil continually. And it repented the Lord that he had made man on the earth, etc." Here we have the plain statement that the entire imagination of man is not only inclined to evil, but firmly fixed and set upon it, and that not at intervals (as people suffering from insanity or fever have seasons of less violence), but all the time. Afterwards we have, 8: 21, "The imagination or thought of man's heart is evil from boyhood." For this is the real sense of the Hebrew, and the Septuagint is not very different, "Since the mind of man is intent upon evil from his youth." But our translation* has: "The feelings and imagination of man's heart are prone to evil," a change in the sense certainly due to man's ignorance. For few mortals reach such a measure of scorn for themselves as to attribute nothing good to themselves, and to confess openly the evil desires of their innermost hearts. Hence it is that we cannot be induced

i. e., the Latin Vulgate.

to admit that our whole heart is evil. And, persistently denying this, we even go to the length, such is our boldness, of changing, or rather corrupting, the word of God to suit our view. This is what has been done here: where the real sense of the Hebrew is quite plainly "is evil," some one has dared to say,* "is prone to evil," so that he may not himself fall under suspicion of being evil by nature. Yet this was done very incircumspectly. For how did it lighten the cause of human wickedness to modify the statement here, when just before it was said that we are flesh and that all our imagination is intent upon evil continually? For since we are flesh we cannot help having always a taste for the things of the flesh; but all these are the very wickedness from which the worst fruits proceed, as Paul has taught, Gal. 5:19-21. The mind of man and the heart of man are, therefore, evil from his early years, because he is flesh, because he is a lover of self, of glory, of pleasure, and greedy of wealth, however he tries to disguise or conceal it. "For we are all hypocrites," Isa. 9:17, "and evil doers, and every mouth speaketh folly." And the Preacher cannot cry out sufficiently how vain we are, saying, Eccles. 1:2, "Vanity of vanities; all is vanity."

Now I turn to the testimony of the New Covenant.

In John 8:34, Christ says: "Everyone that committeth sin is the bond-servant of sin." Adam sinned. Therefore he became the slave of sin.

Paul, writing to the Romans, puts it thus, Rom. 6:16: "Know ye not, that to whom ye yield yourselves as servants to obey, his servants ye are whom ye obey?" Adam yielded himself to sin, for if he had not yielded himself, he never would have touched the forbidden fruit. Therefore he became its servant and slave. For unless, resolved to make himself like God, skilled in the knowledge of good and evil, he had first yielded himself to the counsel of the Devil, he would have had such a repugnance to the apple that he would not have deigned to look at it. Our first parent, then—not to go on offering kindly excuses—willingly and gladly yielded himself to the servitude of sin. Now, by virtue of his condition, a slave neither can nor ought to listen to anyone but the master to whom he has bound

*See above, p. 76.

himself. Man, therefore, meditates the sin which his master orders. But there is sin the moment man, disregarding the law of the Creator, has preferred to follow himself, rather than the standard of his Leader and Lord. He is the slave, I was saying, of him to whom he has gone over. But he has gone over to himself, abandoning the love of God through love of self. He is, therefore, his own slave: he loves himself more than God, more than anyone even. And this, at last, is to be dead, this is the death that is sin, this is the character of corrupted and fallen man.

In John 3: 6, Christ says: "That which is born of the flesh is flesh." It follows, therefore, that they that are born of the dead are themselves also dead. For as soon as Adam turned to himself, he degenerated and became flesh altogether. Being, therefore, flesh, he was also dead; for these are equivalent terms, to be flesh and to be dead, in the sense in which we are here speaking of death, as has been made plain above. Now, it cannot possibly be admitted that one who is dead can beget anything living. Therefore, Adam, being dead, cannot beget one who is free from death. For the dictum is immutable, "That which is born of the flesh is flesh."

In similar fashion Paul speaks, Rom. 7: 18: "For I know that in me, that is, in my flesh, dwelleth no good thing." He is speaking here not of the flesh that we have in common with the camel, for instance. Otherwise, what sense would there have been in saying that there is nothing good in our perishable flesh, a fact that even a blind man can see? No, he is speaking of the whole man, who, though he is compounded of soul and body, two things of diverse nature, is yet called flesh, because he meditates nothing but what is fleshly and death bringing. Paul makes this plain when he says a little before [Rom. 7: 14]: "We know that the law is spiritual: but I am carnal, sold under sin." Here, I say, is made plain what I am maintaining, namely, that Paul is speaking of the character of the sin and death to which we have been given over and sold by the defection of our first parent, as has been said.

I have, perhaps, pursued this theme farther than is necessary, but it will do no harm. The human heart is so vast that it is as hard to explore all its recesses and hiding places as to measure the ocean [cf. Isa. 40: 12] or to cleanse the stable of Augeas.* Hence it can easily hide its wickedness and retire into its depths. But He who is light [cf. Jn. 8: 12] cannot be deceived. From Him nothing can be hid, and He so completely discloses man to us that—if, at least, we believe His word—we can see clearly that man is by nature evil, however much he struggles and shuffles to conceal the fact. He from whose mouth we have heard this is true, and so it must be true. Man is, indeed, clever and bold in denying. If we put faith in him, he will never admit plainly that his nature is vile, but when a καρδιογνώστης ["heart-knowing," Acts 1: 24], God drags him out into the light, he is ashamed to deny that which he is conscious of. Nor here let anyone say: "If everyone admitted that he is conscious of this, what you have said of the wretchedness of human wickedness would indeed be much to the point; but there are some who either do not accede to the words of God and confess themselves evil, or, even if in their hearts they recognize their wickedness, yet, in the hope or desire of concealing it and preserving their reputation, are unwilling to seem to have recognized it." Right, indeed. Here we have coming up of its own accord the very thing I was after, namely, that for man to know himself it is almost as necessary to have God as his teacher as to have a knowledge of God, because man has so many deep caverns, in which he hopes to find such refuge that no one can find his hiding place, or even if he find it drag him out. We require God, therefore, as a sort of diver, and Him alone, in order really to explore man. And what I said above, that one ought not to expect to recognize God from His words unless faith be present (for if that be lacking, whatever you assert of Him will seem an idle tale), is also true in the study of man. For unless faith be present, so that a man believes that every word that proceedeth from God is true, he will be as far from knowing himself as is the distance between spirit and flesh. "For through the law is the knowledge of sin" [Rom. 3: 20]. But the law is spiritual, while we are carnal. Unless, therefore, the spirit enter into us, we shall remain carnal forever. For we are sold under sin [cf. Rom. 7: 14].

*The seventh labor of Hercules was the cleansing of the Augean stables.

Yet as long as we are carnal, we recognize not ourselves. For the flesh in no wise despises itself, but is in its own eyes ever great and fine, yea, even God. Faith, therefore, is just as necessary to a man for knowledge of himself as for a knowledge of God.

Now, your distinguished theologians and hypocrites of animal appetite, not knowing this, are satisfied—to quote but one of their views belonging to false religion—to grant that man's heart is prone to evil, at the same time attributing to him unimpaired power of choice, so as to be able freely to stretch out his hand towards anything he chooses. This is nothing else than trying to weave a rope out of sand or to make an angel of Belial. For as sand because of its character and form cannot possibly be woven together, so Belial* and man cannot be so changed that the one, the author of darkness, lies, treachery, and sin, becomes an angel of light [II Cor. 11: 14], and that the other stretches out his hand to any good thing, unless perhaps his greed and love of self, in the hope of receiving pleasure, pronounce something good, just as the author of our race stretched out his hand towards the apple in the hope of becoming God and knowing all things, a hope that could have had its origin in nothing except love of self. Since, therefore, man would measure all things by himself if God in His wisdom allowed him, theologists in vain attribute to him sound and unimpaired power of choice. But more on this question in the sequel,† if the Lord will grant it.

It will, perhaps, not be inconsistent with my purpose to introduce here, as a sort of imported embellishment, the opinion of a most learned and eloquent man—I mean Cicero—as given in the oration in defense of Archias, in which the passage showing that man does everything from a desire for glory agrees so completely with the divine teachings that the words seem to be due to the direct influence of God, rather than to be the unconstrained utterance of Cicero, the creature of glory. For how could he be revealing his true self in affirming here that we do everything from eagerness for glory, when at other times he wishes everything to seem done from patriotism and

*Cf. II Cor. 6: 15.
†*See* below, Section [24]. Merit.

love of virtue? These are his words:* "For virtue desires no other reward for hardships and dangers than that of glory and praise; and if you take that away, gentlemen, what reason is there why in this span of our life, meagre and short as it is, we should employ ourselves in laborious undertakings? Surely, if the mind had no presentiment of a hereafter, if it bounded all its thoughts by the limits within which the period of life is confined, it would not break itself with such toil, nor torture itself with so many cares and anxieties, nor so often risk life itself in the struggle. There dwells in every man of worth an influence which rouses his soul day and night with the spur of glory and whispers to him that the remembrance of our names must not be suffered to disappear with our life, but be made to endure through all future ages, etc." How Cicero here reveals the inner nature of man! He says there is a force dwelling in the souls even of the best that unceasingly spurs them on to the gaining of glory and summons to the task all their thoughts and plans and labors. But what he calls a "force" we who are the faithful know is nothing else than death and sin and the wretched condition of fallen man, in consequence of which he is forever a lover and devotee of self. And if among the faithful you find any who deny that man does everything for the sake of his own private glory and gain, you may consider it as settled that they are themselves not faithful, but carnal and servants of sin. For as long as we defend ourselves, it is certain that the light of the Spirit is lacking, which shows and discloses man to himself. Thus, even by a heathen writer are we taught that all our thoughts are directed towards ourselves. And let no one be influenced by the fact that Cicero declares the souls of all are possessed by an eager desire for glory; but, on the contrary, let us observe that some are not at all intent upon glory, but rather upon pelf or feasting or lust. For what Cicero said refers to the best, his thought being that it is characteristic of them to make of all right actions so many rungs, as it were, in the ladder of glory. The meaner, or rather viler, spirits, who measure all things by feasting and lust, are considered inferior to those eager for glory. I am speaking of that eagerness for glory which walks in honorable paths; for those

Pro Archia poeta 28-29.

who glory in bad things are sometimes cast out by the bad. But those that are set upon pelf lay their schemes partly with a view in this way to raise themselves on high, partly with a view to supplying the means of satisfying the demands of their gluttony and lust. It remains, however, fixed and unshaken that all the designs of every man are sin, in so far as he forms them as man; for he measures all things by himself, cares for himself alone, thinks of himself more honorably than of others. And although he may see himself surpassed in many things by many men, he yet finds something in which to accord himself the first place, lest he lack glory. Cæsar sees himself surpassed by Cicero in eloquence* and in skilfulness as a counsellor and pleader; but as far inferior as he is in this department, so far superior he finds himself in the nobler arts of command and warfare, for by these he has mounted to the very summit of power, whither all the torrent of Cicero's eloquence cannot carry him. But in such cases, perhaps, one may easily say: "Everyone who in the judgment of all men has some special pre-eminence, gives himself first place. But take some poor Irus,† some pitiful man who can have absolutely no hope of glory or of any distinction, and teach him, who is so thoroughly without ambitions in this life that he would rather die than live, teach him this self-devotion. Then I will accede to your view." Listen, then. Confront Irus himself or the most miserable wretch with Croesus, Hercules, Ulysses. To Croesus he will say, "You are untaught to suffer poverty, I am well trained to misfortune"; to Hercules, "You perform the most marvelous feats, indeed, but you are a slave to passion, while I feel little or none"; to Ulysses, "You are indeed πολυμήτης, a man of many devices, but amid so many cunning devices it is impossible that fraud should not sometimes occur, whereas I enjoy a happy artlessness and live in a condition where fraud is of no use." Thus he will always find some point in which to flatter his vanity. I say nothing now of the malignity with which most people meditate only things that are going to harm others, if only they suffer no loss themselves. We ourselves, all of us who either in early times or in

*Suetonius *De vita Caesarum* I. 55.

†The ragged beggar of Homer, *Odys.* xviii, 1-7.

these times have written about divine things, in the very work which ought to be farthest removed from the selfish desire for glory have not kept ourselves free from it. For how few do not so fashion their speech that it may win the approval of all, so deck it out that it may attract all! This is not yet sin, but its natural result is to beget a fault, unless we are very careful. For there are some who in the warmth of Christian love wish all so well that they desire to have what they know to be pious and right shared with all. There are, on the other hand, some who look to this one thing only, how they may show themselves so eloquent, so wise, such practiced artists, that after the fashion of Gorgias* they can speak admirably on any subject whatever, and handle all themes admirably. Indeed, I think there is no one who does not feel the spur of glory, even when he is doing his best to show that glory ought to be scorned. This is frequently met with in Plato, for whenever he makes Socrates talk philosophy he uses such involutions and such splendor of language that he is clearly seen to have been most bent upon glory just when he was representing Socrates as the greatest scorner of glory.

I have brought in these things from the heathen in order that, if possible, even those who are devoted to philosophy may receive eyes with which to see what man is. Nor let anyone fancy that pious men are insulted by this seeming to put them on a par with the heathen; for I doubt not that there were heathen who wrote with pure purpose. But that was not man's doing, but God's. For if you leave man to himself he measures all things by himself.

So much for what man is in his own nature. Hence, since even among the theologians you can easily find some who treat the word of God as a mere matter of business (for you see how they make their living by it), it cannot be denied that they are zealous for glory. Oh, that it were not true! It has now been quite sufficiently proved that man does everything from self-love, and, unless he undergoes a change, always will do so. Hence I have not improperly counted among those

*Gorgias, the famous Greek Sophist and rhetorician. In 427 B. C. he came to Athens as ambassador from his home in Sicily. There he made a great impression by reason of his oratorical skill.

who, willy nilly, do everything for gain or glory this class of men who handle even divine things for their own personal ends. Therefore, since they see that, because they bear the mark of persons who speak only to win favor and blatantly dissemble their real opinions, it is not hard to perceive what they are inwardly, I beg them to confess with us, *i. e.,* with the faithful, that man is altogether bad and that all his thoughts and actions are controlled by self-love.

[5]. Religion

I must now return to religion, which I put aside for a little while till I should speak, as far as the Lord gave to me, of those between whom religion subsists.

Of the word enough has been said, and I now come to the thing itself.

"God created man in his own image and likeness" [Gen. 1:27], and surrounded him with blessings and indescribable delights, but he foolishly suffered himself to be dragged into the direst calamity by vain hopes. As soon as that happened, he began to see in himself something unpleasing. For it is written, Gen. 3:7: "And the eyes of them both were opened." Good God, were they blind before? By no means, but their hearts, like their eyes, were ignorant of anything base, as long as they kept from eating of the tree of life. There was nothing to sadden them, nothing to make them ashamed. But after they ate the fatal apple, their eyes were opened; for it was plucked from the tree of the knowledge of good and evil. Yet what did they see first that they had not seen before? Something secret that they had not known before? The demon seemed to promise something of this kind, and the poor things no doubt hoped for something of the sort. They saw, then, that they were naked. Now, they had been naked before, but nakedness was not regarded as nakedness: sin was not imputed before the law came, Rom. 5: 13. So nakedness was not known before lack of clothing was felt; and this took place only when man turned away from his Creator, the treasure house of every good thing. From this we should learn that our minds, to whatever part of creation, to whatever design, to whatever hope they turn, find nothing but trouble, disaster, and utter wretchedness (for this is the nakedness in question, to be exposed to all evils and deprived of the protection of God), and that comfort and rest are nowhere to be found save with God. And we see, if we look a little more closely, that such folly is native to us, so that we begin uncertain and difficult things blindly, without intelligent consideration of the end; and when that is finally reached our eyes are opened by hard experience, yet so that we see nothing but the evils into which our own recklessness has plunged us. And the human mind is always after something new, though we find an Epimetheus* oftener than a Prometheus; that is, we are all wise after the event.

We are taught, in the next place, that the nakedness of Adam means nothing else than guilt and the death that is sin, of which so much was said above. For who could believe that Adam was so dull that he could not make the argument: "Suppose you are naked. God Himself created you naked. Let Him see you naked." But it was his consciousness of wrongdoing that made him ashamed to come into the sight of God. If Adam had had a hope that he had anything left with which to coax back favor, he never would have hidden; but he saw that his case was so utterly lost that we do not read of his turning to supplication. Concluding, therefore, from his consciousness of guilt that the worst was in store for him, he hid, and gave his nakedness as an excuse for running away and delaying to appear. What else, then, are we to conclude from all this but that the case of man is so hopeless and lamentable that he dares not appear in God's presence, and even flees from Him, dreads Him when He calls, and refuses to come into His sight? But at the same time we are taught the kindness of God, who receives back into favor this traitorous deserter to the enemy's camp, without his humbly asking it, and though he swiftly runs away and tries to disguise himself. God calls to him, reproaches him, and only so far turns his happy estate into one of woe as His righteousness demands. For what did Adam deserve but death and destruction? But, as far as He could, God considered, with reference to Adam's bold misdeed, how

*Epimetheus: Afterthought, the husband of Pandora, whom he married against the advice of his brother Prometheus, Forethought.

He might give a foretaste even in the beginning of what He would sometime do for the whole posterity of Adam; and when His righteous wrath was still hot at the recently committed crime, He judged more kindly than the guilt deserved.

Before we leave this topic I want to give certain theologians this point to consider. I beg you to give an answer, at least in the form of a probable theory—since you generally employ theories, though they are sometimes far from reasonable—to this question: Does it seem as if Adam would ever have come back of his own notion to ask for grace? You will certainly be forced to admit that on no reasonable inference does it seem likely that one who was so bent upon running away and hiding that he could scarcely be dragged out would have returned if the Lord had not followed him up in his flight. Why, then, will you not acknowledge that the acquired faith about which you talk so much is a fiction (for no man cometh to Christ, John 6:44, unless the Father draw him), and that faith is not of him that willeth, nor of him that runneth, but of God that hath mercy [Rom. 9:16]? Why indeed, when you see that our common parent, whose sin and death have extended to us, was so afraid of God that, yielding to the folly which kept telling him that he could hide, he took himself off in order not to be forced to hear himself upbraided for the sin of his desertion? But what need is there of lengthy discussion? Suppose God lets Adam be; he will never come back to Him from whom he has fled. Suppose He lets man be; he will never seek Him by whom he was created. For everyone is a God unto himself, as is made plain by his worship of himself. For who is there who does not worship himself and give himself the top place in some respect, while demanding of God the reason for all His acts and designs? And what is this but to exalt oneself above God and to exercise a censorship over His works? I have gone on at considerable length, but I wanted to make it plain how far man would wander from God if He from whom we flee did not stop us in our flight; and how far from the true path these theologians are when they talk more pointlessly than the heathen writers about acquired faith and freedom of the will.

Here, therefore, we see more clearly than day that religion

took its rise when God called runaway man back to Him, when otherwise he would have been a deserter forever. For he saw that his nakedness, that is, his guilt, was of such kind and degree that he despaired of a return to favor. But a merciful God pitied his persistence in flight and his bewildered soul; and, like a devoted father who indeed hates the folly or recklessness of his son yet cannot hate the son, He gently calls to him in his desolation and despair, asking him how matters stand: "Adam, where art thou?" Oh, wonderful and unspeakable graciousness of the Heavenly Father! He who places all things where they are—or they would be nowhere—asks him where he is; but He asks for the sake of the unhappy man, that He may show him the more plainly the depth of his guilt; for he did not know where in the world he was. For, frightened by his consciousness of guilt, he saw that it was all up with his home and happy hearth, saw that the words of his Lord were only too true: "In the day that thou eatest thereof thou shalt surely die." He felt how his heart fluttered, how his mind in its distracted state fluctuated between many plans, all unpromising and illusory; and at the same time he feared the destined death was at hand every moment. The Heavenly Father, therefore, asks him where he is, that man may be mindful for ever in what position, in what condition of his affairs, he was when God gently called to him. Here, I say, is the cradle of religion, or rather loyal devotion (for this is the established relation between parents and children, between God and man). The unhappy man saw that he deserved nothing but wrath; therefore he despairs and flees from God. Now see the loyal devotion of the father to his undutiful son. He runs to him in spite of his obstinacy and overbears him amidst his rash designs. What is this but loyal devotion to the son? Loyal devotion, therefore, springs from God even to our day, but for our benefit; for what are we to suppose that God would have lacked even if Adam had immediately expired by the destined death? But pious devotion is complete only when we turn to the one who calls us away from ourselves and our designs. Unhappy, indeed, is the parent (the human parent, I mean) who pursues his son with constant kindness, only to find him constantly resisting or retreating; for his devotion to his son is in vain. But such defeat cannot happen to God; for he whom He calls is forced to respond whether he will or not. This is shown by the prevaricating Adam, the adulterer and murderer David, the persecutor Paul. Pious devotion, therefore, or religion, is this: God reveals man to himself, that he may recognize his disobedience, treason, and wretchedness as fully as Adam did. The result is that man utterly despairs of himself, but at the same time God shows the ample store of His own bounty, so that he who had despaired of himself may see that he has with his Creator and Father an abundance of grace so sure and ready that he cannot possibly be torn away from Him on whose grace he leans. This clinging to God, therefore, with an unshaken trust in Him as the only good, as the only one who has the knowledge and the power to relieve our troubles and to turn away all evils or to turn them to His own glory and the benefit of His people, and with filial dependence upon Him as a father—this is piety, is religion. For as those who are thus minded enjoy God's fatherly care, so they in their turn anxiously and unceasingly pore over,* study, and consider the ways in which they can please Him and deserve well of Him. Piety, therefore, is recognized as surely present where there is an eagerness to live according to the will of God, just as, likewise, perfect devotion between parents and children requires that the son shall study to obey the father as much as the father to benefit the son. Again, true piety is born only when man not only thinks that he lacks many things, but sees that he has absolutely no means of pleasing God, whereas his Creator and Father so abounds in all things that no one in His hands can lack anything, and His bounty and love to man are so great that He can refuse no man anything.

And this can be so abundantly confirmed by the testimony of Scripture that all its teaching, in the Old Testament as well as in the New, and all the pious really sing no other song than that we have nothing, God lacks nothing, by Him nothing is denied. For with the Lord is mercy in exceeding abundance. "With him is the fountain of life" [Ps. 36: 9]. "The earth is his and the fulness thereof" [Ps. 24: 1]. "Salvation is his, and

**relegunt:* The verb echoes the noun "religion" of the preceding sentence, but the English has no means of reproducing the effect.

that so ready that he manifests his blessing, *i. e.,* his bounty and kindness, freely to his people" [Ps. 3:8].

From this it can easily be inferred what further demands true religion makes; and, conversely, it can be quite easily perceived what false religion is. True religion, or piety, is that which clings to the one and only God. Those, therefore, who are pious listen to their one Lord, who so tears them away from the flesh and unites them to Himself that they desire to hear His voice only, and with soul aflame with love cry, Song of Solomon 2:14, "Sweet is thy voice in my ears"; and, "How sweet are thy words unto my taste, yea sweeter than honey to my mouth" [Ps. 119:103]. True piety demands, therefore, that one should hang upon the lips of the Lord and not hear or accept the word of any but the bridegroom. In order to set this faithfulness well before our eyes, the Lord often compares it in the Scriptures to a faithful marriage and, like a constant husband, warns us against adultery and fornication, emphasizing just this one point, that as in marriage faithfulness is required above all else (indeed marriage is nothing but faithfulness given and received), so piety is not piety unless you trust with all your heart the Lord who is the spouse of the soul, fix your eyes on Him only, and lend your ear to none but Him. Therefore He commands, Num. 15:38-39, "that in the four corners of their garments they put ribbons of blue, that when they see them they may remember all the commandments of the Lord, and not follow their own thoughts and eyes, going awhoring after divers things." And Paul makes holy boast, II Cor. 11:2, that he had presented the Corinthians as a chaste and untouched virgin to Christ alone, so that they might hear Him alone, admire Him alone, love Him alone, follow Him alone. And in Ephesians 5:32, he declares that marriage is a great mystery, for it betokens the union of Christ and the Church. By all this I simply wish to show that true piety demands the same faithfulness and purity towards God as are demanded in marriage (I use "same" in a comparative sense and not to denote equivalence). Yet in marriage she is not faithful who listens to another, follows another, obeys another. So also the soul is not truly pious that listens to another than God, follows another than its own spouse. It is evident, then, that those only are truly pious who hang upon the utterances of God alone. How necessary this is to true piety the words of the Lord himself will make clear.

In Deut. 4:1-2, God says: "Now, O Israel, hear the commandments and judgments which I teach thee; that doing them thou mayest live, and entering in mayest possess the land which the Lord God of your fathers will give you. Ye shall not add to the word that I speak to you, neither shall ye take away from it. Keep the commandments of the Lord your God which I command you." And in Deut. 12:32: "What I command thee, that only do thou to the Lord: neither add anything, nor diminish." Faithfulness, or piety, therefore, demands, first, that we learn from God in what way we can please Him, in what manner serve Him. Next, it demands that we shall add nothing to what we have learned from Him, and take away nothing. For they that add accuse God of lack of wisdom and set themselves above God, as if they, clever creatures, indeed! could make good by their wisdom the things that He, they think, promulgated without due consideration. And they that take away make God out cruel, as if from violence He gave commands that they know how to soften in accordance with their own gentleness and humanity. The latter passage quoted above is a weighty one, for upon it depends everything that pertains to the truth or falseness of religion; but, whatever its exact weight, it has force enough and to spare for establishing true religion and confounding false. For "the word of the Lord endureth forever," Isa. 40:8. "Whence it is easier for heaven and earth to perish or pass away than one tittle of the word of the Lord," Luke 16:17. The whole vast universe and the endless host of created things can remove [*cf.* Mt. 5:18] from the words of God or change not a single tittle, *i. e.,* absolutely nothing. Any one, it is true, can easily alter or remove a tittle; but nothing (which is what tittle signifies), nothing (which is what we understand the Lord's words to mean) will perish so as not to come to pass. Those who are faithful, therefore, grasp at the word of the Lord, as a shipwrecked man grasps at a plank. For what is there other than God's word alone with which the conscience can comfort itself? For man liveth "by every word that proceedeth out of the mouth of God," Deut. 8:3; Matt. 4:4. But what sort of man? The man of faith. For what has the unbeliever to do with the word of God? To him the heavenly wisdom is foolishness, and he laughs at you if you trust in God. The pious man, therefore, is the only one who is fed, refreshed, and comforted by the word of God. Conversely, it follows that the pious man cannot feed on any other word than the divine. For as he trusts in God alone, so he is made sure by His word alone; and as he is made sure by God's word alone, so he accepts the word of none but God. Thus again not only from Scripture, but also from the nature of faith itself it becomes manifest that the word of no created being can be accepted in place of the word of God, because the conscience is not given peace and rest by the word of a created being. Nothing, therefore, of ours is to be added to the word of God, and nothing taken from His word by rashness of ours. To this some one might here object: "Yet many have found rest even in the word of man, and still do find it; for today the consciences of many are firmly persuaded that they will attain salvation if the Roman Pontiff absolve them, grant them indulgences, enroll them in heaven; if nuns and monks tell beads for them, and do masses,* hours,† and other things for them." To this objection I answer that all such are either fools or hypocrites, for it must be the result of folly and ignorance if one thinks one's self what one is not. He, therefore, who measures his piety by the fact that he has faith in the contrivances of the Roman Pontiff has had no taste of what is God's, nor has it passed the edge of his lips how sweet is the Lord and how blessed he that trusteth in Him [cf. Ps. 34:8]. But if he is not foolish or ignorant he cannot escape the charge of hypocrisy. For there are a good many who make much of the Roman Pontiff and of frigid ceremonies, because they see that in some respect they will be losers if anything is taken from his dominion; and so they, the sly dogs, take early precaution against what is still afar off. The statement is sound, that the pious heart finds rest in no word

*On April 12, 1525, the Council of Two Hundred abolished the Mass in Zurich.

†The seven canonical hours, *i. e.*, stated times for the offices of prayer and devotion; viz., matins, prime, terce, sext, nones, vespers, and complin.

but God's, and can accept the word of none but God. And this is so unanimously agreed to by the suffrages of all the pious that it needs no testimony beyond this one short and clear sentence: "My soul refused to be comforted; I remembered God, and was delighted," Psalm 77: 3-4. The conscience of the prophet* had nowhere found hope, nowhere rest; but after he recovered the memory of God, at once peace and joy came to him.

But I will hasten on to the testimony of the New Testament, by which I shall show that it is sacrilegious to add anything to the words of God or to take anything away. Thus again it will be manifest that only that is uncontaminated piety which rests upon the words of God solely and alone.

In Matt. 15: 9 Christ quotes the testimony of Isaiah 29: 13, as He is in the habit of drawing His fulminations against the Jews from the Old Testament, though rarely naming the passage: "In vain do they worship me, teaching doctrines and commandments of men." If, then, that worship, that piety or religion, is vain which proceeds from human invention or law, solid and true surely is that religion, on the other hand, which is guided by the word of God alone, and looks to and hears this only.

In John 8: 47 Christ says: "He that is of God heareth the words of God: for this cause ye hear them not, because ye are not of God." It follows, then, that they that are born of God hear His word; and, conversely, they that hear not are not born of God. But those that are born of God and not of the will of man, John 1: 13, are born in this way: not of their own notion and choice have they selected as their God Him who is really God, but by His power in whom they trust it has come to pass that they recognize that they are the sons of God. For He says: "They are born, not of the will of the flesh, nor of the will of man, but of God." Those, then, who are born of God hear His word only of whom they are born. This is the difference between the sons of God and the sons of the flesh, that those who are sons of God know or mind the things that are of God; those who are sons of the flesh mind the things of the flesh, Rom. 8: 5. Furthermore, whatsoever proceedeth not

*Sc. David.

out of the mouth of God is not received by the sons of God, for the Spirit dwelling within them shows them all things and tells them whether what they hear is of the flesh or of the Spirit. Hence it comes about also that "he that is spiritual judgeth all things," recognizes all things, "yet he himself is judged of no man," I Cor. 2: 15; for it is not flesh or blood that judges, but Spirit. I am speaking, indeed, of those only who are Christ's and who have His Spirit, Rom. 8: 9. Those, therefore, who have the Spirit of Christ have not their own, that is, the spirit of flesh and blood and man. But they that have the Spirit of Christ receive the word of none but God, for Christ, God Himself, cannot receive or endure any word but His own; for man cannot be God unto God, but God can be that to man; and unless God is that, man is nothing but a beast. Whoever, therefore, receives the word of man receives the word of the flesh and of a beast. It is dreadful, then, for him who is Christ's to receive any word but God's.

The same teaching is given in John 10: 4f, but clothed in the charming parable of the shepherd and the sheep: "The sheep follow their own shepherd; for they know his voice. And a stranger will they not follow, but will flee from him; for they know not the voice of strangers." The sheep follow the voice of God, their true and eternal Shepherd and Bishop, I Peter 2: 25. For they know His voice and what it is like; but a stranger they do not hear, nor follow, for they know not the voice of strangers. However, you will say: "But how do they flee from strangers, if they know not the voice of strangers? For if they do not know it, they will easily follow a stranger, taking him for the true shepherd." I answer: "They do not know, they do not respect, they do not take to themselves the voice of strangers. For the Lord says somewhere [*cf.* Mt. 7: 23] that He does not know certain persons, and yet nothing can be hid from him. He uses "not know" for "disregard, turn away from, scorn." So also in this passage it is said of loyal sheep that they know, that is, take to themselves, respect, follow, the voice of their shepherd only, and flee from, abhor, refuse to follow, any stranger's voice."

John 15: 4 teaches the same thing: "As the branch cannot bear fruit of itself, except it abide in the vine; so neither can ye, except ye abide in me." We shall never undertake, therefore, anything right and worthy of God, unless we are in the vine, that is, God; for unless we derive our sap and strength from Him, we shall become withered and be cast into the fire. But he abides not in God who draws from himself the sap from which to bring forth fruit. For the things that are of us are carnal, and the things that are carnal and of us are enmity against God, Rom. 8: 7. In God alone, therefore, abideth the truly pious heart, hears His word alone, trusts in Him alone. Moreover, God alone is good [*cf.* Mk. 10: 18], as was made plain above in the study of Him. Therefore good is not to be looked for or even hoped for from any other source than God alone. But we are such strangers to all good that Christ bids us deny ourselves if we would enter into life [*cf.* Mt. 16: 24]. And this was said not to one or two, but to all collectively and individually. Nothing right and good is, then, to be hoped for from any other source than God. He alone is to be listened to from whom alone proceeds all the good there is anywhere. The same thing can be made clear by an illustration. As soon as Adam, to come back to our beginnings, wanted of his own effort to know, it was suddenly all over with him. But if he had turned his attention to those things only which the Lord had enjoined, instead of following his own counsels, man would not be in the position of a son of wrath. From his example, therefore, we can see more clearly than day that the truly pious man ought to shrink away from his own counsels as from sure and immediate destruction. God alone, therefore, is to be listened to, to Him alone is glory to be attributed by all pious souls. For not even the wise man ought to glory in his own wisdom, Jeremiah 9: 23. But if anything right and worthy of God were brought about by our wisdom, surely we might fairly glory. As it is, since God, who is not unfair, forbids glorying, certainly all human wisdom is to be considered of no account. On God alone, therefore, and on His word must we lean.

It is, therefore, as was said at the beginning of this inquiry, very easy to distinguish false religion from true. It is false religion or piety when trust is put in any other than God. They, then, who trust in any created thing whatsoever are not truly pious. They are impious who embrace the word of man as God's. It is, therefore, madness and utter impiety to put the enactments and decrees of certain men or certain councils upon an equality with the word of God. For if their dicta are like God's word, it is the word that must be embraced, not the authority of men; if they are unlike it, they are to be rejected and shunned, as the Children of Isræl avoided marriage with the women of the Moabites and other Gentiles [cf. Ezra 10: 2-4].

The objection, which could be made here, that the Church should be listened to, I shall treat later.*

[6]. The Christian Religion

This age has many scholars who spring up everywhere as if out of the Trojan Horse, and still more who set themselves up as censors of all things. These because of their impiety are unwilling to accept the renascent word,† yet make a pretense of piety and fill the ears of the pious with groundless and fictitious suspicions. Some, when we teach vigorously that all our confidence is to be placed in God our Father, spring up with the impudent suggestion that we must be guarded against; for in all our teaching, they say, our aim is that we may do away with Christ, and, after the manner of the Jews, induce all to believe in only one Person, as we believe in only one God. Others, when we show an inclination to attribute all things to Christ, say they are afraid that we too rashly attribute too much to Him. Yet both make their pronouncements in such a way that you can see of yourself that they are either recklessly ignorant or knowingly impious. For they are so ignorant as to the Father, and the Son, and the Holy Spirit, in their essence, substance, divinity, power, that they do not know what you mean when you speak of one and understand all three; and their lack of knowledge is accompanied by such recklessness that what they are extremely ignorant of they all the more violently drag under suspicion. Or they are so willingly and knowingly impious that they assail with the depravity of a perverted heart what they see is done rightly and piously, and since they despair of accomplishing anything in open warfare,

*See below, Section [13], The Church.

†*i. e.*, the Reformation.

they make an underground attack, alleging a fear that we are too much inclined sometimes towards the Father, sometimes towards the Son. To all such I say, κλαίειν, "fare ill." For I teach that God is to be acknowledged and embraced in such wise that whether you call Him Father, or Son, or Holy Spirit, you always conceive of Him who is alone good, righteous, holy, kind, and all the rest. On the other hand, when I attribute all things to the Son, I attribute them to Him who is what the Father is, what the Holy Spirit is, and whose are the kingdom and the power just as truly as they are the Father's and the Holy Spirit's. For He is Himself that very thing which the Father is and the Holy Spirit, though seen from a different point of view, as they say. What, therefore, these emulous persons are sure to say, namely, that in discussing piety so far I have made no reference to salvation through Christ and to grace, will be groundless croaking: first, because I cannot say everything at once and in the same place; secondly, because all that I have said of the marriage of the soul to God applies to Christ just as much as to God (for Christ is God and Man); finally, because knowledge of God in the nature of the case precedes knowledge of Christ. Therefore, just as grace is first rightly known when sin has been effected through the law, as Paul says, Rom. 7: 25, that is, when sin has been weighed and known through the law, so also Christ, who is the pledge of grace, nay, is grace itself, is first rightly taught and known when from close observation of sin we have learned that by its interposition the way to heaven has been closed to us. For as he that is in sound health lays no store by the physician, but he that is in a desperate condition looks upon him as a god, so Christ is not especially welcome to the whole, but to the sick he is θεὸς ἀπὸ μηχανῆς, that is, unexpected safety sent from above. To this He Himself testifies, saying: "They that are whole need not a physician; but they that are sick," Luke 5: 31; and, "I came not to call the righteous, but sinners to change their former life." In order, therefore, rightly to know Christ, we must first rightly know ourselves; for they that think themselves righteous receive not Christ, as is clear from His own words; and he that feels no sickness wants not the help of a physician.

Christ, then, is the certainty and pledge of the grace of God [cf. Eph. 1:14]. This can be shown in this way: I said before in considering man that his condition is so pitiable that he is dead, the slave of sin, and of such a nature as to care for nothing so much as for himself. For this is what happened to him when he turned away from the good and to himself, for we know that in us is no good thing, Rom. 7:18. Hence arose endless despair of ever coming to God; for how could he ever hope to be received above who by daily evils felt himself exposed to bodily death, and from a guilty conscience felt himself so removed from God that he avoided coming into His sight? But God was better, and pitied His work, and devised a plan to repair so serious a misfortune. Since His justice, being inviolably sacred, had to remain as intact and unshaken as His mercy, and since man was indeed in need of mercy but wholly amenable to God's justice, divine goodness found a way to satisfy justice and yet to be allowed to open wide the arms of mercy without detriment to justice. Not that He thus took precautions against the Adversary or that the potter may not out of moistened clay make or remake any vessel He chooses [*cf.* Rom. 9:21], but that by this example of justice He might remove drowsiness and sloth from us and show us what sort of being He was—just, good, merciful; or, not to presume to say too much of His purposes, because it so pleased Him. For "righteous [justus] is the Lord and upright are his judgments, Ps. 119:137, but, on the other hand, "He is patient and merciful, good to all; and his tender mercies are over all his works," Ps. 145:8-9. For David sings unto Him of mercy and judgment, Ps. 101:1. For He "visits the iniquity of the fathers upon the children unto the fourth generation of them that hate him, and sheweth mercy unto thousands of them that love him," Exod. 20:5-6. While, therefore, God is alike just and merciful, though with a leaning towards mercy (for His tender mercies are over all the rest of His works), yet His justice has to be satisfied that His wrath may be appeased. That, then, God's justice has to be satisfied, the theologians have rightly taught, even those of the new school. For, "if thou wouldst enter into life, keep the commandments," Matt. 19:17. But how shall man satisfy the justice of God? It is so pure, so high, so far removed from any stain, while, on the contrary, any one of us is so truly nothing but sin and blemish that no one would venture to hope to reach the measure that could satisfy divine justice. For who can attain to that purity which David says ascends into the holy mountain of the Lord? In Psalm 15:1 he asks: "Lord, who shall abide in thy tabernacle? or who shall dwell in thy holy hill?" And he answers his own question thus: "He that walketh without blemish, and worketh righteousness [justiciam], and speaketh the truth in his heart. He that backbiteth not with his tongue, nor doeth evil to his neighbor, nor taketh up a reproach against his neighbors. In his eyes a reprobate is despised, but he honoreth them that fear the Lord. He that sweareth to his neighbor and deceiveth not. He that putteth not out his money to usury, nor taketh bribes against the innocent. He that doeth these things shall never be moved." Who, pray, can shine with such purity as to walk without blemish and to work righteousness, when we are nothing but sin and blemish and flesh? Or who among mortals is so single-hearted that neither his heart nor his tongue has ever practiced deceit? Who has done no evil to his neighbor or not suffered others to do it unpunished? In whose eyes have the evil always been despised and the good held in high esteem? Who has not been stained with usury, perjury, and the taking of bribes against the innocent? Who on hearing these words would not tremble, despair, and make ready to flee? But God is such a pure and consuming fire that if any one is troubled with the aforesaid defects he cannot stand in His sight. This is what Isaiah had in mind, 33:14: "Who among us can dwell with the devouring fire? Who among us can dwell with everlasting burnings?" Like David, he answers: "He that walketh righteously, and speaketh truth; he that despiseth the gain of oppressions, that shaketh his hands from taking a bribe, that stoppeth his ears from hearing of blood, and shutteth his eyes from looking on evil; he shall dwell on high, etc." Since, then, this fire demands such soundness and innocence, in order, of course, that there may be no moist or earthly ingredient which must be ejected with hissing and roaring, who is there that would venture, at least if he have any sort of knowledge of himself, to aspire to the companionship of God? Thus it becomes manifest that wherever in the Scriptures the way to heaven is shown, we are driven to despair. For who in this polluted path below can so order his life as to be able to think himself even in his own opinion worthy of dwelling with and enjoying so pure a light, especially when we have all strayed and become so unprofitable that not even one of us does good, when every man is a liar [*cf.* Ps. 116: 11; Rom. 3: 4], and we are all hypocrites and have all sinned and fallen short of the glory of God [*cf.* Rom. 3: 23]?

But since hypocrisy is such a mighty evil that, like certain foolish sufferers who try to hide their ailment, it ventures to deny itself and tries, though in vain, to clear itself of all suspicion, it is necessary for us, after the fashion of skilful physicians, who wrest out the truth by means of various attendant circumstances and symptoms, in the same way to probe and to examine man until we turn his bold concealment into shame and frank confession. For certain clever sick persons, in order to try the skill of the physician, refuse to tell the nature of their disease until the physician pronounces them to be suffering from the very ailment of which they are themselves perfectly aware. Then they entrust themselves more securely to his care, convinced that as he knows the disease so well he will know the cure also. But those who are a prey to obstinate hypocrisy can never be persuaded by the most skilful argument to confess what they really feel and have in their hearts. Yet the more persistently they refuse, the more certainly are they understood by the spiritual physician. For "he that is spiritual judgeth all things" [I Cor. 2: 15]. For in order to make them confess what is discovered by the principles of spiritual medicine, there is need of another than a man, however expert. For man looks on the outward appearance, and God alone on the heart [I Sam. 16: 7]. Unless He excites shame in the human heart, so that it ceases to deny that of which it is conscious, and unless He so humbles it that it recognizes its eagerness for glory, it will never confess that it is such as it really is. For no one tries to descend into his secret self, no one. We come again, therefore, to the conclusion that man has as much need of God for the knowledge of himself as for the recognition of

God. For no man "knoweth the things of a man, save the spirit of the man, which is in him" [I Cor. 2: 11], as was made plain above.

But now I turn to tests by which to wrest from man the admission that he has in him what I assert is in him. I ask, therefore, first: "O thou who art justified by thy works, is almsgiving a good work or not?" The self-righteous answers, "It is." "In whatever way and manner it is done?" The self-righteous: "Not at all, but only when a man does as is in him" (for that is the way these people talk). "Tell me, please, what you understand by the expression 'as is in him'." The self-righteous: "According to his powers." I answer that we beg the question in this way. For whatever the amount given and on whatever account, a man always does as is in him and always does according to his ability. Therefore all almsgiving will be a good work which will justify us. The self-righteous: "Yes." "If I give to be seen of men [*cf.* Mt. 6: 1]?" The self-righteous: "I do not say that." "What, then?" The self-righteous: "I will not argue the point." There you see what this "as is in him" is. It is a figment that makes Christ quite superfluous. For in this way anybody could be justified by works done according to his powers; for anybody can do as is in him, even if in the case of many of his good deeds that be the merest trifle. But I come back to the main point. As many maladies can befall almsgiving to vitiate it as befall vineyards to destroy them. First, if the giving is not in the name of God. Those, therefore, who give only for the purpose of redeeming themselves from the punishments of hell, give in their own name, not in the name of Christ. Second, if people give with ostentation, that they may obtain glory among men, they have received their reward, Matt. 6: 2. Furthermore, if they give grudgingly and dislike to give, and would not give unless they were afraid of malicious comment, they vitiate their almsgiving; "for God loveth a cheerful giver," II Cor. 9: 7. If they do not give in the measure they would want given to them if they were in need, they do not give rightly; for "all things that ye would that men should do unto you, do ye the same to them," Matt. 7: 12. Nor if they give scornfully or negligently; for "cursed be he that doeth the work of the Lord negligently," Jer. 48: 10. Nor if they give because overcome by the wretchedness and misfortunes of the recipient and not from the love of God and their neighbor; for "whoso hath this world's goods, and seeth his brother have need, we know that the love of God is not in him," I John 3: 17. In short, so many vices are wont to attend this quite unquestionable work, that we must not expect any one to be able worthily to perform it. For who does not give in such fashion as to keep the greater portion for himself? Who does not give either to be seen to have given or not to be seen not to have given, etc.? How, then, shall we satisfy God's justice if so pious a work is done by none in such a way that it can be reckoned worthy of reward by an impartial and pious judge? Run through in this way all the things we do, and you will see that they are subject to as great, aye, to greater, vices. Many of us pray, that we may be seen to pray, as the hypocrites do, Matt. 6: 5. We pray that the Lord will give us riches, pleasures, a wife with a large dowry, honors, office, power; aye, that we may be deemed saints and even gods by all men; and, in fact, "we know not what we should pray for," Rom. 8: 26. We fast in the same way, either that our frugality may be heralded [*cf.* Mt. 6: 16-18], or that our thin, pale faces may indicate sanctity; or that dainties and delicacies may be brought to us fasting; or to bring back within an old garment a belly that makes too shameless a show of itself; or to save a penny, as is the case with some who are meaner than Chremes and Euclio*; or that we may reckon as a good work the fasting which ought to be done simply for the purpose of calling us away from the flesh to the better hearing of the voice and bidding of the Spirit. Thus, I say, we measure all things with reference to ourselves, not to Him of whom and in whom we wholly are [cf. Acts 17: 28]. By what sacrifices or offerings, then, shall we be justified, when in our actual works we are so feeble and cold and ineffective; and this so evidently and truly that all the faithful know in their hearts it is just as I have said? For they see that this kind of disease has come to us from Adam, the original cause of this state of death; and they not only see it in the word, but in their hearts feel it true.

Here, I say, the theologians have wandered from the

*Two misers, well known characters in Roman comedy.

straight way, as I began to say a little while ago. For, weighing the justice of God accurately, as they thought, they were forced to see that it must be satisfied, but in regard to the satisfaction they failed to reckon the works of the crowd accurately, although they set a high value upon their own. For they did not rightly know man through and through and see how he is nothing but impurity and corruption and filth, so that even what he learns in its purity he puts forth corrupted. For even when through the heavenly Spirit we reach the point of delighting in that which the law commands, yet the flesh is so rebellious that we accomplish no good thing, Rom. 7: 18. Hence, though the justice of God is so inviolable and holy that our impurity can do nothing towards winning it, these theologians have been unwilling to learn to despair (despair of ourselves, I mean, not of the mercy of God). And this vice also came from too high an estimate of self, for it is hard for man to condemn self and to withdraw from self to such an extent as to have no sense at all of self. And here we have a strange and shameless arrogance. Though they had proclaimed that heaven must be won by our own merits, they offered themselves as ministers and workers to earn merit for others; and on receiving pay they strenuously acquired merit, but with works which they had themselves invented, of which I shall have more to say below. In general, therefore, they have not attained a right knowledge either of God's justice or of man's unjustice, and have had such an ignorant and scornful idea of Christ that they have attributed to Him little more than did the Jews. But this is not strange. For if people in general had begun to rely on Christ—that is, on the grace of God, which is obtained and confirmed through Christ—who would any longer have paid them so much for looking after his salvation? So, not without reason are they raging today; for though they have advertised themselves as agents for securing salvation, nobody hires them, and they sit all the day idle.

But enough has been said about our powerlessness and about our own desperate state of mind. Now I will pass to more cheerful themes, to the gospel, namely, in which a merciful God has not only proclaimed salvation but also sent it, after it had been long foretold and promised. Since this mystery is to be treated with the greatest reverence, the greatest humility and awe, we must prostrate ourselves before the Fount of all grace, that He may so guide, so illumine, our discourse that we shall say nothing unworthy of Him. And since by human discourse, however rich, the untaught mind cannot be persuaded in the things of faith unless the Lord so teach and draw the heart that it delights to follow, we must also appeal to Him who justifieth and who calleth the things that are not as though they were [Rom. 4:17], so to illumine the minds of those to whom we would communicate His gospel that they shall be able to grasp the meaning of the gospel, so to draw and to soften their hearts that they shall be able to follow. For there is nothing that He will not grant to earnest prayer [*cf.* Mt. 21:22]; and there is nothing that we ought to venture or to undertake to do without prayer. May the Lord put right words into my mouth!

Wishing at length, then, to help this desperate case of ours, our Creator sent one to satisfy His justice by offering Himself for us—not an angel, nor a man, but His own Son, and clothed in flesh, in order that neither His majesty might deter us from intercourse with Him, nor His lowliness deprive us of hope. For, being God and the Son of God, He that was sent as deputy and mediator gives support to hope. For what cannot He do or have who is God? Moreover, being man, He promises friendship and intimacy—aye, the common bond of relationship; what, then, can He refuse who is a brother and the sharer of our weakness? Furthermore, this thing so strange and so unprecedented was conceived and prepared from the beginning of human misery. For as God created man through His Son, so He determined through Him to restore man when he had fallen into death, that the Son might be at once his creator and his restorer. For "all things were made through him," John 1:3 and Colos. 1:16-20. "All things have been created through him, and unto him; and he is before all things, and by him all things consist. And he is the head of the body, the church: who is the beginning, the firstborn from the dead; that in all things he might have the preeminence. For εὐδόκησε, it was his good pleasure, that in him should all the fulness dwell; and through him to reconcile all things unto himself, having through the blood of the cross made peace for all things, whether they be in heaven or on earth." Ephes. 2:18: "Through him we both" (Jews and Gentiles) "have access in one Spirit unto the Father." God, then—to go back to the beginning—took pity upon man right after his fall, and when He promulgated the decision of His just judgment He took off something from the hardness of the sentence, that man might not be in utter misery forever. For when He appointed the punishment of the serpent, He made this qualification, in the interest of man: He foretold that there should sometime be seed of the woman that should bruise the head of the real serpent, the Devil, saying: "I will put enmity between thee and the woman, and between thy seed and her seed: it shall bruise thy head, and thou shalt bruise his heel." For this is the real meaning of the Hebrew, as can easily be perceived from the two pronouns, "it" and "his," which in the Hebrew are both masculine and refer to "seed," which likewise is masculine. Hence the Septuagint rendered the statement thus: Odium sive inimicitiam ponam inter te et inter mulierem, et inter te et inter semen tuum et inter semen eius. Ipse tuum caput observabit, et tu observabis calcaneum eius [Hatred or enmity will I put between thee and the woman, and between thee and thy seed and her seed. He shall mark thy head, and thou shalt mark his heel]. Here we see plainly that the holy men understood that there was a mystery underlying these words, and therefore refused to change the gender of the words, though they might properly have done so. For "zaera" [זרע], that is, "semen" [seed], is masculine in Hebrew; so also are "hu" [הוא], *i. e.,* "ipse" [he], and "u" [ו], *i. e.,* "eius" [his]. Not so in Greek; for there σπέρμα [seed] is neuter, like the Latin "semen"; but αὐτὸς and αὐτοῦ, *i. e.,* "ipse" and "eius," are masculine. Hence they might have said: "Ipsum (referring, of course, to "semen") observabit caput tuum, et tu observabis, etc." But, as I said, seeing that there was a mystery concealed here, they refused to change the gender in the pronouns, though they had to change it in σπέρμα. The Latin translator,* however, is everywhere so bold

*The translator of the Vulgate, which reads: Inimicitias ponam inter te et mulierem, et semen tuum et semen illius; ipsa conteret caput tuum, et tu insidiaberis calcaneo ejus.

that I often wonder whether his learning or his boldness was the greater. I come back to the meaning. We see it openly foretold in these words of God that from the woman should sometime proceed the seed which should bruise the head of the serpent, *i. e.,* the Devil; and that, on the other hand, the Devil would try to hurt his heel. Let us, therefore, consider briefly both prophecies. Divine Providence preserved strict verbal propriety. Having first said, "The seed shall bruise thy head," He always uses the same word, "seed." For when He said to Abraham, "In thy seed shall all the tribes of the earth be blessed," Gen. 15,* He used the old word for him who was to be born of Abraham according to the flesh and was to enroll all the race of men among the heirs of God. His calling him "a branch" in Jeremiah 23: 5 amounts to the same thing. And Paul, speaking of the same promise, says plainly: "And to thy seed, which is Christ," Gal. 3: 16, bearing witness that the seed of which so much is said throughout the Old Testament is Christ. Therefore this seed, Christ, crushed the head of the Devil. But the Devil himself tried so hard to hurt His heel, *i. e.,* his humanity, from vexation that it was not subject to the fall, like ours, which is conceived in sin, that he never let an opportunity slip. When Christ had marvelously sustained a fast for forty days and nights, even in the desert, the Devil demanded that he turn the stones into bread, hoping that his teeth and throat would lure him to this. Then he tempted him through the desire for power and wealth, and finally for glory [*cf.* Mt. 4:1-11]. When he accomplished nothing, he armed all his forces and marched out against Him. He roused the hatred of the scribes and priests against him to such a pitch that, in the words of Paul, Rom. 1: 31, they were absolutely ἄστοργοι ἄσπονδοι ἀνελεήμονες, that is, without any human kindness, friendliness, fellow-feeling, or mercifulness towards Him. And, not satisfied with having put such a load of hatred upon Him, he determined to destroy Him utterly; for he feared for his own kingdom more and more each day, seeing His unwavering devotion to the truth in His teachings and His unfailing power in healing disease. Daily he added fuel to the fire of malice, until he drove his aforementioned minions, the

*An error for Gen. 22: 18.

scribes and priests and Pharisees, to the point of forming the plan of slaying Him in any possible way. Christ was by no means unaware of this and often reproached them for their wickedness of purpose. And in the very tumult at the time of His arrest He proclaimed the wiles of the Serpent and the malignity and hatred of the priests, saying [Lk. 22: 53]: "This is your hour, and the power of darkness." The Devil laid a trap for Him even when dead, demanding through his minions that the tomb be watched [Mt. 27: 64-66].

We must, further, consider all the things done by the two Adams, that is, our parent in the flesh and Christ (for so Paul calls them both, Rom. 5: 12 and I Cor. 15: 22), that it may become clearly apparent how Christ by means of the proper antidotes restored man by satisfying the divine justice. I will compare the two in certain respects, as far as the Lord will give it me to do. [1]. Adam was placed in a garden of delights, and then because of transgressions was thrust out of his happy abode into a wild country, with which he had to struggle with spade and hoe and plough. Christ did not arrogate too much to Himself when He made Himself equal with the Father [Phil. 2: 6-8], but coming down from heaven He deigned to take on our form, and in it to break with His word, as with a rod of iron, Ps. 2: 9, them that were nothing but rebellious clay and flesh, that we, who through Adam were in an exile merited by his sin and our own, might through Him return to the place whence He came. [2]. The first Adam wished by knowing good and evil to become God; the second Adam deigned to put on the form and habit of ignorant man, in order to bring him back into the knowledge and favor of Him who alone is good and alone knows what good and evil are. [3]. Adam was prevailed upon by the blandishments of his wife to eat of the forbidden fruit. In Christ human weakness sometimes resisted, not knowing how to suffer, but it always came off worsted. "Let this cup pass from me!" [Mt. 26: 39] cried infirmity, but the divine in Him conquered and subdued the unwilling flesh to the will of the Father. [4]. Adam stretched out his hand towards the forbidden tree, expecting to become happy and wise, yea God. Christ stretched out all His limbs upon the ignominious cross, that we might be made happy through His sorrows, wise through His foolishness ("for the preaching of the cross is to them that perish foolishness," I Cor. 1:18), gods through His poverty. [5]. The author of death reached forth his hand to the deadly apple; the author of life reached forth His hand to the saving wood of the cross. [6]. The sweetness tasted by the one brought death; the bitterness tasted by the other brought life. [7]. The one fled in the hope of hiding himself, for he was afraid to come into the sight of God. The other displayed Himself to the whole world, and submitted to the judgment and the violence of the vilest, in order to recover the lost heritage. He suffered Himself to seem a malefactor in all men's eyes, that through Him we might appear justified unto the Father. [8]. Through a tree we were bound over to slavery, because Adam was not willing to stay his hand; through a tree we were given to liberty, because Christ was willing to suffer anything rather than permit our ruin. For one of the ancient writers says: "He marked the tree at that time as the thing to do away with the damage of the tree"; showing that God at the very moment of death's origin had in view the healing by means of a tree of the disease resulting from a tree. [9]. God laughed at the transgression of Adam, and clothed him and his wife with the skins of brutes. Christ's obedience turned us from brutes into sons of God, and enwrapped us in a mantle of blessed immortality. So far are we from being scorned in the sight of God that we have even been made His heirs, and joint-heirs with Christ [Rom. 8:17]. [10]. In short, the recklessness of our first parent closed the gates of paradise; the humility of Christ opened the door of heaven. I pass over St. Paul's comparisons in Rom. 5:15-21, which all aim to make us see how our ills have been healed by corresponding remedies, and how the divine justice has been appeased for us by the righteousness of Christ alone. For His innocence, given to us, has become as much ours as the life which also we derived from Him. For "in him was life," John 1:4. He is "the way, the truth, and the life," John 14:6, and "in him we live, and move, and have our being," Acts 17:28. As life, I say, was given to us from Him, so also was righteousness, which has been made ours from Him and through Him; for from Him we are all that we are. He put on flesh that He might become ours. He had no need of it, but we had the greatest need of Him. To become one of us, therefore, He, great God that He is, just, holy, merciful, Creator, became man, that we through His fellowship might be raised to gods.

There are also countless other prophecies in the Old Testament which so perfectly set forth His coming, career, death, and in fact His whole life and activity, that no one can deny that He is thus foreshadowed in the Scriptures, His whole activity and teaching correspond so completely with them. But since these prophecies are familiar to all, such as Isa. 11:1-2; Jer. 23:5-6, I will refrain from citing them here and content myself with citing a few figures or types. Jacob went into Mesopotamia [Gen. 28ff], and found there two wives, the elder of whom was dull-eyed, the younger of glad and beautiful countenance [Gen. 29:17]. The elder bore many children, while the younger was persistently barren. By and by the misfortune of her barrenness was changed, and the younger also began to be a mother. What could this presage but that which we see fulfilled in Christ and the Church? The synagogue of the Jews was for a long time fruitful before Christ was clothed with flesh; but after the time foreordained of God was fulfilled, the synagogue became barren and the young church of the Gentiles became fruitful. Jacob returned from Mesopotamia [Gen. 31ff], taking with him much substance, two wives, many children. Christ came down into this world, God became man, so that in Him you recognize Mesopotamia between its rivers, *i. e.,* the two natures, according to which He wrought and suffered all things, ever keeping the boundaries of each intact, faithfully performed the work of His Father, and at length, victorious over death, brought back the whole race of men to heaven. Why should I speak of the selling of Joseph into Egypt? He is such a shining example among the clearest foreshadowings that he needs no painter's brush. And why speak of his great-grandfather, Abraham, whose faith is so proclaimed by God [Gen. 22:16-18] that he is easily seen to be happier than any Alexander or Achilles? For who ever had God as herald? Why, I say, should I speak of his rearing a son by his free wife when he was a hundred years old, seeing that Paul in writing to the Galatians, 3 and 4, paints him as prototype in such lights and shadows that you can fairly touch him? Perez and Zerah, born of Tamar [Gen. 38:12-28], intimated the same thing. It would be tedious to enumerate all the prefigurations, since Paul says that all things happened unto them by way of example, I Cor. 10:6.

He, then, through whom we were all created [I Cor. 8:6], and through whom it pleased God to recreate and renew the world, was, when the time seemed to Him ripe, conceived in the womb of a spotless virgin without any male aid, by the fructification of the Holy Spirit (for He who was to be born thence was sent to make spiritual beings out of fleshly), and began His human life. Read Luke Chaps. 1 and 2, and Matthew 1, and John 1, that I may not have to busy myself here with such well-known facts. Christ had to be born of a virgin* on two accounts: first, because His divine nature could not suffer that any stain of sin attach to it, as has been said above. For God is so thoroughly light, purity, innocence, goodness, that He cannot endure any thing that is in any respect dark, impure, defiled, or evil. Therefore the birth had to be absolutely pure of every stain, because He that was born was also God. Second, on account of the nature of the sacrificial victim. For that had to be free from all blemish, as the law of Moses required, though that applied only to purity of flesh, Heb. 9:9. How much more had that victim to be absolutely spotless which made atonement for the sins not only of all who had been, but of all who were yet to come! And this could not have been unless He had been born of a virgin, and without male intervention. For if the virgin had conceived from the seed of a man, would not the birth have been thereby polluted? And if a woman who had before known a man had conceived Him, even from the Holy Spirit, who would ever have believed that the child that was born was of the Holy Spirit? For nature knows no birth that is not besmirched with stain. For, "Behold, I was shapen in iniquity; and in sin did my mother conceive me," Ps. 51:5. Virgin, therefore, she had to be, and ever virgin, too, who should bear Him in whom there could be not even the least suspicion of a blemish, much less any real blemish. Now I add evidence of these things. That He is a

*Cf. Zwingli's *Eine Predigt von der Ewig reinen Magd Maria.*

victim who expiates every blemish and defect is prefigured in the lamb, *"phase"* [פסח], *i. e.,* of "transitio" [passing over], or rather "præteritio" [passing by], lest in consequence of the ambiguity in the word any one should understand by "transitio" a going forth. For the Hebrew term "paesa" [!] [פסח] signifies a leap or a passing by; for the angel of the Lord leaped over without injury when he saw the door posts smeared with the blood [cf. Exod. 12: 23]. Of this figure I shall say nothing more, since it is perfectly clear in itself and through the notices of all who have spoken of it. Furthermore, the John who baptized the Son of God, as soon as he saw Christ coming towards him, pointed Him out to his disciples with the words: "Behold, the Lamb of God that taketh away the sin of the world!" John 1: 29. He taketh away, therefore, the sins of the world (for sin is used here for "offence and defect of mankind")—not the original defect only, as false religion teaches, does He atone for, nor the sins of those only who were before Him, but of the world; and not those only which the Popes direct are to be remitted by their crowd of priests, but of the world; and He takes away not only those sins which you redeem with money, but the sins of the world independently of any bargain. The sin against the Holy Ghost requires especial consideration, and I shall not go into it here. That He was born of a virgin, Matthew and Luke bear witness, as I have shown; but, lest one miss Old Testament proofs, we have Isa. 7: 14 and Ezek. 44: 2. Since, however, there are persons who, in stout defense of the decrees of the Roman Pontiff, say that not all the facts of our belief are set forth in the Holy Scriptures—inasmuch as the perpetual virginity of the θεοτόκου [God-bearing] and thrice blessed Virgin Mary cannot be established from the Holy Scriptures—it is worth while to oppose to them the invincible shield of the truth, that their eyes may be blinded by its brightness so completely that they shall learn not to blaspheme. Isaiah [7: 14] says that a virgin shall conceive and bear. What is there to wonder at, pray, if a virgin conceives? Did any woman ever conceive who had not once been a virgin, quite apart from our virgin? But the uncommon thing is that she who conceives and bears should remain a virgin. Our virgin, then, remains a virgin, and remaining a virgin is ever virgin; otherwise she would not remain a virgin. And this Ezekiel finely indicates, saying [44: 2]: "This gate shall be shut; it shall not be opened, neither shall any man enter in by it; because the Lord, the God of Isræl, hath entered in by it, therefore it shall be shut for the prince." The objections that could be raised here as to the meaning because of the circumstances can be so easily removed that one aiming at brevity must not delay over them; for "all things happened unto them by way of example, etc." False religion slips up, therefore, when she snarls out that the perpetual virginity does not hold unless it be confirmed by the decrees of the Popes. For, as they cannot by their decrees make her that is defiled undefiled, so they could not with these suspicious dicta of theirs remedy the Virgin's reproach by decreeing that she is ever virgin. For unless she were virgin in her own quality, they could not make her virgin by their decrees. Her virginity is based on the fact, not on the decrees of men.

The ever virgin, then, brought forth Christ, God's Son and hers, while on a journey to Bethlehem, according to the predictions of the prophets, Mic. 5: 2, Matt. 2: 6, Luke 2: 7, and laid her babe in a manger, because there was no room in the inn on account of the crowd of people who had then gathered there to be taxed. Thus Divine Providence ordained that as Adam by sinning had made himself naked and exposed himself to need, so Christ, that the divine justice might be appeased, should experience want, cold, and all the ills that had been brought upon man for his sin. For this was required by justice, that He through whom we were all created, in whom there is no sin, and from whom we had gone astray, should, though innocent, bear what we had deserved through sinning, but bear it for us. For "he did no sin, neither was guile found in his mouth" [I Pet. 2: 22]. What He bore, He bore for us. He needed nothing, but was made needy for us, that we might enjoy His riches. In like manner, He who was to be the food of the soul was laid where the cattle fed, that we might in the very beginning see that He was to be our food who without the knowledge of God are nothing but beasts—the food by which we should be made of the Spirit. He is exposed to the harshness of winter who clothes the flowers of the field more richly than any Solomon [Lk. 12: 27]; who feedeth the ravens [Lk. 12: 24] and giveth sustenance to the beasts [Ps. 147: 9]. And He is born in a place where a multitude of people had assembled. For He is to belong to all; and He is born in a manger, while we snore on downy couches. For He is the true shepherd, who ever watcheth over His flock. He is circumcised on the eighth day, though unless circumcision had looked forward to Him it would have profited nothing. And He is given a name which is above every name [Phil. 2: 9], and which fully signifies just what Christ is. For He is the Savior, and is called Jesus [Lk. 2: 21] for the very reason that He is nothing else than Savior, for He saves the people from their sins. He grows in years and knowledge [Lk. 2: 52], that we may recognize His true humanity. He is accepted by Simeon and Anna [Lk. 2: 25-38] and is proclaimed to be the light of salvation unto all nations, that His divinity also may be seen. At twelve years of age, unto the same end he sits in the midst of the doctors, talks with them, vanquishes and confutes them [Lk. 2: 42-47]. And straightway, that we may not doubt His true humanity, He goes down with His mother and foster father to Nazareth and is subject to them [Lk. 2: 51]. And He is so entirely subject that, following the trade of his foster father, He at length wins for Himself so famous a name in it that men say [Mk. 6: 3]: *οὐχ οὗτός ἐστιν ὁ τέκτων,* "Is not this the carpenter?" And when He has reached the fulness of His time, so that He is presently to be taken up from the earth, He so proves Himself in every way the Son of God, both by His teaching and by doing wonderful miracles, that not only men but even demons against their will are forced to confess that He is the Son of God [Mk. 1: 24]. Now He feeds hungry crowds on a few loaves [Mk. 6: 34-44]; again, He gives as drink water turned into wine [Jn. 2: 1-11], cleanses leprosy, drives away disease, quenches fever; endows the blind with sight, the lame with power to walk, the palsied with movement; straightens the crooked, restores the dead to life with a word [Mt. 11: 4-6]; and there are no ills at all of body or mind so deep-set that He does not take them away. But when He boldly uncovers the deceits and schemes of the hypocrites, then wickedness, which like an owl cannot endure coming into the light, resists, as is its nature, and finds a way to save its reputation though at the loss of its soul. They determine, therefore, to slay Christ the innocent Son of God and the Virgin, caring nothing how much hurt they did their consciences, provided they could make the simple believe that they were just persons, and that Christ was the wicked one, in that He had unjustly heaped abuse upon the just. And since the power of trial had been taken from them, they found a way of bringing accusation against Him before the governor. But, lest something should intervene to prevent His being taken, or He should escape when taken, they made it their business to take Him themselves, thinking His destruction more certain if they brought Him in person than if they made information against Him in His absence. Having, therefore, taken Him they brought Him before the governor, and accused Him of lèse majesté, declaring that He had forbidden the giving of tribute to Cæsar [Lk. 23: 2]. And in order to arouse the enmity of the rabble also against Him, they suborned false witnesses to allege that He had said He had power to destroy the Temple and to build it up again in three days [Mt. 26: 60f.]. In this way they hoped that, even if they found the magistrate pretty firm, His death could, nevertheless, be accomplished through the uproar and shoutings of the degraded rabble. And this is what happened. For the magistrate, as he repeatedly confessed, found no cause of condemnation in Him [Lk. 23: 4, 14, 22], though he made many attempts; yet, not daring to acquit Him, gave Him over to the madness of His accusers. Therefore did wickedness maltreat innocence, iniquity righteousness, the limbs of Satan God, traitors the champion of peace, ingratitude its benefactor, murderers the incarnation of life, parricides their deliverer; and did so spit upon, bruise, and buffet Him, so tear Him with thorns and scourges from the top of His head to the soles of His feet, and so utterly trample upon Him, that pitying children and women could not restrain their tears at His woe [Lk. 23: 27]. But He, no way crushed by these ills, no way angered, yet warned His murderers of the ills they were calling down upon themselves by a wrong so atrocious. They, therefore, inflicted the most ignoble punishment upon Him, nailing to the cross along with murderers

[Mt. 27:38] Him through whom they had life, and against whom they could have done nothing unless through Him they had received the breath of life. Never untrue to Himself when thus miserably exposed to the elements, the stars, and the derision of man, He prayed for His enemies [Lk. 23:34] that the Heavenly Father would not lay this madness to their charge; for such was their barbarity that when He thirsted amid His tortures they gave Him vinegar mixed with gall to drink [Mt. 27:34]. And when He saw that the things committed to Him by the Father were accomplished, He gave a sign, saying, "It is finished" [John 19:30]—His own work, namely, by which through His own innocence He had removed from us the claims of the Devil and of death over us. His task performed, as He was about to give up the ghost, He commended Himself to the Father thus [Lk. 23:46]: "Into thy hands I commend my spirit." With these words He expired. Then suddenly all things begin to be troubled on account of the wrong to their Maker. The sun hides its brightness, that it may be apparent to the cruel murderers, as in an uprising by night, how atrocious the deed was. The veil of the Temple is rent with pain on account of the vast insult to God. The rocks split asunder from impatience, that we might see that the perverseness of the Jews was harder than the hardness of stone. The earth, scorning to bear such savage brutes, quakes, threatening destruction. The dead creep forth from their tombs at the commotion [Mt. 27:51-53; Lk. 23:45]. But the hearts of the impious hypocrites are unmoved. They go to the magistrate, ask him to station a watch to keep guard over the dead body, obtain their request [Mt. 27:64-66]. When the third dawn was breaking, in spite of the soldiers He came to life again through the glory of the Father. When they saw what had happened, they reported it to the priests. Bribed by them for a large sum to lie, they agreed to spread the report that the disciples had secretly taken away the body while they were asleep [Mt. 27:11-15]. Such is the course of insane madness; and hatred, ever blind, refuses to yield to the truth, and fancies that it hides itself well; nay, when it has become very deeply rooted, it has no shame, nor cares whether it is seen or not. This Solomon taught finely in Proverbs 18:3, saying: "The wicked man, when he is come into the depth of sins, contemneth." But Christ, after His triumphant return from the dead, immediately showed Himself to His disciples and, having had intercourse with them for forty days, ascended of His own motion to the Father in sight of the disciples [Acts 1: 3]. All this I have briefly narrated the more willingly, in order to make clearer to every beholder the righteousness of Christ by which He healed the wound of Adam. For we are still dealing with the point that Christ is our righteousness, our innocence, and the price of our redemption. For to this end He died for us and rose again, that He might declare the mystery of our deliverance and confirm the hopes which, when men saw that He had died and afterwards by His own power had become alive again, could not but be made sure in regard to life everlasting after this life. For "in that he died, he died unto sin," Rom. 6: 10; but not unto His sin, for He was absolutely free from sin, but unto ours. And He rose again in order that we may know that we have been made alive through Him.

[7]. The Gospel

Christ suffered all these things for us. If we could have won salvation by our own works or our own innocence, He would have died in vain, Gal. 2: 21. The nature of the Gospel may, therefore, now be briefly expressed as follows. As regards the name, to preface the subject with that, it is known to all that it means nothing but "good tidings." But what those tidings are must be learned from the words of Him who brings them. He sent forth His disciples with the injunction, Mark 16: 15: "Go ye into all the world, and preach the gospel to the whole creation. He that believeth and is baptized shall be saved; but he that believeth not shall be condemned." Here we learn, first, that the gospel is a thing which saves the believer We have, then, what it does, but we do not yet have what it is. We must, therefore, consult another Evangelist, which is by far the most convenient way of coming to an understanding of the Holy Scriptures. Luke, then, 24: 45-47, writing of the same idea and of what happened on the same day, namely, that on which Christ rose, says: "Then opened he their mind, that they might understand the Scriptures, that it is written so and so, and that it behooved Christ to suffer so and so, and on the third day to rise from the dead, and that repentance and remission of sins should be preached in his name unto all nations." Here we have clearly what the gospel is and how it ought to be preached. This is the gospel, that sins are remitted in the name of Christ; and no heart ever received tidings more glad. But it is desirable to explain the plan thereof a little further, for when that is known we shall get a closer view of the thing itself. Christ taught [Lk. 24: 47] that repentance and remission of sins were to be preached in His name unto all nations. First, I think it is generally agreed that "name" is used here for "force, power, might, majesty," as in Mark 16: 17: "In my name," *i. e.,* in my might or power, "shall they cast out demons." And in Acts 3: 6 Peter says: "In the name," *i. e.,* through the force or power, "of Jesus Christ of Nazareth rise up and walk." And, a little later [3: 16]: "And by faith in his name hath his name made this man strong, whom ye see and know, etc." "By faith in his name"—what else can it mean than having faith in His power and force? "His name hath made strong," *i. e.,* His power and majesty? Through Christ, therefore, it is brought about that we repent of our former life. For I showed clearly enough, where we were considering man, that without the grace of God man knows himself just as little as without it he recognizes God. It has to be through the power of God that man knows himself. In order, then, that one may repent of one's errors, it is necessary that one shall know that one's errors are errors, which certainly is not in the power of the flesh, *i. e.,* of man. For he is so blind in his own concerns that he never condemns himself in anything. If it comes to pass that he condemns himself, it comes to pass not through his own power but another's. But this other's power cannot be the power of other flesh, for the nature of all flesh is the same. The other power, therefore, that brings man to a knowledge of himself must be of the Spirit. And this I constantly inculcate in the sense that I leave nothing to man, to whom some, on the contrary, ascribe so much. It is a result wrought by the Divine Spirit alone that man knows himself. But unless knowledge precedes, no self-abasement follows. For who would abase himself unless he saw in himself something offensive? Christ teaches first, therefore, how repentance should arise and be preached in His name; *i. e.,* that it is through His power that man knows himself and is disgusted with himself when known. Then, to return to the exposition of Luke's words, unless we repent, are disgusted with ourselves, ashamed of ourselves, Christ does not become saving and valuable to us who now know what law is and what sin is.

Hence I must tell, in the second place, how repentance must take its beginning.

When, therefore, Divine Majesty formed the plan of redeeming man, it did not intend that the world should persist and become inveterate in its wickedness. For if this had been the plan, it would have been better never to have sent a redeemer than to have sent one under such conditions that after redemption there should be no change from our former diseased state. It would have been laughable if He to whom everything that is ever to be is seen as present had determined to deliver man at so great a cost, and yet had intended to allow him immediately after his deliverance to wallow in his old sins. He proclaims, therefore, at the start, that our lives and characters must be changed. For to be a Christian is nothing less than to be a new man and a new creature [II Cor. 5: 17]. Therefore, when He had sent His forerunner,* he began by saying, "Repent! For Divine Justice is so exasperated that unless you change your character you are sure to suffer bitter punishment, yea, utter destruction and death. I proclaim no far off event, lest forsooth you scorn me, as once happened to Ezekiel [Ezek. 33: 30-32], but one which is already at your doors. For now is the axe laid at the root of the trees, so that, unless you change your life, you will be utterly rooted up" [Mt. 3: 10]. Thus it came about that those who were influenced by the preaching of that most blameless man saw clearly that their way of life must be absolutely changed; and so they came to him in crowds, and were washed by him in the River Jordan as the sign by which he marked those who, having reviewed their former lives, found nothing in them which did not deserve condign punishment, and, understanding this, turned their

*John the Baptist.

hearts to repentance. This was an initiatory rite with which he initiated all the repentant, not a cleansing. This Peter also teaches, I Pet. 3: 20-21, saying that we are washed in baptism in the same way in which the men of old were once purified by the flood. And, that we shall not understand here the baptism of water but the internal change of the old man through repentance, he adds that this is not effected by "the washing away of the filth of the flesh" (for that is all the water could do), but by the conscience asking itself how it stands towards God and giving a good answer. Hence it is manifest that the famous baptizing of Christ by John in the water is nothing but an initiatory rite, and not a washing away of the filth of the soul, for that is the function of the blood of Christ alone. For as the flesh has no shame when it is away from witnesses (for it is blown hither and thither by any wind), it would have been easy for anyone to pretend that he had been deeply impressed by the preaching of John, and yet to live irreverently and impiously. This evil was met by the symbol of baptism. For, having received that mark, one did become ashamed to be openly sealed with the seal of repentance and then openly to defile oneself with the old vices. Thus briefly on the symbol of Baptism, on which much elsewhere* on account of those who think that it wipes away sins or is the seal and certification of their having been wiped away. Both sets of men speak what pleases themselves, not what the word of the Lord has taught. —I come back to repentance. When, then, John taught that man must review his life and change it, what hopes, pray, did he hold out? Did he ever teach, "By doing so and so ye will be saved"? By no means. But, knowing very well that it could not but be that, when man examined himself thoroughly, nay, the oftener he did it, the oftener and more surely he would despair of himself and his own righteousness (whence it is sure that disgust with one's self first arises), he presently pointed out Him through whom salvation should come, directing his discourse to Him who was to come, Acts 19: 4 and John 1: 19, 27, 29-30, and declaring that salvation lay with Him who came after him in time, but in His divine birth and dignity was long before him. He says in Matt. 3: 11, "I indeed

*In *Von der Taufe, von der Wiedertaufe und der Kindertaufe.*

baptize you with water unto repentance": (by the baptism of water, therefore, they were inducted into repentance) "but he that cometh after me is mightier than I, whose shoes I am not worthy to bear: he will baptize you in the Holy Spirit, and in fire." But what else is it to baptize with the Holy Spirit than to make the conscience glad and at peace through His coming? And how can it be made at peace unless it have a firm hope in someone who it knows for certain cannot deceive? To baptize with the Holy Spirit is, therefore, nothing else than Christ's giving us His spirit, which so enlightens and attracts our hearts that we trust in Him, lean on Him, who is the Son of God, who was sent for us, whose brothers we become by His mercy, not by our own merits. John, therefore, shows that our life is such that it needs correction, although when we have corrected it we find not in ourselves anything through which we can hope to be saved. John, then, sends us to Christ, saying that it is He in whom we shall find salvation, even free salvation. This the divine Evangelist and Prophet thus set forth, John 1: 26-27: "I" (John, namely, who was baptizing) "baptize in water; but in the midst of you standeth one whom ye know not. He it is who will come after me, who was before me, the latchet of whose shoe I am not worthy to unloose." Here we rightly understand that John sends us to one who stood among them, or was born in the midst of them. A little while after he says [Jn. 1: 29-31]: "John seeth Jesus coming unto him, and saith, Behold the Lamb of God, that taketh away the sin of the world! This is he of whom I said" (notice how he repeats his previous words), "After me cometh a man who was before me, who was mightier than I. And I knew him not: but that he should be made manifest to Israel, for this cause came I baptizing in water." The divine Baptist shows by these words that Christ is the Lamb that atones for the universal disease of sin, and that he himself is preaching a baptism of repentance before Him that He may be made manifest to Israel. For when man through repentance has come to the knowledge of himself, he finds nothing but utter despair. Hence, wholly distrusting himself, he is forced to take refuge in the mercy of God. But when he has begun to do that, justice makes him afraid. Then Christ appears, who has satisfied the divine justice for our trespasses. When once there is faith in Him, then salvation is found; for He is the infallible pledge of God's mercy. For "he that gave up a Son for us, how will he not with him also give us all things?" Rom. 8: 32. The justice of God and a heart conscious of all its sins frighten us. For what do we not all meditate and concoct? What hopes do we not indulge in of pleasure, pelf, and greed for glory? Hence, when we are so terrified by the righteousness of Him to whom we are hastening, and by our consciences, which are driving us headlong to despair, Christ, the Son of God, comes to help our distress; for with Him as Redeemer, with Him as Advocate, with Him spending everything for us, we may hope all things in the hands of the Father. O unspeakable wisdom of God, O measureless bounty, O still greater mercy, surpassing all men's hopes! God enlightens us, so that we know ourselves. When this happens, we are driven to despair. We flee for refuge to His mercy, but justice frightens us. Here Eternal Wisdom finds a way by which to satisfy His justice—a thing wholly denied to ourselves—and at the same time to enable us, relying on His mercy, to enjoy Him. He sends His Son to satisfy His justice for us, and to be the indubitable pledge of salvation; but on condition that we become new creatures, and that we walk having put on Christ [II Cor. 5: 17]. The whole life of a Christian, therefore, is repentance. For when do we not sin? Hence Christ, when He first sent out His disciples to preach, bade them preach the same thing which John and which He Himself had preached, Matt. 4: 17 and 10: 7; Mk. 6: 12; Lk. 9: 2. For they, too, warned men to change their very wicked lives, and declared that the kingdom of God was at hand.*

But I ask your attention to what follows, in order that the nature of repentance may become still clearer and that at the same time I may answer an objection, which is to this effect: If we are to understand Christ in this way, as the sacrifice which, offered but once, made satisfaction for the sins of all, we shall all be more inclined to follow our lusts, inasmuch as all these sins can be committed with impunity; for Christ is

*Compare with this treatment Zwingli's *Eine kurze Christliche Einleitung*, the section on the Gospel.

the pledge that all sins are washed away.

answer

I will first of all show by the Holy Scriptures how Christ is the only One through whom there is approach to the Father, and that He alone blots out all sins. For then the argument that these people use will find its place. That Christ, then, is the only One through whom there is approach to the Father will be plain for this reason, that if God could have been reached in any other way there would have been no need of Christ's death.

It is well, however, to bring His own words before us. Of these I will first set down those by which He bears clear witness that He is One sent for the salvation of all; then those by which He bears witness that He is the only One through whom salvation is given; for "is" precedes "is the only."

John 3: 16 says: "God so loved the world, that he gave his only begotten Son, that whosoever believeth on him should not perish, but have eternal life." By these words the whole reason and meaning of the Gospel are explained—the reason, that God gave His Son because He so loved the world; the meaning, that whosoever believeth on Him attains eternal life.

A little later the divine Baptist says [Jn. 3: 35-36]: "The Father loveth the Son, and hath given all things into his hand. He that believeth on the Son hath eternal life; but he that believeth not the Son shall not see life, but the wrath of God abideth on him." This passage makes for both points; that is, as well for the point that Christ is a means of salvation for all, as for the point that He is the only means of salvation for all.

In John 6: 53-58, Christ's main purpose is to show that He is such food that whosoever eateth Him shall live; that is, He is such a treasure of the soul that whosoever fixes his heart and hope on Him will have eternal life. For He came down from heaven, He says, that the world through Him might have life. In this same chapter He says: "Verily, verily, I say unto you, He that believeth on me hath eternal life." To all, therefore, whose hope is in Him He is a means of salvation.

In John 8: 12 He says: "I am the light of the world. He that followeth me shall not walk in the darkness, but shall have the light of life." To everyone that follows him, therefore, He is light; to all the faithful He is, therefore, a means of salvation.

In John 10: 9 He says: "I am the door; by me if any man enter in, he shall be saved."

Thus, by ever varied metaphor, He teaches the same thing, namely, that He is our light, salvation, leader, shepherd, father, all.

In John 12: 31-32 He speaks after this fashion: "Now is the judgment of this world: now shall the prince of this world be cast out. And I, if I be lifted up from the earth, will draw all men unto myself." He cast out the Devil from his kingdom, and suffered Himself to be set up as an ensign for all the nations, according to the prediction of the Prophet, Isa. 5: 26-30 and 11: 12, that all the nations might come to Him. For on that account was He stretched upon the four arms of the cross, that they might come from the north and the south, from the east and the west, as the same prophet foretold, 43: 5, and that Abraham, and Isaac, and Jacob might sit down with God, Matt. 8: 11.

The passages testifying to this idea are too many to be all brought together here. The very thing that recommends the gospel is just this [Mk. 16: 16], that "whoso believeth the gospel when it is preached shall be saved, and whoso believeth not, shall be condemned." The gospel, as from what precedes is now clearer than day, is nothing else than sure salvation through Christ, than which no tidings more pleasant, more healthful, more precious, can be brought to us. For when our consciences are laboring amid the narrows and cliffs of despair, what tidings more joyful can be brought us than that there is at hand a Redeemer who will "bring us forth into a large place," Ps. 18: 19, and a Deliverer and Leader who can do all things, for he is God? Hence also Paul, Rom. 1: 16, gives this definition: "The gospel," he says, "is the might or power of God unto salvation to everyone that believeth"; that is, the gospel is nothing else than the might of God by which He gave His own Son for us. Whosoever, therefore, believeth on Him, whether he be Jew or Gentile, will be saved.

The sum and substance of this section, therefore, is that Christ is a means of salvation unto all men of all nations and races. For He "would have all men to be saved, and to come to the knowledge of the truth," I Tim. 2:4. And He is not only so good that He would have it, but also so rich that He can. For "of his fulness have we all received," John 1:16. For "he is rich unto all that call upon him," Rom. 10:12.

Now I will show that Christ is the only means of salvation.

In John 6:53 He who is alone our salvation Himself speaks thus: "Verily, verily, I say unto you, Except ye eat the flesh of the Son of Man, and drink his blood, ye have no life in you." I will first of all give a summary of this sixth chapter. Christ had fed many thousands of people on a few loaves of bread, and they afterwards followed Him the more eagerly in order to fill their bellies without trouble. For there were but few who came to Him in order to be made better by His teaching. When Christ, who knows the heart, saw this, He reproved their hypocrisy and insatiable gluttony and warned them to seek the true and life-giving food of the soul; that this was the work most pleasing to God. And although they, remembering their former feast, understood by food or bread nothing but that provision by the eating of which we sustain our strength, Christ was yet ever speaking of that food which restores the famished heart. For He had come to refresh hearts ahungered for heavenly things. He says, therefore, that He is the bread of life [Jn. 6:33, 51] which cometh down out of heaven, and which giveth life unto the world. What else would they think of here who had come for their belly's sake than how Christ could be eaten? And so they recoiled in horror. But He, to show plainly in what way He is food or bread, says: "The bread which I will give is my flesh, for the life of the world." His meaning is this: "Ye are turning over many things in your minds as to this food which I am promising. One wonders at its charcter, another is aghast at an apparent barbarity. Why do ye ever stay so close to earth? See ye not that I am trying to rouse your sluggish minds with parables? Why rise ye not, therefore, at last to higher things? Again, see ye not that, though I sometimes seem to those who are still too much given over to the flesh to do it rather violently—see ye not, I say, that I purposely go from these external and crude things to the internal and spiritual? I came not to feed the body, but to bring back the human heart to God. While ye are occupied with the memory of bread for the body, I am occupied with the way in which I may put into the mouth of your souls food that is spiritual. And while ye are thinking of bread for the body, I am teaching that there is a food that can renew the heart, which bread made of flour cannot in the least do. This food is myself: the bread which I promise to give is my flesh, which shall be given up for the life of the world. This makes the heart glad and secure of salvation, if it believes unshakenly that I have been given up for the life of the world through the glory and grace of the Father. This is the food in the strength of which ye shall walk even unto the mountain of God" [*cf.* Ps. 15:1; Isa. 2:3]. But the more the Jews were taught, the less they understood and the more they shrank from the flesh and blood of Christ, imagining that it was these they were invited to crunch and to drink, and thinking it a monstrous and savage thing that they should be summoned to such a feast. Christ, perceiving that their stolidity proceeded from unbelief, smote them still more heavily, and according to the prophecy of Isaiah 6:10 [cf. Jn. 12:40] made their heart fat, and their ears heavy, and shut their eyes, saying [Jn. 6:53]: "Verily, verily, I say unto you, Except ye eat the flesh of the Son of Man, and drink His blood, ye have no life in you"; as if to add, "however much commotion ye make among yourselves, I certainly must be eaten and must be drunk." And after much more He says plainly [Jn. 6:63] that the flesh of which they were thinking profiteth nothing, eaten, of course, in the physical way they shrank from; that it is the spiritual manducation of which He was speaking that quickeneth; that by the words which He was going to speak the human heart becomes alive and strong. "If you eat bread, I say, the body is strengthened; if you eat me, *i. e.,* if you trust in me, your hearts will be strong unto God."

So much on the subject of this chapter, at greater length, perhaps, than brevity allows, and yet more briefly than the occasion demands; but it has been done for the sake of those who do not see the allegory here and have found therein occasion for many errors, while yet Christ meant to teach by it nothing other than the sum and substance of the Gospel, namely, that He was sent from heaven to suffer death for poor mortals. This fact would have such saving virtue for the poor creatures that the soul that would rely thereon would be far more strengthened and be rendered far stauncher than the body is by the use of bread.

But now I come to the words I quoted [Jn. 6:53]: "Except ye eat," *i. e.,* except ye firmly and heartily believe that Christ was slain for you, to redeem you, and that His blood was shed for you, to wash you thus redeemed (for that is the way we are in the habit of showing bounty and kindness to captives—first freeing them by paying a ransom, then when freed washing away the filth with which they are covered), "ye have no life in you." Since, therefore, Christ alone was sacrificed for the human race, He is the only One through whom we can come to the Father.

In John 10:1 He teaches the same thing in other words: "Verily, verily, I say unto you, he that entereth not by the door into the sheepfold, but climbeth up some other way, the same is a thief and a robber"; and a little farther on: "I am the door: by me if any man enter in, he shall be saved." Since, therefore, to enter by any other way than by the door is the mark of thieves and robbers, and since Christ is the door, they are thieves and robbers who either seek, or teach others to seek salvation in any other way than through Christ. Christ, therefore, is our only means of salvation. And let no one at this point raise the objection that this passage applies to the shepherds only and not also to the general method of salvation; for it is so pregnant with meaning that it teaches just as clearly by what way everyone can come to God as it does how they to whom that charge has been committed ought to feed the sheep of Christ. For He speaks just as solemnly and anxiously of the sheep as of the shepherds, as is easily apparent to one who considers attentively.

In John 8:36 He says to the Jews: "If the Son shall make you free, ye shall be free indeed." But there is one only Son of God; it is, therefore, only through Christ that we are freed from the yoke of sin and made sons of God.

To the same effect is the allegory of the vine and the branches, in John 15, since Christ deduces the following: "As the branch cannot bear fruit of itself, except it abide in the vine; so neither can ye, except ye abide in me" [15: 4]; and, a little later: "If a man abide not in me, he is cast forth as a branch, and is withered, etc." On Christ alone, therefore, must they be grafted who would attain salvation. But His reply to Thomas in John 14: 6 is the clearest statement of all: "I am the way, the truth, and the life: no man cometh unto the Father, but by me." Since He is the way, by Him alone must we enter in. And again: "To the Father no man cometh but by him." He, therefore, is the only one through whom and in whom we find salvation.

And Peter says in Acts 4: 12: "For neither is there any other name under heaven given among men, wherein we must be saved." There is no name, no force or power, which can make us blessed save that of Christ. Christ, therefore, is the only one in whom we are blessed. Paul, I Tim. 2: 5-6, confirms this: "There is one God, one mediator also between God and men, the man Christ Jesus, who gave himself a ransom for all." Now it is sure that "unus" [one] is used here in the sense of "solus" [only one], as in the passage, Matt. 19: 17, "Unus," *i. e.,* "solus," "bonus est deus," "One," *i. e.,* "only one," "is good, God"; for Luke 18: 19 expresses the same idea by the words, "nemo bonus, nisi solus deus," "none is good but God alone."

I think it is now sufficiently clear that through Christ alone we are given salvation, blessedness, grace, pardon, and all that makes us in any way worthy in the sight of a righteous God.

However, from these premises (namely, that Christ is the expiation for the sins of all and the way of salvation, and that He alone is this way and expiation, and this to him only who trusts in Him), those who either have not faith enough in the gospel or have not taken it in in its full purity think it follows that all who lean upon it must degenerate from over freedom. For, they reason, when the human heart learns that all sins are so bountifully pardoned through Christ, it quite naturally must become more prone to vice. Hence some of them, out of a foolish prudence, have wished to guard against anything of this sort happening, and have proclaimed that Christ made atonement either for the original guilt only, or only for those sins which were committed before He came.* These errors arose from the fact that, while thinking themselves profoundly versed in the nature of Christianity, they were profoundly ignorant of it; for it is based upon faith, not upon wisdom, knowledge, or prudence; and since they had not faith they became vain in their reasonings [cf. Rom. 1:21]. For Christian faith is a thing that is felt in the soul of the believer, like health in the body. Any one can easily feel whether that is bad or good. So the Christian feels how his heart is in a bad plight because of the burden of sin, and, on the other hand, feels how well off it is in that there is a sure remedy in Christ. It usually happens, also, that those who are always well do not make sound health of so much account as do those who suffer from long or severe illnesses. So Christ is not so priceless a possession to those who feel no sickness of the soul as to those who feel and suffer pain. Hence it has come about, since we do not know ourselves thoroughly, *i .e.,* deep in to the core (for we know nothing of the illness and its gravity), that for us Christ has never been the means of salvation and priceless treasure that He is. But if we had ever truly suffered pain from our disease, *i. e.,* if we really know ourselves, what worthless and diseased cattle we are, while we yet wish to appear to all men as great, noble, righteous, holy; how completely given over to evil desires, so that we let our passions guide us in everything—if, I say, we had ever been sensible of our disease, our pain would have been so great that after the physician had relieved it we never should have thought of saying, "I will be ill again," *i. e.,* "I will sin again." The man who has broken a leg, and has found a good physician who has restored the injured limb, does not say to himself, "You are lucky to have found such a physician. Go and break your leg often; for that physician can cure anything." But all through his life, wherever he goes, whithersoever he turns, he looks out and takes care not to break his leg again. For he has felt how painful it is to restore a broken limb, how tedious to lie a whole month upon one's back or upon the one side only. So those who, when they hear that Christ has made atonement for the sins of all, exult-

felt need for Xp

*This Romish doctrine Zwingli has refuted at length in his *Ad Fridolinum Lindoverum expostulatio.*

antly exclaim, "We will sin, for all things are freely pardoned through Christ," have never felt the pain of sin. For if they had ever felt it, they would take care with all their might not to fall into it again. I have made this preamble in order to be able to speak more clearly, as I promised to do, about repentance.

[8]. Repentance

We have till now regarded repentance as a forced and feigned pain for sins committed, and as the paying of the penalty set upon the sin by the judge, *i. e.,* the father confessor. We repented of our evil doing only when the Pope ordered, or when the celebration of Easter was approaching, or when our health demanded it. What was this but hypocrisy? Or whence came it except from ignorance of ourselves? For he who has attained to knowledge of himself sees such a vast slough of wickedness that he is driven not only to grieve, but to shudder, to despair, to die. For what lust is so filthy, what greed so bold, what self-esteem so high, that every man does not see it in his own heart, scheming or working or hiding something? And as no one can deny this, how has it happened that we have not felt the pain that is born thereof? It has happened from the fact that, as was said above, no one tries to go down into himself, no one. When, therefore, we do so go down, real pain and shame immediately follow. But this was by no means the case before in the repentance of the Popes. For how should any one be disgusted with himself when no one knew himself, but thought rather that he was righteous either through his own works or through hired efforts? The second part of the gospel, then, is repentance: not that which takes place for a time, but that which makes a man who knows himself blush and be ashamed of his old life, for one reason because he is greatly dissatisfied and pained at himself, and for another because he sees it ought to be altogether foreign to a Christian to waste away in those sins from which he rejoiced to believe that he had been delivered. When, therefore, Christ and John and the Apostles preached, saying, "Repent," they certainly did not speak of that feigned and counterfeit repentance which I mentioned in the first place;

nor of that which is felt once for all and straightway thinks license to sin given it, for this kind, as has been sufficiently set forth, is just as much a counterfeit as that performed by order of the Popes. But they spoke of the repentance in which a man goes into himself and diligently investigates the reason of all his acts, his concealments, pretences, and dissimulations. When he has done this honestly, he is driven by the vast extent of his disease to despair of his own righteousness and salvation, just as a man who has received a mortal wound keeps expecting black and everlasting night. Then, if some Machaon* should bid him be of good cheer, that the wound could be sewed up and all made good again, I think nothing more acceptable and cheering could happen to him. So our sinner, too, having thus probed his wound and despaired of safety, betakes himself to begging for mercy, and presently after seeing Christ understands that all things are to be hoped for (for "if God is for us, who is against us?" [Rom. 8: 31.]) He rises up who had lain prostrate. He lives who had learned and felt to his horror that he was dead. But neither Christ, nor John, nor the Apostles spoke of this side of repentance in such a way as to imply that it is to last a certain time and then can be put aside. It is to last permanently, as long as we carry about this pitiful burden of the body. For this is so given over to vanities that it never stops teeming with evil growths, which, as soon as they spring up, must be crushed, cut off, stifled, as things highly unbecoming a Christian. And this labor, this struggle, this watchfulness—what is it if not repentance? Therefore when Christ and John and the Apostles preach saying, "Repent," they are simply calling us to a new life quite unlike our life before; and those who had undertaken to enter upon this were marked by an initiatory sacrament, baptism to wit, by which they gave public testimony that they were going to enter upon a new life.

Now I will come to the testimony of the word, lest I seem to anyone to have brought forward my own rather than heavenly testimony.

Christ called a certain man to the service of the gospel, Luke 9: 59-62: "But he said, Lord, suffer me first to go and

*Son of Æsculapius and physician of the Greeks at Troy.

bury my father. Jesus said unto him, Leave the dead to bury their dead; but go thou and preach the kingdom of God. And another also said, I will follow thee, Lord; but first suffer me to bid farewell to them that are at my house. But Jesus said unto him, No man, having put his hand to the plough, and looking back, is fit for the kingdom of God." These words of Christ are perfectly clear in themselves, for they plainly require that we shall neglect everything else and follow God at once, and not look back. And though they might seem to apply to those only to whom the ministry of the word is entrusted, they do apply to all; as do also those two parables in Luke 14: 28-32, in which He teaches that they who determine to follow Him must examine their strength—the one that of the man who wished to build a tower, the other that of the king who was going to make war against a foe; each of whom before starting upon his undertaking counted the cost and his resources, lest he might be forced to leave everything unfinished. Finally, Christ makes this application: "So likewise, whosoever he be of you that renounceth not all that he hath, he cannot be my disciple." But what does it amount to to have renounced riches unless you have renounced those sins on account of which we are taught that riches should be scorned?

The same thing is taught by the parable in Matthew 22: 11-13 of the man who had been cordially invited to a marriage feast, but had not on a wedding garment, and therefore was cast into outer darkness. Thus those who are called to the marriage feast of the heavenly bridegroom should look to this only, that they so clothe themselves and so walk as not to disgrace themselves and insult the bridegroom.

Again, Christ says, John 8: 31: "If ye abide in my word, then are ye truly my disciples." Therefore they are disciples who abide in His word.

He speaks in like fashion, John 14: 12, 20-26.

And Paul, Rom. 6: 3-4, most clearly teaches that those who have enlisted under Christ must begin a new life, saying: "Are ye ignorant that all we who were baptized into Christ Jesus were baptized into his death? We are buried therefore with him through baptism into death: that like as Christ was raised from the dead through the glory of the Father, so we also might walk in newness of life." What else does Paul teach here than that all we who have been baptized have been admitted to the death of Christ, as the act of baptism bears witness, which first plunges us into the water to recall the death and burial of Christ, and then draws us out again, signifying nothing else than that, as Christ rose again from the dead to die no more, so we while buried in baptism are dead to the world and our former life, but when drawn out begin a new life, that is, one worthy of Christ? This the Apostle himself expounds in the following verses, saying [Rom. 6: 5-11]: "For if we are united with him in the likeness of his death, no doubt we shall be also in the likeness of his resurrection. By this likeness we learn that our old man was crucified with him, that the body of sin might be done away, that we should no longer be in bondage to sin. For he that hath died is justified from sin. But if we died with Christ, we believe that we shall also live with him. By this we see that Christ being raised from the dead dieth no more; death no more hath dominion over him. For in that he died, he died unto sin once: but in that he liveth, he liveth unto God. Even so reckon ye also yourselves to be dead indeed unto sin, but alive unto God in Christ Jesus our Lord." In these words of Paul, clearer than the sun as they are, there is nothing which everybody cannot easily grasp except the one expression, "to be dead unto sin"; for this expression Paul uses in different senses. When he teaches that Christ died unto sin, he means that Christ died because of sin, that sin might be slain; but when he says that we are dead unto sin, he means that we are freed from sin and hence no more subject to it.

In Gal. 6: 15 we read: "In Christ Jesus neither circumcision availeth anything, nor uncircumcision, but a new creature." It is not enough, therefore, to be baptized, but we are baptized in order to be new creatures. It is not enough to say, "Lord, Lord" [cf. Mt. 7: 21], but we must live according to the will of the Father. This new life and the laying aside of the old is thus taught in Rom. 13: 11-14: "Since we know this, namely, the time, that now it is high time for us to awake out of sleep: for our salvation is nearer than when we believed. The night is far spent, the day is at hand: let us therefore put away the works of darkness, and let us put on the armor of light; and let us walk honestly, as in the day, not in revelling and drunkenness, not in chambering and wantonness, not in strife and envying: but put ye on the Lord Jesus Christ."

The same thing is taught in I Peter 4: 1-11. Let him who will look for it there.

All the writings of the Apostles are filled with this idea, that the Christian religion is nothing else than a firm hope in God through Christ Jesus and a blameless life wrought after the pattern of Christ as far as He giveth us. It is plain, therefore, that repentance is not only knowledge and abnegation of self, but guarding against the abnegated self, so as always to have something to hope for while you walk in hope, and not to be without something to fear, namely, a relapse into sin. This also is clear, that not repentance but hope in Christ washes away sin, and that repentance is the being on guard lest you fall back into the ways you have condemned.

But here there seem to be many obstacles to prevent us from hoping that blamelessness can be preserved. First: "All men are liars" [Ps. 116: 11], and where lying flourishes all things are depraved. Then: "In many things we all offend," Jas. 3: 2, and as many as offend, sin, Matt. 18: 7-8. Therefore, since we all offend in many ways, we all sin in many ways. Furthermore, St. John declares, I John 1: 8: "If we say that we have no sin, we deceive ourselves, and the truth is not in us." How, therefore, even when Christ is kept before our eyes, can we be saved, since He demands a new life and other ways, but we see ourselves constantly turning back to our natural disposition? Here it is a hard task to satisfy some wise and learned persons; for since they have the clearest testimony of Scripture on both sides, namely that the redemption brought by Christ is mighty and effective for all that pertains to salvation, and that, on the other hand, blamelessness is so uniformly demanded, two difficulties seem to them to follow: one, that those who dauntlessly and constantly inculcate faith in Christ seem to be traitors to zeal for blamelessness; the other, that, seeing blamelessness so insistently demanded, they begin to doubt how much Christ can do. These persons, therefore, are very hard to satisfy; for since they are devoid of that which is wrought here in the pious by faith in Christ, they do not grasp that which is spoken spiritually. For piety is a matter of fact and experience, not of speech or knowledge. For as Abraham knew that the voice of God which bade him slay the son [Gen. 22:1-14] through whom a holy posterity had been promised was the voice of Him who had made the promise, even though human reason might fairly have maintained something else, namely, that it was the voice of the tempter, the Devil—"How could it be that he should bid you slay him whom he had but just given you for raising up a posterity?"—he girds himself with unshaken faith, arranges the wood for the fire, inexperienced as either lictor or priest he binds the loved and tender form, draws the sword with hardly less pain surely than if he were drawing it through his own heart, and raises it, oh, with what trouble of soul! over the blameless neck so often covered with his kisses. All of which was the work of God alone, that He might be marvelous in our eyes [cf. Mt. 21:42]. For if He had not so impressed Himself upon the understanding of Abraham that he had no doubt the voice was God's, the command would have been given in vain. As, I say, that voice was known to Abraham only as the voice of God, while everybody else would have thought it the voice of an impostor, so the things that I am going to say about faith in Christ and Christian blamelessness will not be understood by those whose faith is a matter of teaching rather than of experience. For I see them here at once scoff and say: "I have faith. It is you who lack it. Why do you judge me?" We will, therefore, bring right before you those who dare solemnly to boast of themselves, saying, "Seek ye a proof of Christ who speaketh in me?" II Cor. 13:3—and whose faith is would be impious to doubt—and we will hear what they have to say on this question. When Paul magnified grace so highly, there were not lacking persons to snarl, as some also do today: "If the goodness and bounty of the grace of God are made manifest in my sin, what forbids my sinning almost without limit, that the bounty of God may become known to all?" Rom. 3:7. And again: "Shall we continue in sin, that grace may abound?" [Rom. 6:1]. He replied to them in the way I quoted a little while ago from chapter 6. On the other hand, when he saw that some were beginning to have confidence in themselves because the law so emphatically demands blamelessness, he says that Christ is of no use to us if righteousness come from our works, Gal. 2: 16; and that grace through Christ is of no avail if salvation be due to works, Rom. 4: 4 and 11: 6. Placed, therefore, in this dilemma, he shows his true self and gives us an example from which we can learn what really happens to those who trust in Christ: how, namely, through faith they are sure of salvation, but through the weakness of the flesh are constantly sinning, though their sins are not imputed to them as such because of their faith.

[9]. The Law

Others have told at more than sufficient length what the Law is and what sin is. Therefore, I shall treat these topics briefly.

The Law is nothing else than the eternal will of God. For I shall say nothing here of civil laws or ceremonial laws, because they have to do with the outer man, and I am now talking of the inner man. Besides, these laws vary according to the exigencies of the times, as we often see in the case of civil laws; and ceremonial laws were abolished altogether by Christ, for they were made to be amended at some time, as was also done at the proper time, Heb. 9: 10. But the divine laws, which have to do with the inner man, are eternal. The law will never be abrogated that you are to love your neighbor as yourself; and theft, false witness, murder, etc., will always be regarded as crimes. And that the Law is the eternal or permanent will of God is proved by what is written in Rom. 2: 14 of those without the Law: namely, that they show the law has been published in their hearts, in that they do the things which the law commands, though the tablets of the law have not been set up before them. But none writes in the heart save God alone. Likewise, through the Law comes the knowledge of sin, Rom. 7: 7, and, "where no law is, there is no transgression," Rom. 4: 15. We are forced to admit, therefore, that the Law proceeded from God; for of ourselves we should not know what sin was unless God had manifested in His word what should be done and what not done. The Law, therefore, is nothing else than teachings as to the will of God, through which we understand what He wills, what He wills not, what He demands, what He forbids. But, that the will of God is permanent, so that He is never going to change any part of that law which has to do with the inner man, is evident from the words of the Lawgiver Himself. In Matthew 7:12 Christ says: "All things therefore whatsoever ye would that men should do to you, even so do ye to them: for this is the law and the prophets." If all our acts are to be done in accordance with this rule, it must be eternal; for if it be not eternal, all of them are not to be fashioned according to it. Then, in Rom. 13:19, Paul teaches that all laws are gathered up and comprehended in this one law, "Love thy neighbor as thyself." Every action, every design, therefore, and whatever regards one's neighbor must be comprehended under this law. With these points briefly settled, you will easily understand a very difficult problem of which some persons complain that no one has given a solution satisfactory to them. This is: How does it happen that from the same Law we keep some things and cut out others? Those things which, on being referred to and tested by this rule of the permanent will of God, "Love thy neighbor as thyself," are seen to be comprehended under it, can never be abolished; but those that are not were rendered obsolete by Christ. "For Christ is the end of the law," Rom. 10:4, and "the end of the law* is love," I Tim. 1:5. Christ, therefore, and love must be the same thing. "God is love," I John 4:8. They, therefore, who serve under Christ are bound to do that which love orders; what love does not order or what does not proceed from love either is not enjoined or is unprofitable, I Cor. 13:3.

[10]. Sin†

Sin is taken in a twofold sense in the Gospel teachings: First, for that disease which we contract from the author of our race, in consequence of which we are given over to love of ourselves. Of this I spoke to the best of my ability when considering man. It is this disease that Paul has in mind when he says, Rom. 7:20: "It is no more I that do it, but sin which dwelleth in me." This sin, therefore, *i. e.*, this defect, is the

**legis:* Vulgate, *praecepti;* Greek, τῆς παραγγελίας

†*Cf.* Zwingli's *On original sin*, in vol. 2 of this series, pp. 1-32.

disease native to us in consequence of which we shun things hard and burdensome and pursue things pleasant and agreeable. In the second place, sin is taken for that which is contrary to the Law, as through the Law comes knowledge of sin, Rom. 7: 7. Any course of action, therefore, which is contrary to the Law is called sin. Let us see, then, how they are related to each other, the sin that is disease and the sin that is transgression of the Law. The disease does not know that it is disease, and thinks it has a right to do whatever it likes. God does not think so, but when the disease tries to get everything for itself and thinks all things bound to serve it and to minister to its greed, He prunes this luxuriant growth with the sickle of the Law. For the Law "was added because of transgressions," Gal. 3: 19. For the Searcher of hearts is aware that the nature of all is the same, and that Thersites* has just as much self-love as Agamemnon.* Now if all were alike given loose reins, the only consequence would be that every man would subject everything to himself, according to the measure of his strength; whence a harvest of robbery, plundering, murder, parricide, and all that kind of enemy to human association would spring up. He therefore confines this far-reaching greed within fixed limits, and commands us not to do to others what we do not want done to us, and, conversely, to do to others what we want done to ourselves [Mt. 7: 12]. And that we may do it more readily and recognize the wisdom of God, He sweetens this law of nature, as it is called, with the seasoning of love, saying: "Thou shalt love thy neighbor as thyself" [Mt. 22: 39]. Love is a sweet thing, but it takes even the most bitter things cheerfully, for nothing is hard to him that loveth. Therefore, though it seems a great and difficult thing to do to your neighbor what you want done to you, it becomes pleasant and very easy if you love. But here the old man, the disease, the flesh, Adam, sin, rebels—for these are the names by which the teaching of the Apostles calls this vice of φιλαυτία, [self-love]. The flesh, or the old Adam, I say, rebels, scorning everything but itself; for it would rather that all things should serve its own lust to their own destruction than put any limit to its greed and its passion

*Thersites was the meanest, as Agamemnon was the highest, of the Greeks before Troy.

for glory and pleasure. Hence anger against the Law and the Lawgiver, hatred and machinations—hatred, because it cannot avoid or escape the Law or the Lawgiver, for if it ascendeth into heaven, He is there, if it descendeth into hell, He is there [cf. Ps. 139: 8]; machinations, because it struggles with all its might to deceive Him who yet cannot be deceived; it ponders, devises, schemes, hustles about, and after many attempts comes to this conclusion: "He is a tyrant who demands these things, for how is it possible for anyone to love another as much as himself? Nevertheless, since He makes such severe demands, His vengeance must be guarded against. You will do, therefore, as crafty slaves are wont to do with good and ἀδόλοις [guileless] masters—think up some clever dodge to blind Him so that He will not see your design." Hence the usurer endows a priesthood or some sacred office, the whoremonger keeps a season of thoroughgoing fasting in honor of the Virgin, the betrayer puts up trembling and desperate prayers. By this more than silly cajolery they hope, forsooth, to overwhelm their unsuspecting Lord, or to throw dust in His eyes, so that they can indulge with impunity in adultery, usury, and betrayal. Thus was the Law no more listened to, nor men's ways modeled upon it, nor the things that cause dishonor put away, but man became a god unto himself; for though the Law might slay, yet man none the less made himself alive in his wiles and hopes. Hence impiety gradually increased to such an extent that it said in its heart: "There is no God" [Ps. 14: 1]; though by disguising its face it was openly posing as piety itself. I have spoken thus at rather great length that we might see how the sin that is transgression is born of the sin that is disease.

The next thing is to show how we have been made free from the Law and from sin.

We have not been made free from the Law in the sense of not being bound to do what the Law bids; for the Law is the unchangeable will of God. For not one tittle of the Law shall fail, Luke 16:17. How then are we through Christ dead to the Law, so that we are subject to something other than the Law, as Paul taught by the analogy of the wife in Rom. 7:1-4? This is the way we have been made free: He that loves does all things freely, even the hardest. God, therefore, has put into our hearts a fire by which to kindle love of Him in place of love of ourselves; and He desires this fire to burn, Luke 12: 49. The Baptist had promised this fire, and so had Christ Himself as He was going to heaven, Acts 1: 5; which fire is love, and God is love [I John 4: 8]. If this burn in us, we shall do all things no longer from compulsion, but freely and cheerfully. For love is the completion of the law [Rom. 13: 10]. For the Law was performed with repugnance and feigning, when the fire of love was not yet burning; but now that that is kindled, the Law is not regarded, so far are we from fearing it; but love draws us in all things and to all things. And as we say of those who are bound by their passions that they are carried away, so those that are on fire with divine love are carried away by the spirit that burns in them. We have, therefore, one kind of freedom from the Law, that through which we do for love that which we know will please God. For Paul teaches in Rom. 12: 2 that this is acceptable to God. A second kind of freedom from the Law is that the Law cannot condemn any more, which yet before wrought the wrath and indignation and just vengeance of God, Rom. 4:15 and Gal. 3:10; and Deut. 27: 26, where divine justice sternly thunders: "Cursed is everyone who continueth not in all things that are written in the book of the law, to do them."

Christ, therefore, "redeemed us from this curse of the law, being made a curse for us," that is, being nailed to the cross for us, Gal. 3: 13 and Rom. 6: 10. We are no longer under the Law but under grace; and if under grace, the Law cannot condemn us, for if the Law still has the power to condemn, we are not under grace. It is, therefore, Christ who has broken the wrath of the Law (that is, who has appeased God's justice, which would have caused Him deservedly to rage against us), and who by bearing the cruelty of the cross for us has so softened it that He has chosen to make us not only free instead of slaves, but even sons. And if we are sons, as we surely are, Rom. 8: 14 and Gal. 4: 6, we are above the Law. "For if the Son hath made us free, we are free indeed and free-born," John 8: 36. We are, therefore, freed from the Law, now that love has been substituted for the fear of the Law. For since

God so loved us that He gave His Son for us, has He not above all kindled a responsive love? For one might, perhaps, undergo death for a righteous friend; but God, when we were His enemies, sent His Son to free us and to make us joint heirs with Him [cf. Rom. 5: 7-10]. Again, we are freed from the vengeance of the Law; for Christ has paid by His suffering that penalty which we owed for our sins. Indeed, we have been so completely freed from sin, as far as it is a disease, that it is no longer able to harm us if we trust in Christ. For "there is no condemnation to them that are in Christ Jesus, who walk not after the flesh" [Rom. 8:1]. And in so far as it is transgression, we have been freed from harm from it in the same way as from the wrath of the Law, Rom. 8: 2: "For the law of the Spirit of life in Christ Jesus made me free from the law of sin and of death." For when we say, "The Law condemns," we are simply saying, "The sin which is done contrary to the will of the Law condemns." Hence I said, we must determine about freedom from sin in the same way in which we have determined about freedom from the condemnation of the Law. When after all this we find in our own case that the disease is still so potent that we are constantly sinning, and have said that those have absolutely no hope of salvation who have not been made new men, we are, of course, driven into the old despair. Therefore, having made the needful preparations for removing this difficulty, I will now show how we are new men, even when we still are full of the old man; that is, to speak plainly, how it happens that those who are in Christ, even though they sin, yet are not condemned.

In order to do this more easily and fitly, I will treat the words of Paul in Romans 7. Paul was forced to ventilate this question when he was settling the controversy about justification by faith and justification by works. One party raised the objection, Rom. 6: 1, "Shall we then continue in sin, that grace may abound?" His answer to this objection he does not set forth until the eighth chapter, and I refer the diligent reader to that chapter. I shall begin with the words that seem best adapted to clearing up our problem. Paul asks, then, Rom. 7: 7-8: "What shall we say then? Is the law sin? God forbid. Howbeit, I had not known sin, except through the law: for I had not known that coveting is sin" (to speak for the moment in paraphrase) "except the law had said, Thou shalt not covet. But sin, finding occasion, through the commandment," as with a sun-dial or a plumb line (for there is personification here), "measured out* in me all manner of coveting." That is, when the Law came into sin's hands, she wanted to measure and weigh everything, and finally brought it about that I learned that all manner of human coveting is sin. For all teem with it in consequence of the disease. And that this is the meaning is shown by what immediately follows: "For apart from the law sin is dead." I, Paul, will take myself as an illustration for you. "I was alive apart from the law once," still ignorant because of my age of even the name of law; "but when the commandment came, sin revived." There was the disease of φιλαυτια [self-love] and coveting in me, but I did not know that these were sin, thinking allowable what love of self persuaded to. But when the law, Thou shalt not covet, was promulgated, sin revived; not that any new change took place in me, but what I had not before known to be wicked I perceived through the Law was wicked. And as soon as I saw this, "I died." For all that I saw in me was the lust of the flesh, of the eyes, the hands, the belly, and a sort of vast pride of life. Hence nothing but despair of life could arise within me. But I must not omit to state that no one should from this death of mine accuse the Law of poisoning, so to speak, as if *it* killed me. The Law displayed itself to me to show me that I was dead before, but to my undoing did not understand what death or what life is; and it tried to restore me to life and innocence. But this resulted for me in death, through the fault not of the Law but of myself. For sin, being a curious but stupid evil (note the personification!), having got hold of the Law as a standard, began to measure everything. And the Law deceived me; for in great part at least I thought myself righteous, but I was mightily mistaken. Indeed, everything so teemed with sin, was so polluted and impure, that, as I said, I straightway died. For, to speak frankly, no blame for this death of mine ought to be imputed to the Law. "The law is holy, and the commandment holy, and righteous and good" [Rom. 7:12]. If you

***dimensum est:* Vulgate, *operatum est;* Greek, κατειργάσατο

think I am now saying these things in order to defame that which is good, as if it were the cause of death unto me, you are wrong. For the Law did not kill me, but at the Law's so showing I found myself dead. For [Rom. 7:13] "sin" (personification for the third time), "that it might be shown to be what it is, through the law, which is good, rendered me dead; that through the law sin" (personification again) "might make itself the greatest of sinners." That is, sin, seized with admiration of the Law, wanted to try all things by it, but only established the fact that it is itself a sinner beyond measure.

This is the first part, in which we learn that we are nothing but corruption.

The second part contains the battle of the flesh and the spirit. There follows, therefore [cf. Rom. 7:14-25]: "For we know that the law is spiritual: but I," to come back to myself, whom I had begun to set before you as an illustration, "am carnal, sold under sin," like some Κἀρ ὅλος, *i. e.*, poor, mean slave, who, like the enslaved Cappadocians, knows how to be nothing but a slave. For, that you may understand my bondage, now that I have turned to Christ I see so much of the old disease still remaining that when I begin to do anything faults immediately so assail me on all sides that there comes out a work contrary to what I desire through faith. And so it happens that "that which I do, I know not," nor approve. For what I had determined upon according to the counsel of faith, "that I do not; but, on the contrary, I rather do that which I hate." Now notice whether I accuse the Law at any point. When, as I have said, "I do that which I would not, I silently consent unto the law, and bear witness to it that it is good." For I had myself determined to do what the Law bids, for the reason that it seemed to me good. When, therefore, I determine one thing according to the teachings of faith, but do a widely different thing, "it is no more I that do it, but sin that dwelleth in me," that is, the disease to which we are all subject. "For I know that in me, that is, in my flesh, dwelleth no good thing." And think not that I mean here the flesh that we have in common with the cattle (for who does not know that there is no good thing in that?). Or what of importance would he have said who proclaimed that no good is in it? That would be too frivolous a remark for apostolic seriousness. I am speaking of the whole man, who is nothing but flesh if left to himself (as God Himself said in Genesis 6:3), and neither meditates nor determines aught that is not evil. Yet if the Spirit of God comes to him to illumine him, so that man knows himself and God, the man pulls in his direction, promising nothing but pleasures, and the Spirit pulls in its direction, promising troubles but finally eternal bliss. Hence a contest arises. While I give ear to the Spirit, I excite the soul to pious living; again, when I listen to the flesh, that is sluggish and refuses to follow. Thus it happens that the will is present with me, but when I am to carry out the thing all my members are so slothful that I do nothing. "For the good that I would, I do not: but the evil which I would not, that I do" [Rom. 7:19]. When, therefore, what I would not (in so far as I obey the Spirit), that I yet do, it is no more I that do it, but that violent disease of sin which dwelleth in me. I find, then, a law, that, when I would do good, evil at the same time clings very tightly to me. For I feel no little delight in the inward man—that is, the man that gives ear to the Spirit—when I hear the law of God and begin to regulate myself by it; but at once I see another law in my members, warring against the law of my mind when that would obey the Spirit, and bringing me, whether it be law or force, into captivity to the law of sin which is in my members. I am speaking to you of deep and serious matters, but in simple language, though I do my best to season it so that it will slip down successfully. I mean just this, that when with the inward man, taught by God, I consent to the law of God and begin to fashion myself according to it, the force of the old man suddenly springs up and drags me in another direction, so that I abandon my determination and desert to the camp of the flesh. I am so torn asunder, so fluctuating, so neither crow nor dove, that I am beyond measure disgusted with myself. For when my heart is given to God and I would only cling to Him and do what is pleasing to Him, straightway the violence of the flesh seizes me, like a fierce whirlwind, and throws me captive into the fetters of sin. Then do I utter without ceasing such groanings as these: "O wretched man that I am, who through the grace of God recognize what is true and right, but when I try to follow it am dragged elsewhere by this unclean way,* or rather impotence and death, of the flesh! What God will grant me deliverance from this body, which should more properly be called death than body?"

Thus far, dear brethren, I have been showing the discordance between the Law and the old man, and, rising from the Law and the old man to the old man and the new, I have made of one man two, the inward who obeys the Spirit and the old who never varies from his own law, that is, from self-love and self-estem. Between these you will ever find war. "For the flesh lusteth against the Spirit, and the Spirit against the flesh" [Gal. 5:17]. Hence continual battles. Sometimes the flesh wins: and though it does not rout all the forces of the Spirit, it yet brings it about that we do not what we would. As a result, though nothing may happen to him from external things, the life of a Christian is yet a continual battle. And this so often saddens and troubles me and disturbs my pious vows, that, as I have just said, I frequently cry out in impatience and on the brink of despair: "O wretched me! who will free me from this misery?" But now, in the third place, that you may have the whole matter, I will show you what conclusion comforts me in such straits. Know, therefore, that when I have battled and sweated long and much within myself in this fashion, nothing inspires me with a more grateful sense of relief than the remembrance of Christ. Laying hold on Him, I, who was very near shipwreck, joyously make land. For I say to myself: "The God who gave His Son for you can refuse nothing, and knows your weakness [cf. Rom. 8:32]. Since, when you were once much farther away from Him, in fact His enemy, He took you back into favor, much more will He save you now that His Son has come to life again," Rom. 5:21. Then my fevers and fears begin to abate, and my soul to be at rest and my whole being to revive. And when this takes place I gird myself for the thanksgiving I would make to God, my Father, through Christ Jesus our Lord [cf. Rom. 7:25]. But there are further battles—and this I mention that you may not in security and carelessness after one or two battles fall unawares into danger—

**viam:* the reading of the first and second editions and of the Egli-Finsler text, which Schuler and Schultess silently change to *vim,* "power."

and after these still others, so that the life of a Christian seems to me just like a ship that is tossed hither and thither by a great storm, which the sailors now steer for a little with the rudder, and now are compelled to let run before the fierce gale. And this I, if any man, have experienced in myself; for, in spite of what I am, I find myself serving sometimes God and sometimes the flesh. My heart persists in meditating upon those deeds which the Law of God commands; it loves God, trusts in His mercy, is eager to please Him in all things. And the flesh persists, nor changes its nature any more than does a fox or a wolf. It at last makes me sin against my will, though my heart be unwaveringly fixed upon God in unchanging hope. And I doubt not that, as what can happen to anyone can happen to everyone, your experience is the same as mine. For as no one is exempt from this disease, so, of course, none is exempt from the battle. In this matter, therefore, the sacred anchor, as it were, to which we must hold fast is in spite of everything by no means to let ourselves fall from the hope and glory of the sons and heirs of God.

If we hold fast firmly to this [cf. Rom. 8:1-11]—to put the finishing touch to this problem—no condemnation can touch us; but only on condition that we walk after the Spirit and not after the flesh. But, that you may understand what it is to walk after the Spirit, as far as that is granted to us while we sojourn in this world, note this: The Spirit of life in Christ, which by contrast may be called the law of the Spirit if one pleases, through which I feel in my inmost heart that I am free through Him from the just vengeance of God and made His co-heir, that Spirit, I say, has made me free from the law—*i. e.,* from the power and necessity of sin and of death. For when on account of the weakness of the flesh we could not be saved through the works of the Law, God sent His Son, clothed in flesh like unto our diseased flesh in every respect except the disease; and He condemned the disease which daily called out so many sins in us; and He condemned it with His own flesh, that is, by Himself enduring death for us according to human weakness, that the righteousness of the law, which no man could fulfil, might through His help be fulfilled in us. For all that He did or bore He bore for us. Hence, also, His righteousness is our righteousness, if only we walk not after the flesh, but after the Spirit. For they that are fleshly do mind, meditate, pursue, fleshly things; but they that are spiritual meditate and pursue the things of the Spirit; though faults often intervene, so that our life does not come out as we had fashioned it in the inward man. The citadel must be stoutly defended, that we may not surrender ourselves wholly to the desires of the flesh. Even though we understand that, against the will of the Spirit, we are frequently drawn by it into sinning, yet we must ever deny its sway, and ever open our eyes again, even though we have been blinded by the mists of the flesh seven times in the day, and ever look afresh to the Law, *i. e.,* the will of God, and struggle anew for blamelessness. We must, therefore, be on our guard vigorously against scorning the desires of the Spirit and following the flesh; for the desires and counsel of the flesh bring speedy death, whereas the counsel of the Spirit brings forth life and peace. The desires and thoughts of the flesh are enmity against God; for it in no wise obeys the law of God, nor can it be made to obey. Hence you can easily see what it is to live carnally and what spiritually. To live carnally is to be wholly given over to the sway of the flesh and to be averse to the Spirit; to live spiritually is to obey the Spirit, never to abandon faith, even though the flesh sometimes is not free from the infection of sin. They, then, that are in the flesh cannot please God. But ye are not in the flesh, but in the Spirit, if so be that the Spirit of God dwell in you. And it dwells in you if you trust in the Son of God, although for the time being you are enveloped in the flesh. Now if any man have not the Spirit of Christ, he is none of His. But when Christ is in you (to speak with perfect clearness), the body is dead because of the disorder of sin; but the Spirit is life because of righteousness, not yours but His who has been made your righteousness. Such is the Christian that with respect to the body he is ever dead; but when his heart clings to God, with respect to the Spirit he is ever living.

By these words of the Apostle I think the very perplexing problem with which we are struggling is cleared up, namely, how it happens that a blamelessness is demanded which we cannot possibly offer, and yet Christ is the efficient guarantee for the sins of all; because the two propositions cannot stand together, that salvation must be won by blamelessness, and that all things are condoned to the righteousness of Christ for the very reason that we cannot attain salvation of our own effort. And although I have overcome the objection which I mentioned above, yet, that certain uneducated persons may feel entirely satisfied, I will answer it again. It was objected that this magnifying of grace through Christ makes those who are called Christians frivolous and dissipated. I answer, therefore: Those who trust in Christ become new men. How? Do they lay aside their original body and take on a new body? By no means; the original body remains. Does, therefore, the disease that we have inherited also remain? Yes. What is it, then, that is renewed in us? The heart. How? In this way: Beforetime it knew not God, and where there is no knowledge of God, there is nothing but flesh, sin, self-esteem; but after God is known, man sees himself within to the core, and repudiates himself thus known. As a result, he sees that all his works, even those which he had always thought were good, are of no value. When, therefore, through the enlightenment of heavenly grace the heart comes to know God, the man is made new. For he who before trusted in his own wisdom, in works or resources or strength, now puts his hope in God alone. He who before turned all his thoughts towards securing his own interests without regard to virtue or God now devotes himself only to retaining nothing of his original habit, and to so fashioning himself according to God's will as never to offend Him. And as the body is ever bringing forth dead works, our new man is also ever bewailing this unhappy and disastrous condition: Alas! kind God, what am I but an inexhaustible sink of iniquity? I sin again and again and make no end. When wilt Thou set my wretched self free from this mire in which I am caught? See in passing whether the Christian life is continual repentance or not. And this despair, what is it but death? Yet when in these circumstances the heart through the Spirit of God refuses to give up hope, does not the conscious self, which had just before collapsed, now revive? This, then, is the Christian life: when the hope in God through Christ never wavers, even though man through the weakness of the flesh is not without sin, yet comes out victorious because he does not surrender himself to it, but as often as he falls always rises again, sure that He who said to Peter that one must be forgiven seventy times seven times [Mt. 18:22] will Himself grant the full measure of pardon that He taught. We see, to use an illustration, that something not unlike this occurs in the grafting of trees. The husbandman digs up a wild pear, and transplants it to rich, cultivated ground. As soon as the stranger tree has taken root in the new soil, its top is cut off, and shoots of cultivated trees are grafted upon it, which then grow along with the trunk. But see what different fruit they put forth! The superior graftings bud, and render the farmer branches loaded with pears in due season. But the trunk arms itself with thorns and with rough shoots, which if not pruned away venture to produce fruit of their own; and the more you suffer them to grow, the more strength is taken from the true cultivated graft. We men are wild pears (for I do not wish, after the fashion of Paul, Rom. 11:17-24, to talk of the olive, a tree unknown to the Germans and nearly so to the French), and when we are imbued with the heavenly teachings we are planted in new earth. For he that would follow Christ must deny himself [cf. Lk. 9:23] and listen only to what He orders or suggests. And what is this but being transferred from the forest to the rich soil of a garden, transplanted from the earth to heaven? But see what great and hard things must be done here, or we essay this planting in vain. The top must be cut off, *i. e.,* our desires, wisdom, thoughts, designs, and in their place must be grafted heavenly shoots, *i. e.,* the knowledge and hope of things divine. We are, therefore, grafted from on high; and as the trunk grows along with the grafts, so our body retains its own nature, even though the heart be changed through the heavenly Spirit. Then does the spiritual heart bring forth the fruits that Paul describes in Gal. 5:22. And the flesh puts forth its vicious growths, just as the trunk does shoots and thorns. Yet, just as these are constantly cut away, so also must the faults that spring forth from the trunk of the flesh be continually and assiduously pruned off, that they may not grow to such dimensions as to be able to smother the cultivated fruit or to dwarf it by drawing away the sap. Now, the thorns are sometimes allowed to flourish on the stem that they may keep off the destructive goat until the tree grows high enough to avoid his harmful tooth. So, too, in us, when the heart is pious the sins that spring up perform some service; for "we know that to them that love God all things work together for good," Rom. 8: 28. But they do not render such service that they ought to be tolerated permanently, but only till the accomplishment of the purpose which the Lord wishes effected through them. David [II Sam. 24: 10] had committed as shameless a sin as was ever done among the Jews, but the Lord made use of his recklessness to keep him all his life from being puffed up. So also pious men who in their hearts cling to the Lord learn through the frequent springing up of thorns, *i. e.,* through the flood of their sins, to recognize their own weakness and to be humble, lest, puffed up with their own fancied blamelessness, they fall into the snares of the Devil. Christ weaves this idea beautifully into an allegory in John 13: 10, when He teaches Peter thus: "He that is bathed needeth not save to wash his feet, but is clean every whit." But, most wise Master, how is he clean or bathed who has such dirty feet that they have need of washing? Are not the feet a part of the body? How then is he clean every whit whose feet are still unclean? Christ adds, therefore: "And ye are clean, but not all." "For he knew," says the evangelist, "him that should betray him." They were all clean save one, because they had remained steadfast in faith. Christ bears witness to this in Luke 22: 28: "Ye are they that have continued with me in my temptations." But Judas was unclean; for he had already covenanted with the Jews to betray Him. The rest of the Apostles still had defects, but these could not harm them as long as the citadel of faith was held. When, therefore, the Apostles are pronounced clean, because they had not fallen away from their faith, even if some dust had clung to them from walking in this high road of corruption, it is quite evident that if faith in God is safe and its power unimpaired nothing that can happen can destroy. It is all washed away by that constant repentance of which I have spoken and by faith in Christ. Paul deals with the same idea in Rom. 8: 10. For after having said that "the body is dead because of sin; but the

Spirit is life because of righteousness" found in Christ, he adds, to prove his point: "But if the Spirit of him that raised up Jesus from the dead dwell in you, he that raised up Christ shall quicken also your mortal bodies through his Spirit that dwelleth in you." But He will only so quicken that the body be forever dead. For thus he speaks afterwards [Rom. 8:20-23]: "For the creation was subjected to vanity, not of its own will, but by reason of him who subjected it in hope, because it is itself delivered from the bondage of corruption and restored into the liberty of the glory of the children of God. For we know that the whole creation," *i. e.,* all men (for thus Christ also calls all men in Mark 16:15: "Preach the gospel to the whole creation") "alike groan and are in pain as long as they are now, *i. e.,* in this present time, living. Even ourselves, who are the chief apostles (because we were the first to receive the Holy Spirit) [cf. Rom. 8:23], no one ought to except from this groaning and pain, for on account of the rebelliousness of the flesh we groan just as much as the rest, desiring to be released and to be with Christ." And a little later he explains the groaning and anguish more clearly [Rom. 8:26]: "Likewise the Spirit also aids our weaknesses." By "Spirit" here he means the spiritual man, who is so raised to God through the Spirit of God that he looks up to Him alone. This Spirit of ours, then, which is nothing else than faith in and through God, constantly grieves for our weaknesses. For we see not what we should pray for. For it often happens that we pray to be saved from poverty, illness, humiliation. Then the Spirit, that is, the faithful heart, maketh intercession for us with groanings which cannot be uttered. For what great pain, think you, is begotten in the heart consecrated to God when it sees the flesh—*i. e.,* man, hopelessly subject as he is to the flesh, *i. e.,* to self-love—forever praying for those things only which it selfishly desires—vengeance, or the favor of man, or wealth? Groanings, therefore, spring up in the heart from this constant folly of the flesh, groanings which only he knows who is caught in these straits. That this is the true meaning of this passage of Paul is proved by what follows: "For he that searcheth the hearts knoweth what is the counsel or meditation of the Spirit" [Rom. 8:27]. That Holy Spirit through which we all breathe and trust in God has no heart. Paul is speaking, therefore, of the Spirit which has a heart, *i. e.,* of the spirit of man, *i. e.,* the pious mind. And the meaning is: "Man ventures, so zealous for himself is he, sometimes to ask of God things which it is not right for Him to give or for man to receive. Then the pious mind forthwith sweats because of the recklessness of the carnal man (for Paul makes two of every man here), and cries to God with weepings and groanings inexplicable to us, grieving for its persistent folly and praying for forgiveness. And if this happens when he goes wrong in praying, how much more when he fails by sinning! The Spirit flees for refuge to God, laments the disobedience of the flesh, and is filled with shame at the constant recurrence of the weariness with life and the flesh that comes therefrom. But God, who knoweth the hearts, sees plainly what faith, or the pious mind, meditates: namely, that it is anxious for the salvation of the man and never ceases to cry to God in behalf of the saints, *i. e.,* of the faithful, themselves to wit. And a kind God grants that these things work together for good to them on whose behalf the pious mind is troubled." Man, therefore, is ever dead, as is shown by his works; at the same time he ever lives, as is perceived from the anguish of his soul.

See now whether they can take in this teaching who have not a lively faith in God.

[11]. The Sin Against the Holy Ghost

Since from what has been said above it can easily be inferred what the sin against the Holy Ghost is, I have thought it seasonable to speak of that in this place.

When, therefore, Christ says, Matt. 12: 31: "Every sin and blasphemy shall be forgiven unto men: but the blasphemy against the Spirit shall not be forgiven unto men. And whosoever shall speak a word against the Son of Man, it shall be forgiven him; but whosoever shall speak against the Holy Spirit, it shall not be forgiven him, neither in this world, nor in that which is to come," it is clear from the above quoted words of Christ, John 13: 10, "He that is bathed needeth not save to wash his feet," that if you have faith, there is no sin at all which is not blotted out. For where faith is, even though you are always a sinner you yet never cease to deplore the unfortunate propensity to sin and are always trying to fashion yourself anew. On the other hand, where faith is not, there no account is taken of sin or of the fear of God. Let one meantime make whatever pretence one will, murmur prayers, fast, feed the hungry; if one has not faith in God, all these things are shams and the price of vainglory. It is, therefore, the utmost blasphemy against God not to trust in Him. From this then proceed palpable slanders. "For the impious man says in his heart, There is no God" [Ps. 14: 1]; and in saying this he blasphemes also against the work of God, as the hypocrites did in the aforesaid passage in Matthew 12: 23-37. They seemed to the simple people most ardent worshippers of God, when they were His fiercest foes; hence they blasphemed against the work of God. For when Christ by divine power had driven the devil out of his human habitation, they slanderously said it was done by the power of the prince of the devils. And this slander could have emanated from nothing but lack of faith. For their not believing that Christ is the Son of God was the reason why they spoke slanderously of His work. And the fact that they were absolutely ἄθεοι, *i. e.,* without God, was the reason why they did not believe in Christ. For if they had trusted in God they could not have helped recognizing God. It is, therefore, lack of faith alone, which we call infidelity or disbelief, that is never forgiven; for it never lays hold of or worships God, never fears Him, never orders itself according to His will, never avoids sin in order not to offend Him. Piety, on the other hand, does so. It clings constantly to God as its one treasure, cleaves to Him alone, worships Him alone, hangs upon His nod, is on its guard against the things that offend Him, and when from weakness it has been guilty of them bewails its error with troubled tears. Here there is no careless indifference to sin, but watchful and faithful guard to prevent sin from creeping in anywhere. There is no watchman, therefore, so diligent in guarding you against sinning as faith. What John says, I John 5: 16, about a sin unto death refers to nothing else than disbelief, as is easily apparent to one who looks at it closely. "If," he says, "any man see his brother sinning a sin not unto death, he shall entreat, and he shall obtain and shall give life to him, and, indeed, to all them that sin not unto death. There is a sin unto death: concerning that I do not command that one should pray." But there is other sin that is not unto death. Concerning this, therefore, you ought to pray. For instance, when anyone wrongs another it is a serious thing; but the more serious it is, the more should we who are members one of another pray God to forgive an offence so great. But, that the sin against the Holy Ghost and the watchfulness of faith may be more clearly understood, he adds [I John 5: 18]: "We know that whosoever is born of God sinneth not." How is it, disciple beloved of Christ, that he does not sin who is born of God, when you yourself say that no one is clean? Is no one born of God? For we all sin and offend in many things, all of us. Are we born of God, then? And you who have received the first fruits of the Spirit groan [cf. Rom. 8: 23]. Is it sin you groan for? How, then, are you born of God? See, therefore, how the divine man answers and explains himself. He says [I John 5: 18]: "He that is born of God guardeth himself, and an evil demon toucheth him not." Behold the watchfulness and care not to sin, and, when you have sinned, the anxiety to wash the sin away with tears and not to sin again! This anxiety the unbelieving do not share. Many persons may want much more said about the sin against the Holy Ghost, because the men of old involved themselves in so many ambiguities and sinuosities on the subject that they could hardly see what its character was; but I am content with the above. For not even an angel from heaven by teaching otherwise [cf. Gal. 1: 8] could make the faithful mind believe that there is any sin that is not atoned for through Christ. This is what solid faith in Christ means. It remains, therefore, that disbelief is the only thing that is denied pardon.

Now as to those impostors who, not to keep silence when they cannot endure that all sins should be washed away through the grace of Christ (for they would rather, though they cannot make atonement, yet for pay received seem to do so)—who, I say, not to keep silence assert that Christ made atonement for original sin only, or for the sins merely of those who were before Him. Their error might be at once overthrown by that single proclamation of the Baptist [John 1: 29]: "Behold the Lamb of God, that taketh away the sin of the world"; for original sin is not the only sin in the world, and Christ takes away all the sins of the world. Yet I would by no means pass over the very clear testimony of I John 2: 1-2, that they may not be able to plead any excuse. "Little children," he says, "these things write I unto you, that ye may not sin. And if any man sin, we have an advocate with the Father, Jesus Christ, the righteous: and he is the propitiation for our sins; and not for ours only, but also for the sins of the whole world."

With this testimony, then, I shall here be content, since it has been abundantly proved above that Christ is the means of salvation to all.

The true religion of Christ, then, consists in this: that wretched man despairs of himself and rests all his thought and confidence on God, sure that He can refuse nothing who has given His Son for us; and that the Son, who is equally God with the Father, can refuse nothing, since He is ours. But false religion merely juggles with the name of Christ, having its hope elsewhere. For, to wash away his sins, one man hires drunken singers, another monks to engage in empty psalmody; one thinks to purchase blessedness by building pretentious churches, another by having costly raiment made for some saint; one rests on his own works, another on those of somebody else. In short, there are as many gods as there are cities, for each has some special saint to whom it entrusts its salvation. So also Jeremiah laments, 2: 28: "According to the number of thy cities are thy gods, O Judah."

Almighty God, grant that we may all recognize our blindness, and that we who have thus far clung to creatures may henceforth cleave to the Creator, that He may be our only treasure and our heart abide with Him [cf. Mt. 6: 21].

So much on the chief and essential point of the Christian religion; for I think this, such as it is, is enough to enable the pious to see where they should fix their hopes and from what keep them away.

[12]. The Keys

Since the subject of the Keys is not only closely related to the Gospel but is really nothing else than the Gospel itself, in no other place than this can it be more suitably treated. In my "Conclusions,"* written in German, I said a thing absurd in the judgment of certain persons who think nothing right except what they themselves do. But I do not repent of that view; for it did not originate with me, but was sent from heaven. For I asserted nothing about the Keys that had not been put forth by the Son of God Himself, the Mouth of truth, Knowledge unchangeable. Now let the Pontifical crowd rage; let the creatures of vainglory concoct any device they please. I shall cling to my view so tenaciously that I can no more be torn from it than from God.

False religion is not consistent with itself in explaining either what the Keys are or when they were given. Some think the Keys are the authority given to the priest† by which he can loose and bind according to his own free-will; and therefore they introduce the formula of absolution, as it is called, with the distinct words: "The Lord Jesus Christ absolve you, and I by virtue of the authority from Him which I exercise absolve you, etc." Others attribute all the power to the word of God, administered by the priest merely as an instrument or organ. And it was well for these that they put forth this view of theirs before the sway of the Roman Pontiff attained its present dimensions. For today they could not say these things with impunity—albeit their view is not correct, as will be clearly shown. And as to when the Keys were given, they are so at variance with each other that it is strange the Roman Pontiff (since he alone, as they dream, has the right to judge the Scriptures) has not pronounced in some bull when they were given, that there might not be such divergence in a matter of such moment—or rather emolument. And he could easily have done so, for he has made a decree that the soul shall not

*His *Auslegen und Gründe der Schlussreden*, 1523.

†From early in the thirteenth century the view prevailed that the priest forgives sin in God's stead. Accordingly, the precative form of absolution, "May God (or, the Lord) absolve thee," was finally superseded by the indicative form, "I absolve thee."

die when the body is destroyed.* But let us not laugh when piety hears shameless impiety speaking so wantonly. This, then, I once said of the Keys: "The word keys, in the sense it has here, was transferred from keys that unlock to the setting free of the mind, because things that are hidden away and fastened keys open and uncover. In the same way one's consciousness is closed and unknown to all but one's self. As, therefore, things that are locked up cannot be got at without the proper key, so one's consciousness cannot be released and made free unless it be done with the appropriate key." This would be clear from the mere fact that God alone can release the mind, if we had to treat the matter by argument and illustration. But let us hear what the mouth of the Lord our God says. When, as we read in Matthew 16: 15-19, Christ asked of the disciples who they thought He was, Peter answered in the name of all, as also all had been asked: "Thou art the Christ, the Son of the living God." And Christ said to him: "Blessed art thou, Simon Bar-Jonah: for flesh and blood hath not revealed it unto thee, but my Father who is in heaven. And I say unto thee, that thou art Peter, and upon this rock I will build my church; and the gates of hell shall not prevail against it. And I will give unto thee the keys of the kingdom of heaven: and whatsoever thou shalt bind on earth shall be bound in heaven; and whatsoever thou shalt loose on earth shall be loosed in heaven." Here the first thing is to examine the way in which they who trot out false and counterfeit keys, wondrously and artfully wrought, defend themselves with a sort of Hercules' club. It is, indeed, just this: "We see," they say, "more plainly than day that Peter alone made answer to Christ, and that Christ spoke to Peter alone. Hence the Keys can belong to no one but Peter and him with whom he may have shared them." We must observe, therefore, that as Christ had asked the question of all the disciples, so also Peter answered in the name of all, although the Evangelist makes no mention here of any other. But John, 6: 67-69, makes mention of all twelve when he records the same reply, thus: "Then said Jesus unto the twelve, Would ye also go away? Simon

*Under Leo X, the Fifth Lateran Council, in December, 1513, condemned those who deny the immortality and individuality of the soul.

Peter answered him, Lord, to whom shall we go?" (Notice that he said in the name of all, "shall we go," not "shall I go.") "Thou hast the words of eternal life, and we believe and know that thou art that Christ, the Son of God." Now, if the answer, "Thou art Christ, the Son of God," deserved the promise of the Keys, as they certainly did, then the Keys were promised to all; for all proclaimed Christ to be the Son of God, as we have now seen here in John 6: 69. And it is characteristic of the Evangelists that they sometimes attribute a speech to all the disciples in common, as Luke, 22: 35, "Lacked ye anything? And they said, Nothing"; sometimes to one disciple, as here in Matt. 16: 16 and in John 6: 68, where both represent only Peter as replying, but the latter manifestly in the name of all. Again, you will find that one of them attributes to some particular one what another attributes to the disciples in general. So Luke 9: 13: "But he," *i. e.,* Christ, "said unto them, Give ye them to eat. And they said, We have no more than five loaves and two fishes." We see here that the words, "We have, etc.," were said by all; though John 6: 9 expressly assigns them to Andrew, the brother of Simon. You will find also, in the third place, that Christ sometimes promised a thing to one or two individually, and then gave it to all. For example, in Matt. 4: 19, when He calls Peter and Andrew, He says: "Come ye after me, and I will make you fishers of men." And a little later the Evangelist says of John and James [Matt. 4: 21]: "And he called them." So in Matt. 9: 9: "Follow me"; where He adds nothing about the function of fisher, and yet they were all made fishers of souls. So, too, in our passage no one can doubt that what was said to Peter was said to all, especially as they all had the same idea in regard to Christ, as I have proved from John. Mark 8: 30 and Luke 9: 21 also contain something that contributes to the matter, the second saying: "He charged them, and commanded them to tell this to no man"; and the first saying, "And he charged them that they should tell no man." He commanded all to keep silence, because, of course, all had confessed Him. From all this it is evident that Christ promised the Keys not to Peter alone, but to all who on being asked recognized that He is the Son of God. For this is the essential thing in preachers, that they themselves believe what they preach to others. Therefore, since He was about to send them forth to preach, He wanted the point brought out clearly, not in order by asking to learn something He otherwise would not have known (for He searches the hearts and reins), but as an example to us not to lay hands hastily upon any man [cf. I Tim. 5: 22]—He wanted the point brought out, I say, whether they held the right view of Him; for it is especially conducive to the advancement of the word, that is, of the Keys, if he who administers the word is no hypocrite. And altogether He did in the promise of the Keys what everybody does in his own affairs. Suppose you have twelve sons and ask them how they are minded towards the commonwealth; and suppose they, delegating or according to custom yielding the office of answering to the eldest, promise to endure all things in its behalf; very likely you will promise Cato (for suppose that is the name of your first born) that for this judicious answer so worthy of your sons you will seek for him a wife who shall be of good character, beautiful, noble, rich, so that he may have the hope of an unenfeebled posterity. Well, do you not propose to do the same for the others? Of course you will secure wives and dowries for all; nor have you set up the first-born as lord of the others. So, neither was Peter by this promise of the Keys set over the others. The right of the first-born, "Be lord over thy brethren" [Gen. 27: 29], came to an end in Christ. For He, being the only real Lord and Son, took away all mastery from us, and commanded that he who is elder be as the younger, and the superior as a servant.

Now I think it is firmly established that the Keys are not Peter's as sole possessor or as lord of them. And if anyone desires more, let him wait till we come to the section, "What the Keys are and when they were given"; then it will be easily manifest that they were given to all alike.

The name of Peter was not bestowed upon Simon for the first time here, but at that first meeting in which his brother Andrew had brought him to Christ, John 1: 42. For then Christ said to him: "Thou art Simon the son of John: thou shalt be called Cephas (which is by interpretation Peter)." Hence it is also probable that he was afterwards often called by that name, as the narrative of the Gospels indicates as it goes on. Especially in Mark 3: 16 can we see that Simon had had the name Peter some time before the event described in Matt. 16: 15-19. Therefore the words "Thou art Peter" are an explanation of the reason why He had previously given him that name: as though Christ were saying, "I was right to give thee the name Peter; for thou art Peter. For staunchly and clearly and unwaveringly thou confessest that which has saving power for all. I, too, will build my church upon this rock, not upon thee; for thou art not a rock (*petra*). God alone is the rock on which every building should be built. There are also two others, called the sons of thunder,* not because they are themselves to be proclaimed, nor because they are to thunder out their own word, but because they are to trumpet forth the word of God unwaveringly. So thou, Peter, art not a rock." For how would the Church have collapsed when he, trembling at the feeble voice of her who kept the door [John 18: 17] began to make denial! "You must be staunch and firm in preaching the true rock, that all may find shelter upon it who would weather the force of all gales and storms." That the divine Apostle so understood the words of Christ he himself bears witness, I Pet. 2: 4-5: "Unto whom"—Christ, that is —"coming, a living stone, rejected indeed of men, but with God elect and precious, ye also, as living stones, are built up a spiritual house." "Behold, as Christ is a rock," you say, "so are we rocks." But see in what sense Christ is a rock, and in what sense we are rocks. Christ is the rock upon which the building rises, we are the common stones in the building which has its foundations in Christ. Christ alone, therefore, not Peter nor any creature, is the rock, built upon which the Church stands fast against all the vicious fury of all the storms. This would be the place to speak of the Church, but in order to avoid confusion I will inquire about the Church after we have found the Keys. One thing had almost escaped me. Hitherto reckless Rome has fought for the primacy of Peter so shamelessly that it has distorted to this end everything that gave any appearance of supporting this contention. Yet, if they had but examined with care and faith the words

*John and James. See Mk. 3: 17.

of Peter in his first epistle, 5: 1-3, they might have understood how rashly they scorn and corrupt the truth. He says: "The elders among you I exhort, who am a fellow-elder" (he is the colleague of the elders, not their lord or head: where, then, are those who fancy that the Christian Republic must fall to pieces unless some single one be set over all?) "and a witness of the sufferings of Christ, and also a partaker of the glory that shall be revealed. I exhort you, I say, feed the flock of Christ entrusted to you, being attentive and watchful, not of constraint, but readily and willingly; not from desire for filthy lucre, but from kindness and inclination of heart; neither as oppressing with lordship God's heritage, but as being patterns and examples to the flock." Behold the grandeur of the Christian shepherd! He feeds the flock with painstaking watchfulness; does not use constraint except so far as the word itself constrains; looks not at profit, but does all things of a ready mind, *i. e.,* with faith and love of God; claims no lordship for himself, but aims at this one thing, to be a blameless example to the flock.

The next thing would be to speak of the gates of hell, on which some have said much that I do not disapprove; but I want to hasten on to other things, satisfied with this one observation, that the gates of hell signify the force and power of hell. For cities are usually so built that the towers, moats, ramparts, and all the fortifications about the gates shall be exceedingly strong. Christ adopted this fashion of speech, wishing to teach that all the power of hell, all its fortifications and defences, were demolished by the advent of Christ, and that this same power of hell can do no harm to them that are in Christ Jesus. For the Devil has been led captive in the triumph of Christ and his authority torn from him [cf. Col. 2: 14]. The gates of hell, therefore, *i. e.,* its force and power, can do nothing against those that trust in Christ the rock, much less against Christ. "For the prince of this world came and he had nothing in Christ," John 14: 30. For his hope to destroy Him and win the victory was vain.

There follows, therefore [Mt. 16: 19]: "And I will give unto thee the keys of the kingdom of heaven." Some contend that the keys were delivered here, than which nothing more foolish can be said; for He says, "'I will give," not "I give," nor "Lo, take," as some of the Popes, falsifying the words, have had engraved on coins.* The Keys, therefore, are promised here, not bestowed. Although some of the learned schoolmen openly proclaimed this, it was not laid up against them; but now a man is declared a heretic who asserts this thing which the words so undoubtedly express. "But," they say, "Christ said it, and what He said must have taken place." Thank God that they have come to the point of attributing so much to Christ; but I am afraid their wish to seem to attribute it to Him is not genuine, and that it does not come from the heart but from contentiousness, which turns every possible thing into a weapon, even if it wounds itself. For when they say, "Christ said it, and therefore it must have taken place," they immediately tack on this: "But we nowhere read of the Keys having been bestowed; therefore they were given here." They are right, then, when they say, "Christ said it, therefore it took place"; but their weapon shall now be turned against themselves. For, "We do not read of their having been given, therefore they were not given except on this occasion," does not follow. It can easily happen that a man who has been present at some business agreement or contract is absent later when the transfer is made. Does this on that account follow: "He did not see the goods transferred or the money counted out; therefore it was not counted out or else was counted out at the time of the agreement"? So also these persons, not knowing what the Keys are, know not when they were given; for even if they had been present when they were given, they simply would not have understood what it was that was given. They should, therefore, argue thus: "Christ said, 'I will give them'; therefore they were given." Then we must see when they were given, instead of arguing thus: "We do not know that they were given anywhere; therefore they were given when they were promised." But suppose we were so blind as not even to know Christ, much less the Keys? Here those who are so hard pressed on account of the future tense of the verb are at vari-

*Coins of Paul II, Alexander VI, and Julius II bear the legend, "Accipe claves regni caelorum." Many other issues of papal coins show crossed keys, or Christ delivering the keys to Peter, or Peter with a key or keys.

ance. Some of them say that the Keys were given to Peter at the time when Christ said, Luke 22: 32, "I have prayed for thee, that thy faith fail not: and when thou art converted, strengthen thy brethren." How, I ask, is one to deal with persons of this kind? Christ's only object here was to teach the self-confident Peter that human powers are such that unless the Lord strengthen them all that we ourselves enjoin will go to pieces. Therefore He says: "I have prayed for thee, that thy faith fail not." For if He had not prayed, Peter would have fallen from the faith. And this not only would have happened to Peter, but would happen every day unless the Lord with His hand upheld our weakness, so that we should not for even a moment halt in the faith. But is this equivalent to saying, "Receive the promised keys"? Christ is strengthening the wavering faith of Peter, not offering the Keys; for they could not well be handed over then on the eve of the final struggle. But they say, " 'When thou art converted, strengthen they brethren' shows clearly that he was set over the others." That is the way contentiousness goes to work. I am diligently trying to discover when the Keys were given, and you intrude, where you should not, new mention of precedence. But see how out of place this is. Scarcely has the sound of the words died away in which Christ utterly does away with all ambitions aiming at superior place [Lk. 22: 24-27], and do you venture to reassert what He had just forbidden? Peter was going to deny Christ more shamelessly than any other. In order that this might not cause him harm by making impossible his restoration to his former position (for there was great pride in these things), He foretold that he should be a prop to the rest, not because he alone remained steadfast in faith, for he did not, but because he was perhaps the only one who, on account of his inconsiderate promptness in promising, needed that Christ should point out the remedy before the disease which nevertheless had to come actually came. In fact, the faith of St. John the Evangelist—in my opinion, that is—as far as we can infer from the Gospel writings, was far and away ahead of Peter's. For he went in, and he secured for Peter an opportunity of going in [Jn. 18: 15-16]. Nor can the fact that he was known to the High Priest weaken my view; for, when you have gone over to one who is an enemy, to be known is rather a hindrance than a help. It seems clear that John has disguised this out of courtesy, in order not to seem to have claimed greater strength of mind for himself than for Peter. But John was not always eager and forward in displaying his faith, as was Peter, who on that account needed more than he the strong support of the Lord. For to John He entrusted His mother—his dear mother to his most whole-souled disciple. And when both disciples hastened together to the sepulchre, though he was not the first to enter, he yet was the first to see the empty sepulchre and the linen cloths, feeling no fear as to whether the guards had left or not [Jn. 20: 2-8]. But whither am I wandering away from the subject? Is "And when thou art converted, strengthen thy brethen" equivalent to "Receive the promised Keys"? But others, not having full reliance on this passage, pass by all other passages and fly to the twenty-first chapter of John, to see if they can anywhere find that the Keys were delivered to Peter alone, for then they think the Papacy wins and holds the field. Since Christ there three times entrusts the sheep and lambs to him to be fed [Jn. 21: 15-17], they proclaim: "Behold, this is the place where we see more clearly than day that the Keys were given to Peter, according to the promise made in Matt. 16: 19." Here (to say nothing of the inconstancy that caused them to contend a little while ago that the Keys were given in Matt. 16: 19, and now makes them incline to this passage) I feel a lack of fairness in them. For do not those with whom we are dealing incessantly cry, "The Fathers! the Fathers!"? How is it, then, that they do not listen to the Fathers in this place, when all the old writers say that this threefold inquiry of Christ's was made to take away the shame of the thrice-repeated denial? I subjoin the words of Augustine, who says this: "A threefold confession is rendered for a threefold denial, that the tongue may serve love not less than it served fear, and impending death not seem to have drawn out more speech than actual life."* But perhaps they refuse to be overcome by one witness, so let them hear another. Cyril, on John, Book 12, Chap. 64, says: "For since Peter, honored along with the others by Christ Himself with the name

Commentary on John, Tract cxxiii, §5.

of Apostle, thrice denied Him at the time of the Passion, now a triple confession of love is properly asked of him, that the triple denial may be balanced by a similar triple confession. Thus the sin committed with words is cured with words, etc." So these writers. But our opponents will perhaps say: "These men's testimony does not at all prevent the Keys from having been bestowed on this particular occasion; for the reason why Christ demanded the love was that He might be able to place the Keys in a worthy place." To make plain, therefore, how these devotees of darkness invariably becloud the light and obscure its brightness, I will ask, in the first place (granting for the moment that the Keys were given then): When Christ says, "Feed my sheep," what do you think the Keys are? Here they will no doubt be just as much puzzled as the Jews were when Christ asked them directly: "The baptism of John, was it from God, or from men?" [Mk. 11: 30]. If our friends say, "The Keys are feeding, inasmuch as He says, 'Feed my sheep,'" (for what they say about dominion was demolished above by the words of Peter himself from I Pet. 5: 1-9)—if, then, the Keys are feeding, as they certainly are, how will it afterwards be made clear where the dominion and primacy rest, since the office of feeding with the word was entrusted to the other Apostles equally with Peter, as is plain from John 20: 21-23? Therefore the Keys were not given on this occasion, but before. If, on the other hand, you say that "feeding" is not used here in the sense of "refreshing" with the word, you will again fall into your old-time error of taking away the natural meaning of words and forcing upon them a new one which they cannot possibly bear. This is plain from the fact itself and from Peter's example—from the fact, because the soul is not fed except with the word of God, as has been shown above, and because man lives "by every word that proceedeth out of the mouth of God" [Mt. 4: 4]; from Peter's example, because by "feed" he understood "refresh" with the word, as is shown by his insisting so stoutly on the word as to hold with the rest of the Apostles that "it is not fit that we should lay aside the ministry of the word to serve tables," Acts 6: 2. Also, because we nowhere read that Peter inaugurated anybody by his own power or authority, but was rather sent out by other

Apostles, as in Acts 8:14, where he is sent to Samaria with John to aid Philip. Furthermore, Peter did not understand by "feeding" the making of regulations; for in Acts 15:10 the view which Peter had advocated did not prevail. But why do I talk so long with these chatterers, when I see that all they utter they utter for no other reason than not to seem to get the worst of the argument by keeping silent? This disease was depicted by some heathen writer who said a certain man's object was just to talk, without caring what he said. Christ was in the habit of dealing with the disciples as faithful instructors do; hence they called Him Master and Lord, John 13: 13. Though an instructor desires to train fitly all who are entrusted to his care, yet he draws out and questions or examines different ones at different times and places, and sometimes teaches a particular one in the hearing of all, that all may learn together. So Christ took Peter, though it was certainly the disciples whom Christ wished to teach two definite things. First, that his triple denial of Him might not tend to Peter's detriment, He asked him in the presence of his fellow disciples whether he loved Him, that when the disciples heard him doing this they might understand that Peter had regained Christ's favor and was restored to his place, as has been made plain. The other thing was that all should learn by the example of Peter (for all were sent forth to feed the sheep) that God demanded this one thing in a shepherd, that he should love Him and not himself, assured that he who loves God will faithfully do His work. Thus it is manifest that the Keys were presented neither here nor to Peter alone. However, they were presented at the time when Christ, the life of the soul, having overcome death, rose again, as we see in John 20:23. We shall here kill two birds with one stone, as the saying is; for first we shall show what the Keys are, and when that has been done it will also appear when they were given. Christ, then, metaphorically called Keys the delivering and comforting of the soul; and these take place when under the illumination of the Holy Spirit we understand the mystery of Christ and trust in Him. To loose, therefore, is nothing else than to raise to sure hope the heart that is despairing of salvation; to bind is to abandon the obstinate heart. These things will be explained separately in the sequel.

The Keys, therefore, have a certain mark by which you can easily discover them when you look through the Gospel writings for them. Christ gave a forewarning of this mark in Matt. 16:19, namely, that we are loosed and bound by them. The first thing of the kind that occurs is in Matt. 18:17, when Christ orders him who sins with shameless persistence to be cast out like "a heathen man and a publican," at once adding: "What things soever ye shall bind on earth shall be bound in heaven; and what things soever ye shall loose on earth shall be loosed in heaven." It seemed to me at one time that the Keys were given here, as I taught in "Archeteles."* But since the question here is only about those who sin with shameless persistence, and who having been cast out are taken back when they have mended their ways, I have been compelled to go further and to see if I could not somewhere find such Keys given as fit all cases alike. But before we leave this point (lest anyone should persist in dinning into our ears that the Keys were given here, as I have confessed that I once thought myself), we ought to know that with faith itself as instructor we learn the Keys were not given here. For the question is simply about the casting out of the wicked and taking them back again; while yet the Keys must be of such a character as to set free and comfort all consciences, and not those only who have dared to sin openly with brazen face. And if you ask, "Why, then, does Christ Himself put forth this law, the mark, as it were, by which the Keys are recognized?" I reply that Christ uses it here as a sort of major premise, and then makes a descent, as the logicians call it. For since by the word of God consciences that have not shamelessly prostituted themselves are loosed and bound, much more are those that have prostituted themselves to be bound, that is, to be avoided; and again, when we see that by the pain of repentance they have been changed, they are to be taken back into the former fellowship. It is, therefore, proved on the authority of Christ that this casting out, avoiding, excommunicating, of shameless sinners can righteously be done among Christians by the power and intent of the law of the Keys, in whose competence it is that unbelievers may be shunned, and just as much those who

*See vol. I, p. 256.

with their lips profess to be Christians, but deny it in their deeds. Similarly, since it is the function of the Keys to loose the impious from his impiety and admit him into the number of the brethren, the man who sins openly, if he changes his ways, can just as much be taken back again.

From this [Mt. 18: 18] passage on, though one looks closely everywhere, one nowhere finds this mark by which Christ has taught us the Keys are recognized until one comes to John 20: 21. There, after Christ had risen from the dead, He greets the disciples with these words: "Peace be unto you"—the same word the angels had uttered at His birth, "And on earth peace"—that it may be plain that He is the peace and refreshment of soul. And this we can understand from the fact that the disciples "were glad" when they saw the Man [Jn. 20: 20]. That the words may be more firmly fixed in their minds, He repeats them, saying, "Peace be unto you: as the Father hath sent me, even so send I you." Notice that what Mark said [16: 15]: "Go ye into all the world, and preach the gospel to the whole creation," John thus expresses: "As the Father hath sent me." Now, He had sent Him to be the salvation of all nations even unto the corners of the earth. So now He sends the disciples to proclaim that this salvation is everywhere at hand. For, to remind you of this meanwhile, the same event on the same day is described here in John 20: 21, in Mark 16: 15, and in Luke 24: 47; which some persons have not seen, thinking that as these passages are read in the churches at different times the events took place at the seasons at which they are read, especially what I have quoted from Mark. If you compare the three accounts, what I say will easily be manifest, though one has certain special features which you do not find in another; for Christ did many things, nay, endless things that are not written in this book [cf. Jn. 20: 30]. And John took particular care to leave out nothing in the essentials of the gospel, and to add by diligent gleaning what the others had passed over.

But that the slow of comprehension may be fully satisfied, I will make a few comparisons.

It is perfectly clear in itself that the event given in Luke [24: 36-49] took place on the very day of the Resurrection. For of the two who were going to Emmaus he says [24: 13-35] that they set out on the very day on which the women had come and reported that they had seen the vision of angels. And afterwards, when they were returning to Jerusalem, he says they left Emmaus in the same hour in which Christ had walked with them and they had recognized Him in the breaking of bread. And when they had reached the city, they found, he says, the Eleven, who told them that Christ had risen and had appeared to Simon; and the two in turn told also how He had appeared to them. All these things are most clearly seen to have happened on the very day of the Resurrection. There follows in Luke [24: 36]: "And as they thus spoke" (notice how clearly the words designate the time), "as they thus spoke," he says, "Jesus stood in the midst of them, and saith unto them, Peace be unto you." John does not mention the episode of the two going to Emmaus, but plaintly indicates that the event* took place on the very day of the Resurrection, saying: "When therefore it was evening on that day"—the day, namely, on which He had appeared to the Magdalene, and she had told the news to the disciples [Jn. 20: 14-18], when those who afterwards went to Emmaus had not yet started; for when Christ was talking with them they told Him [Lk. 24: 22] they had been frightened by the report of the women who said they had seen a vision of angels, and these women could not have been other than the Magdalene and her companions, whose tale Mark [16: 9-14] describes vividly, at the same time mentioning those who were going to Emmaus, and telling how, when they returned and said that Christ had appeared to them, some did not believe them. "Postea" (afterward) Mark says, where our version has "novissime" (finally), as if that was the last appearance of Christ, though the Greek is ὕστερον, which cannot possibly mean "novissime," but "postea"—he says, then, "afterward," when the men returning from Emmaus had told what had happened to them, as the Eleven sat at meat on the very day of the Resurrection. For Luke [24: 36] says, "'As they thus spoke," and John [20: 19] "When it was evening." Clearly it must have been quite dusky, for those who went to Emmaus had seen the day decline [Lk. 24: 29].

***i. e., the event related in Luke 24: 36-49.**

Next I will compare John's words [20: 20], "The disciples were glad, when they saw the Lord," with Luke's [24: 37-38], "But they were terrified and affrighted, and supposed that they beheld a spirit. And he said unto them, Why are ye troubled? and wherefore do questionings arise in your hearts?" John describes what took place after this that Luke describes, for Luke thought the behavior of the disciples when they first saw the Lord ought not to be passed over in silence. Therefore he says that at first they were troubled and began to question whether perhaps it was not the trick of some spirit that they saw. Christ knowing this upbraided them. See also Mark's words [16: 14]: "He upbraided them with their unbelief and hardness of heart, because they believed not them that had seen him after he was risen." And He said [Lk. 24: 38] (I return to Luke): "Why are ye troubled? And why do ye suffer your hearts to be filled with absurd questionings?" Then Luke adds: "See my hands and my feet, that it is I myself: handle me, and see; for a spirit hath not flesh and bones, as ye see me having. And when he had said this, he showed them his hands and his feet. And while they still disbelieved and wondered for joy, he said, etc." Here is where John begins, saying: "And when he had said this, he showed them his hands and his side." Luke had said, "his hands and his feet." John added "side" also, for Jesus certainly showed all the wounds He had received on the cross, and Luke had said nothing about the side. John continues: "The disciples therefore were glad, when they saw the Lord," clearly explaining what Luke had said rather obscurely with "wondering for joy," namely, that, although they had been troubled in the beginning, yet as their recognition grew through his displaying his wounds their stupefaction changed to joy.

We will content ourselves with these notes, from which skeleton, as it were, it is clear that all three of these Evangelists are describing the same event of the same day. Therefore, what John says [20: 21], "As my Father hath sent me, even so send I you," Mark expands in the words [16: 15], "Go ye into all the world, and preach the gospel to the whole creation," while Luke has [24: 47], "It behooved that repentance and remission of sins should be preached in his name unto all the nations." For this, finally, is the gospel, as has been shown at length above. There follows in John: "When he had said this, he breathed on them, and saith unto them, Receive ye the Holy Spirit." This Luke explained more fully, saying: "Then opened he their mind, that they might understand the Scriptures; and he said unto them, Thus and thus" (these words are to be understood deictically) "it is written. And thus it behooved that Christ should suffer, and rise again from the dead; and that repentance should . . . be preached," etc. And John, as usual, seeing that Luke had told with great fulness how and what Christ had taught the disciples through the Holy Spirit, contented himself with saying: "He breathed on them, and saith unto them, Receive ye the Holy Spirit." But what else is it to open the mind or understanding than to inspire with the Holy Spirit? Moreover, they that were to spread Christ through all the world receive also the Spirit of Christ. For as He had been sent, so also are they sent [Jn. 20: 21]; therefore they had to have the same spirit, being engaged in the same work.

Now we are very near the mark by which we shall discover the Keys. For having inaugurated the disciples into the apostleship, and having given them His spirit, by which we might know forever that those who undertake to preach the gospel will labor in vain if they burn not with the Spirit of God, He presently discloses what they must bring to men to make them free, and says in Mark [16: 15-16]: "Preach the gospel to the whole creation. He that believeth and is baptized shall be saved; but he that believeth not shall be condemned." It is not necessary to remind you that "believe" is used in this place and in many other places for "trust." Here, then, are the Keys which Christ committed to the Apostles, by which they unlocked the gates of heaven—they preached the gospel. They that believed the gospel when it was preached felt the deliverance and comforting of their consciences. For the gospel, as I think has been said sufficiently, teaches us to embrace not only grace but a new life. Furthermore, one does not begin a new life unless one is disgusted with one's previous life. Hence Luke says [25: 45-49] that Christ opened the minds of the Apostles, that they might understand from the Scriptures "that it behooved that repentance and remission of sins should be preached in his name"—that is, by His command and power—"unto all the nations." Since, therefore, even by the teaching of the Popes it is admitted that the remission of sins is brought about by the power of the Keys, it is certain that the Keys are what sets free the captive conscience. But as to what the Keys are, in their teaching we are farther from the truth than heaven is from the earth. For the Papalists say they are the authority conferred upon man by God; but Christ says that they are the faith by which the gospel is believed, that is, by which we trust in the righteousness and merit of the Son of God, and utterly deny and cast ourselves aside. For from the teaching of Christ we find that "it behooved that repentance and remission of sins should be preached in his name." Here then are the Keys which make a man known to himself, so that knowing himself he despairs of salvation, and after that has happened sees that all his salvation is placed in Christ, and knows this salvation to be so sure and so thoroughly his own that he has not the slightest doubt that through Him he has been made truly a son of God. Will not the conscience then straightway leap for joy? Will it not feel itself freed, exhilarated, sustained? The word of God, then, by which we learn to know ourselves and are taught to trust in God, is the Keys by which the ministers of the word set us free; for they who, taught by it, put all their trust in God are henceforth free indeed. That, therefore, which Mark said, "Preach the gospel to the whole creation. He that believeth, etc.," John, in order to show what were the Keys once promised (for none of the Evangelists before him had expressly shown this mark), expresses in the words, "Receive ye the Holy Spirit: whose soever sins ye remit, they are remitted unto them; and, on the other hand, whose soever sins ye retain, they are retained." Thus far I have spoken only of the remission of sins; but how the Apostles should retain sins is a matter of wonder, since Peter is taught [Mt. 18:22] to pardon the offender seventy times seven times. I find only two ways in which the Apostles retained or bound sin. One in I Cor. 5: 4-5, but this has to do with the excommunication which is effected by the power of the word, of which I spoke a little while ago. The other Christ has made known in Matt. 10:14: "Whosoever shall not receive you, nor hear your words, as ye go forth from that man or that city, shake off the dust from your feet." It appears here that to bind is simply to leave one to one's error. In this way Paul bound, Acts 18: 6, shook off the dust against the Jews when they rejected the word, and went unto the Gentiles. So likewise Acts 13: 46. To bind by the word is, therefore, nothing else than to abandon, according to Christ's command, those who do not receive the word, and to have nothing to do with scoffers. For the divine vengeance will be milder to Sodom and her companion cities than to those who, when the light has been offered them, love the darkness better than the light. The followers of the Popes still cry out that the Keys were delivered to the Apostles out and out, and that therefore the word cannot be the Keys; for the word is not of the Apostles but of God, and what the word does, or God through His Spirit, cannot be bestowed upon man. Moreover, since the Keys were delivered to the Apostles, clearly it is not the word that was delivered; for the word is not of the Apostles, but of God. I reply that throughout Holy Writ there are endless things that God has bestowed upon us which are so far from being ours except when communicated by His grace that they cannot possibly be in man's power. As when in Matt. 10: 8 He says: "Heal the sick, raise the dead, cleanse the lepers, cast out demons." Yet these things are as little in the Apostles' power as it was in the King of Israel's power to deliver Naaman from leprosy, II Kings 5: 7. And so, a little later on, when Jesus says [Mt. 10: 14]: "Whosoever shall not hear your words," etc. Yet they could not have committed a more serious sin than to have bestowed their own words upon men; and blessed is he that heareth not the word of a man, for "in vain do they worship me," he says, Matt. 15: 9, "teaching the commandments and doctrines of men." From these and countless other passages, I say, we see plainly that the most kind Father makes things ours which cannot be anyone else's at all than His; but it is not strange that He so bestows them who gave us His Son to be ours. How shall He not with Him give us all things [cf. Rom. 8: 32]? Now I think the real Keys have been pretty well cleared of the rust of human traditions, so that anyone can see that they are nothing else than the administering of the gospel, and the withdrawal of it where there is obstinate unbelief. Let them snarl: "Would you catch a weasel asleep, or propose to teach your masters?" I will not turn a hair, for He on whose word I rest is more ancient than the oldest and wiser than the wise men of today. We know that though the human conscience can be set at rest by the faith with which we cling to God alone, yet it cannot be set at rest by human deliverance or absolution, as some have proclaimed. We are taught by the word, administered, 'tis true, by man, but we are not made sure by the word unless the Spirit of the Lord soften our hearts so that the word can be sown there and our hope planted in God. It is, therefore, established that it is by faith, and not by absolution, as they call the made-up formula of Papal authority, nor by any sacrament whatever, that the inward man can be made secure. For faith alone knows how much trust it has in God through Christ. Away, therefore, and away quickly with these counterfeit Keys of the Popes from the Church of the faithful! For by means of them nothing is sought but dominion over the conscience, and when this has been acquired it opens the way for greed to the treasures of all. When it has opened these, it takes all it wants, in order to have the wherewithal to minister to lust. Hence a carnival of every kind of crime so unrestrained and so widespread that no tongue, no pen, can describe what a quantity of evils of every kind have been let out by these Keys. You committed adultery and then allowed your strong box or wallet to be entered with these Keys; your adultery was nothing. You crushed the poor man with usury, and then gave something to the Keys; your gains were holier than a heritage from one's mother. What but just before was usury, extortionate interest, and such an obstacle that you could not possibly be saved; what you had called poisoning, treachery, robbery, perjury—all this the power of the Keys wiped away; but hardly unless you first laid out a tidy sum of money. Nay, the strange thing was that the more washing away they did, the more efficacious for washing away they became, if only money was poured out unstintedly. Who, by immortal God, is so blind as not to see that this folly could not have grown so rampant without the wrath of God? But, thanks be to God, who has bolted the door with the bolt of His word, which no force, no skill, can break, so that however these Keys turn they cannot get into the consciences or the strong boxes of them that trust in God. Although, therefore, the subject of Confession is closely related to the discussion of the Keys, I will first speak of the Church and afterwards of its Sacraments.

[13]. The Church

Human presumption has distorted the name Church as well as the thing itself so as to make it apply to some few persons only, just as if you should say that the whole body, the entire assemblage, the entire people or congregation, meant some few. For the Church is a congregation, an assemblage, the whole people, the whole multitude gathered together. He, therefore, who says that the Church means some few is just as wrong as he who says that the people means, or is, the king; or who says that the general assembly, the assemblage or congregation, of the citizens is or means the Council. I have, therefore, often written* of the Church, with the hope that men otherwise learned would be turned from the error of conceding that the Popes are the Church. But these men are partly unbelievers, partly arrogant persons. The unbelieving are so averse to the word that they study it in vain; for in their hearts they are wholly disinclined towards it. And the arrogant persons so utterly refuse to accept anything but their own teachings that you see clearly that they suffer from the disease of wishing to appear to have taught everything and to have taught it correctly. Hence the writings of some of them are so contaminated, as far as the truth is concerned, though the outward show is very fair, that you do not know but it would have been better never to have taken up the pen than to have wrapped the truth in such shameless allurements. Yet they are so pleased with themselves that, unless you walk in their footsteps and show yourself, in a way repugnant to the feelings of a Christian heart, either a shameless flatterer or a fawning coxcomb, even at the expense of the truth, they shrink from your works as a dog does from being washed. Things that are

*In his supplementary statement to the Second Zurich Disputation and in his *Der Hirt*.

true are to them brutally rough. They say the disease is too serious to be curable by strong remedies. Fine fellows! Did they ever see a serious disease cured by mild remedies? Slow diseases are cured by mild remedies. If the disease of the Popes were now for the first time beginning slowly to grow worse, the use of such remedies would be quite proper. But when all the members have been permeated with the disease, is it not time to administer the one and only effective remedy that can restore the original health? Slow remedies would perhaps make death slow, but vital ones will restore life and health. Not that I greatly approve those persons who make a great fuss about trifles, but who are such strangers to Christian love that they can neither endure nor do anything for God's sake; persons who have the one most holy name of Christ upon their lips, but in bitterness, contentiousness, clamorousness, bickerings, whisperings, and meddlesomeness, outdo Envy, the Furies, and Cerberus himself. I have myself—and I say it solemnly, with God and my conscience as witnesses—winked at the hallucinations of many people, even when they were plainly at variance with the truth, but only under conditions where I hoped they would return to the right way. When they were too slow in coming to their senses, or refused to come to their senses at all, without giving their names I brought forward to the best of my humble ability what I saw in the Holy Scriptures. So obnoxious in my eyes are these contentions, which cannot be noised abroad without offence to brothers, especially contentions in regard to things which are not vital to Christianity, that I see no more deadly poison can be given to a growing Christian than contentiousness. For are not love and contentiousness diametrically opposed? And what is the Christian life altogether but love? Therefore, when you sow the seeds of contentiousness, at the same time you banish love; for they are as unwilling to be guests in one and the same house as Christ is to associate with Belial [cf. II Cor. 6:15]. But one who desires to speak of the Church has to make these introductory remarks, because some men persist in calling certain most shameless men the Church, though they are, in fact, straining every nerve to destroy the Church of Christ. Let them flatter and by their adulation squeeze out as much money as possible, but let them not mix up Christ with these practices, since it is clearer than day (such a revealer of the heart is speech) that they seek not the honor of God, but mountains of gold or the speedily vanishing smoke of vainglory. Let them, therefore, call things by their right names, and suffer Church to mean "assemblage," and say that the Church of Christ is simply the people, the assemblage, the company of Christ, especially as they nowhere in all Holy Writ find the Church of Christ or of God taken to mean a few bishops, or rather mumblers. Many things are to be tolerated, as I myself not only assert, but daily put in practice; but they are to be tolerated in such fashion as to fall away by and by. Those who are jealous for Cæsar's fame say in his praise that when he saw that he must fall in death he gathered his garments and limbs together so as to fall decently.* Christ could have overwhelmed all His enemies with one word [cf. Jn. 18: 6], but to give an example of peace He tolerated the worst class of men with a tolerance of which you will nowhere find the equal recorded, and did it to abolish the Synagogue in the suitable way. So, too, these men will show themselves well-mannered when they teach that they must fall, and that therefore everything must be arranged so that they may fall with decent dignity and no crash. In this matter they should not imitate physicians, who bid you hope even when no hope is left, but, rather peacemakers, who vigorously reprove the errors of both sides in order that obduracy may be broken down with the least friction. I come back to the word "Church." And since last year in the month of August I wrote upon this same subject in reply to that thoroughly impious and corrupt person, Jerome Emser, and since on all sides such a flood of tasks besets me that I can employ here only what little time I can steal from things not absolutely necessary, I have directed that what I there said about the Church be here incorporated verbatim; although we shall now hear some few things that we have just been hearing, but written for another purpose and not without result.

[14]. The Church ("Reply to Emser")

[For this section, taken entire from the "Reply to Emser,"

*Suetonius *De vita Caesarum*, I: 82.

see below pp. .]

[15]. The Sacraments

I promised to speak of the Sacraments after having considered the Church.

I heartily wish this word "sacrament" had never been adopted by the Germans without being translated into German. For when they hear the word "sacrament" they think of something great and holy which by its own power can free the conscience from sin. Others again, seeing the error of this, have said it was the symbol of a sacred thing. This, indeed, I should not entirely disapprove, unless they also insisted that when you perform the sacrament outwardly a purification is certainly performed inwardly. A third group has asserted that a sacrament is a sign which is given only when atonement has been made in the heart, but is given for the purpose of rendering the recipient sure that what is signified by the sacrament has now been accomplished. I do not like to differ from great men,* especially at this time when they are so flourishing and are writing with such success that they seem to have clothed the world in a new guise and to have changed it from a rude to a very refined state. But I beg them to consider what I am here going to adduce in the same manner in which I always weigh their own writings. The one thing upon which I fix my attention in reading the writings of others is the spirit in which the author seems to have written; for all his purpose becomes plain in his very language. If I see that a thing was written from love of God and one's neighbor, I overlook many errors, just as many persons, no doubt, considerately overlook mine. When, however, occasion offers, I fill in the gaps, reverse the order, unravel the knots, connect wandering thoughts, without, however, discourteous strictures on anybody by name, that peace may be preserved, which some are so bent upon disturbing. I make two exceptions, Emser and Eck, for they are pests to the teachings of Christ. Their own wanton recklessness has forced me to write pretty sharply against them and by name. For the former without any warning so arrogantly attacked me unawares that I should have been a renegade to Christ's teach-

*Luther and his associates.

ings (for it is His work, not mine, in which I am engaged), if I had retired before a man singing his song of victory before he had come into my sight. For he wrote against me in such a way (and published the book) that he tricked me into waiting for six months to see if he were going to send me a copy.* The other laid a snare for my destruction, and sending most absurd and lying slanders to the assembly of the Swiss tried to get the start of me, so that, if his scheme succeeded, I might seem to have been rightly slain, and that he might sell himself for a high price to the Romans and the tyrants of Germany. When I disclosed his crime† (and it could not be denied), good gods, how he raved! So I beg all the readers of this Commentary to judge it with a free mind and without passion, and to remove what they see is foreign to the purest teachings of Christ, employing not decrees and condemnations of their own but the spear of the heavenly word drawn from the writings of both Testaments.

With your good permission, then, I will end my prefatory remarks, and tell what I have found as to the signification and force of this word.

"Sacrament" for Varro‡ is a pledge which litigants deposited at some altar; and the winner got back his pledge or money.

Again, a "sacrament" is an oath, and this use of the word is still found among the populace of France and Italy.

Finally, there is also the so-called "military sacrament," by which soldiers are bound to obey their general according to the rights or laws of war. For wars also have laws, but laws of their own, for the regular laws are silent in the midst of arms.§

It does not appear that the word was used among the ancients to mean a sacred and secret thing. Hence I have given no space to this acceptation of the term, nor to the one which the Latin translation of the New Testament has, of

*The preface of Emser's *Defense of the Canon of the Mass against Huldreich Zwingli* was dated April 15, 1524. The preface of Zwingli's *Reply* was dated August 20, 1524.

†In the second half of 1524 Zwingli issued two pamphlets against Eck.

‡*De lingua Latina*, V, §180.

§Cicero *Pro Milone 11.*

"sacramentum" for mystery [cf. Eph. 5: 32]. For the word does not express that, nor do I know any Latin word which really gives the meaning of μυστήριον, because "arcanum" [secret] has a wider application than μυστήριον, and "sacrum" [sacred] is of somewhat narrower scope.

So I am brought to see that a sacrament is nothing else than an initiatory ceremony or a pledging. For just as those who were about to enter upon litigation deposited a certain amount of money, which could not be taken away except by the winner, so those who are initiated by sacraments bind and pledge themselves, and, as it were, seal a contract not to draw back. I will not say here how disgracefully ignorant even as to the meaning of the word "initiation" the gentleman was who, in answer to a letter of mine in which I had said that baptism was an initiation, remarked: "Even if it is an initiation, it is not a perfecting or justifying." He did not know that "initiation" is used here not for "beginning" or "commencement" merely, but also for the solemn and serious τελετή [perfecting] for some order or society or office, that is, a mystery or occult final sealing which is effected by a set form of words. When this has been accomplished, the person initiated is bound to perform for the office, order, or institution to which he has devoted himself what the institution or office demands. A sacrament, therefore, since it cannot be anything more than an initiation or public inauguration, cannot have any power to free the conscience.* That can be freed by God alone; for it is known to Him alone, for He alone can penetrate to it, as has been abundantly shown in considering man and the gospel. How, therefore, could water, fire, oil, milk, salt, and such crude things make their way to the mind? Not having that power, how will they be able to cleanse it? In fact, what is the cleansing of the mind? Is it a sort of contact with some clean thing? But what can the mind touch, or what touch the mind? Since, therefore, no creature can know a man within to the core, but only God, it remains that no one can purge the conscience save God alone. Solomon, in II Chron. 6: 30, is a witness: "For thou only knowest the hearts of the children of men." Also the Pharisees, in Luke 5: 21: "Who can forgive sins, but God

*Refutation of the Catholic conception.

alone?" And lest anyone should wonder about this latter testimony, I will remark that testimony from an opponent is the strongest. They are wrong, therefore, by the whole width of heaven who think that sacraments have any cleansing power. The second group,* seeing this, taught that sacraments are signs which when they are performed make a man sure about what is performed within him. But this was a vain invention; as if, forsooth, when a man is wet with the water something happens in him which he could not possibly have known unless water had been poured over him at the same time! They did not know, if they will allow me to say so, what faith is or how it is born in a man. I said some time back that faith is a matter of fact, not of knowledge or opinion or imagination. A man, therefore, feels faith within, in his heart; for it is born only when a man begins to despair of himself, and to see that he must trust in God alone. And it is perfected when a man wholly casts himself off and prostrates himself before the mercy of God alone, but in such fashion as to have entire trust in it because of Christ who was given for us. What man of faith can be unaware of this? For then only are you free from sin when the mind trusts itself unwaveringly to the death of Christ and finds rest there. And if meanwhile you had been deluged with the whole Jordan and a sacred formula been repeated a thousand times, your mind would yet have had no feeling of being in a better state, except in so far as this trivial and fleeting notion that the sacraments purify, so persistently beaten into it, gave a false impression of having persuaded it. For they that have not faith gape with wonder at anything applied to them that is said to have any power, and fancy they have found, nay, actually felt, salvation, when they have not felt anything at all within, as is shown by their subsequent lives. For if we become new men, that is to say, if we love God and our neighbor, we shrink from sin, put on Christ and daily grow more and more into the perfect man, are changed by the action of the Holy Spirit. But who would not feel this change? If, however, pleasing ourselves for a time with the freedom from guilt we have acquired, we presently, when this hallucination has worn off, return to the old life, like a dog to

*The Lutherans.

his vomit [cf. Prov. 26: 11], it is evident that we have not felt any change of heart, but only the awe of the water. Many are baptized, therefore, who during baptism feel nothing beyond awe of the water, and not also remission of sins, that is, the deliverance of the heart. And this was generally the case with those who were baptized by John and those who after the ascension of Christ at the preaching of the Apostles and disciples received baptism before they were sure of salvation through Christ or were fully taught in regard to it, as in Acts 19: 2-6 and 10: 44. Cornelius and his house had received the Holy Spirit before they were baptized: they had, therefore, been sure of the grace of God before baptism. Therefore this second view has no value, which supposes that the sacraments are signs of such a kind that, when they are applied to a man, the thing signified by the sacraments at once takes place within him. For in this way the liberty of the divine Spirit which distributes itself to individuals as it will, that is, to whom it will, when it will, where it will, would be bound. For if it were compelled to act within when we employ the signs externally, it would be absolutely bound by the signs, whereas we see that really the opposite takes place, as has been made clear by the testimony above. Consequently, in the third place, there came forward men* who, seeing clearly that the sacraments cannot purify, nor the operation of the divine Spirit be such a slave to the sacraments that, when they are performed, it is compelled at the same time to operate within (for it is established that the Holy Spirit was sometimes given before baptism, sometimes afterwards, as in Acts 10: 44-48 and 19: 2-6), taught that the sacraments are signs which make a man sure of the thing that has been accomplished within him. Hence, for example, they refuse baptism to all who have not previously so well learned and confessed the faith that they can respond to all its articles. Their view is just as far from the truth as was the preceding. For those who have so learned and confessed the faith have been sure for some time already of salvation, as was made plain a little while ago in the refutation of the error of the second group. For if the heart already trusts, it cannot be unaware of its trust. What need, therefore, has he

*The Anabaptists.

of baptism who has already for some time been sure through his faith in God of the remission of his sins? The sacraments are, then, signs or ceremonials—let me say it with the good permission of all both of the new school and the old—by which a man proves to the Church that he either aims to be, or is, a soldier of Christ, and which inform the whole Church rather than yourself of your faith. For if your faith is not so perfect as not to need a ceremonial sign to confirm it, it is not faith. For faith is that by which we rely on the mercy of God unwaveringly, firmly, and singleheartedly, as Paul shows us in many passages.

So much for the meaning of the name. Christ left us two sacraments and no more, Baptism and The Lord's Supper. By these we are initiated, giving the name with the one, and showing by the other that we are mindful of Christ's victory and are members of His Church. In Baptism we receive a token that we are to fashion our lives according to the rule of Christ; by the Lord's Supper we give proof that we trust in the death of Christ, glad and thankful to be in that company which gives thanks to the Lord for the blessing of redemption which He freely gave us by dying for us. The other sacraments are rather ceremonials, for they have no initiatory function in the Church of God. Hence it is not improper to exclude them; for they were not instituted by God to help us initiate anything in the Church.

All this will be made clearer in the sequel.

[16]. Marriage*

Of Marriage I am going to say only enough here to prevent anyone's thinking its dignity impaired when I do not count it among the sacraments, while Paul nevertheless calls it a sacrament, Ephes. 5: 32. I will say this, therefore, that two errors have been committed as to this passage: the first by the [Latin] translator, who, when he should have rendered "mystery" by "secret" [arcanum], always translated it "sacrament," although the latter word does not correspond to the former; the second by us, who do not examine with due care the meaning of this passage, in which Paul simply wished, by

*See, further, Section 21 (p. 257).

comparing Christ as bridegroom and the Church as bride with husband and wife, to show that as Christ died for His own and was made theirs, so those united in marriage ought to bear and do all things for each other: the husband, since he is the image of God, should especially love his wife, protect her, and spend himself for her; and the wife should cling only to her husband in faith and love. Thus should a married couple be as like unto God as possible, since God, in turn, does not disdain to have Himself and His Church called by the names husband and wife. Therefore, wedlock is a holy thing: neither Christ nor His spouse the Church, nor any faithful soul, scorns comparison with it. But if you contend that marriage is a sacrament for the reason that it typifies Christ and the Church, I have no objection. It is not, however, an initiation, but a compact for life, a union of all fortunes, and a common lot. When, therefore, the union of Christ and the Church is learned by comparing it with marriage, what is the need of reckoning it among the sacraments? Suppose this word "sacrament" had never been heard by Christian ears. Would not marriage be marriage, and baptism be content with its name, and likewise the Lord's Supper? Since, however, the name has come into use, I do not wish to be obstreperous, but only to see that it confine itself within its proper limits. Marriage is a most holy thing, and is not made any more holy or any clearer by being called a sacrament, but darker and less clear. For everybody knows what wedlock is, but hardly anybody knows what a sacrament is. So everybody knows what baptism is, but few know what a sacrament is. Let us recognize, therefore, that marriage is a most holy compact, even if we never count it among the sacraments. Have not the Greeks wedlock, baptism, the Lord's Supper? But they have not this word "sacrament." Also, the Germans have nothing corresponding to this foreign word, and hence they ignorantly borrowed it. Since, therefore, sacraments are initiations and nothing else, while marriage is a compact existing between two persons only, let us not allow it to be obscured by that word.

[17]. Baptism

John, who from baptizing got the name Baptist, has disclosed in his own words what baptism is: namely, an initiation by which those marked themselves out who were going to mend their lives. I am speaking now of baptism pure and simple, in which those who are going to enter upon a new life are dipped in water; not of baptism as embracing the whole matter of preaching as well as dipping. Those who today battle so stoutly against the baptism of infants—not seeing this distinction, namely, that baptism is used sometimes for the whole procedure of both teaching and sacrament, sometimes only for the sacrament, that is, the sign—fight blindfolded, as gladiators sometimes did. Thus, then, the divine Baptist speaks in Matt. 3:11: "I indeed baptize you with water unto repentance." What else is this than to say: "I dip you in water, that you may repent of your old life, that is, be so ashamed of your former life that you will utterly cast it off and begin a new one? By this sign I am simply teaching you, who are ignorant of heavenly things, that henceforth, if you wish to be saved at all, you must put on an entirely different life. As those who are washed come out new, as it were, so I first bring you by a visible act to the wiping out of your past life." Mark, 1:4, keeps the same sequence when he says: "John was in the desert baptizing and preaching the baptism of repentance for the remission of sins." Not that I mean that John began to baptize before he taught, but that he readily baptized any who came to him, although he did not know how honestly they had received the word, and did not demand to know. But when he saw that many of the Pharisees and Sadducees had come to his baptism, and knew through the Holy Spirit that their hearts were not right and whole with the Lord, he upbraided them sharply, saying: "Ye offspring of vipers, etc." He meant: "Ye have come, indeed, to baptism, not in order to lay aside your old life, but that you may seem to men to belong to the number of those who by the sign of baptism bind themselves, as by an earnest or an oath, to a change of life, while within ye are not a whit better and make no change in your bad life. Since ye wish to be counted in the company of the repentant, show the fruits of repentance! Do as becomes the repentant!" From all this it is plain that baptism is an initiatory sacrament by which those who were going to change their life and ways marked themselves out and were enrolled among the repentant. And this was a preparation for the coming of Christ, as Luke, 4:17, proves from Isaiah [61:1-2]. For when everybody, having reviewed his whole life, not only found nothing in it on which he could rely for salvation, but also saw at the same time that he lacked the strength to tear loose from his former life and steadfastly to prosecute a new one, he needed someone to lend a hand in this wretched state of things. Such a one is pointed out not only by the divine Baptist, but also by the Evangelist, as was highly necessary. For, knowing that repentance begets despair, he immediately shows that one had come who should raise up again the fallen hopes. He says, John 1:26: "I baptize with water; but in the midst of you is and was born, yea even here among you stands, one whom nevertheless ye know not; he it is who will come after me, who yet was before me; the latchet of whose shoe I am not worthy to unloose." "He will baptize you with the Holy Spirit and with fire," Matt. 3:11. John, therefore, at the same time taught repentance, and said that He who should destroy sin was at hand.

But before we go further I must speak of the baptism of the Holy Spirit, since some men not rightly taught concerning it have put forward in consequence wrong views of baptism.

The baptism of the Holy Spirit, then, is twofold. First, there is the baptism by which all are flooded within who trust in Christ, "for no man cometh to him, except the Father draw him," John 6: 44. "And all shall be taught of God," Isa. 54:13. Second, there is the external baptism of the Holy Spirit, just as there is the baptism of water. Drenched with this, pious men once began at once to speak in foreign tongues [Acts 2:4-11]. This was a sign to others rather than to the speakers, for the speakers felt within themselves faith and enlightenment of soul, but the others did not know this of them. It, therefore, turned their tongues into foreign speech, that others might know that what was taking place was done by the divine Spirit. And this latter baptism of the Holy Spirit is not necessary, but the former is so very necessary that no one can be saved without it; for no one is saved except by faith, and faith is not born save at the instance of the Holy Spirit. John said that both baptisms were to come, when he said [Lk. 3:16]: "He shall baptize you with the Holy Spirit, and with fire." Now, we are not all imbued with the sign of tongues, but all of us who are pious have been made faithful by the enlightenment and drawing of the Holy Spirit. The baptism of John, therefore, preceded both baptisms of the Holy Spirit, as far as Christ is concerned; for otherwise it is evident that repentance cannot begin without the Holy Spirit. Yea, the baptism of John even antedated repentance, as has been made plain in the case of the Pharisees and Sadducees, and in Luke 3: 7. The first is plain from the fact that John sent those whom he had frightened to Christ, of whom they were still ignorant, and promised that they would find salvation in Him. For thus is it recorded in John 1: 28-31: "These things were done in Bethabara where John was baptizing. The next day John seeth Jesus coming unto him, and saith, Behold the Lamb of God, that taketh away the sin of the world! This is he of whom I said to you, After me will come a man who was before me, because he was first in regard to me, and I knew him not; but that he should be made manifest to Israel, for this cause came I baptizing with water." Behold how John baptized with water those whom he sent to Christ, and baptized them in order to send them to Christ! The second point, namely, that Pharisees and Sadducees also were baptized by John is made manifest thus. In Luke 3: 7 we read: "He said therefore to the multitudes that went out to be baptized of him, Ye offspring of vipers, who warned you to flee from the wrath to come?" And the same thing that Luke says here of the multitudes that went out to be baptized of John, Matthew, 3: 5, expressed thus: "Then went out unto him Jerusalem, and all Judaea, and all the region round about Jordan; and they were baptized of him in Jordan." It is, therefore, logical for us to understand the words, "But when he saw many of the Pharisees and Sadducees coming to his baptism, he said, etc.," in the sense that both Pharisees and Sadducees were baptized. For as Luke says those went out to be baptized who Matthew explicitly writes were baptized, so also Matthew said "came to his baptism" for "were baptized." This view will be plainer if one considers closely the words that follow: "Ye offspring of vipers." But what is written in Luke 7: 29-31 took place on another occasion and had to do with other persons, as Matt.

11: 7-19 clearly shows.

How the baptism of John and that of Christ differ is a question much mooted both in the past and today; but it is an unprofitable question, for there really is no difference at all as far as the reason and purpose are concerned, although as far as the procedure or form is concerned there is some slight difference. Yet the latter is not, properly speaking, a difference, for we can employ the same thing in various ways without detriment to faith. John's dipping effected nothing—I am speaking here of the baptism of water, not of the inward flooding wrought through the Holy Spirit. Christ's dipping effects nothing; for Christ was satisfied with the baptism of John as well in His own case as in that of His disciples. But if His baptism had had anything richer and fuller in it, He would no doubt have given His disciples a supplementary baptism, and not have suffered Himself to be baptized according to John's way. That Christ was not baptized by any other baptism than John's, as far as the dipping is concerned (for I want to reiterate that constantly, lest I should seem to hold that Christ imparted nothing further through His Spirit than John did), is quite evident in Matthew, Mark, and Luke, where we see Jesus coming to baptism like the rest, though He had no need of repentance. Hence, also, it is manifest that John made no express requirement, as some maintain. But clearest of all is what John wrote, 1: 32-34, where he makes the Baptist say: "I have seen the Spirit descending as a dove out of heaven; and it abode upon him. And I knew him not: but he that sent me to baptize with water, he said unto me, Upon whom thou shalt see the Spirit descending, and abiding upon him, the same is he that baptizeth with the Holy Spirit. And I have seen, and have borne witness that this is the Son of God." Since, therefore, John would not have known Him unless he had afterwards seen the Spirit descending upon Him from heaven, he baptized Him just as he did any others whatsoever; although this seems to be contradicted by what is written a little before, where, as Jesus was coming to him, John called Him the Lamb of God that atoneth for the sin of the world. But here we must consider that the Evangelist is not looking so much at the sequence as at the essential point of the matter. The earlier of the two events he describes after the other. Having pointed out the Lamb that destroys the sins of the world, he then, in order not to seem to anyone to have spoken with more boldness than truth, proves that the world can be washed clean through Him for this especial reason, that He is the Son of God. For he says: "And I have seen, and have borne witness that this is the Son of God." Furthermore, that He is the Son of God he proves by the fact that the heavenly Spirit descended upon Him in the form of a dove, and rested upon Him. Thus, what had taken place before, the Evangelist narrates afterwards. For a visible sign had been given to John, that by it he might recognize Christ. Having recognized Him, he proclaimed to others also that He was the Lamb that destroys the sins of the world. For there follows a little later the statement that on the next day he pointed Him out again to two of His disciples, who left him and followed Jesus [Jn. 1:35-43]. All this makes it manifest that John led to Jesus Christ, and as soon as it could be done sent his own followers to Him. While this is all so, another point meets us, namely, that Christ was not unknown to John when he baptized Him; for we have it plainly put in Matt. 3:14 that when Jesus came to John to be baptized by him John said: "I have need to be baptized of thee, and comest thou to me?" These words apparently cannot have been said to one unknown; hence it seems possible to infer that Jesus was known to John even before he saw the Spirit descending upon Him. Since it would take too long to disentangle this knot here, I refer you to Augustine's "The Agreement of the Evangelists,"* Book 2, Ch. 15. My object is simply to make plain that there is but one baptism, whether we call it of John or of Christ. For there is "one faith, one baptism," Eph. 4:5. This can also be inferred from the fact, Matt. 3:14, that John pleaded that he needed rather to be baptized by Christ, meaning, of course, "I send to Thee those whom I initiate with water, because I, too, ought to be sent to Thee, and comest Thou to Me?" Christ, therefore, solved his difficulty thus: "Suffer it: for whatever is right, that is, whatever ought to be done, we will fulfil." Thus Jesus was baptized in just the same way as other men, for nothing is said of any change, and mention of that

**De consensu evangelistarum.*

would not have been omitted if any had been made; nor indeed would Christ's being baptized have had any great significance if it had been done by a method different from the common one. But now, as the Son of God was baptized by John, by whom sinners were baptized, it is a wonderful thing that the spotless Son of God accepted that sign which is given to those who have to be changed, though He is Himself the unchangeable God.

Finally, and this is the strongest point of all, men who had already heard Christ and justified Him, were still baptized with the baptism of John, Luke 7: 29. If you maintain that βαπτισθέντες in this passage clearly signifies that they had already been baptized before, I have no objection, for my conclusion follows just the same, namely, that the baptism of John and the baptism of Christ are the same thing; for unless they were one and the same, Jesus would have rebaptized these persons through His disciples. Since, therefore, even here He was satisfied with the baptism of John, we must agree that it was the same as the baptism of Christ. Still, the first-mentioned meaning appeals to me more, namely, that after hearing Christ they were baptized with the baptism of John; or, what is much nearer the truth, "baptizati" is used in this passage for "imbuti," so that the meaning is that these men had hitherto been taught by John, but having heard Christ, about whom they had heard much while with John, they justified Him, that is, they had an exalted opinion of Him such as we are wont to have of a just man. That the disciples of Christ were washed in the baptism only of John is plain from this: In John 1: 37 we read that two disciples of John the Baptist had heard the heralding of Christ by their master, "Behold the Lamb of God," etc. One of these was Andrew, brother of Simon. Now, if he was a disciple of John he was undoubtedly baptized; for there were baptized by him even those who did not care to be his disciples, much more, then, those who followed him as their leader. Again, in John 3: 26 we read that John's disciples brought him word: "Rabbi, he that was with thee beyond Jordan, to whom thou hast borne witness, behold, I say, the same baptizeth, and all men come to him." From this it appears that Christ through His attendants baptized in the same way and form as John did; for if He had baptized otherwise, the disciples of John could not have failed to mention it. In the third place, John 4: 2 has, "Although Jesus himself baptized not, but his disciples." Since, therefore, we nowhere see that the disciples were baptized by Christ (for He baptized not), and at the same time see that His disciples baptized, it is not likely that they baptized others, but had never been baptized themselves. Since, then, they were baptized, they were baptized with no baptism but the baptism of John; for Christ baptized not. Since, therefore, Christ received the baptism of John and made no change in it either in his own case or that of the Apostles, it is clearly established that baptism had its beginning under John, and that there was no difference between the baptism of John and that of Christ, as far as the nature, effect, and purpose are concerned. For it is evident that Christ was baptized on our account, in order to commend baptism to us. What baptism, then, did He wish to commend? Some other than John's? Why, then, was He not first Himself baptized with that other? Since, therefore, He wished by means of the baptism of John to commend baptism to us and made no change in it, it is apparent that the baptism of John and that of Christ are the same baptism.

But this view seems to be opposed by what is written in Acts 19: 1-10 and Matt. 28: 19. For this passage of Acts plainly bears witness that twelve men were baptized over again in the name of Jesus, who yet had been previously baptized with the baptism of John. But if the baptism of John and that of Christ are the same, there was no need of their being baptized with the baptism of Christ. We must, therefore, consider the character of both baptisms. John baptized, then, unto the entering upon repentance, as has been said,* and proclaimed that salvation was at hand in Him who was to come after him; for He was the Lamb that alone took away sin, and he taught trust in Him; for he said [they should believe] on Him which should come, that is, on Christ, Acts 19: 4. The baptism of John, therefore, demanded a new life and made known hope in Christ. And this was a baptism of teaching; for the water was the same in both cases. The baptism of Christ required

*See p. 186.

nothing different, for He, just like John, "began to preach, Repent!" Matt. 4: 17. The fact that Christ was Himself the hope, and that John was not the hope (for he was not himself the Light, John 1: 8, but sent men to Christ), produced no difference in the baptisms; for both tended to Christ, that is, demanded a new life which should be modeled after the pattern of Christ. Nay more, no difference is argued by the fact that Christ's baptism had the author of salvation at hand in person, while John's promised that He was coming, for the lot was the same of those who were baptized in the baptism of John as of those who were baptized in the baptism of Christ, if they died before Christ ascended into heaven. For "no one hath ascended into heaven but the Son of Man, who is in heaven," John 3: 13. Those, therefore, who died before the departure of Christ into heaven could not reach heaven, even though they changed their life and set all their hope upon Christ; for He is Himself the first fruits of them that rise again [I Cor. 15: 20]. Much less could their having been washed with water bring about the opening of heaven. For Christ in all things must have the pre-eminence, Col. 1: 18. Since, therefore, John taught that the life must be changed and modeled after the pattern of Christ, to whom he sent men, and since he proclaimed that Christ Himself is our hope, and since Christ taught the same thing (for what does all the teaching of Christ demand but a new life formed according to the will of God and having unwavering trust in Christ?), it follows that if their baptisms of teachings were the same, their baptisms of water also were the same. The character of their teachings is the same. For what difference does it make that John said He was coming forthwith, and that Christ exhibited Himself in person? Did not John also show Him when he said: "Behold the Lamb of God," etc.? For not even the Apostles could have spoken of Christ's first coming otherwise than John spoke; nay, rather, no one without exception could have exhibited Christ but Himself. As, therefore, the Apostles drew men to Christ, so also did John. Hence Luke not without reason said of his preaching, 3: 18: "With many other exhortations preached he good tidings unto the people." For what else did John teach than the Apostles taught? Besides, that deeply significant speech which John the Evangelist sums up in Chapter 3: 35-36 expresses the nature of the gospel most clearly, as given in these words: "The Father loveth the Son, and hath given all things into his hand. He that believeth on the Son hath everlasting life; but he that hath not faith in the Son shall not see life, but the wrath of God abideth on him." What else is this, pray, than "He that believeth when the gospel is preached shall be saved; but he that believeth not shall be condemned" [Mk. 16: 16]? Since, then, the baptisms of teaching are altogether the same, how is it that we suppose a difference in the baptisms of water, when each applied the water to the end that we might come forth new men and might model our lives according to the teaching which each proclaimed?

We must now come back to the nineteenth chapter of Acts, where there seemed to be something opposed to the view that there is but one baptism, whether you call it Christ's or John's or that of the other Apostles also. "When Paul had come to Ephesus and found certain disciples, he said unto them, Did ye receive the Holy Spirit when ye believed?" What is Paul asking here? Is it whether they have spoken with tongues? He seems to be asking this, for afterwards when he "had laid his hands upon them, they spake with tongues." What, then, is this new inquiry? Was this thing demanded for faith? Certainly not, for we see that the miracle of tongues rarely occurred. He was not, therefore, asking about the gift of tongues, although this gift followed afterwards, but about the inward strength of their faith. For he knew that they had been baptized, that is, taught, by Apollos; who, however, was first taught "the way of God more exactly" by Aquila and Priscilla [Acts 18: 24-28] after he had come to Corinth from Ephesus. Hence Paul, very properly fearing that these disciples might perhaps be lacking in something, asked whether they had been taught inwardly through the Holy Spirit, so as to have all confidence in salvation through Christ. They, therefore, not having yet attained this, tell him that they have never heard any mention of a Holy Spirit. Paul wondered at these words, and asked into what they had been baptized. They replied, "Into John's baptism." Notice how he here uses "baptism" for "teaching," as does also Christ, Matt. 21: 25, when He asks the Jews:

"The baptism of John, was it from men or from God?" Here it is manifest that Christ is not speaking of the baptism of water, for that is decidedly of the earth, whereas the teaching had come down from heaven. And in John 3: 26 the disciples of John say: "Behold, the same baptizeth, and all men come to him"; when nevertheless He did not Himself baptize, as later on we see in the fourth chapter. But Christ did baptize with teaching, since He taught just what John also taught, as far as the substance of it was concerned; for in other respects no one so taught, as one having authority. In the same third chapter, a little before the passage already quoted, John says [3: 22]: "After these things came Jesus and his disciples into the land of Judaea; and there he tarried with them, and baptized." While there is here no mention at all of teaching, it is manifest that the Evangelist uses "baptize" for "teach." Here I warn those persons who do not interpret this passage quite correctly to give careful attention. What now follows Paul said not for the purpose of belittling the dignity of John's baptism or the estimation in which it was held, as we have generally believed, but in order to bring out its character plainly, for when this had been explained these disciples could tell whether they had come to repentance and Christ in the way John had preached. So he says [Acts 19: 4-5]: "John verily baptized the baptism of repentance"—what else is this than "preached repentance"?—"saying unto the people, that they should believe on Him that should come after him, that is, on Christ Jesus. And when they heard this, they were baptized into the name of the Lord Jesus." If, therefore, these men had the form of baptism which Paul tells of here, what, pray, was lacking to them? For if they repented of their former life and set all their hope on Christ, they were already born again. It becomes manifest, therefore, that they were not adequately instructed in the teaching of John, however far they thought they had progressed therein. For what one of the Apostles preached the Gospel of Christ more clearly than John, as was seen a little while ago? But Apollos himself had been somewhat deficient, as we see in Acts 18: 24-28, so that it is not likely that disciples still new to the faith were better equipped than a master so famous for his knowledge of the law and the prophets. Having, therefore, believed up to this time that they held the teaching of John correctly, they found, as Paul recited its essentials, that they were still far from the complete teaching. They are baptized, therefore, that is, led by Paul into Christ. For I must not fail to note that, however the Latin translators render it, the Greeks uniformly have in this passage [Acts 19: 3] "Into what were ye baptized," not "in what"; and again, "Into John's baptism," not "in John's baptism." Also, a little later, "baptized the baptism of repentance," not "with the baptism"; and, finally, "They were baptized into the name of the Lord Jesus," not "in the name." I am well aware that figurative expressions of this kind are sometimes translated in that fashion, but in this passage the recurrence of the locution warns us not to think it used casually. Nay, not to waste time with such critics, what the Greeks have in Matt. 28: 19—"Baptizing them into the name of the Father, and of the Son, and of the Holy Ghost"—is much more vivid than "in the name," as the Latins have it. For to be "baptized into the name" is to be grafted into faith in God. That "name" in this place signifies "power, majesty, grace," is nothing new, for Christ Himself says, Mark 16: 17, "In my name shall they cast out demons," that is "in my strength"; for the Apostles had naught either of words or of deeds that they could fairly attribute to themselves, as Paul tells us, Rom. 15: 18; and in the fourth chapter of Acts Peter says that there is no other name under heaven than that of Christ whereby we can be saved, that is, it can be done only through the grace of Christ. However, as far as the external baptism of water is concerned, I still would not oppose using these sacred words as we dip a man, or initiate him with baptism, although to "baptize into the name of the Father, and of the Son, etc.," is in reality nothing else than to dedicate, devote, consecrate, those who were previously of the world and the flesh to the Father, Son, and Holy Spirit. From what has been said, answer can easily be made also to the second objection, in which it was said that Christ's baptism was different in form from John's; for these words that are written in Matt. 28: 19, "Baptizing them into the name of the Father, etc.," were not said simply for the purpose to which the theologians have confined them. For the real meaning of these words is that those who are about to put on Christ are thus dedicated to the Father, Son, and Holy Spirit, that is, joined and bound to them. But it is a mere outward thing, this dipping to the accompaniment of the sacred words, "In the name of the Father, and of the Son, and of the Holy Ghost"—a sign and ceremony signifying the real thing. As, when something is delivered by hand, the joining of hands is not the delivery of the thing, but is the visible sign by which we testify that a contract has been performed on both sides, so are ceremonies outward signs which prove to others that the participant has bound himself to a new life or will confess Christ even unto death.

So much on baptism. Now as to the baptism of infants, which some men today so persistently refuse to them that if they as steadfastly held aloof from contentiousness, faction, strife, evil speaking, arrogance, and impatience, no one could praise them enough. You ask whether baptized infants are damned or not, and they reply that they are not damned; and, on the other hand, if you ask whether infants are damned if not baptized, they reply that they are not damned. So you infer that infants are not included under the law, "He that believeth" (when, of course, he has heard the gospel preached) "and is baptized shall be saved; but he that believeth not shall be condemned" [Mk. 16:16]; for this, you urge, was said to adults and not to those who are incapable of listening, and therefore infants cannot be cast out of the general salvation, especially those born of believing parents, for otherwise their condition would be worse than that of carnal Israel. If, then, the children of Christians are not less God's than those of the Israelites, who would forbid their being baptized according to the words of Peter, Acts 10:47? Yet, after all this, they do not abate their obstinacy one whit. Therefore when I have finished these Commentaries, I shall, God willing, treat of the Baptism of Infants in a separate book.*

*The preface of Zwingli's *Von den Taufe, von der Wiedertaufe und von der Kindertaufe* was dated May 27, 1525.

[18]. The Eucharist

Two years ago I wrote among sixty-seven articles* one, the eighteenth, on the Eucharist, in which I wrote many things with a view rather to the times than to the thing itself. For not even Christ could praise enough the faithful steward of His word who in due season sets meat before the household of his Lord; of whom He speaks with admiration in Matt. 24: 45: "Who," that is, how great, "is the faithful and wise steward to whom his lord hath entrusted his household to give them food in due season?" I determined, therefore, unceasingly so to dispense the word as to reap the largest harvest for my Lord. For who would not cast off a servant who should proceed to plough the ground in the dead of winter and to sow seed in it? These things are to be done in the spring time. So I made many concessions at that time to the tender minds of those for whom I wrote, but all for their edification. After the example of Christ I distributed and kept in store as well; for after He had instituted the Eucharist, He said [Jn. 16: 12-13] that He had yet many things which must be told to the disciples, but they could not bear them then; therefore He determined to keep them until the coming of the Holy Spirit. When, therefore, kind reader, you come upon some things here which you have not seen in my earlier writings, or some things said more plainly here than elsewhere, and some things said differently, do not be astonished. I did not wish to give food when the time was unseasonable, or to cast pearls before swine [Mt. 7: 6].

Indeed, even if I could have done it without any danger, I did not wish to put things forth at a time when no one would receive them. I repeat here, therefore, what I said there, with the understanding that what I offer here, in the forty-second† year of my age, shall outweigh what I offered in the fortieth, when, as I said, I wrote rather with a view to the times than to the thing itself, according to the Lord's command that we shall do our edifying in such fashion as not to be torn to pieces by the dogs and swine at the start [cf. Mt. 7: 6]. For I fear that if there is anywhere pernicious error in the adoration and wor-

**Auslegen und Gründe der Schlussreden.*

†Zwingli was born January 1, 1484.

ship of the one true God, it is in the abuse of the Eucharist. If this had retained its proper use, according to the institution of Christ, there would not have crept in such atrocious sins against God's people, the Church. Now we are all bent upon handling holy things, or upon having them about us—yea, I will say it plainly, upon making holy by our own merit, forsooth, things that perhaps are not holy (for everybody knows how much has been expended on the bones of the pious to provide for their worship)—rather than upon making ourselves holy. The result is that we worship with embraces and kisses wood, stones, earth, dust, shoes, vestments, rings, hats, swords, belts, bones, teeth, hair, milk, bread, quadras, tablets, wine, knives, jars, and anything that pious men have ever handled. And (most foolish thing of all) we think ourselves distinctly blessed if we have got just a look at any such thing; we promise ourselves the remission of our sins, prosperous fortune, and the whole world. But true piety, which is nothing else than blamelessness preserved through love and fear of God, we have abandoned so completely that not even among infidels do we see ordinary, that is, human, righteousness so utterly prostrate as among Christians. We have fancied that we do something worth while if we have high sentiments about holy things, though holiness has been ascribed to them by ourselves, or if we talk about them in most polished terms, and yet ourselves teem the while with all uncleanness, just like whited sepulchres [cf. Mt. 23: 27]. To be one who trusts in God and is holy—this it was to be a Christian. Let no one, then, when he hears me talking of the Eucharist, form such a judgment about me as to think that because Zwingli has said a thing it must be accepted—if, perchance, there are any who have sworn such allegiance to the man, though I fancy there are few or none. On the other hand, let no man cast aside what he sees brought from the fountain-sources of the hidden things of God because he who brings them is a humble writer. I see sins committed in both these directions. In every instance judgment is to be suspended until the cause has been heard to the end and we see clearly what verdict should be pronounced.

The Greeks gave the name Εὐχαριστία to the Lord's Supper, having always, if I may be permitted to say so, been more pious and more learned men than the Latins, as their written works bear witness clearer than day. And they undoubtedly gave it this name for the reason that they understood, both from faith and from the meaning of the words of Christ and the Apostle, that Christ wished to have a joyful commemoration of Himself made by this supper and thanks given publicly for the blessing which He has bountifully bestowed upon us. For the Eucharist is a thanksgiving. He, therefore, that would take part in this public thanksgiving should prove to the whole Church that he is of the number of those who trust in the Christ who died for us: to remove, to withdraw, or to estrange one's self from that number, whether by desertion or by uncleanness of life, would be the height of faithlessness. Hence, also, the Eucharist is called Communion or Communication by Paul, I Cor. 10: 16. From this comes excommunication, too, or denying someone access to this communication of the faithful on account of impurity of life. We therefore now understand from the very name what the Eucharist, that is, the Lord's Supper, is: namely, the thanksgiving and common rejoicing of those who declare the death of Christ, that is, trumpet, praise, confess, and exalt His name above all others. But since that most significant discourse of Christ's which is embraced in the sixth chapter of John is not correctly understood by the great majority, though they boldly distort it into other meanings, I have determined above all things to declare the primary sense of this passage, that they who force all Scripture willy-nilly to serve their own view may not be able to get here weapons to defend their error.

When Christ saw that those who were coming to Him were given over to their bellies and came to Him on that account [Jn. 6: 26], according to His custom He took occasion to teach a lesson from the situation. Therefore, soon after they were filled He thus addressed them: "Ye come to me for the sake of being filled with food; but I came into this world not to act as a steward of bodily food, but to feed the mind. Ye work and sweat, following me for the food of the belly. Ye slothful ones, work for the food that surely will not perish; for that which thus far ye seek perisheth with the belly; but the food that I will give you is spiritual, and hence cannot perish but abideth forever. For my Father, God, hath sealed me, that is, confirmed me to be the sure salvation and pledge of life." The Jews, therefore, not understanding what Christ meant when He bade them work for—that is, seek—the food that could not perish, said: "What must we do, that we may work the works of God?" For they thought that He was speaking of some outward work which He required of them. Jesus, therefore, answered and said unto them [Jn. 6:29]: "This is the work of God, that ye believe on him whom he hath sent." See what the work is that God requires of us. Christ here mentions nothing at all save to believe on the Son of God, that is, Himself. See also what the food is which He had just before bidden them acquire, saying [Jn. 6:27]: "Work for the food that perisheth not." We shall find it to be no other than that we believe on Christ. This food, then, of which Christ speaks here is faith. Therefore here is placed the first mark by which we discover that they are utterly wrong who think that Christ in this whole chapter is saying something about sacramental food.

[I.]. Christ bids us seek the food that perisheth not, and this is nothing else than to work the work of God. Furthermore, the work of God is that wherewith we believe on the Son whom the Father hath sent [Jn. 6:29]. The food He bids us seek is, therefore, belief on the Son. Faith, therefore, is the food of which He talks so impressively all through this chapter. The Jews say, therefore: "What sign doest thou then, that we may know" (namely, that we must trust in Thee) "and believe? What dost thou work, by which we can recognize that Thou art God, to whom alone the Law commands us to cling? Thou knowest that our fathers in the desert did eat bread that rained from heaven [Jn. 6:31], as is sung in the Psalms [78:24]: He gave them bread from heaven." Jesus answered [Jn. 6:32]: "Verily, verily, I say unto you, Moses gave you not that bread from heaven; for even if it fell from above, it was not of heaven; but my Father giveth you the true bread out of heaven. For the bread of God is that which cometh down out of heaven, and giveth life unto the world. The bread of Moses supported bodily life, but the bread which the Father gives refreshes the soul; and it is so abundant and efficacious that it gives life to the entire world." The Jews, therefore, not comprehending the words of Christ, which were nothing else than the explanation of the gospel (for by "eating bread" He means believing the word of the gospel), say to Him [Jn. 6: 34]: "Lord, evermore give us this bread." Jesus, therefore, said unto them [John 6: 35]: "I am the bread of life: he that cometh to me shall in no wise hunger; and he that believeth on me shall never thirst." Hearing Christ say that the bread which came down out of heaven gives life to the world, the Jews desired that this bread be evermore given to them. Jesus, understanding that they did not comprehend the meaning of the gospel, explains what this bread is, so life-giving that it can make the whole world live, and says [Jn. 6: 35]: "I am the bread of life. He, therefore, that cometh to me, that is, who is grafted upon me, who receiveth me, shall in no wise feel hunger." And that "cometh to" is here used for "receiveth," the following words indicate: "He that believeth on me shall not thirst." It is faith, therefore, that allays all hunger and thirst. But what hunger, and what thirst? Those of the soul, of course. Faith in Christ is, therefore, the only thing that can give such food and drink to the heart that it shall want nothing further. Christ continues: "But I said unto you, that ye have seen me, and yet believe not." What else is this than, "Ye wonder that I said that 'he that cometh to me shall neither hunger nor thirst,' when yet ye are here present with me and subject to hunger and thirst. This comes from the fact that ye have looked upon me and even still look upon me with the eyes of the flesh. But I am not speaking of this kind of sight or nearness, but of the light of faith. If any man has that, he shall want nothing. He will not seek by night for some one whom he may love and to whom he may lament his burnings [cf. Jn. 3: 2], nor will he wander distractedly about. For he is sure that He whom he holdeth is the true spouse and only treasure of the soul, and he will thirst for no other. Ye have not this light of faith, for ye do not trust in me. Hence ye do not understand how I am the food, that is, the hope, of the soul. And the reason for your blindness is, to say nothing harder, that the Father hath not drawn you into knowledge of me. Otherwise ye would receive me [cf. Jn. 6: 44]. For [Jn. 6: 37-38] all that which the Father giveth me shall come unto me. And I for my part cast out none that cometh to me. For I am come down from heaven not to do my will, the will that you attribute to me just as to other men (I am, indeed, true man, and according to that nature also have a will of my own, but one much more obedient than yours; for your will often resists the will of God, but mine always obeys)—I am come down from heaven, then, to do the will of him that sent me. And that you may know what is the will of him that sent me, I say; This is the will of my Father, who sent me, that of all that which he hath given me I should lose nothing, but should raise it up at the last day. But that ye may know this also, what ye ought to understand by the words, 'The Father giveth me' and 'The Father hath given me,' I will speak more plainly: This is the will of him that sent me, that every one that seeth, that is, knoweth, the Son, and believeth on him, should have eternal life: and I will raise him up at the last day" [Jn. 6: 40]. Behold the food of which he is speaking! God has sent His Son into this world that we may have life through Him. Who, then, are to have life through Him? Those who rely upon His grace. But how will they rely upon Him unless they recognize Him? He said, therefore: "Every one that seeth the Son," that is, who understands why the Son was sent into the world, "and believeth on him, shall have eternal life." Here it seemed to the flesh that Christ was taking to Himself too much when He said [Jn. 6: 48]: "I am the bread of life." For He had shortly before said [Jn. 6: 33]: "For the bread of God is that which cometh down from heaven, and giveth life unto the world"; from which it followed that He is Himself that bread which came down from heaven. Therefore the flesh, that is, the Jews, murmurs, and says [Jn. 6: 42-43]: "Is not this Jesus, the son of Joseph, whose father and mother we know? How is it, then, that he saith, I came down from heaven?" Jesus therefore answered and said unto them: "Murmur not among yourselves. Have ye not heard me say already, All that which the Father giveth me shall come to me? Your unbelief, from which follows slowness of understanding, compels me to say the same thing over and over again. This is the fact: No man can come to me, that is, no man approaches me as the one pledge of salvation, except the Father that sent me draw him: and him whom He draweth to me, that is, uniteth with me in faith, I will raise up at the last day [cf. Jn. 6: 44]. It is strange that ye constantly think my words are such peculiar utterances, when I say nothing or very little that is not written in your own law or prophets. And this also is written in the prophets, Isa. 54:13 and Jer. 31:34: 'And they shall be all taught of God.' Why, then, do ye wonder at my saying that on account of your unbelief knowledge of me is denied you by the Father, when even your prophets teach that this knowledge must be given by the Father? But what can be said more simply and plainly than what I am now going to say? And I am going to say it, that ye may not have left any cause for just complaint. What I expressed before by the words, 'What the Father giveth me cometh to me,' or by the words 'No man can come to me, except my Father draw him,' hear now in other, clearer terms, thus [Jn. 6: 45]: 'Whoever hath heard the Father and learned from him, cometh to me' as to the one and only anchor of salvation. Not that any man hath seen the Father [cf. Jn. 6: 46], lest perchance ye should refer these words 'hear' and 'learn' to the senses rather than to the mind, that is, to inward illumination. No man hath ever seen the Father—although he works within us so that we may hear and learn what he wills—save he is that is from God: he hath seen the Father. Verily, verily, I say unto you [Jn. 6:47], He that believeth on me hath eternal life. Now ye have the essence of this teaching of mine, aye, of the whole mission entrusted to me, namely, that he that believeth on me hath eternal life. I am that bread of life, the nature of which I explained in the beginning of this discourse. No one denies that your fathers did eat manna in the wilderness, and they died [Jn. 6: 49]; but he that eateth of this bread, me to wit, that is, that believeth on me, hath eternal life. This is that bread which cometh down from heaven, that a man may eat thereof, and not die" [Jn. 6:50].

[II.]. We must note in passing that Christ is our salvation by virtue of that part of His nature by which He came down from heaven, not of that by which He was born of an immaculate virgin, though He had to suffer and die by this part; but unless He who died had also been God He could not have been salvation for the whole world. This, then, is the second mark that in this chapter Christ means by "bread" and "eat" nothing else than "the gospel" and "believe," because he who believes He was slain for us and who relies on Him has eternal life; and that He absolutely is not speaking of sacramental eating. For to make this idea still clearer He says again [Jn. 6: 51]: "I am the living bread which came down out of heaven: if any man eat of this bread, he shall live forever. But, that I may not keep you longer in suspense, I will explain briefly what the reason is why I am salvation unto the whole world, or how it comes about. Listen! The bread of which I am saying so much, and which I am going to give you, is my flesh, which I will give for the life of the world."

[III.]. This, then, is the third sure mark that Christ is not speaking here of sacramental eating; for He is only in so far salvation unto us as He was slain for us; but He could be slain only according to the flesh and could be salvation bringing only according to His divinity. In this way, then, is Christ the food of the soul, because the soul, seeing that God spared not His only begotten Son but delivered Him to an ignominious death in order to restore us to life, becomes sure of the grace of God and of salvation. And let no man try to be subtle here because He said His flesh was given for the life of the world, and so venture to argue that Christ is a means of salvation to all according to His human nature only, since He says Himself that His flesh was given for the life of the world: therefore His flesh quickens. For as Christ is God and man in one, it comes about that, albeit He was slain in the flesh (for who could kill God?) and His death was made life for us, yet on account of the unity and community of His natures that is sometimes attributed to one of the natures which belongs to the whole Christ. After these words, then, "The bread that I will give is my flesh, which I will give for the life of the world," the Jews were none the wiser, because of their unbelief and obstinate hatred. For they did not grasp the meaning of Christ's words, that He is a means of salvation to us not by being eaten but by being slain; for the human mind is made sure of the mercy of God when it sees that He spared not His Son, etc. [cf. Rom.

8:32]. They murmured, therefore, the more recklessly and wildly the more ignorant they were, indignantly saying [Jn. 6:52]: "How can this man give us his flesh to eat?" For they still thought only of the flesh which stood before their eyes. Hence they very properly shuddered, though our theologians shudder not. Christ, therefore, seeing that all His efforts to draw them into knowledge of Himself were vain, treated them as Isaiah was once ordered to treat the people, Ch. 6:9-10, where the Lord says: "Go, and tell this people, Hear ye indeed, but understand not; and see ye indeed, but perceive not. Make the heart of this people fat, and make their ears heavy, and shut their eyes; lest they see with their eyes, and hear with their ears, and understand with their heart, and turn again, and I heal them." Christ, I say, seeing that He was accomplishing nothing, made their ignorance yet the more crass, as He shows by His own words, Matt. 13:13-17. Therefore, when they spoke of Him so hatefully, He said [Jn. 6:53-55]: "Verily, verily, I say unto you, Except ye eat the flesh of the Son of man and drink his blood, ye have no life in yourselves. He that eateth my flesh and drinketh my blood hath eternal life; and I will raise him up at the last day. For my flesh is meat indeed, and my blood is drink indeed"—Christ's flesh, I say, in so far as it was delivered to death for our deliverance; and His blood, in that it was shed for our cleansing; as is made very plain in what has been said. For when they would not take in His mystical language, which He had yet so perfectly explained that they ought not to have wanted anything more, He smote them harder and made them blinder, for that was what they deserved, and such is the judgment of God.

[IV.]. Hence after all this He adds [Jn. 6:56]: "He that eateth my flesh, and drinketh my blood, abideth in me, and I in him." This is said for the hardening of unbelievers, but for the enlightening of the pious. And it is the fourth mark by which we perceive that Christ is speaking here not of sacramental eating (for there are numberless persons, alas! who eat and drink the body and blood of Christ sacramentally, and yet are not in God nor God in them, except in the same way He is in the elephant and the flea), but of the eating of faith; for he that believeth himself set free by the delivering up of

Christ and washed clean by the shedding of His blood surely abideth in God. For he casts all his confidence securely upon the Son of God, and directs his hopes nowhere else; for he cannot thirst for any other good who already enjoys the highest good (I mean as far as is meet for wayfarers to enjoy, and not use or enjoyment to the extent the theologians talk about; for the pious enjoy God while they are here, although this is unknown to all whose hearts burn not with love of God). And, on the other hand, God abideth in them, for (as is plain from Christ's very words [Jn. 6: 44]) no one approaches Christ unless the Father draw him. He, therefore, who learns by inward teaching from the Father surely has God in him; and, at the same time, whoso abideth in Christ, in him abideth Christ also. For to abide in Christ is to cling firmly to God through the love with which He gave Himself for us; but "God Himself is Love," I John 4: 8. "Whoso, therefore, abideth in the love of God, God is in him and he in God" [I John 4: 16]. But love follows faith in the order of the understanding. It is, therefore, through the faith with which we rely upon the grace of Christ that we abide in God, and He in us. That this is the meaning is proved by Christ's following words [Jn. 6: 57]: "As the living Father hath sent me, and I live because of the Father; so he that eateth me, he also shall live because of me." "The Father sent me," He says, "hence also I obey his will in all things; for I am the Son of the Father. So, surely, they also that eat me, that is, believe on me, will fashion themselves to my pattern. Ye will eat in vain, that is, ye will in vain pretend that ye believe, unless ye also change your life. I came not only to redeem but also to change the world. They, therefore, that believe on me will transform themselves into my pattern. This is the bread which came down from heaven, as is shown by its results; for he that eateth of this bread shall live forever; not so he that eateth bodily bread. This ye can see from the fact that your fathers did eat the manna that came down from above, and died. No bodily food, therefore, can make any one last forever." This language offended not only those who hated Christ, but also some of His own disciples; and they, not to do anything too rudely, said [Jn. 6: 60]: "This is a hard saying; who can hear it?" They still clung to the visible flesh just as tenaciously as His enemies did. Jesus, therefore, knowing that even some of His disciples were murmuring at this, said unto them [Jn. 6: 61-62]: "Doth this cause you to stumble? What, then" (supply "will ye say," or "will ye think," or some such phrase) "if ye should behold the Son of Man ascending where he was before? Ye do not take in my words because ye do not believe that I am the Son of God. But what will ye say when ye shall see me ascending to heaven by my own might? Will not the fact itself then force you to confess that I am the Son of God? Ye do not trust in me because ye do not believe that I am the Son of God, and your not believing is the reason why ye do not understand what I say. I try to lift you to the things above by comparisons and pleasant allegories, but ye are always sinking to the depths by the weight of your unbelief. The thing of which I am speaking is a spiritual thing, and has nothing to do with bodily things. The Spirit teaches spirit. The Spirit of God, I say, deigns to draw the wretched spirit of man to itself, to unite and to bind it to itself, and wholly to transform it into itself. This thing feeds and rejoices the heart and assures it of salvation. What else is this than the food of the soul? By what comparison can it be more fitly expressed than by that of food? For as the starving stomach rejoices when food comes into it, wherewith the used-up breath and heat and strength are replenished, so the starving soul, when God discloses Himself to it, leaps for joy, and daily grows and increases in strength more and more, being transformed into the likeness of God until it develops into the perfect man. It is, therefore, spiritual food of which I am speaking, for only the Spirit gives it, since the Spirit alone draws the heart to itself and refreshes it. Ye are very thoughtless when ye imagine that I am speaking of the flesh that is built up with veins and sinews. That profiteth nothing. How long will ye be without understanding [cf. Mt. 15: 16]? I tell you plainly, so far am I from speaking of bodily flesh or essential body, that I bear open witness that my flesh profiteth absolutely nothing."

[V.]. And this is the fifth and most distinct mark by which we discover that Christ is in no wise speaking here of the Sacrament of the Eucharist; and not only this, but in these words He is providing by law, as it were, against our ever indulging in dreams about bodily flesh. For since Christ says that it profiteth nothing, human rashness ought never to dispute about eating it. But if you say in objection that the sense must be different (for the flesh of Christ does profit something, since by it we have been redeemed from death), I reply: The flesh of Christ profiteth very greatly, aye, immeasurably, in every way, but, as I have said, by being slain, not eaten. Slain it has saved us from slaughter, but devoured it profiteth absolutely nothing. The Truth has said so, and the fact cannot be otherwise. For the Jews were disputing about eating the flesh, not about offering it as a sacrifice, hence Christ's words must refer to that. However much, therefore, the theologians dispute about the essential body of Christ or bodily flesh, they will never accomplish anything, except to show themselves more stupid and more reckless than the Jews towards all the painstaking kindness of the Savior. For the Jews, clinging ever to the visible flesh, deserted Christ rather than let themselves understand His benign teaching, although, as becomes a loving Master, He plainly points out their error so that they may not perish in it, and says that the flesh they were looking at profiteth absolutely nothing. But our theologians by their actions virtually say: "O Jesus, there is no need of this explanation; we understand the idea correctly. We know that you are speaking of visible and tangible flesh. We must eat that if we desire to be saved. You, who know the hearts and the thoughts of men [I Chron. 28: 9], were prudent to no purpose when you said that the flesh is absolutely without profit to us; for we, who in our realm are mightier than you, shall easily succeed in compelling all men to confess even in express words that they eat your flesh, and that as they eat it they also perceive by sense that they are eating flesh and drinking blood. Therefore withdraw that statement, 'The flesh profiteth nothing,' until you see that we, outdoing the stupidity of the Jews (who turned away from Him who knoweth the hearts of all, rather than flatter Him by pretending to understand that which they were ignorant of), have prevailed upon the mass of men to confess that they understand, believe, or perceive by sense that which they never have understood, believed, or perceived by sense. For instance, there is our friend Berengarius,* whom we compelled (as appears in Section 2 of the De Consecratione, beginning 'I Berengarius') to confess that after consecration the true, that is, the corporeal and essential, body and blood of Christ are present, and that the sacrament is not only as a matter of sense but in reality handled by the hands of the priest, broken and torn by the teeth of the faithful, etc. So also will we drive to this all who venture to utter a syllable to the contrary. If you insist altogether upon the statement, 'The flesh profiteth nothing,' we will turn from you; for it is better for us to withdraw from you than to have our revenues and gains vanish." Do not be scandalized, kind reader, by this sharp irony of mine. You will see presently why one has to deal in this way with so stupid a class of men, who have even compelled the senses to confess something other than what they have experienced. When, therefore, Christ had taught clearly that it was spiritual and not oral manducation of which He was speaking—for, He said, the flesh profiteth absolutely nothing—He added [Jn. 6: 63]: "The words that I speak unto you are spirit, and are life." That "word" is used by the Hebrews for the whole matter, the whole event and case, is everywhere evident in Holy Writ. Luke 1: 65: "And all these words were noised abroad throughout all the hill country of Judaea." Hence in this passage Christ is to be understood as having said: "This case that I have been setting forth to you is one of the heavenly Spirit, and begets life in those who intrust themselves to it. And the reason few of you understand it or receive it is that the great part of you do not believe."

[VI.]. This is the crown as it were of the whole discourse: "I announce the gospel to you, but ye do not believe it. Now the gospel is nothing else than myself, though in the beginning I expressed myself modestly and darkly, in order not to give an

*Berengar of Tours, 998?-1088. He was twice (in 1059 and again in 1079) forced to recant his denial of the Real Presence. The former recantation was in these words: Ego Berengarius . . . et ore et corde profiteor, de sacramentis dominicae mensae, . . . panem et vinum, quae in altari ponuntur, post consecrationem non solum sacramentum, sed etiam verum corpus et sanguinem domini nostri Iesu Christi esse, et sensualiter non solum sacramentum, sed in veritate manibus sacerdotum tractari, frangi et fidelium dentibus atteri.

impression of arrogance or temerity; but what the Father wills has to be said. Therefore I said that I am He whom the Father promised to your fathers, the true food of the soul, sure salvation, and the infallible pledge of hope. He, therefore, who trusts in me is already saved; for he felt within himself, as soon as he set all his trust on me, how glad his conscience became, how his soul was raised from despair to the sure possession of salvation."

I have amplified at somewhat greater length than before the substance of this sixth chapter [of John], as far as it pertains to the Eucharist, but I hope not fruitlessly. For I think we can clearly see from this that the theologians and experts in Pontifical Law, in distorting to the abuse of the Eucharist everything they have drawn from this passage, have acted recklessly or ignorantly, and, therefore, their authority ought to have no value where it is not based on the truth. But if you absolutely insist upon forever thrusting it in my face as an invincible shield, I will simply say that faith itself dictates this meaning for this passage, unless I am very greatly wrong in my faith when I unwaveringly believe that there is one and only one way to heaven, firmly believe that the Son of God is the infallible pledge of our salvation, and trust in Him so completely that for the gaining of salvation I attribute no power to any elements of this world, that is, to things of sense. And if now anyone asks pertly for what purpose I have explained this section of John with such pains, I answer: That the truth may come into the light. And if in any part I have fallen short, this ought to be made manifest by Scripture testimony, and not by somebody's accusations. It was easy to accuse Christ before His judge with false and made-up slanders. Yet when the latter asked [Mt. 27:23]: "What evil hath he done?" no witnesses were brought forward, but all was threats and outcry. Unless, therefore, we wish to become like the impious enemies of Christ, we ought not in deference to papal authority to rage against the innocent truth, which is Christ Himself. If, then, this is the genuine meaning of this passage, no man's authority ought to outweigh it, the flesh ought not to be guilty of preferring any man's authority to the truth. Human wisdom ought not to prevail over divine truth. Whatever, therefore, has been plucked from this chapter and distorted into any other meaning than this native one which the Lord has explained through me, whether it be read in decrees of Popes or works of theologians, or heralded in churches or pulpits, ought to have so little effect that we should all declare it would have been more pious for those who have done this thing never to have touched the undefiled truth than in their presumption so to have defiled it.

What, therefore, will their authority avail, however great and excellent they are? The truth is more excellent. To the others, who break out with, "You seem to me to hold that the bodily flesh and also the blood of Christ are not present in the Eucharist," I answer: Do you say this of yourself or have others said it to you? If you are a believer, you are aware how salvation comes; and then the word of God has such power with you that you raise no question about bodily flesh. But if others have told you that this is my view, I say to them that in this matter I hold as the Church of Christ holds. She will not even brook the question whether the body of Christ is in the Sacrament of the Eucharist in actual, physical, or essential form. For when you bring up these elements of the world, she will thrust this buckler in your face: 'The flesh profiteth nothing' [Jn. 6:63]; why, then, do you dispute about the flesh? Even if you now cry out, "O heaven! O earth!" nay, even "Stars and seas!" I shall simply say, "The flesh profiteth nothing"; why, then, is it better for you to be curious rather than anxious about it? Be this, then, a wall of bronze, "The flesh profiteth nothing." Go now, and bring up all your engines of war, catapults, battering-rams, sheds, and every kind of weapon; far from shattering this wall, you will be able not even to shake it. We must, then, hold a different view of the flesh and blood of this sacrament from that which the theologians have thus far laid down, whose opinion is opposed by all sense and reason and understanding and by faith itself. For I do not think we have to listen to those who are so bold as to say, "I have always firmly believed that in this sacrament I eat the essential body, or the bodily and sensible flesh, of Christ." As if in saying this they could persuade any one to believe that his senses perceive what they do not perceive! When, therefore, thy say that the whole thing is established by faith and therefore cannot be denied, for we must firmly believe that we have a sense perception of the bodily flesh, I reply: "I know what faith is and I know also what sense is; but you, either not having this knowledge or supposing that I have it not, are trying to cast darkness upon my light. Faith exists in our hearts through the Spirit of God, and we are sensible of it. In fact, that there is an inward change of heart is not an obscure matter, but we do not perceive it by means of the senses." But now these persons come and, because they fancy that faith is a violent and deliberate turning of our hearts towards some even quite incongruous thing, they therefore aver that here the belief that the bodily and sensible flesh is present is held with unwavering faith. Yet in this they make two mistakes: First, in thinking that faith has its origin in man's decision and election. They make a mistake here because, although faith is hope and trust in things quite remote from sense, nevertheless it does not rest upon our decision or election. The things upon which we set our hopes themselves cause us to put all our hopes upon them; for if we were made believers by our own election or determination, all men could become believers by their own strength, even the impious. Since, therefore, faith has not its origin in sense or reason and looks not to the things of sense, it is easy to discover how they err in the second place. They err in the second place, then, in applying faith to things of sense, and in saying that through these it brings us certainty. But of that there is no need, for what is perceived by sense owes nothing to faith. Why should any one hope for that which he already sees? For things which are perceived when presented to the senses are things of sense. Let us see now how finely these things fit together: By faith we believe that the bodily and sensible flesh of Christ is here present. By faith things quite remote from sense are believed. But all bodily things are so entirely things of sense that unless they are perceived by sense they are not bodily. Therefore, to believe and to perceive by sense are essentially different. Observe, therefore, what a monstrosity of speech this is: I believe that I eat the sensible and bodily flesh. For if it is bodily, there is no need of faith, for it is perceived by sense; and things perceived by sense have no need of faith, for by sense they are perceived to be perfectly sure. On the other hand, if your eating is a matter of belief, the thing you believe cannot be sensible or bodily. Therefore what you say is simply a monstrosity. Observe, too, that the theologians asserted here another thing, which even the senses knew not, namely, that bread is flesh; for if this had been so, it would have been established by the verdict of sense, not by faith. For faith springs not from things accessible to sense nor are they objects of faith. Nor do I think we have to listen to those who, seeing that the view mentioned is not only crude but even frivolous and impious, make this pronouncement: "We eat, to be sure, the true and bodily flesh of Christ, but spiritually"; for they do not yet see that the two statements cannot stand, "It is body" and "It is eaten spiritually." For body and spirit are such essentially different things that whichever one you take it cannot be the other. If spirit is the one that has come into question, it follows by the law of contraries that body is not; if body is the one, the hearer is sure that spirit is not. Hence, to eat bodily flesh spiritually is simply to assert that to be body which is spirit. I have adduced these things from the philosophers against those men who, in spite of Paul's warning to be on our guard against philosophy, Col. 2: 8, have made it the mistress and instructress of the word of God, that they may see clearly how nicely they sometimes weigh their decisions and pronouncements. In short, faith does not compel sense to confess that it perceives what it does not perceive, but it draws us to the invisible and fixes all our hopes on that [cf. Heb. 11: 1]. For it dwelleth not amidst the sensible and bodily, and hath nothing in common therewith. Come now, understand what happiness is born in you if you believe that you eat the bodily and sensible flesh of Christ, or, as others say, eat His bodily flesh spiritually! You will undoubtedly admit that nothing arises therefrom but perplexity, dulness, and, to speak freely, suspicion in regard to other things of faith which are most certain and most sacred. Yet these fine fellows were all the while saying that this monstrous eating of sensible and bodily flesh is a prop to faith, and sometimes they brought it forward as a miracle, which yet no man perceived. Who, pray, ever made up such nonsense, and that before the eyes of those who clung in their hearts to the true and most high God, and who, as soon as they examined their faith, saw that there was no need of paradoxes of this sort? For what did God ever promise to those who believed that bodily flesh is eaten here? Did not those who were truly faithful know for certain that salvation is found in relying upon the mercy of God, of which we have the sure sign or pledge in Jesus Christ the only begotten Son of God? What, then, do you imagine this invention—subtle forsooth, since it consists of words only (for no mind can take it in, and neither does faith teach it, as we have seen)—effected with the pious? Nothing, by heaven. Hence it undoubtedly came about that those who were truly pious either believed nothing of the kind, or when pressed to believe took to flight in their hearts, even though with their lips they confessed that they believed it was as the impious declared. For who, when confronted with anything so monstrous, did not flee, saying: "Do not examine this thing; believe the Fathers." And whenever the goading voice of the Truth said: "It is a strange thing. How can it be that you should be compelled to believe that which you cannot see to be possible? When the Jews did not comprehend it, Christ showed that it was to be understood spiritually, but now these persons say it is done in a bodily and material sense, which yet you do not perceive nor experience," did not everyone say to himself: "It is not for you to take anxious thought about these things"? But these fellows had taught men thus to run away that the truth might not shine forth and be understood. And as to the impious, they did not trust even in Christ, so far were they from giving Him thanks for the redemption given to us. What, then, did they do but tyrannically thrust upon us what it is impossible that they themselves believed, even though they said so a thousand times? For faith is the gift of God; and since God never taught this thing, He surely has not drawn men to believe it. That He did not teach it is clear, because the flesh profiteth absolutely nothing. And much the strongest and clearest proof is, that we all, as has been said, when we consider this spiritual-bodily manducation (for I am forced to speak thus against my will), always turn away in heart, chiefly for the reason that truth is always victorious; but the indifferent or fearful heart would not resist, because it saw something different enjoined by the Pope. What, then, is the reason of this, when nothing so delights the soul as partaking of the word of God?—as David bears witness, Ps. 119: 103: "How sweet are thy words unto my taste! Yea, sweeter than honey to my mouth!" And again [Ps. 19: 9]: "The commandment of the Lord is pure, enlightening the eyes"; and [Ps. 119: 105]: "Thy word is a lamp unto my feet, and light unto my path." Since, I say, the veil that softened the brightness of the light for Moses' gaze has been taken away, what is the reason why we all fight shy of considering this manducation? If it rested upon the authority of the word of God, it no doubt would have, in common with the rest of God's words, the quality of becoming clearer and more acceptable the more it was considered. We discover, therefore, since faith is the sweetest and pleasantest thing known to the soul, while this bodily and sensible manducation oppresses or saddens the heart, that it has proceeded from the notion of reckless men rather than from the word of God; though, not to be unfair to anyone, some men can plead ignorance as an excuse for their fault because of the words of Christ which we call the words of consecration.* For, as we show the bread we say plainly: "This is my body." Of these words I am now going to speak.

I have now refuted, I hope, this senseless notion about bodily flesh. In doing that my only object was to prove that to teach that the bodily and sensible flesh of Christ is eaten when we give thanks to God is not only impious but also foolish and monstrous, unless perhaps one is living among the Anthropophagi. Meanwhile I leave everyone free to hold what view he will of spiritual manducation, provided he rests on Christ's dicta and not his own, until he has weighed what I am going to bring forward about the words of Christ. Then he may choose what the Lord will give him to choose, for I impose no law upon any man.

I bear witness, therefore, by the one only God Almighty, Father, Son, and Holy Spirit, who knoweth the hearts of all, that what I am presently going to put forth, I shall put forth for no other cause than that of finding out the truth. I know

*In this connection see Zwingli, *De canone missae epichiresis.*

the insatiable thirst of the old Adam for glory, and, if I had ever striven overstrenuously for it, opportunity for satisfying my ambitions had been offered me in earlier days by the greatest princes of the Christian world, though about this I shall maintain a steadfast silence, and not tell of it even deprecatingly as some persons do. I know also how hard it is to combat an idea implanted in all men's minds, for as a rule we are the sort of worshippers of Christ that pose as having done something worth while if they have stoutly defended those external signs which we call sacraments, even if they never or very seldom review their lives and prop up what is in a tottering condition; although it ought to be our especial care to come as near as possible to the pattern of Christ, whose name we bear. It is a perilous thing, therefore, to venture into such danger, where you are bound to meet so many savage enemies, and where everyone wishes to seem tremendously pious through raging tremendously. What are you to do, then? The law bids us to restore to its master the straying ox of even an enemy [cf. Exod. 23:4]; and if you see the whole world straying, shall you not give warning, especially when in these days of ours you see Hercules after Hercules unhesitatingly going forth to proclaim every kind of pernicious doctrine? The King of Heaven has entrusted various talents to various people, and some make diligent use of them, while some are slothful [cf. Mt. 25:14-30]. To me also He has given a mite, concern for which ever burns within me, constantly reminding me not to let it be consumed by rust [cf. Mt. 6:19]. Hence, while others sail undaunted over the boundless sea of Scripture, because all their equipment is strong—masts, topsails, rigging, poles, oars, prow, beam, stern—and bring back vast stores of merchandise from every quarter, my little skiff, roughly put together, has cautiously to hug the shore, and still more cautiously to bear its slender load. I will do my best, therefore, to have everything that I bring forward on this subject so strong and solid that it cannot easily be torn to pieces. And I pray all who have given themselves to Christ, not to judge until they have heard the whole case. Then I shall take it calmly whatever verdict they render. If they agree with me, I shall certainly be grateful; if, on the other hand, they reject, condemn, and execrate my effort, they will do it, if they are wise, by the force of the Scriptures. Then I shall be not a little obliged to them, for they will bring me back from error to the right way. For I am thoroughly determined to listen most gladly to any one who duly admonishes me according to the heavenly teachings. But if anybody goes to work with clamorings, he will shout as vainly as Hercules did for Hylas. I am deaf to such words as, "It is heretical, erroneous, an offence to pious ears." They have so often smitten upon these ears that they have made them callous. Therefore let no man say, "Who will put up with this? The whole world thinks differently." Let him rather reflect that often an entire nation, except a few persons, has been in error, as happened in Noah's time [Gen. 6:17-18]. Elijah [I Kings 18:32] thought himself entirely alone, and Micaiah [I Kings 22:9-28] stood a true prophet against the entire crowd of reckless prophets. The truest is always known by the fewest. So perhaps those who think otherwise than the majority about the bread of the Eucharist do so not without reason. Following the example of Moses, I will see what this fire means [cf. Exod. 3:3]. Now, I frankly confess, before my God and the Lord Jesus Christ and the whole creation, that I am more inclined to this sense for Christ's words which I am going to put forth than to that other sense which we have thus far given them, though I make no rash declaration; but if anyone will put forth something clearer and more consonant with faith, I promise to receive it with open arms in great thankfulness.

I have said, then, that this hard view of the bodily and sensible flesh of Christ was occasioned by ignorance of Christ's words, "This is my body, etc." If their meaning had been decided from the Holy Scriptures rather than according to the dicta of avaricious men, we never should have stumbled unawares upon so many absurd questions. Now, these words, "This is my body," should not have been so handled with unwashen hands, but we should first have examined every corner of Scripture to see what meaning they could bear and what not, as, for example, we see done in other cases. Some men today attribute to works what belongs solely to the grace of God, but they do it not without Scripture authority, for there is found just as much Scripture testimony attributing to works what belong to the grace of God as there is testimony attributing it to the grace of God alone. What opinion, then, in these circumstances ought properly to prevail? That which faith dictates. And faith dictates this: We are the work of God, of Him we breathe, in Him we move and have our being [Acts 17: 28], to Him we tend; therefore all things are His, and we are unprofitable servants who are not sufficient for anything [Lk. 17: 10], but all our sufficiency is from God [II Cor. 3: 5]. Those who hold this view easily free themselves from difficulty when they come upon mention of works in the Scriptures. For they see it belongs to God's grace and friendliness to ascribe to our works that which yet He Himself works; nay, that it is His work and not ours; and so they sail safely all through Scripture. And this is what ought to have been done in this passage. After Christ had said to the Jews, "The flesh profiteth absolutely nothing" (for so emphatic is the Greek expression οὐκ ὠφελεῖ οὐδέν), no lips should have ventured to talk further about bodily flesh, especially when it is clearly seen that the Jews took offence at this same bodily flesh, and that Christ met their offence with these words, so that no one can fairly even dream that there can be any disagreement on this point. For nothing else offended the Jews than the thought that bodily and visible flesh must be eaten; but Christ met their error by saying that the flesh profiteth absolutely nothing; that it is the Spirit that quickeneth the soul; that He spoke words of salvation—namely, that he who trusted in Him who was to give His body and blood for us should have everlasting life; that these words were brief, but life and the heavenly Spirit breathed from them. Why, then, did we fall so incautiously into such a hard view, when we had a charm potent enough easily to lay bare all the tricks of human viciousness? Is not this saying of Christ's a barrier which the pious heart neither can nor would leap over? Is it not a ruler with which he who has wholehearted faith in God smooths and straightens everything that otherwise would be hard and rough? Who that understands the central point, namely, that those who trust in Christ have thereby the power of becoming sons of God, nay, recognize that through one and the same Spirit they are already sons and heirs of God [cf.

Rom. 8:14-17],—who of these, I say, will be stupefied, as the Jews were, at these words, "This is my body," when he hears Christ so plainly say, "The flesh profiteth nothing"? Into such darkness, most merciful and righteous God, when we fail to trust in Thee, Thou dost suffer us to fall that even at midday we grope blindly like those who have lost their sight. For if there had been sound faith, it would have driven off this darkness, just as the sun at its appearing dissipates the night. O inscrutable are Thy judgments [cf. Rom. 11:33]! For as it was proper for Thy justice to smite our faithless selves with blindness, so it was proper for Thy mercy to open our eyes again and to raise us to the bright light, as they say eagles do their young, that we, finding we can bear the light, may also recognize this blessing, because of our own power we never could have opened our eyes to the light hadst not Thou, who callest even the things that are not yet [cf. Rom. 4:17], led us into Thine admirable light.

Therefore the words of Christ, "The flesh profiteth nothing," force every thought into the obedience of God [II Cor. 10:5], so that by no reasoning either can you or should you now understand the words, "This is my body," of bodily flesh or sensible body, as has been made plain. We shall have to see, therefore, what sense the words must have; for (not to pass this point by) there is no weight in the foolish objection, "Why do we not force the words, 'The flesh profiteth nothing,' into conformity with the words, 'This is my body,' and say the former must be squared with the latter, rather than make the latter fit the meaning of the former?" First, the things Christ is there discussing are so perfectly clear that no one can base any purely allegorical or symbolical meaning upon what either precedes or follows. Second, faith sees that the true meaning is the one which the words bear upon their face. For who will believe that Christ thrust His own into a darkness in which He did not allow the Jews to remain? Christ is light, the Gospel is light. Who can believe that we should be driven into a thing from which the Jews, lest they should feel abhorrence, were led away? Finally, the senses do not here make such protest and rebellion as when faith has the daring to say that it believes that bodily flesh is eaten. For the senses cannot be persuaded to say that they perceive what they do not perceive at all. For in other matters they hardly allow faith to believe things that they do not themselves experience, even when nothing is demanded of them beyond their nature and laws. And now, when this counterfeit faith, which has reached this decision about sensible flesh, imposes it upon the senses in spite of themselves, so that contrary to all their own laws they are forced to confess that they perceive what they do not perceive, they constantly refuse to submit; even if you tyrannically force them to confess in spite of themselves what they do not perceive, they constantly remonstrate. But now I come back to the point itself. We must see, I say, what the native meaning of these words of Christ is, for they cannot have this crude material one. There have come forward in our day those* who have said that a symbolical meaning is to be found in the word "This." I commend their faith, if only it is not counterfeit. For God seeth the heart, we poor wretches judge from the face [I Sam. 16: 7]. I greatly commend, therefore, not the faith which makes them venture thoughtlessly to treat these words, but that through which they see that it is untenable for us to understand bodily flesh here. I will not, however, speak now of the Charybdis the fear of which drove them upon this Scylla, for it has no bearing upon this matter. When, therefore, in three Evangelists as well as in the Apostle Paul they read: "Jesus took bread, and when he had given thanks, he brake it, and said, Take, eat; this is my body," they maintain that there is here a change of reference, so that the pronoun "this" does not refer to the bread which he had taken, broken, and handed to the disciples, but to the sensible body itself of Christ. Their view undoubtedly is (for except one pamphlet and that a small one I have read nothing of theirs†) that Christ wished to show His disciples that this body of His was the one of which the prophets had said much as to the treatment it would suffer. This view would get very strong

e. g., Carlstadt. Cf. Zwingli, *Ad Matthaeum Alberum de coena dominica epistola*, (1524).

†It is evident from Zwingli's *Ad Matthaeum Alberum de coena dominica epistola* that he had read Carlstadt's *Von dem widerchristlichen Missbrauch des Hern Brodt und Kelch.*

support from Christ's declaration in John 6:51: "The bread that I will give is my flesh, which I will give for the life of the world." For this is equivalent to saying: "Behold this very body, which I very recently declared must be sacrificed for the life of the world! It will presently be hurried to the altar. But have no fear or anxiety. I am here, and show myself. And, that you may not fall into any error, for instance, the error of believing that because I am the Son of God I am not going to give this body to be slain, but am going suddenly to produce another, as angels have often been seen to do—that you may not, I say, with the recklessness characteristic of human imaginings, fancy that I am going to give another instead of this body, I say to you plainly and clearly that I am going to deliver up for the redemption of the world this body which you see before you."

With their kind permission, then, I will say what I think, and what, we shall very clearly see, is the real fact of the matter. If in this fashion we twist the word "this" so as to make it refer to Christ, the whole incident loses its point; and yet it has been set down with such painstaking care by all the writers that it is impious to suppose that it has been so carefully portrayed for no good reason: "Jesus took bread, and blessed it, and gave thanks, and brake it, and gave it to the disciples, saying, Take, eat; this is my body which is given for you." What was the need of all this circumstance, which the Evangelists have set forth so vividly that even to this very day whenever we hear these words we seem to see Christ Himself acting and speaking? What need, I say, had Christ of all this circumstance, if all He wished to say was simply that this body of His was already between the hammer and the anvil, as the saying is? Or is He, like a generous host, inviting the disciples to eat, although they have already dined, so that the meaning is, "Be of good cheer, and eat in joy"? To what purpose, then, the words, "blessed," "gave thanks," "brake," "gave to"? Would they not have eaten unless Christ had divided the bread and given it to them? We are forced here either to let go all the actions and sayings—perish the impious thought!—or to confess plainly that this body of His which Christ gave with such careful distinctness and majestic solemnity was a symbolical one. Nor is it an obstacle that the word for bread in both Greek and Latin is masculine, while that for body is neuter, for you will hear in almost any language countless like forms of expression by which one passes from the finished product to the material, as, "Take this bowl; it is the purest gold among all the royal vessels." See how "crater" [bowl, a masculine] signifies the finished product, while "aurum" [gold, a neuter] signifies the material; for the bowl is made with artistic skill, and gold is the material of which it is made. We pass, therefore, from the finished product to the material, that the value of each may be recognized. Hence by this argument weapons would rather be supplied to the old view than wrested from it, if we rushed into a sickening battle of words. For our flesh-eaters will say: "See, here there is a transition, from the product, namely, the bread, to the material, namely, the body, so that the sense is: 'This bread, as far as its material is concerned, is the very body of Christ.' " This would be a quibble, however, which I speak of only for fear someone may perhaps try the thing in the way I have mentioned. For in ordinary parlance we go from the product to the material which the hand of the maker had taken up to work with. Hence here we ought to go from the bread to the flour, and say, "This bread is flour." But these things are petty subtleties and accordingly not very solid, and I have mentioned them not to attribute any force to them, but merely to show that expressions of this kind are found in quite all languages. Thus it becomes apparent that the argument drawn from the change of gender is unsound. In the third place, when Christ subjoins, "This do in remembrance of me" [Lk. 22: 19; I Cor. 11: 24], what, pray, are they bidden to do in remembrance of Him? If you say, "To eat," I shall object; "What, then, shall we make of the words, 'This is my body,' which come between?" Does it not seem exceedingly violent, when all the actions and all the sayings that precede and all that follow these words clearly lead to the conclusion that what is offered the disciples to eat is the body of Christ, albeit a symbolical one, and when the command to do this in remembrance of Him sets forth the whole reason for this eating—does it not, I say, seem violent to twist these intervening words into a reference to something else? It does, indeed. We must not do violence to words in this way even when faith does not contend that the sense is different.

The entire difficulty, then, lies not in the pronoun "this," but in a word no larger as far as number of letters is concerned, namely, in the verb *"is."* For this is used in more than one passage in the Holy Scriptures for "signifies." I hear (to mention this point first) that Wycliffe* earlier held and the Waldensians† today hold this view, that "is" was put here for "signifies," but I have not seen their Scripture basis for it. It is possible for persons to hold right views and not rightly support the right views they hold. Perhaps that was the reason why their view was condemned as impious. For I, having through the grace of God often joined battle with many adversaries in regard to the meaning of Scripture passages, have often found that persons, even when they held right views, were sometimes forced to abandon their cause and to surrender it to others because they could not strongly support their right views. Hence I shall without fear of these words, "He is a Wycliffian," "He is a Waldensian," "He is a heretic," bring forward the passages of Scripture in which it cannot be denied that this word "is" certainly is used for "signifies." Afterwards I shall prove clearly that in this passage also "is" must be taken in the sense of "signifies." This will be plain from the testimony following. In Gen. 41:26 Joseph, interpreting Pharaoh's dream, says: "The seven beautiful kine, and the seven full ears, are seven years of plenty: and both contain the same meaning of the dream." What is this, pray? Are the seven fat kine seven years? Certainly not, but the kine he had

*John Wycliffe (1324?-1384) opposed the doctrine of transubstantiation. Although he denied that after consecration the bread and wine are changed into the body and blood of Christ, he held that by concomitance the bread is in a figurative and sacramental sense the body of Christ, which the believer receives spiritually. He was condemned by the Council of Constance, 1415 A. D.

†For a long time the Waldensian doctrine of the Eucharist scarcely differed from the Roman. Under the influence of Wycliffe and Huss, the Waldenses first turned against the doctrine of the real presence. As Luther often designated the Bohemian Brethren as Waldenses, it is possible that Zwingli is doing the same here. They had been violently persecuted in the early years of the sixteenth century.

seen portended seven fruitful years, and nobody but a fool can deny that this is the force of the words. "Are" is used here, therefore, beyond controversy for "signify." A little later there follows [Gen. 41: 27], "And the seven lean and thin kine that came up after them, and the seven thin ears that were blasted with the burning wind, are seven years of famine to come, etc." Here again we have "are" used for "signify." Now I come to the New Covenant. In Luke 8: 11, when Christ had signified by the parable of the seed falling upon the ground the varied attitudes of people in receiving the word of God, and the disciples failed to understand and asked what He meant by this parable, He discoursed thus: "The seed," of which they had heard so much—"The seed is the word of God." But no seed is the word of God—the word of God was signified by this term. Here, then "is" is again used for "signifies." A little later [Lk. 8: 14] we have: "And that which fell among the thorns, these are, etc.," that is, "and that which I said fell among the thorns signifies those, etc." And a little later [Lk. 8: 15]: "But that in the good ground, these are, etc."; that is, "but the seed which I said fell in the good ground signifies those, etc." So in Matt. 13: 1-23, in the same parable, "is" is used for "signifies," although the language is a little less direct. In the same passage, when explaining the parable of the tares sown after the wheat, He says [Mt. 13: 38]: "The field is the world." But the field is not the world; but it signified the world in this parable. In the same verse: "The good seed are the sons of the kingdom"; that is, the good seed signifies and denotes the sons of the kingdom. Again, "But the tares are the sons of the evil one"; that is, are the symbol of the impious or the evil. Again [13: 39]: "The enemy that sowed them is the devil"; that is, signifies the evil spirit. Again: "The harvest is the end of the world; and the reapers are angels"; here "is" and "are" are used for "signifies" and "signify" respectively. I think testimony enough has now been adduced to prove that "is" and its cognate forms can be used to mean "signify." But since I hear some persons blurt out indignantly, "If we are to force any word we please thus to signify anything we please, nothing in the Holy Scriptures will retain its integrity, for license will be given the impious to twist everything into anything you like," it is worth while to give them an answer rather more polite than their objection. Who does not know, then, that there is absolutely no word that is not sometimes taken out of its native soil and planted in a foreign one, where it has a far higher value than if you had left it in the home ground, that is, in its literal meaning? This was specially customary with the Hebrews beyond other peoples, as is most plainly apparent all through Christ's discourse, even when translated into a foreign tongue.* Take the despised term "dung." When Christ, in Luke 13: 8, makes the husbandman intercede for the barren tree, undertaking to put dung about it, how could He more delightfully have signified a kindly minister of the word, whose duty it certainly is to encourage the backward in every way, and to commend them to the Lord in constant prayers, lest He judge them according to their deserts? Take another term, "stone." Does not this term occupy a more honorable position when it signifies Christ [Mt. 21: 42] the stone, than when it means an inert rock projecting in the field, or even one used in the construction of a building? So also with verbs. Does not Paul use with great effect the verb "run" when he says to the Galatians [5: 7]: "Ye were running well," for "ye were walking uprightly in all diligence"? And when our Saviour says, "I am the door" [Jn. 10: 9], was he a door? Yet, according to the intolerance of those who refuse to admit any extension of the meaning of verbs and nouns, He must be a door. Of wood, then, or of stone, or of ivory or horn, as in Pliny and Homer? "I am the way" [Jn. 14: 6], "I am the vine" [Jn. 15: 5], "I am the light" [Jn. 8: 12], etc., force us in spite of ourselves to allow them a signification other than the literal one. Is He a vine? No, but He is like a vine. There is, therefore, no need of this senseless wail: "Look out, fellow citizens, your interests are in jeopardy, you are going to lose your language"; for we cannot conveniently use even every-day speech without metaphors and metalepses. With faith as teacher, then, we shall see in what sense we ought to take each expression; for otherwise we should be doing a thing absolutely unworthy both of Christ and of ourselves in regarding him as actually a lamb or a ram in John [1: 36; 21: 15-17], and as a fatted calf in Luke [15: 23].

*Namely, Greek.

When, therefore, He says [Jn. 15:5], "I am the vine," He is saying nothing else than, "I am like a vine to my disciples." Who will make an uproar here? Who complain that an outrage is done? So, also, in our passage we must consult faith, and if she says that in the expression, "This is my body," this verb "is" must not be taken in its literal meaning, we must by all means obey faith and have no fear whatever of those whom we see daring everything in their impiety, for they cannot, however much they rave, wrest the truth out of the hands of the pious. If, however, faith cannot endure this meaning, then the signification of this word in this passage—as was made plain above by many arguments and is made singularly and solidly plain by the expression, "The flesh profiteth nothing"—will be an altogether different one, whatever outcry is made by the ignorant and impious. This verb "is," then, is in my judgment used here for "signifies." Yet this is not my judgment, but that of eternal God; for we cannot boast of anything which Christ wrought not in us, Rom. 15:18; and it has been abundantly shown above that since faith is from the unseen God, it points to the unseen God and is a thing absolutely independent of all sense. For whatever is body, whatever is an object of sense, can in no way be a matter of faith. Hence, when I say that in my judgment this word is used in this way in this passage, I speak thus for the sake of certain weak persons, and not because this view can truthfully be shattered by means of any passage of Scripture. For either we must reject "The flesh profiteth nothing," which yet it were impious to do (for "it is easier for heaven and earth to pass away than one tittle of the word of God" [Lk. 16:17]), or this alone must be the one simple meaning.

We must, then, now first of all see how everything squares if we use "is" for "signifies" in this fashion. And as everything will square beautifully, it will be proved at the same time that "is" in this passage as well as in others must be taken for "signifies," which was the second thing I undertook to prove. Thus, then, Luke [22:19] has it, and we shall content ourselves with him from among the Evangelists: "And he took bread, and when he had given thanks, he brake it, and gave to them, saying, This signifies my body which is given for you: this do in remembrance of me." See, faithful soul but captive of absurd notions, how everything squares here, how nothing is violently taken away or added, but everything squares so perfectly that you wonder you have not always seen this meaning, and wonder all the more that the beautiful harmony of the discourse in question has been so recklessly mangled by certain persons. "He took bread, gave thanks, brake it, and gave to them, saying." Behold how there is no missing link here! "This (that I offer you to eat, namely) is the symbol of my body which is given for you, and this which I now do, ye shall do hereafter in remembrance of me." Does not the saying, "Do this in remembrance of me," plainly indicate that this bread should be eaten in remembrance of Him? The Lord's Supper, then, as Paul calls it [I Cor. 11:25-26], is a commemoration of Christ's death, not a remitting of sins, for that is the province of Christ's death alone. For He says: "This which I now bid you eat and drink shall be a symbol unto you which ye shall all use in eating and drinking when ye shall make commemoration of me." And that nothing needful for the true understanding of this commemoration may be lacking, Paul, in I Cor. 11:26, after having said with regard to the bread as well as with regard to the wine, "This do in remembrance of me," explains as follows: "For as often as ye eat this bread" (symbolical bread, namely, for no one of them all calls it flesh), "and drink this cup, proclaim* the Lord's death till he come." But what is it to "proclaim the Lord's death"? To preach, surely, to give thanks and praise, as Peter says, I Pet. 2:9: "That ye should shew forth the excellencies of him who called you out of darkness into his marvellous light." Paul, therefore, reminds us that even unto the end of the world, when Christ will return and contend in judgment with the human race, this commemoration of Christ's death should be so made that we proclaim the death of the Lord, that is, preach, praise, and give thanks. For this reason the Greeks called it "Eucharist."

Now we will come to the words of the cup, in which our view is found more clearly expressed. But first I will remind

*Annunciate: Gk. καταγγέλλετε. Luther, also, and the margin of the King James Version represent the Greek verb as imperative. The Latin Vulgate has *annunciabitis*.

you that "cup" here is used for "drink," the container for the thing contained. Thus, then, it reads [Lk. 22: 20]: "This cup, the new testament in my blood, which is shed for you, etc." We will examine the individual words here. The cup is called the new testament. We know the article ἡ in this place has the same force as "is," as also in Hebrew "hif" and "hu" [הִוא and הוא]; for Paul in I Cor. 11: 25 used both the article and the verb "is": ἡ καινὴ διαθήκη ἐστίν, illud novum testamentum est. Yet, lest some detail should be wanting, I have preferred to say "illud," [the], that there may be no point open to captious criticism in what I say. Well, then, is the cup this new testament? Certainly it is. Truth says so. But this new testament has its force nowhere but in the death and blood of Christ; nay, the death and blood are the testament itself. But if the cup is the testament, it is argued that this cup is the true and sensible blood of Christ; for this, shed for us, sanctified the testament, ratified and confirmed it. Here also I shall disagree with great men, though it is not I that disagree but the fact itself. For what would it matter if I disagreed ever so widely, if the fact yet were otherwise? "Testament," then, is used here in an unusual sense for the "sign" or "symbol of the testament," just as a document is said to bear witness, though it does not breathe or speak, but is the sign of something said or done by somebody who did once breathe. Another even clearer illustration: The document is sometimes spoken of as the testament, as is often the case in Cicero: "The testament was opened, read, etc."; yet not the writing but the goods bequeathed were the testament. For what would it have profited to have had the writing bequeathed? But the writing merely contained what legacy should be given to each heir. So also in this passage the testament is the death and blood of Christ, and the document, in which are contained the subject and description of the testament, is the sacrament in question; for in this we commemorate the blessings that Christ's death and the shedding of His blood have brought us, and enjoying these blessings we are grateful unto the Lord God for the testament which He has freely bestowed upon us. The testament, therefore, is opened and read when Christ's death is proclaimed; the testament is distributed when each man trusts in the death of Christ, for then he enjoys the heritage. And that this cup is used thus as the symbol of the true testament the words themselves indicate, when He says, "This cup, the new testament," that is, the sign and instrument of the testament, "is in my blood." He does not say, "This cup, which is the new testament, is my blood," but, "This cup is the new testament in my blood." And these things, of which one is in the other, are distinct from each other, as thing and thing, in their real nature, as the philosophers say. Furthermore, things which in their real nature are distinct cannot possibly so coincide as to be the same thing. For what is in something else is not that very thing in which it is. What reason, then, was there, when the other Evangelists, Matthew [26: 28] and Mark [14: 24], had said, "This is my blood of the new testament," for Luke [22: 20] and Paul [I Cor. 11: 25] to say, "This cup is the new testament in my blood"? There seems to be a strange discrepancy here, for the former call it the "blood of the testament," the latter "the testament of the blood," that is, "the instrument and sign of the testament which has its force in the blood of Christ." This was all done designedly. For Luke and Paul, writing after the others, introduced new clearness into their words. They saw that the words, "This cup is my blood," were too bold for the comprehension of some persons, although (as we see in Tertullian, of whom later) clear enough to the men of an earlier time, and therefore they thought that not every one would be sure to understand the expression as meaning, "This cup is the symbol of my blood, which is the blood of the new testament" (for that is the force of the article τὸ *). Consequently, they shaped the expression differently: "This cup is the new testament," that is, "This is the cup of the new testament, which new testament has its force in my blood"; for both Matthew and Mark said in the genitive case, "Novi testamenti," what Luke and Paul said in the nominative, "Novum testamentum." Hence also they used "is the new testament," in an unusual sense, for "is the symbol of the new testament," just as we call the document in which bequests

*In Mt. 26: 28 the Greek text used by Zwingli had: τοῦτο γάρ ἐστιν τὸ αἷμά μου τὸ τῆς καινῆς διαθήκης. The second τὸ is referred to in his comment.

are contained a testament, and name the statue of Caesar "Caesar." It is, then, the symbol of the new testament. This idea will be made more clear if we consider carefully the articles in all four writers. For these, namely, ἡ and τό*, are by no means relative, but point out something as distinct and solid. When, therefore, the words of the cup run: "This cup is the new testament in my blood," where "in my blood" can have no other meaning than that the testament "has force in my blood," it is plain that the words of the bread must in like fashion be taken in the sense: "This (that I bid you eat, namely) is a symbol of, or signifies, my body which is given for you." Now I want no one to suffer himself to be offended by this painstaking examination of words; for it is not upon them that I rely, but upon the one expression, "The flesh profiteth nothing" [Jn. 6: 63]. This expression is strong enough to prove that "is" in this passage is used for "signifies" or "is a symbol of," even if the discourse itself contained absolutely nothing by which the meaning here could be detected.

Paul must be consulted in another passage also, that we may see more clearly how Christ's disciples used this sacrament in the time of the Apostles. In I Cor. 10: 16 we have: "The cup of blessing," *i. e.,* of the bounty and munificence of God, "which we bless," *i. e.,* with which we give thanks, "is it not the communion of the blood of Christ?" That is, when we drink together from this cup which Christ has given us as a symbol of His bounty, do not we alone drink who share in the blood of the testament? He, therefore, who drinks here, shows himself to all the brethren as one of the number of those who trust in the blood of Christ. For that this is the only natural meaning of these words is clearly proved by certain marks which presently follow. "The bread which we break," with one another, namely, "is it not the partaking of the body of Christ?" [I Cor. 10: 16]. That is, when we break the bread with each other, do we not all, as many as are the body of Christ, mutually disclose and show to one another that we are of the number of those who trust in Christ? Now follows a mark by which it is seen that this is the sense here, and that '"body" is here used otherwise than "symbol of the body," namely, for "the

*With διαθήκη and αἷμα respectively.

Church." For He says [I Cor. 10:17]: "Seeing that we, who are a multitude, are one bread, one body: for we all partake of the one bread." We see here and in Chapter 11:17-34 most clearly that the use of this sacrament in Paul's time was as follows: The disciples of Christ came together and ate their whole supper together from the beginning, and some made rather pretentious and sumptuous provision for themselves. Hence arose shame and scorn unto those who had little. Some hurried, while others were slow; and so it came about that some had finished and were waiting for the symbolical bread, while others were still without supper when the bread and cup began to be carried round. So Paul bids them eat at home, and not contemn the church, that is, the congregation of God. However, he bids them eat at home not the symbolical bread and blood, but their ordinary supper. When, therefore, they were gathered together in this way to give thanks and praise unto the Lord, they were warned not to eat without judgment; whence he says [I Cor. 11:28-34]: "But let a man prove himself, etc." For whosoever eats of this symbol shows himself to be a member of the Church of Christ. Therefore he may not thereafter eat of the things offered to idols [cf. I Cor. 8:1-13], nor sit at such meals [cf. I Cor. 10:17], who has sat at the symbolical board of Christ (for that is Paul's trend in this passage). For those that eat and drink at that board become one body and one bread; that is, all who assemble there for the purpose of proclaiming the Lord's death and eating the symbolical bread certainly show that they are the body of Christ, that is, members of His Church, which, as it has one faith and eats the same symbolical bread, so is one body and one bread. Thus it becomes clear that Christ wished to give us bread and wine as food and drink, because as these two are combined each into one body from numberless grains or atoms of flour or drops of the juice of the vine respectively, so we come together into one faith and one body. Hence also the Greeks called the Supper by the other name, σύναξις,* [gathering], because by this symbol all who had thus assembled were gathered together

*cf. Stephanus, *Thesaurus linguae Graecae*, vii, 1219: σύναξις peculiariter dictus est a quibusdam theologis conventus, qui fiebat ad celebrandam coenam domini, item celebratio ipsius coenae.

into one body.

But the passages in Acts which speak of the breaking of bread especially make for this view, if, as some think, they are to be understood of the communication of the symbolical bread. And it plainly cannot be denied that the first mention of the breaking of bread, in Acts 2: 42, must be understood of this symbolical bread, since it reads: "And they continued steadfastly in the apostles' teaching and fellowship, and in breaking of bread, and in prayers." For, a little later [Acts 2: 46] mention is made of bread, that is, bodily food, and of their habit of breaking it from house to house. It is, therefore, plainly apparent that this bread was in use with the Apostles in the way I have said, as you can easily deduce from what precedes and what follows. Hence also it is clearer than day that circumcision and the Passover, which could not take place without blood, were through Christ, who puts an end to all blood with His blood, changed to these elements so kindly to man, so that we see the savagery of the Law transformed into the blessing of Grace. The Law was consecrated with the blood of beasts, and initiation into its service was by the blood of circumcision. Into the service of Christ, who with His own blood consecrated an eternal testament, we are initiated by the outpouring of water, so that we may see that the fire of burnt offerings was put out by the blood of Christ. The Passover was a commemoration and festival celebration by which thanks were rendered unto the Lord for the deliverance from the slavery of Egypt. But, that no trace of the bloody Law might remain, He wished His festival or commemoration to be celebrated with the symbol of things most kindly to man, namely, bread and wine, and in this fashion baptism is our circumcision, the Eucharist our Passover, that is, the commemoration, festival, or celebration of our redemption. It is, therefore, false religion which taught that the use of this symbolical bread destroys sins; for Christ alone destroys sins by His death. But He died once only, as we see in Rom. 6: 10 and in the whole Epistle to the Hebrews [cf. Heb. 7: 27; 9: 12, 26]. Having, therefore, died once, He forever has power to blot out all the sins of all. It is false religion which taught that this bread is a work or an offering which, offered daily, expiates our sins, as I have showed elsewhere by many proofs, but most briefly of all against Jerome Emser the Ibex,* where I reduced the whole matter to two very short syllogisms, which I shall not be sorry to insert here. But first I must make here the introductory remarks that I made there.

From the "Reply to Emser"†

The New Testament is eternal, as is clear from Isaiah 9:2 and Jeremiah 31:31. Therefore the blood also on which the New Testament rests and with which it is sprinkled must be eternal; for it is the blood of the eternal Son of God, I Peter 1:19; Heb. 9:14.

1. The blood of Christ alone takes away our sins; for He is the only one who takes away the sins of the world and who has reconciled all things through His blood, Col. 1:20. For if sins could have been expiated in any other way, Christ would have died for nought, and those who eat Him would still hunger, those who drink Him would none the less thirst. Far be this from the minds of believers. He Himself, lifted up from the earth, has drawn all things to Himself [cf. Jn. 12:32]. But sin also is not removed without blood, Heb. 9:22.

II. But the blood of Christ was offered once only; for it is the eternal blood of God's eternal Son. Heb. 9:12: "Through his own blood he entered in once for all into the holy place."

III. Therefore the blood of Christ, offered once for all, endures forever to remove the sins of all men.

In the second place, observe the following:

I. Christ is offered only when He suffers, sheds His blood, dies. In fact, these are equivalent. Proof: Paul says, Heb. 9:25-26: "Nor yet that he should offer himself often . . . else must he often have suffered since the foundation of the world." Therefore "to offer Christ" is for Christ to suffer; for Paul proves that the offering of Christ must be the only offering of the kind, from the fact that He was slain only once. Therefore there is offering only when there is death; for offering follows

*An epithet suggested by the figure of this animal on Emser's coat of arms. See p. 345.

†cf. pp. 392-393.

death. For the offering is accomplished only when that which is offered has been slain.

II. Christ can no more die, suffer, shed His blood, Rom. 6: 9-10: "Christ, who rose from the dead, dieth no more; death no more hath dominion over him. For the death that he died, he died unto sin, and that once; but the life that he liveth, he liveth unto God."

III. Therefore Christ can no more be offered up; for He cannot die.*

From this it is clearly manifest how recklessly the Pope of Rome and all his minions have imposed upon the simple-mindedness of Christians. For what have they not acquired by celebrating the Mass? Whole kingdoms have been given them that they might eat the Lord's Supper for us, and yet they did not eat it at all, but pretended that they were offering Christ for our transgressions. If this custom had come down from the Apostles or from those first brethren of Christ, it would have had something to show for itself; but, as it is, since this ritual of the Mass has absolutely no basis in any institution of Christ or of the Apostles, why, in the Temple, that is, in the Church of God, do we endure this shameless traffic, which breaks out so openly to the dishonoring of Christ? Why do we not bid all these mass-mongers to cease this atrocious insult to Christ? For if Christ has to be offered up daily, it must be because His being offered once on the cross is not sufficient for all time. What greater insult can be named than this? All masses should be immediately abolished,† and the Lord's Supper used according to its institution by Christ. Yet no wrong should be inflicted upon the mass-reciters who have been chosen for this office, but they should be supported in peace as long as they live; but afterwards none should be put in the places of the dead, and their goods should be devoted to benefiting the poor. The objections that are raised to this from the Fathers so-called, from the Councils and Pontifical laws, are so trivial that it is not worth while to refute them. For as, before

*Here ends the quotation from the *Reply to Emser.*

†On April 12, 1525, the Council at Zurich decided that the Mass should be done away with, and on the following day for the first time the Lord's Supper was celebrated in Zurich according to Zwingli's directions.

Christ was born, no one could effect that any offering should save us, so, now that He has reconciled us to God by having once suffered death on the cross, no congegation, no Council, no Fathers, can effect that He be offered up again. For as He has atoned for the sins of all from the founding of the world, so is He even unto the end of the world the bearer of salvation to all who trust in Him; for He is everlasting God; through Him we were created and redeemed. If, therefore, you find anything from Holy Writ distorted into the contrary, do not be troubled, but hasten to the passage thus twisted, and you will immediately discover theft or violence. For example, many men have argued a great deal about the priesthood of Christ, with the object of making themselves out His priesthood; and to support this error they have brought forward the statement in Hebrews 5:1: "Every high priest, being taken from among men, is ordained for men," and many other passages from the same epistle. Yet, when you examine the case more closely, you will see that there is not a better club with which to destroy all their arguments than this epistle; and I advise you to study it carefully. When, therefore, you come to the aforesaid passage, Heb. 5:1, you will find plainly that Paul is explaining the priesthood of Christ by comparison with the high priest of old. It is not a series of sacrificing priests ordained in succession, with new men substituted for the dead. For how could Christ be "a priest for ever" according to the utterance of the prophet [cf. Ps. 110:4], if any one were to succeed to His place? Is He dead or deprived of His office, that any one has to be substituted for Him? Nay, since He sits forever at the right hand of the Father [Mk. 16:19], and forever destroys our sins by the one offering made upon the cross, He does not need that any one should supply His place. And no one can supply His place, save a righteous being who dies for the unrighteous [cf. I Pet. 3:18]; and since none can be or do that save the Son of God, it is impious to talk of an offering priesthood at all. I am not speaking of the ministers of the word and the Church. They are the dispensers of the mysteries, that is, the hidden things of God [cf. I Cor. 4:1], and are not the priesthood of Christ; for that can be nothing else than Christ Himself making satisfaction with the Father for us forever. So priceless is He. And if any one raises also as an objection what is found in Acts 13: 2 in the new translation* of the New Testament, "And as they were sacrificing† unto the Lord," let him know that the Greek is λειτουργούντων; and this word means "ministering" as well as "sacrificing," nor is it used in the Greek anywhere in the whole New Testament where the Lord's Supper is spoken of. Hence it becomes manifest that in this passage "sacrifice" is used not for "offering" or "slaying a victim," but for administering the word; for frequently, all through Paul's Epistles, λειτουργοί is used for "ministers," as in Heb. 1: 14; and λειτουργία for "the ministry of the word," as in Phil. 2: 17. But he explains most clearly in Rom. 15: 16 that by a metaphor he is calling the ministers of the word λειτουργοί or ἱερουργοί because they make offerings, as it were. For as the ancient priests of the mysteries slew animals for a sweet savor unto the Lord [cf. Lev. 1: 9], so shall the ministers of the word turn beastlike men into real offerings to God. For he says [Rom. 15: 15-16]: "But I write the more boldly unto you in some measure, brethren, as one who is reminding you, because of the grace that was given me of God, that I should be a λειτουργός, that is, a minister of Jesus Christ unto the Gentiles, ministering, ἱερουργῶν, the gospel of God, that the offering up of the Gentiles might be made acceptable, being sanctified by the Holy Spirit." By these words of Paul it is made abundantly clear what we ought to understand by "liturgia" in Acts 13: 2 also. For the men enumerated there were ministering the word with painstaking and great soberness, and except for this no mention would be made there of the ministry of the word, which would be foreign to the usage of the Apostles, whose one occupation was preaching the word [cf. Acts 6: 4].

The "Eucharist," then, or "Synaxis," or Lord's Supper, is nothing but the commemoration by which those who firmly believe that by Christ's death and blood they have become reconciled with the Father proclaim this life-bringing death, that is, preach it with praise and thanksgiving.

*By Erasmus; *i. e.*, his second edition, 1519.

†Cum autem illi sacrificarent. The Vulgate has, Ministrantibus autem illis. The Greek is, Λειτουργούντων δὲ αὐτῶν

It follows, therefore, forthwith that those who come together for this practice or festival, to commemorate, that is, to proclaim the Lord's death, bear witness by this very fact that they are members of one body, are one bread; for all who trust in Christ are one body, as Paul bears witness in more than one place, and especially in the above mentioned I Cor. 10:17. He, therefore, who joins with Christians when they proclaim the Lord's death, who eats with them the symbolical bread or flesh, certainly ought afterwards to live according to Christ's directions; for he has given evidence to others that he trusts in Christ. They, therefore, that trust in Him "ought to walk even as he walked," I John 2:6. Hence it came about that those who shared in the communion of this bread expelled from their fellowship by the institution of excommunication any one who too shamelessly went a-whoring or a-drinking, or practiced usury, or worshipped idols, or was a reviler or an extortioner [cf. I Cor. 5:11]. And if this usage had never died out of the church of Christ, the life and conversation of Christians could not help being very good. See, pious heart, how we become feeble and frail when we follow after our own devices. We all wanted to attain salvation by masses, when yet the Lord's Supper, even if celebrated according to Christ's institution of it, would not expiate sin; for that belongs to Christ alone. But it was a sacrament which witnessed before the church that we had sworn allegiance to Christ; and if we did not faithfully live up to this witness we should have been removed from the fellowship of the brethren, that Christian integrity might the better be maintained. What, then, has happened since we have turned this rule of life and discipline of Christian morals to another use? That which we all see with our own eyes: we have become more shameless in our lives than even the Turks and Jews. For you do not find among them such frequent adultery, so many unscrupulous forms of extortion, such beastly drunkenness, such bold robbery, to say nothing of the arrogance of high and low, of the continual wars, vile blasphemy, obscene talk, lying, cheating, and overreaching. Have we not all had our hands full with trying by hearing or hiring or reading masses to drain this universal swamp of evil? This, I believe, no one will deny, that we have all fled for refuge to the mass, as to a sacred anchor [cf. Heb. 6:9]. Nay, we have gone even to such a pitch of madness as to fancy that we saw a bread that brings salvation. Nor have we been content with this; but what we saw we also worshipped, forgetting our own articles so-called, according to which it is agreed among all who have written on the subject, whether of the new school or of the old, that not even the pure humanity of Christ is to be worshipped. "Only God is to be worshipped" [cf. Mt. 4:10], and "No man hath seen God at any time" [Jn. 1:18]. Why, then, do we worship a thing we see, when only God is to be worshipped and we have never seen Him? Whither will they now turn who teach that the Eucharist, so-called, is to be worshipped? Who ever worshipped a thanksgiving? For what is a thanksgiving, or where is it, or how is it? Does it not exist only when thanks are given? So, what is a Synaxis? Nothing, by thunder, but a gathering together, an assembling, a concourse. But who will ever be able to worship that? It is an action, a usage, and exists only at the time when it takes place. The same view is to be taken of the Lord's Supper. It is a supper and a thanksgiving, when it is eaten in conjunction with the proclaiming of the death of Christ. Do we read that any one of the Apostles worshipped the supper when Christ was instituting this commemoration of Himself? Alas for our souls, which are so given to error that, I fear, even though we see the truth itself set before our eyes we yet do not receive it! Whither, then, does our faith tend, or upon what is it based? Does it not tend to God? Why, then, do we still delay to tear our hearts away from ceremonies? Why do we set our hopes upon things upon which the Lord has not commanded us to? Is not our salvation based upon Him who is the Savior of all nations? Why, then, do we seek it in the bread of commemoration? I may add, however, that it is my conviction that this bread and chalice of commemoration are to be treated with all reverence in the church, in which all things should be "done decently and in order," I. Cor. 14:40. But more in my concluding paragraphs.

Now I will cite those of the ancients who, as we shall see clearly from their own words, did not understand that there was in this sacrament or this symbolical bread any bodily flesh or indeed any flesh whatever (for what is the use of calling flesh spiritual, when that would be the same thing as calling fire watery or iron wooden?). Next I will cite those who are silent about the flesh, evidently because they hold the same view as myself, but are by no means silent as to the object for which the Supper was instituted. Thus it will be established that the use of the Eucharist among them was far different from the tradition the Roman Pontiffs have given us. Tertullian in his first book against Marcion* says, "Nor did He, God namely, disdain the bread by which He represents His own body." See how plainly he says that the body of Christ is represented by the bread, not that Christ's body is represented by any visible bread whatsoever, but by the symbolical bread which was used in proclaiming the Lord's death. Hence also I have called it symbolical, because it is at once both sign and seal.

Augustine, though speaking differently in different passages on this subject, yet seems in two places to express clearly what he understands by "body." The first† makes for the view of Tertullian. It is in the introduction to the third Psalm, where he speaks of Christ and Judas thus: "And in the New Testament narrative itself our Lord's patient endurance is so great and so marvellous that He bore so long with him, namely Judas, as if he were good, though He knew his thoughts when He admitted him to the feast at which He committed and delivered to His disciples the figure of His body and blood." How clear this is which Augustine says here! He tells us that Christ bequeathed to His disciples a figure of His body and blood. But in what way did He bequeath to them a figure? By bequeathing, of course, the use of this symbolical bread, by which the Lord's death was represented and figured in a commemorative act by a sensible sign and observance. Or, as manna in the Old Testament foretold and prefigured Christ as the bread to come of the soul, so this bread

*Against Marcion, I: 14. *See* Robertson and Donaldson, eds., *The Ante-Nicene Fathers*, III: 281.

†*Expositions on the book of Psalms;* Psalm 3: 1. *See* Schaff, ed., *The Nicene and Post-Nicene Fathers*, First series; VIII: 4-5.

should call to mind the body of Christ that was slain and His blood that was shed for us.

The same writer in Tractate 27* on John manifestly rejects bodily flesh. First he says: "And He set forth the manner of the gift He was bestowing upon them, the way in which He was giving them His flesh to eat, saying [Jn. 6:25]: 'He that eateth my flesh, and drinketh my blood, abideth in me, and I in him.' The sign that one has eaten and drunk is, namely, this: if one abides in Him and is His abode, if one dwells and is dwelt in, if one clings and is not abandoned. This, therefore, He has taught and in mystic language has reminded us of, that we may be in His body, in His members under Himself as head, eating His body and not giving up unity with Him. But of those who were there most from lack of understanding were offended; for on hearing these words they thought only of flesh such as they were themselves. But the Apostle says, and says truly: 'To understand according to the flesh is death' [Rom. 8;6]. The Lord gives us His flesh to eat, 'and yet to understand it according to the flesh is death.' Yet He says of His own flesh, that it is life eternal. Therefore not even the flesh ought we to understand according to the flesh, as is shown in the words: 'Many therefore'—not of His enemies but—'of his disciples, when they heard this, said, This is a hard saying; who can hear it?' [Jn. 6:60]. If His disciples found this saying hard, what of His enemies? And yet it behooved that to be said so as not to be understood by everybody. The secret things of God ought to make men earnestly attentive, not hostile, etc." From these words of Augustine we see plainly that he held the view that the flesh of Christ is not even to be considered, as a little later in the same tractate† he declares more openly, saying: "If Christ has profited us much through His flesh, how is it that the flesh profiteth nothing? But through the flesh the Spirit wrought for our salvation. The flesh was a vessel. Note what it held, not what it was." Lo, again he says that we are not to trouble about what the flesh is! Why, then, do we look only at the

**Homilies on the Gospel of John,* Tractate 27, §§1-2. *See* Schaff, ed., *The Nicene and Post-Nicene Fathers,* First series; VII: 174.

†§5.

flesh here, which profiteth nothing?

Now I will come to those who have explained the use of this food in such fashion that we see plainly that not only as regards the thing, but as regards its use this sacrament was an altogether different thing to the men of old. Hence I am easily induced to believe that Augustine, an exceptionally keen and clear-sighted man, did not venture to proclaim the truth explicitly in his day, because it had already largely fallen into disrepute. An altogether pious man saw what the sacrament was, and for what purpose it had been instituted, but the notion of bodily flesh had grown very strong.

First, therefore, I quote Origen in two passages for the reason that he seems both in regard to the thing and in regard to the purpose to agree with me. The first passage is in the Homily on Matt. 23: 23, upon the words: "Ye pay tithe of mint and anise and cummin, etc." He says:* "But if we are to adopt a moral interpretation for such words in the gospel, we must know that as mint and anise and cummin are seasonings for foods, not themselves chief articles of food, so in our behavior some things are of prime and necessary importance to the justifying of our souls, such as these weighty points of the Law, judgment, mercy, and faith; while there are other things that season our acts, as it were, commend them, and make them sweeter, as, for instance, abstinence, laughter, fasting, genuflexion, remaining for the collects, assiduity in the communion, and the like, which are not themselves righteousness but are looked upon as adding savor to righteousness." See how he relegates the communion, which in old times was partaken of more frequently than in our day, to a place among unimportant things and ceremonial acts, which he surely never would have done if he had felt and boasted about bodily flesh, as we do. The other passage is in Homily 35† upon the same Evangelist, on these words: "This is mẏ body, etc." Here he immediately adds: "This bread, which God the Word acknowledges to be His body, is the word that nourishes the soul, the word proceeding from God the Word and the bread from the bread

*_Series veteris interpretationis commentariorum in Matthaeum._ Homilia 20.

†_Ibid._ §85, on Matt. 26: 26. (Sometimes cited as _Tractate 35._)

of heaven which was placed upon the table, of which it is written, 'Thou has prepared a table before me in the presence of those who afflict me.' [Ps. 23: 5]. And this drink, which God the Word acknowledges to be His blood, is the word that gives to drink and in goodly fashion exhilarates the hearts of the drinkers; and it is in the cup of which it is written, 'And thy cup which exhilarateth me, how goodly it is!' And this drink is the product of the true vine which saith [Jn. 15: 1]: 'I am the true vine.' And it is the blood of those grapes that, cast into the winepress of the Passion, brought forth this drink. So also the bread is the word of Christ made of that wheat which falling into good ground brought forth much fruit" [cf. Mt. 13: 8]. But why did He not say, 'This is the bread of the new testament,' as He said, 'This is the blood of the new testament'? Because the bread is the Word of Righteousness, by eating which the soul is nourished; while the drink is the Word of the Knowledge of Christ according to the mystery of His birth and passion. Since, therefore, the testament of God was made for us in the blood of the passion of Christ, that we, believing that the Son of God had been born and had suffered according to the flesh, might be saved, and not in righteousness, in which by itself there could be no salvation without faith in the passion of Christ, on this account it was of the cup only that He said: "This is the cup of the testament, etc." It would take too much space to transcribe the whole passage here.

We see by these words that Origen held the view that the essential thing in this sacrament is the faith by which we believe that Christ made sacrifice for us; for He is the food of the soul. And afterwards in the same passage he explains the procedure, saying: "And Jesus always, taking the bread from the Father for those who are keeping this festival with Him, gives thanks, and breaks, and gives to the disciples according as each is capable of receiving; and gives, saying [Mt. 26: 26]: 'Take and eat.'" Lo, he calls it a festival, that is, a celebrating assemblage or gathering of the church! Further, he says that Christ gives according to the capacity of each, which cannot possibly be understood of bodily flesh, for, according to our friends, this is the same in the case of all to whom it is given; but since He gives faith and thanksgiving not in the same measure to all, it is apparent that these are what is spoken of. What follows here in Origen will at first sight seem to his inexperienced reader to have somewhat the appearance of being said of bodily flesh, though nothing is less true, as readily becomes plain if one looks more closely. But what he adds at the end shows with perfect clearness what the Eucharist is to him and what its purpose, when he says: "Then he taught the disciples, who had celebrated the festival with their master" (observe "festival") "and had received the bread of blessing, and had eaten the body of the word" (see whether he thought there was sensible body here) "and had drunk the cup of thanksgiving, etc." Behold the Eucharist, a commemoration, celebration, or proclamation of the death of the Lord! Hilary in Canon 9, treating of the fasting of John's disciples and Christ's, says:* "But in answering that while the bridegroom is present the disciples have no need of fasting, He is teaching the joy of his own presence and the sacrament of the holy food of which none shall be in want while He is present, that is, while he keeps Christ before his heart; but when He is taken away, He says they will fast, because none who believeth not that Christ has risen shall have the food of life. For the sacrament of the bread of heaven is received in faith in the resurrection, and whosoever is without Christ shall be left fasting as far as the food of life is concerned." Hilary means here that the mystery of Christ is the food of the soul, and that as long as He is at hand none need fast, but that when He has been taken away, then shall men fast. They, therefore, for whom Christ has risen, that is, they that attribute to Christ resurrection from the dead, alone properly eat the sacramental bread which is the symbol of the heavenly, while they that are without Christ are left fasting as far as the food of life is concerned. He thinks, therefore, that the Lord's Supper is the symbol of those that trust in Christ, in whose hearts He has risen again, that is, who firmly believe He has risen. For those who believe He has risen must believe that He is true God; and those who believe He is true God cannot help trusting in Him. Therefore, this great authority says: "The sacrament of the bread of heaven is received in faith in the resur-

**Commentary on St. Matthew*, ch. 9, §8.

rection."

And in the thirtieth Canon he says of Judas: "Nor, indeed, could he drink with God who was not to drink in the kingdom, etc." [cf. Mt. 26: 29]. This language also seems to contain something from which we may learn that Hilary did not have the idea that in the Lord's bread is eaten the body of Christ which hung upon the cross, or wailed in the manger, as our friends say; for he says "drink with God," "not "drink the blood." This view about Hilary is strengthened by the fact that he says nothing else at all about the Lord's Supper than these few words. I quote Jerome upon Sophonias, Chapter 3, not because it contributes much to the subject but because it shows a far different view of the Eucharist from that of the Pope. He says,* then: "Even the priests who minister in the Eucharist, and distribute the Lord's blood to His people, are guilty of impiety against the law of Christ, thinking that the words, not the life, of the officiating priest are the essential thing for εὐχαριστία, the Eucharist, and that only the solemn prayer is necessary, not the worthiness of the priest, etc." First he says: "And distribute the Lord's blood to His people"; from which it becomes clear that in Jerome's time the priests did not eat alone, but still administered the Eucharist to the whole congregation, and that they used not only the bread but also the cup. Next he says: "Thinking that the words, not the life, of the officiating priest were the essential thing for εὐχαριστία, the Eucharist." In this statement he is evidently opposing the teaching of the Popes, who do not deny to the worst of priests the right to officiate at the Eucharist; but Jerome holds the contrary. Yet neither Jerome—begging the pardon of all who are his sworn adherents—nor the Pope speaks rightly about officiating at the Eucharist. Finally, if by "the worthiness of the priest" he means the works of the Law, he is just as much in the wrong as is the Pope, though it is not to the worthiness of the priest but to the solemn prayer that the Pope attributes all efficacy. But if by "worthiness" he understands a Christian life modeled on faith, and holds that this is the essential thing for the Eucharist, he is right; for the Eucharist is the giving of thanks to the Author of their being

**Commentary on Zephaniah,* III: 1-7.

by men, assembled together, who have been renewed through faith and life in Christ.

Augustine in Tractate 84 [§1] upon John, on the words, "Greater love hath no man than this, that a man lay down his life for his friends," [Jn. 15:13], says a little further on: "This doubtless is the thought in the Proverbs of Solomon 23:1-2: 'When thou sittest to eat at the table of a ruler, consider diligently what is set before thee, and put forth thy hand, knowing that thou must provide the like.'* For what is 'the table of a ruler' but the table whence are taken the body and blood of Him who laid down His life for us? And what is 'sitting at it' but approaching it in humility? And what is 'considering diligently what is set before thee' but pondering worthily the great favor shown you? And what is it 'to put forth thy hand, knowing that thou must provide the like' but what I have already said, that as Christ laid down His life for us, so we also ought to lay down our lives for the brethren? For this the Apostle Peter also says [I Pet. 2:21]: 'Christ suffered for us, leaving us an example, that we should follow his steps, etc.'" See for what purpose Augustine says that we eat the body and blood of Christ: for the purpose, namely, of pouring out our life for the brethren just as Christ did for us.

However, lest anyone think that Augustine means by body and blood these bodily things, I will quote also what he had said just before in Tractate 26, after this fashion, "Finally, He sets forth how that is done of which He is speaking, and what it is to eat His body and to drink His blood: 'He that eateth my flesh, and drinketh my blood, abideth in me, and I in him' [Jn. 6:56]. This, then, is to partake of this food and drink this drink: to abide in Christ and to have Him abide in us; and consequently he that abideth not in Christ, and in whom Christ abideth not, beyond a doubt neither partakes (spiritually) of His flesh nor drinks His blood (though he physically and visibly crush with his teeth the sacrament of the body and blood of Christ), but rather eateth and drinketh the sacrament of this great thing to his own judgment, etc." What, pray, could be said more clearly and openly than this?

*The text of the Septuagint is followed in these verses.

What at the same time could be said more carefully? For having said, "though he physically and visibly crush with his teeth," he at once adds, "the sacrament of the body and blood of Christ," that you may not think this is to be understood of the bodily flesh of Christ. This, he means, is to eat carnally, when one eats sacramentally; but to eat sacramentally cannot be anything else than to eat the sign or symbol. Again, let no one think it a trivial thing that he spoke of "eating sacramentally," as if such partaking detracted from Paul's words in I Cor. 11: 27: "He that eateth and drinketh unworthily, eateth and drinketh judgment to himself, etc." For someone might say: "If I eat only sacramentally, how can I 'be guilty of the body and blood of the Lord?'" Augustine, therefore, blunts the point of this thoughtless objection by saying, "but rather eateth and drinketh the sacrament of this great thing to his own judgment." See first how he says not "this great thing," but "the sacrament of this great thing." Of what thing? Of this, that through faith we are in Christ and He in us. Therefore, continuing to speak carefully, he declares that those who merely eat the sacrament of faith in Christ eat and drink judgment to themselves; meaning, besides, that this sacrament ought not to be eaten by anybody but one who trusts in Christ.

Also in Book 3 of "The Agreement among the Evangelists," Chapter 1, giving the reason why John said nothing about the body and blood when he was describing the supper and the washing of the feet, he says: "John says nothing in this passage about the body and blood of the Lord, but he plainly bears witness elsewhere much more fully as to the Lord's having spoken upon this point." Augustine, therefore, thinks the same kind of eating necesary here, as far as the thing itself is concerned, that is treated in the sixth chapter of John. And this is to have faith in the Gospel word. We do not, therefore, according to his opinion, in any other way eat Christ than through faith, trusting in Him as the sure pledge of salvation.

I have quoted these things from the weightiest of the Fathers, not because I wish to support by human authority a thing plain in itself and confirmed by the Word of God, but that it might become manifest to the feebler brethren that I am not the first to put forth this view, and that it does not lack very strong support. For I call God to witness that for the glory of Him alone I secretly considered this matter with various learned men for several years, for the reason that I was unwilling to spread among the crowd thoughtlessly and recklessly anything that might give rise to some great commotion. But the more persons I conferred with, the more I found who assented to this view. Therefore I prayed frequently that the Lord would show a way by which all should learn to know how much less difficult than we all thought is this thing which in the judgment of the simple is by far the most difficult; and a way, too, by which, as far as usefulness is concerned, it would be of more service and use in the church than anything else. For what has opened the door more widely to all sorts of vice than that when sinning shamelessly we have not kept away from this communion? Or what could have more persuasively invited to mutual love and favor than the frequent pouring into the ear and the heart that Christ of His own free will died for poor mortals and His enemies? Or how could any one have better defended himself against the risk of shame from adultery, usury, vanity, pride, arrogance, greed, and the other vices, than by sitting again and again at the table from which many had been turned away in dire disgrace, where daily examples were made? Seeing, therefore, that the original use of this sacrament would do so much good, I prayed earnestly to the Lord, as I have said, that He would show me the way to approach so delicate a matter wisely, and He answered my earnest prayers. Thus at length I came to the conclusion that it would be of advantage if the mass should be overturned; and I hoped that when that had been overturned the Eucharist could be restored in its purity. I saw no more effective armor for this conflict than the sixth chapter of John. There that indestructible adamant, "The flesh profiteth nothing," is so firmly imbedded in its form and substance that it stands uninjured, however you beat upon it, and all opposing weapons are shattered without even making a dent in it. Next to this passage the best adapted to the purpose seemed to be John 1:18: "No man hath seen God at any time." This forbids the worshipping of anything that is the object of sight or touch. Finally, it was necessary that the original use of it, of the Eucharist, I mean, should be set forth. When this was once understood, those empty hopes and monstrous notions would fall to pieces of their own accord. I communicated this plan to many persons; but before the matter had come to anything, some pamphlets came out breathing threats;* and then those who had not strength or light enough attacked the subject on a side where victory could not be won. Thus does divine power make a laughing-stock of human affairs. In these circumstances I was forced against my will to publish this view of mine, since many brethren everywhere demanded it, even to the point of harshness. And I sent to the Evangelist of Reutlingen, a man personally unknown to me, a letter,† which I hedged about with such a stringent oath that no one should publish it that by the gift of God I have not yet seen it published, though many sincere brethren in the Lord have seen it. But when afterwards I began these Commentaries, what other view was I to hold than that which I had held in the letter mentioned? For I was obliged to furnish the Commentaries: I had promised this to not a few of the best and most learned men in France. I pray the Lord, therefore, before whom I stand today and lift up hands clean of every desire to make trouble or win renown [cf. I Tim. 2:8], that, if this which I have set forth is the true purport of this institution of His, as in my own mind I am absolutely sure that it is, He will through that grace with which He has pitied the whole human race open the eyes of all, that each and every one may recognize and cease to worship the abomination (for it must be the greatest of all abominations when the creature is set up in God's place) which has established itself in the place that is God's. For since God alone is to be worshipped [cf. Mt. 4:10], and absolutely no creature, so that even the theologians declare that Christ's pure humanity cannot be worshipped without risk of idolatry, is it not the height of impiety to worship the bread? And what does it amount to when they say they worship not

*At the end of the year 1524 and in January, 1525, appeared, in two parts, Luther's pamphlet, *Wider die himmlischen Propheten, von den Bildern und Sakrament.*

†*Ad Matthaeum Alberum de coena dominica epistola.* (Dated November 16, 1524.)

the bread, but the body of Christ? Do they not worship the creature? Where, then, are their decrees, by which, as I have said, they forbid the worship of the human? But, again, they say: "We worship and even eat the spiritual body of Christ." What, by Almighty God, is the spiritual body of Christ? Do we find anywhere in the Scriptures any other spiritual body of Christ than either the Church, as in Eph. 4: 4 and Col. 1: 18, or our faith, which believes He paid the penalty for us upon the cross and is sure of salvation through Him? Why, pray, do we burden pious hearts with words of this kind, which no intellect can comprehend? "Spiritual body" man comprehends as little as if you were to say "bodily mind" or "fleshy reason." Do we not eat Christ's body spiritually when we believe that He was slain for us and trust in Him? Are not spirit and life forthwith in us? Why do we continue to link together incongruous words simply to weave this long rope of contention? Let us speak plainly! We eat spiritually when through the grace of God we come to Christ. To eat the body of Christ spiritually, then, what is it but to trust in Christ? Why do we think up strange inventions which cannot possibly hold together? "I am the light of the world," says Christ [Jn. 8: 12]. Since, then, He is the light, who will believe that He has thrust us into such darkness as this, in which faith is weakened rather than strengthened? What I say is true and found to be so. For when the human heart is safe through Christ by faith in God, does it not possess the crowning blessing of salvation? It certainly does. What, then, do you suppose happens to it when it is driven into things so disparate and so abhorrent to all understanding? It simply begins to waver, by Heaven. You will say: "Faith can do all things; and unless you have it, you cannot be saved." I answer, that in this way everybody is imposed upon. Those who hold this hard doctrine demand faith tremendously in this instance, though at other times they do not attribute very much to it. That is about what those do who out of their fleshly minds, as Paul says, Eph. 4: 14 and Col. 2: 18, assert anything they please. When you press them so hard that they are forced either to give in or to turn and flee, they take refuge in faith; when if they really had faith they never could have made any such assertion. For those who trust in Christ neither hunger nor thirst for anything else [cf. Jn. 4: 14]; for they have already the food by which the soul is revived. Therefore they ascribe to faith what she does not recognize nor suffer to be attributed to her, as has been abundantly proved above.* Hence they do her no small wrong when they give her credit for establishing the presence of the bodily flesh of Christ. And this for two reasons: [I.] First, because they say that this bodily flesh exists through our faith; for faith protests. And it will have to be admitted that this great thing, as they represent it, exists of itself rather than through our faith. For faith is directed to things that exist before you put faith in them. Our faith, therefore, cannot produce this flesh. This I should not have said if there were not certain persons who seek such poor shelter under faith as to venture to say that this flesh exists through faith. What more foolish than this can be said? Can our faith cause bread to be flesh? This must be proved conclusively by the word of God, where faith has its abode, not thrust upon faith by force. [II.] Second, they do wrong to faith because they say it saves us. This is, to be sure, true in itself, but in this instance it is as far from the truth as darkness is from light. For they are putting up a pretext, as if this faith saves which believes that bodily flesh is in the bread or is the bread itself. But this is said without the authority of the word; for nowhere do we read: "Verily, verily, I say unto you, that he that believeth that in this bread he eateth my bodily flesh shall be blessed." Nay, another very great error would follow, namely, that there are two faiths effective for salvation: one that by which we trust in Christ, the other that by which we believe that this bread is flesh. For they say: "Unless you believe that the thing is so, you cannot be saved." See how human reason, willingly and knowingly, finds darkness in the midst of light, in order to grope in it and by groping and searching to gain a reputation for cleverness among the simple. For where in Scotus and Thomas† is there such zeal and diligence in investigating the changing of the bread and wine into body and blood as there is display of cleverness? They imitated physicians

*See p. 199.

†Duns Scotus (1265?-1308?) and Thomas Aquinas (1225?-1274).

unskilled in their profession, who, in order to seem learned, by means of drugs cause you at a period foretold by them to experience a more severe attack of some trifling ailment, that by their affording relief they may be regarded as gods. Do we not see that this is like the case we have under discussion? These men taught, in the first place, that the bodily flesh of Christ, as it wailed in the manger and as it hung upon the bloody cross (they might at least have said, as it entered into the disciples through closed doors after the resurrection), is eaten here. And, in order not to seem bad teachers, they got up a wonderful maze of argument to show that the thing was so, and they led about in a labyrinth, as it were, the stolid minds that never really believed the thing or at least refused to take a clear look at what is the truth, showing them one form after another until they took away all concern for the way out. After this was in great measure taken away, they proceeded to tyrannize over those who wanted to look into things a little more carefully. They called those heretics who strove to teach that which is true. Why go into detail? When they were going to sell this bread of communion like any other commodity, they needed to make it something that all should look upon with wondering admiration, so that they could increase the price. They began, therefore, to make the bread flesh, disregarding the saying, "The flesh profiteth nothing." I beg all, therefore, who read these words of mine, by that faith by which we all are saved, not to condemn or reject forthwith what they hear, even if it seems to them perfectly absurd, but to pray the Lord to give them the true light of understanding, by which they shall be able to see what is true and right and holy. The face of Truth is glad and by no means arrogant, but she is also inaccessible to flattery. Hence they whose consciences are bad dare not at first sight gaze upon her steadily and fearlessly; but when they have again and again got a taste, as it were, of looking at her, she will begin not to disturb them. Almighty God grant that we may all learn that that only is true religion by which our hearts cling to Him solely and alone, imitate Him alone, desire to please Him alone, hang upon His will alone. And may He grant, on the other hand, that we may see that these elements of the world make us not a whit better, but that, if you concede too much to them, they rather draw you away from the true worship of God. Thus shall we convert to the benefit of the poor (and thereby truly worship Christ) the expense that we have hitherto lavished in gold and silver and gems and other precious things upon the worship of the god Maozim,* whom we have honored in the holy place, according to the words of the eleventh chapter of Daniel, though we knew him not; and our hearts, which hitherto have been tossed hither and thither by false hopes, will be fixed upon the one God through the everlasting pledge, His Son. Amen.

[19.] Confession

The truly sacred writings know of no other confession than that by which a man comes to know himself and to throw himself upon the mercy of God, according to the word of the prophet, Ps. 32: 5: "I said, I will confess my transgressions unto the Lord; and thou forgavest the iniquity of my sin." As, therefore, it is God alone who remits sins and puts the heart at rest, so to Him alone ought we to ascribe the healing of our wounds, to Him alone display them to be healed. For who ever uncovered a wound to any other than the physician or the person who he hoped could give him helpful advice? Just so is it with confession: it is God alone that heals our hearts; to Him alone, therefore, is the wound to be disclosed. But if you do not yet quite know the physician or are not sure where he dwells, no one forbids your unbinding your wound before a wise counsellor and begging him to give you advice. And if he is a wise and faithful man, he will be sure to send you to a physician who is so skilled in his profession that he can sew up your wound. I will now explain the parable. The man who knows not the physician is he that has not yet come to a right knowledge of grace through Christ, and yet, such is the nemesis of conscience, is seeking to lay down the burden by which he is oppressed. The sage and faithful counsellor is the minister of the word of God, who, like the good Samaritan, pours wine and oil into the wounds [Lk. 10: 34]. The wine signifies the sharpness of repentance, to which he leads the man

*So the Latin Vulgate: Daniel 11: 38.

when he sets him before his own eyes so that he may learn to know himself, or sometimes drags him in spite of his resistance to a knowledge of his hypocrisy. It is a bitter and sharp thing that you are thoroughly bad within to the very core; it is a still more bitter thing that you cannot deny your wickedness; it is the most bitter thing when you realize that you are dead and that your hopes have failed. Then the wound begins to burn. Presently, therefore, the minister of the word should pour in oil, that is, Christ, who is anointed beyond all with the oil of gladness, that is, he should show what grace has bestowed upon us through Him. When the man has learned this, he can no longer be kept from hastening to Him. Auricular confession, then, is nothing but a consultation in which we receive, from him whom God has appointed to the end that we may seek the law from his lips, advice as to how we can secure peace of mind. Behold the Keys, therefore, behold the Gospel, of which enough has been said. The minister of the word, therefore, evangelizes you; and when you have been evangelized, that is, when you have received Christ, you are absolved and delivered from the burden of sin, and this relief you feel in your heart, even if no pontiff pronounces the words of any formula over you. Nonsense and sheer trumpery, therefore, are the promises of the Papalists concerning the Keys. In the same category belong the doctrines of certain reckless persons who have asserted that a man is made sure by the Keys. Unless he is sure within through faith, you will say in vain, "Thou art free." For you can no more make him sure by your words than you can make an elephant of a fly by saying, "You are an elephant." You may teach and expound the meaning of the Gospel, but you do it in vain, unless the Lord give inward teaching. For how many are there who hear and do not receive it [cf. Mk. 4:15]! What is the reason they do not receive it? God hath not drawn them [cf. Jn. 6:44]. As soon as He draws them, they leap over to Him without your help. Unless a man has this certainty of faith, he will be absolved a thousand times by the priest in vain; for he will always go from him in despair and unbelief. And the things concerning confession that have been invented and handed down are as the ocean and Cimmerian darkness, so that it is not at all worth while to refute them. If you examine properly the few things that I add here, you will sail safely through the whole of Scripture, as far as Confession is concerned, easily perceiving that of the auricular confession we have hitherto practiced absolutely no mention is made therein. [I.] To confess is, first, to praise and to give thanks to the Lord; as, "Confess unto the Lord, for he is good," as the children of Israel sang when Pharaoh was drowned.* [II.] Next, to confess is to trust in the Lord, to confess that He is our rock and refuge, as Ps. 105: 1-25 and I John 4: 15-16: "Every one that confesseth that Jesus is the Son of God, etc." [III.] Further, to confess is to acknowledge that of which you are reproached or accused; as those whose consciences were pricked by the preaching of John acknowledged that the case was as he taught. So today those confess their sins who when they hear the word of God are conscience stricken so that they recognize their trouble, and straightway betake themselves to the physician. [IV.] Finally, we confess our sins when we inform our neighbor or some learned scholar of our secret guilt, in order that he may join us in asking forgiveness of the Heavenly Father, or may find counsel, as has been said, that will enable us to resist evil thereafter. Of this confession, James, 5: 16, says: "'Confess your sins one to another, and pray one for another, that ye may be healed; for the continual prayer of a righteous man availeth much." Relying upon this passage, the Papalists have defended auricular confession hitherto, though St. James is not speaking of that, but of the confession which every man makes to his neighbor when he discloses to him some internal and hitherto hidden wound. Hence, nothing more can be wrung from this passage than that every man should go to his neighbor and ask him to pray with him for his shortcomings. And in order that he may do this more earnestly, he exposes the foulness of his wound. In a word, he makes sufficient confession who trusts in God, as was said in the second article above; who praises Him and gives thanks for blessings bestowed, as in the first article; who acknowledges his sins and deplores them before the Lord, as

*The quotation is not from Exod. 15, as one might surmise from the words that follow, but from Ps. 136: 1. Probably verses 13-15 led him to think the whole Psalm was sung on the occasion of Pharaoh's destruction.

in the third; who fervently prays for forgiveness with the help of brethren, as in the last. He, I say, makes sufficient confession who is so minded, and he has no need of any priest. But he who has not been taught after this fashion certainly has very great need of a priest. But of what sort of priest? Not of one who gets into the treasure chest with false keys, but of one who by the word of God teaches men to recognize their misery, and grace as well. Secret confession, therefore, is a consultation, the Keys are the expounding of the gospel, and all else is mere windy gabble of the Papalists. But there are those who say that many persons will perpetrate many misdeeds when they are not obliged to confess. To such I answer: You are either inexperienced or hypocrites; inexperienced, because you have not learned that nobody ever refrained from misdoing on account of confession, whereas we know that, on the contrary, if they were ashamed to confess, many have refrained from confessing what they had done; hypocrites, because no person can help knowing how recklessly he conceals things and even feigns righteousness where he wishes to give the impression that he has made a clean breast of everything and has felt sincere sorrow. Yet, we still venture to defend a thing which has been nothing but a means of getting men's goods away from them; for unless the Lord of Hosts had left us the seed [cf. Isa. 6: 13], *i. e.*, had brought back again the light of the gospel, it would have been all over with everybody's goods, earnings, and possessions. Was not the Pope of Rome saying that all realms are his? We have ourselves seen the legate of the Pope of Rome putting up the claim at Zurich that a certain house belonging to the priory, as they call it, was his. Let us, therefore, confess frequently to the Lord, let us begin a new life frequently, and if there is anything not clear let us go frequently to a wise scholar who looks not at the pocket-book but at the conscience!

[20]. The Other Sacraments

Confirmation had its beginning when the custom of baptizing infants became common, since among the earliest Christians only those infants were baptized who were engaged in a struggle for life. And yet why was this? Does the danger of death make people more learned in Christian things? No, but an error had been imbibed which held that next after faith baptism washes away sins; and then this error, proceeding in the usual manner to harsher lengths, ventured even to deny salvation to infants, as if, forsooth, Christ were less merciful than Moses, under whom those that had been circumcised or initiated by offerings were counted among the children of Israel [cf. Gen. 17:10-14; Exod. 12:48], even if they did not yet emulate the faith of Abraham, which, indeed, they could not.

Extreme unction, as they call it, is a human office of kindness. The Apostles sometimes anointed the sick, and those began to feel better who just before had been in a poor state of health, Mark 6:13. This James, 5:14, bids men do all the time; that is, visit the sick, and if occasion demands or the sickness allows, the older persons should rub the sick man, anoint him, and pray God to heal him.

Ordination, which, they say, impresses upon the soul a special character, is a human invention, and what is adduced concerning the laying on of hands from Acts [4:30] and from I Tim. 4:14 is trivial. That was an external sign by which they marked out those upon whom the gift of tongues was about to descend, or those whom they were going to send out to the ministry of the word. What has this to do with fashioning the character? The episcopate, that is, the ministry of the word, is an office, not a rank. He, therefore, who administers the word is a bishop, and he that does not is no more a bishop than a man is mayor or judge who does not fill the office.

[21]. Marriage†

I am forced to come back to marriage, because a point which I ought especially to have treated was overlooked above. Marriage is an honorable thing, as the Apostle says, Heb. 13:4. Why, then, do we forbid to some persons a thing even by God's testimony holy and pious and good: to priests, for instance, monks and nuns, and bishops, that is, ministers of the word?

†Cf. Zwingli's *Supplicatio ad Hugonem* (*See* Vol. 1, pp. 150ff.) and his *Eine freundliche Bitte und Ermahnung an die Eidgenossen* (*See* Vol. 1, pp. 166ff.).

(Those others, whom you are forced to acknowledge as bishops because of their official rank, are, as I have said, not "episcopi" [overseers] but rather "aposcopi" [away-seers].) Those, therefore, who forbid wives to ministers of the word build up with words to tear down with deeds. For there is no need of my saying anything here about the lust of the flesh: we all know by experience how chaste and pure we are! Why, then, do we voluntarily invite a scandal into the church of God, when nowhere are wives forbidden by God's commandment? We all know that marriage is a respectable thing, as I have said. Why, then, are we unwilling to allow it to the minister of the word? Instead, when we see that any is weak, we prefer to put up with a whoremonger, to the offence and disgrace of the whole church, rather than with a lawful husband. And yet some say that they shudder at any ministering of a priest who has a wife; for they cannot bear, they say, to see a priest celebrating mass in the church or teaching while his wife is listening and praying, though yet they endure without any offence a most shameless whore, sometimes sitting in one of the very front seats. At this point I might properly deal savagely with men not foolish but wicked; for theirs is the voice not of foolishness but of unrighteousness. The mass is not only worthless but an abomination; and I am not sure but the profit-seeking traffic of masses has deserved that God should have so long endured in His church such foul "spots" (for that is what Peter calls this kind of men [II Pet. 2: 13]). Why, then, does He not wish to see the priest celebrating Mass? Because that which is abominable so pleases us that nothing right either can or ought to please us. We demand masses: therefore let whoremongers celebrate masses, for they are better suited to this abomination than respectable husbands. But let the husband of one wife [cf. I Tim. 3: 2] administer the word in the church of God, lest, when he is teaching that it is not permissible to defraud a brother in his matrimonial affairs, he see present many women whom he has defiled with adultery, and, smitten in conscience, not dare to speak out and to rebuke unfalteringly his own and other men's sins. But more a little later upon marriage, when we come to vows. Here meanwhile I will suggest that the one and only reason, it seems to me, why we refuse marriage to our bishops, in spite of the fact that Paul in making a selection above all prefers a married one, I Tim. 3: 2 and Tit. 1: 6, is that such a countless crowd of priests given over to leisure seems to be a menace if they may take partners to themselves. Some monk will be an heir along with his brother; some nun will put in a claim for an inheritance that has passed to some one else; some priest will be elected into the Council, or perhaps succeed to a magistracy. This is really, in my opinion, the kind of meanness that yet screens itself behind something other than the fact. But why not obviate these evils? Can it not be enacted by law that no priest shall be chosen into the Council? When such a law has been passed, what further danger will threaten? Thus other dangers also could be duly met, and this shameless nastiness be removed from the sight and presence of the faithful. And as far as the exceedingly great number is concerned, why do we not let them die off in peace, and not put any more men into their priesthoods, but convert their goods to the use of the poor, especially since the poor have gone hungry long enough while those others have been filled to bursting? What disturbance, pray, has for some time arisen anywhere in all the kingdoms of the Christian world that was not raised either by the Pope of Rome himself or by those mitred and hatted disciples of his, the bishops and cardinals? Do they not regulate all the policies, fortunes, and decrees of kings? But whence comes this great power? From riches. And whence come the riches? From so many priesthoods, rates, tithes, and other oppressive burdens which would be harder to count up than the stars. Their means, therefore, must be narrowed down to modest limits. But, that no one may be able to complain that the action is taken out of covetousness rather than from zeal for divine things, these persons must be endured until they die off in peace, as I have said. But if some of them with characteristic pertinacity continue to disturb the peace of a commonwealth or kingdom by their power, their wings must be clipped until they no longer can fly so high. But look here, you; what boldness have you? See how ready you are to make a disturbance and to take to plundering! You will crush only those who make a disturbance; those who make no disturbance you will leave free, lest you make a still greater disturbance. Faith must be kept with them as long as they keep it themselves, lest through the habit of breaking faith we degenerate from men into beasts. Look here, you, too; come back and hear the thing out. No private person is to do this, for thus it gradually would come about that anybody could make an attack upon anybody else on some made-up, empty pretence. Leave these things to be arranged by king or magistrate. But look here, you also, you kings and magistrates. Why do you put this money into your own treasury unless forced by extreme need in the defence of your people? Adopt the following rule:

Put the proceeds from the priesthoods, monasteries, rates, revenues, of the departed into the treasury of the poor, not into your own. What these persons have hitherto impiously extorted, give back. Otherwise you would increase more than ever in power and wealth, which render no one humbler or kinder; and so it would eventually come about that on account of your oppressive rule you would make yourselves more hated than you ever would have been if this great increase of wealth had not come to pass. Fortune is accompanied by envy, and the more the former grows, the more the latter at the same time glows. So much briefly as to abolishing the useless priesthood and converting its goods to the use of the poor. For Christians ought to have no priesthood save Christ's; and He is an everlasting priest [Heb. 6: 20], so that none should succeed to His place. But ministers of the word, bishops, that is, watchers who watch over the flock of the Lord, are to be honored with due honor according to Paul's direction [I Tim. 5: 18]. These alone, therefore, we shall have some time in the church of God, when within at most forty years all those that now make us sick and impatient will have moved elsewhere. So long were the Israelites in going from Egypt into the land of Canaan [Exod. 16: 35]; in patient endurance we shall not, I hope, be inferior to them.

[22]. Vows

Some kinds of vows are as impious and as stupid as if one should give a pledge to a king to bring to him without harm to oneself the heads of a thousand enemies. We find that David* and Hercules† made themselves responsible for a number demanded or a task, but no one has ever been so presumptuous as to promise to return safe with that many heads.

When, therefore, certain persons promise chastity, poverty, and obedience, see how they are not acting from knowledge, and how their very zeal is either foolish or feigned.

First, as to chastity. Christ says, Matt. 19:11, that not all men have this, but only those to whom it is given from above. Let those, then, to whom it is given, practice it. Impious, therefore, and quite as ill-mannered as if I should promise a friend to live for a whole year out of his purse, will it be if I promise God to give Him what I cannot even have unless He gives it to me. For is this not promising a friend that you are going to draw your expenses out of his purse? In I Cor. 7:9, St. Paul solves this difficult problem of chastity clearly and at length, saying: "If they have not continency, let them marry: for it is better to marry than to burn." Do you burn, then? Marry; for you do better and more rightly in quenching the flames of ungovernable passion by marrying than in carrying about a mind restless and filthy from burning. And how long you ought to bear the burning no man can tell better than yourself. There are very, very few in the whole number of mortals who do not burn; and I am not sure that there has at any time, to say nothing of today, been one who has not felt the fires of passion; but how fiercely each burns no one can know save Him to whom the heart is known. Since, therefore, no man knows what is in a man, save the spirit of the man, which is in him [I Cor. 2:11], no one can judge for you when you ought to marry or when to remain single. You will, therefore, have to decide alone for yourself whether to take a wife or not. But you will take one when you see that nearly all your thoughts are carried away by the violence of this fire as by a torrent; that fear of God is thrown to the winds, love of Him killed, prayer hindered.

You can, in fact, infer this from the chapter of Paul men-

*See I Sam. 18:25-27.

†An allusion to the twelve labors of Hercules, performed in the service of Eurystheus.

tioned. For when he says [I Cor. 7: 5], "Defraud ye not one the other" (he is speaking of a husband's or wife's withdrawal from intercourse), "except it be by consent for a season, that ye may give yourselves unto prayer. Afterwards come together again, that Satan tempt you not because of your incontinency," it is evident that, to avoid the temptation of Satan, that is, the defilement of fornication and adultery, it is permissible to marry; likewise when our praying is hindered. But how far any one is hindered none knows better than he who feels the thing. If, therefore, you feel, as I have said, your mind reel at the mention of Venus, so that you say, "I would if I might," the flesh surely has the upper hand and will never rest until it has accomplished what it wants. In order, therefore, not to be perpetually burning, marry; "for it is better to marry than to burn." Whoever desires fuller knowledge of this matter should study carefully the chapter mentioned [I Cor. 7].

We, see, therefore, that all alike were spoken to. "If thou hast not continency, marry [I Cor. 7: 9]; and, "if a virgin marry, she hath not sinned" [I Cor. 7: 28]. Therefore, all alike may enter into marriage. For as to the objection made on the score of your vow,* it has no force to invalidate the law of God, so that it is even the height of impiety to override that because of our traditions, as Christ, in Matt. 15: 3, reproached the scribes and Pharisees with doing, when He said: "Why do ye transgress the commandment of God becauuse of your tradition?" I will not mention now how foolish it is to promise a thing which is not in your power. All vows of chastity, therefore, are impious.

The objection, raised by some on account of the Nazarites, Num. 6, has long been obsolete. For the Lord commanded many things of the children of Israel of which He had Himself no need and in which He had no pleasure; but He bade them be done for Him that they might not be done for the Devil. Such were various sacrificial rites. And this is the view to be taken in regard to the Nazarites. There was danger that the Jews would desire their sons to live after the manner of other nations according to some peculiar way of life, and that they would forthwith make vows to that effect. The Lord, therefore,

*The priest's vow of chastity.

gave them a way of life Himself, with which they would be so content as not to turn aside to idolatry. Others, again, cite in objection, "Pay thy vows unto the Most High" [Ps. 50: 14], and "Vow and pay," Ps. 76: 11; but in doing this they only betray their own ignorance, namely, that they have not yet learned that "vows" is used in the Holy Scriptures for voluntary gifts and offerings, not for taking an oath or dedicating the heart. This last is what was demanded by the law [Deut. 6:5]: "Thou shalt love the Lord, thy God, etc." As, therefore, offerings were abolished, so also were vows. For "näder" [נדר] in Hebrew signifies the voluntary offering of anything customarily used by the priests as an offering. In general, all vows can apparently be reduced to two classes. We vow either the things the Lord orders or of our own free will certain things over and above those which the Lord orders. Those, therefore, who vow what the Lord has commanded act presumptuously, for they pretend that they will do more zealously what the Lord orders if they add their own vow or oath than if they listen to the command alone of the Lord. And what else is this but extreme folly and weakness of faith? The faithful man ought to be eager to do the will of God for the reason that his God has ordered this or that, not because he has taken upon himself to do this or that. For, those who are eager to do the commands of God for the reason that they have taken a vow make themselves of more account than God. The man is insubordinate who does not obey the orders of the commander unless he has first promised that he will do so. Everyone ought to do without any vow what is ordered by the law and the government. Moreover, if we vow certain other things than those contained in the law of God, it is in vain; for "in vain do they worship me," says Christ in Matt. 15: 9, "teaching doctrines and commandments of men"; and, in the same chapter, "Every plant which my heavenly Father planted not, shall be rooted up" [Mt. 15: 13]. And what is more foolish than to promise some new things to the Lord, as if we had fulfilled all that had hitherto been commanded and were generously adding on also something extra of our own? Who has ever fulfilled even this one commandment, "Love thy neighbor as thyself"? [Mt. 22: 39]. It becomes plain, therefore, that when we make such vows we fall into what Paul calls ἐθελοθρησκεία [will-worship], Col. 2: 23. For this is nothing else than a worship got up of our own will, and that is nothing but hypocrisy and contempt of the divine law. No one thus far has fulfilled what the Lord has commanded. Why, then, do we who have not attained to the divine commands make up new ones? I will say openly what is true: These vows of chastity, poverty, and obedience are an avoidance and evasion of the divine law, as will be evident presently when I have spoken of poverty and obedience. What is the use of vowing poverty? The Christian heart is not Christian unless it is poor; for "Blessed are the poor in spirit" [Mt. 5: 3]. According to the law, therefore, we ought all to be poor; and those who are not fail to obey the law. Why, then, do they make a vow of the law itself, as if they could keep it better having vowed than by obeying the commandment of God? But if they vow poverty and want of material things, again they act foolishly. For why do you vow what is not in your power? First, if you are rich, it is not necessary for you to vow poverty, but, according to the words of Christ, to sell all you possess and give to the poor [Mt. 19: 21]. This the Lord enjoins. Why do you vow what the Lord enjoins? If, on the other hand, you are poor, why do you vow poverty, which you have to bear whether you will or not? Suppose you vowed that you would be deformed, when you were so before vowing! Next, if God wishes you to be very rich, a king, for instance, or a prince, but to the end that you faithfully dispense what has been entrusted to you, will you vow poverty? Again, when the Lord has refused you riches, but given you a patient heart, so that you can endure cheerfully, and you then vow poverty, are you not more likely to ascribe your bearing a very hard situation with equanimity to your vow than to the grace of God? For if you credited all things to the grace of God, you never would make the vow, but would constantly accommodate yourself to His will.

Now, obedience we all owe to all, for "if anyone shall compel thee to go one mile, go with him two," Matt. 5: 41; and, "Love seeketh not her own," I Cor. 13: 5, but is eager to help others; and, "All things whatsoever ye would that men should do unto you, do ye also the same to them," Matt. 7: 12. The church of Christ is one body, Rom. 12:5, and this body requires before all things that none of its members shall be at variance. Therefore, those who are members of the church of Christ, from the very fact that they are members of one body, ought honorably to direct or to obey each other as the case may be. What need, then, that you should promise obedience, when you owe it so completely that unless you give it you will find an ungracious judge? And as to the emphasis certain persons so arrogantly put upon what is written in I Sam. 15:22, "To obey is better than sacrifice," I answer briefly that, as a rule, it comes to pass by the will of God that if any one tries to abuse His word to serve his own desires he defeats his own ends. And that is the case here. Samuel said to Saul: "Obedience is better than sacrifice"; but of what obedience was he speaking? Of that by which a man binds himself to some party? Not at all, but of that by which he obeys God in spite of all the schemes of man, however fair and good these are in appearance. Saul had been ordered to destroy everything that belonged to the Amalekites [I Sam. 15:3, 9, 21-22]; but he, thinking it better that things should not perish uselessly, saved many sheep for a burnt offering unto the Lord. The Lord is angry at this, and says by the mouth of His Prophet, that it is better for you to obey the voice of God than your own counsel. Obedience, therefore, is preferable to sacrifice, but obedience to God. How necessary to salvation that is has been abundantly said already.

Now I will show, as I promised, that these vows of poverty, chastity, and obedience are an avoidance and evasion of the divine law and will.

Take chastity first. They vow this, which is not in their own power, and on account of it they scorn marriage, and when they ought to be begetting and bringing up children, they defend themselves with their vows; but see how nicely! They go a-whoring more shamelessly than dogs. And if you advise them to abandon the monastery and marry, since they see that continence is denied them, they reply that they are bound by the terms of their vow. See, now, whether this be not overriding the law of God on account of human tradition. I will say nothing of those vile and filthy things that the majority of monks secretly devise from uncontrollable passion, so that it is quite plain that their hearts, and sometimes their bodies also, are defiled with fouler lusts than those living in wedlock; nay, are so vile that they cannot even be compared with respectable marriages. But, however filthy and foul they are, they fail to obey the law of God on account of their vow.

Their poverty is such a no-poverty that nowhere can you find greater riches along with greater peace and quiet than in the monasteries. If you live in the world, even though you are very rich, you have to attend to many things, to run about from place to place, to fear rain, hail, and other inclemencies of weather. These friends of ours neither fear nor trouble themselves about any of these things, but without sweat and blood all things come to them; they toil not, neither cleave the soil with the ploughshare, yet when no market has any pheasants or pigeons, hares or goats, there is nothing in the way of stockfish, sole, mullet and eels that is not brought to them. Truly it is a great achievement to bear their want! Why should I speak of raiment? In winter they keep themselves so warm with skins and wool and fires that they sometimes have to sweat in spite of themselves; in summer their robes are so open to the breeze, they lay aside so completely all heavy clothing, that you might think they could live on air.

Further, their obedience is such that if a parent is in want they are not allowed to help her, even if she has spent all her substance in getting this cuckoo* into that nest. If she is ill, they are not allowed, in consequence of this obedience, to go out and to nurse, to relieve, and to help, in this illness. (I say nothing of the rest of the poor.) When the government demands contributions, they are exempt; when it assigns posts of duty, they object that, bound by their allegiance to God, they cannot fill these. Why continue? They have nothing in common with their toiling neighbors and fellow-countrymen. If war breaks out, they sleep not under the sky, but snoring peacefully in the pleasantest habitations, so that Solomon in all his glory [Mt. 6: 29] could not have enjoyed the delights of this world in such peace and quiet. They owe nothing to anyone but themselves, they look out for no one but themselves. And

*Her own son. The cuckoo is proverbial for ingratitude.

the most outrageous thing of all is that the more wealth they heap up, the more they lavish upon their own pleasures; the more unyieldingly they have resisted the government in bearing the common burdens, the more they expect to be looked up to and to be considered lords of all. They are adored, worshipped, made gods of. You will never see them forbid that being done to them which ought to be rendered unto God alone.

Such are these impious vows, which to these fellows, nay to us fools also, seem so fine. They promise chastity, but are content with having promised, and are more lascivious than goats; poverty, though the King himself has greater lack than they; obedience, which is manifest disobedience to God and foreign to all Christian love. Therefore they betray Christ who bind themselves by these vows. They revolt from the law of God, for they follow their own laws, scorning and rejecting the divine, and they lay aside humanity towards their kin and neighbors. For who is more cruel in commands than they, who holds on more greedily to his own than they? No one can help seeing that this kind of life has been sown by the enemy, that is, Satan, like tares among the wheat of the Lord, Matt. 13: 25. Paul, that most watchful bishop, had zealously tried to guard against this evil, Acts 20: 29 and Col. 2: 18, but we have kept a poor lookout. Now, however, since God has opened our eyes again, let us walk in the light [I John 1: 7], as it were. Let us do away with these evils, but with sense and order, lest the last state become worse than the first [II Pet. 2: 20].

So much on vows, on which I have said more in my "Conclusions."* But, as far as their confutation is concerned, enough Scripture and arguments therefrom have been brought forward here.

[23]. Invocation of the Saints

Invoking the saints has become such a deeply rooted custom everywhere that I was afraid in the beginning that this subject would hardly get a hearing. But my anxiety was groundless, for as soon as faith took root, it brought with it

*His *Auslegen und Gründe der Schlussreden.*

such a clear light of truth that all who saw it cast away hope in any created thing whatever.

The doctrine that the saints are not to be invoked has been for two years now so thoroughly examined, in my books if not elsewhere, and has gained such currency that I can dispose of the matter here in fewer words than would be required if it had never been discussed before. I treated it in the "Archeteles"* first, then in the "Conclusions,"† afterwards in the "Refutation of the Canon of the Mass,"‡ and finally in the "Reply to Emser," where I reduced the whole discussion to the briefest dimensions and so have decided to insert that part of the work here without alteration.

[For this extract from the "Reply to Emser" *see* below, pp. 382-388.]

So much I wrote in answer to Emser.

I have seen meanwhile a pamphlet by a certain great theologian§ among the French (if you take him at his own valuation), but I have been prevented from reading it carefully both by my occupations and by pity for the pamphlet and its author. For the unhappy man is so ignorant of what is meant by God, by man, by faith, hope, saint, pilgrim, advocate, mediator, everything, that if I had never before had faith in the saying, "No man can come to me except the Father draw him" [Jn. 6:44], and that other, "Everyone that hath heard from the Father, and hath learned, cometh unto me" [Jn. 6:45], I should, nevertheless, now be forced to recognize them as most true; since I see so great a theologian taking the Holy Scriptures in hand like a donkey running a solemn ceremony, as the saying goes. I call God to witness that I am sorry for his efforts, which I have not seen. But why should I be sad? The ape is as proud as a peacock of his offspring. Certain good and learned men from France had suggested that I

**See* Vol. 1, p. 286-287.

†*Auslegen und Gründe der Schlussreden.* (July 14, 1523.)

‡*De conone missae epichiresis.* (August 29, 1523.)

§Josse van Clichtove, bishop of Chartres, whose pamphlet, *De veneratione sanctorum,* was published at Paris in 1523. The title page states: Primus, honorandos esse ab ecclesia sanctos, et sedulo a nobis orandos, ostendit. Secundus, rationes eorum, qui contendunt non esse venerandos nec orandos a nobis sanctos, dissolvit.

should write a reply to him by name; but when my brother, Oswald Myconius,* had carefully examined the book, because I had not time to make a résumé of it, and had put the main points together, we both of us had to laugh, for there was such a complete absence of anything solid in it anywhere that we thought the author and his pamphlet quite unworthy of attention. This babyish person does not know that "sancti" are not the same thing as "divi," since those also are called "sancti" who are still on earth; as, "To the saints (sancti) who are at Rome" [Rom. 1: 7]. He does not know what the church is, but thinks that by authority of the church it can be decided that "sancti" are to be invoked and to make intercession. Suppose the church should decree some time that they are all at one and the same time to come down to us! Do things take place in heaven so exactly in accordance with the pronouncements of the church? The fact that Moses prayed, and Abraham, and others, he twists into, "Therefore the saints (divi) are to be worshipped." The way he decks out a worship for them, you would think he had been Master of Ceremonies. He speaks of the saints in heaven as he would of a little brother. He makes no distinction between the promises to the fathers, which all pointed to Christ and concerned things to come, and the promises to us, which likewise point to Him, but have been already fulfilled and are immovable. They had to remind God often of the fathers with whom He had made the covenant; we already enjoy the fruits of the covenant and have no need to pray to God through any save Christ. "For there is none other name under heaven wherein we must be saved but the name of Christ" [Acts 4: 12]; and He Himself tells us: "Whatsoever ye shall ask in my name, he will give it you," etc. [Jn. 16: 23]. But when he [Clichtove] tries to demolish the arguments of his opponents, he so sinks in with one foot while pulling out the other that in spite of his sweating and struggling he is forced to give himself up as lost. And when he brings in Jerome arguing thus:† "Stephen prayed here, therefore he prays in heaven also," and when he does the

*There is no trace of this work of Myconius'. Probably it was never printed.

†In his *Contra Vigilantium*, I: 6. cap. 6.

same with Paul, he is as pleased with himself as if he were riding in a triumphal chariot. Yet meantime he is not equal to upsetting such a frivolous argument as this: If this is logical, "Paul prayed here, therefore he prays there," this also is logical, "Paul wrote epistles here, therefore he writes them there." For if he should send down from heaven to us epistles by which the biggest disputes between theologians could be settled, he would do quite as much good as by interceding. But why ridicule with many words a man who ought rather to be wept over? The man who truly possesses and truly teaches faith will not need many words to refute such a notion; for by faith is learned disregard of the saints in this respect, and by faith is learned the true "worship of the saints." We "worship" them rightly when we all cling firmly to that God to whom they also in their lifetime clung and taught others to cling. For how could it be that while they were still under the weakness of the flesh they should arrogate nothing to themselves, and now when they are utterly removed from all such weakness should have changed their minds, and having previously led men to the one and only God should now bid them come for refuge to themselves? I want my friends, therefore, not to take it ill that I have not gratified them by reducing that pamphlet to pulp, for it was quite superfluous. Faith, as I have said, will of itself thoroughly eradicate the error; though every position that he supports in his whole pamphlet will be found so completely overthrown by these few considerations urged in reply to Emser, if only one will read and weigh them faithfully, that no one will want anything further. God is such that He is sufficient unto all. He is so kind a Father that He refuses nothing, so bountiful that He loves to bestow Himself. Whom, then, are we procuring as our advocates? Faith does not know this spurious foresight. Hence it is perfectly plain that those who still cling to the creature do not lean on the one true and holy God. What, then, does their faith amount to? Would it not have been better to keep silent than to make such a shameless display of want of faith? I know the Jeromes and the Augustines and the rest, but I know also Christ and the Apostles, and none of them ever taught any such thing. And what is gained by violently twisting Scripture to such purpose, or by refusing to understand the underlying allegorical sense when such sense is present? Faith leans upon one God, clings to One, trusts in One, hopes on One, flies to One for refuge, knows for certain that it will find with One everything that it needs. May He who draweth hearts to Himself grant that we may cleave to Him alone, and may that hypocrisy which parades as piety be banished from the souls of all! Amen.

[24]. Merit

Since those who have mortgaged their hopes to the saints place chief reliance upon their merits, and since in the church of God hitherto the merit not of what I call saints but of most shameless whoremongers has been sold at the highest price they ventured to put upon it, the next thing is for me to speak of merit.

I have said earlier* that these four things are related: Providence, Predestination, Free Will, and Merit. Not that the last two are really related to the first two, but that the man who rightly understands the first cannot help understanding the last. Now providence is the mother of predestination, as it were, and having spoken of it to the best of my ability in considering God, I need not repeat my words here. I there represented God as providing for all things; for all things exist through Him. All things, therefore, are maintained and disposed through Him. And the reason our minds fail to reach an understanding of this is because they are so narrow and circumscribed; though there are not a few things the proper consideration of which enables us to fashion for ourselves a sort of image of Divine Providence, of which things I am going to bring forward only the principal one, namely, man himself. He submits to the control of reason, so that all his members wait upon its nod; and by reason I mean the entire power by which man determines and decides to do this or that. I am speaking of external activity, not of the internal government or alteration of the soul. He bids his feet walk, and they move; his hand to grasp the plough, and it obeys. He never moves a finger without the reason. Yet, far stronger and surer is Divine Providence in controlling the whole uni-

*See p. 70.

verse; for—if one may compare little things with great—God is in the universe what reason is in man. Since, therefore, we see reason presiding over all our activities, whether of movement or rest, so that we see nothing done without its command, how is it that we do not confess that in the same way all things are so done and disposed by the providence of God that nothing takes place without His will or command? We are anxious; for we fear that we shall be forced to confess that God is the author of evils also. This, however, is because we do not observe man carefully enough, for sometimes sickness and diseases come upon him, when, if they did not, he would die altogether. He burns with fever, so he refrains meanwhile from drinking too much, and presently he is restored to his former health. He suffers from gout, a thin and acid humor retires from the vital parts to the extremities; but if this had not taken place the man would have died long before. Thus, as long as certain things take place of which we know not the cause and purpose, we refuse to recognize Divine Providence in them, though it uses us, and, in fact, all things, as it will. Nor is what is base to us base to Providence, for its baseness to us comes from the fact that the Law has been placed over us. And the Law has been so placed because our passions overstepped all bounds. But since God is not subject to such, He is not under the Law, but is Himself that which He demands of us through the Law. Hence that is not base with Him which is base for us. The promiscuous pairing of animals, even in our judgment, is not base, though such pairing of human beings is most base. But what is it that absolves them but condemns us? The Law. For by the divine law we are confined within the barriers of matrimony. So nothing can be base for God which yet cannot help being base for us. Let us, therefore, not be anxious and fearful, and exempt certain things from the Providence of God as not becoming to it. For things that are base for us are not so for it; and things which we think pernicious are on another side profitable. And predestination, which is only another word for foreordination, is born of providence, nay is providence; for even the theologians distinguish providence from wisdom, in that the former proceeds to act and to dispose, while the latter simply sees what should be done and how. For it would be incongruous for the Supreme Good to know all things before they took place and not to be able to dispose and to order all things. Again, to control all things, to have all knowledge and all power, and yet not to do it would be ungenerous, nay, mean, and of this it were impious to suspect the supreme deity. By the providence of God, therefore, are taken away together free will and merit; for if it disposes all things, what part have we that permits us to think anything done of ourselves? And since all things are done by His activity, how are we to have any merit? That all things are done by His activity was abundantly told in considering Him. For "in him we live, and move, and have our being," etc. [Acts 17:28]. Yet, because of the weight of the flesh, it has always happened that some men have failed to attain to this measure of knowledge of God. Hence Paul in writing to the Colossians, 1:9, bears witness that he prays for them unceasingly that they may grow in the knowledge of God. Those, therefore, who have not attained to this knowledge have had much to say about free will and merit, but their utterances were not made of much account by those who had reached real knowledge of the providence of God. At the same time, however, we see that some who really had come to the knowledge of providence have magnified the merit of works; but this, again, for the benefit of those who did not clearly understand providence, to keep them from committing such great sins as they otherwise would. Such were the prophets, who strongly urge men to good works. But what sort of men? Those poor in faith? Yes, for after faith and (according to Christ's words [Mt. 24:12]) love had waxed cold, these holy men were anxious to do their full duty to the glory of God and the peace of the state; and although they strenuously inculcated faith and fear of God before all things, yet, seeing that God had blinded the minds of the people so that οὐδὲν ὑγιές [nothing sound] was to be expected of them, they at the same time did not omit the preaching of works also, although they were well aware of the providence of God. For thus, after many things by which he tries to draw men to God, Isaiah says, 45:24: "Therefore shall they say, In the Lord have I righteousness and strength." For some men are so stupid that, however much you cry to them and insist, they yet measure God only by their own foot-rule; and recognizing that they do all things without generosity, that is, for a return, they cannot be induced to take any other view of God. Hence they think that God ascribes everything to merit, and that where that does not exist it is vain to hope for His favor. God takes advantage of their weakness, or rather want of faith, and invites them to good works by the hope of reward, that meantime His own may lack nothing. But if you say to me, "Since all things are done by the providence of God, why does He not cause those who are so far astray in their knowledge of Him, and who accordingly do all things under compulsion and without generosity, to be better enlightened, that with the clear-sighted they may see the thing that is most to be looked at?" I answer: "Go to Him who created them, and ask the reason of His action from Himself." For we were not His counsellors [cf. Jer. 23: 18], nor did we first give Him anything so that we have a legal right to demand something of Him in return. We know that the potter has the power to make of the same clay one vessel unto honor and another unto dishonor [cf. Rom. 9: 21]; and why shall we say to our Lord and God, "Why didst thou make me after this fashion?" Because, therefore, no one denies that in the Holy Scriptures there are almost more utterances that attribute merit to our works than the reverse, we are not on that account to decide that after the manner of referees we are to take something from either side and give it to the other, in order that peace may be made between our merit and God's grace, between our free will and God's providence or predestination. God is not as man. But we ought rather to do that which we see those holy men did, as I have just said. Knowledge of God must be strenuously inculcated, and faith aroused. If we are successful here, the most excellent fruit will be put forth spontaneously by the good tree [cf. Mt. 7: 17]. At the same time, the sluggish must be stirred up with the hope of reward and the fear of punishment, that the work of God may nowhere halt.

But if you say that thus dissension will arise between the pious and the mercenary, I answer: Nothing whatsoever of the kind. For the pious are not contentious, but teach from love;

and those who in these days, having advanced a step farther than they see generally done, leap up and scorn everyone but themselves are less pious than those who rely upon works. Piety endures all things, does all things, and never fails, ἐκπίπτει [cf. I Cor. 13: 8]. It puts up with the feeble, therefore, has sympathy for the weaker vessel, is not carried away before smoking flax [cf. Mt. 12: 20]. But, if it were permitted to expose here the hypocrisy of certain persons who do just nothing but make a show of their own learning and who cannot endure to see anyone regarded as more learned than themselves, we should give offence, to be sure, but should safeguard the simple. In order, therefore, not to exasperate all the wrath of this turbulent small fry, I content myself with the kind of teaching that I have given above. Only let us at the same time note that, if we ever see ascribed to us by the very mouth of God what cannot belong to any but God, we are to recognize the grace which He shows towards us so lavishly as to ascribe to us what is His alone, and let us not boast or rush into contentious argument. "For we can do nothing against the truth" [II Cor. 13: 8], and we are placed here to build up, not to destroy. The Christian life is guilelessness, as I have often said already. But no soil will bring forth guilelessness more fruitfully than disregard of self. And disregard of self is more luxuriant the more of the dew of the knowledge of God it has drunk in; for the fuller one is of God, the emptier one is of oneself. Those, therefore, who from piety, and not from puffed-up knowledge, rightly recognize and confess God's providence, devote themselves to guilelessness and nothing else. But those who do not find this path ought to be goaded on by the law, by hope, and by fear, to doing the same thing the pious do. This will seem to some rather indiscreet doctrine, but I shall not care a snap for their opinion, seeing, as I do, that the Prophets, Christ, and the Apostles walked in this path. But in order fully to meet the expectations raised by the earlier part of this treatise, which ascribed all things to providence and nothing to free will and merit, I have ordered that the brief remarks which I made on merit in answer to Emser be incorporated here. For I am too busy to do otherwise.

[For this quotation from the "Reply to Emser" *see* below

pp. 388-392.]

But what are we to say of those works which have been invented according to the tradition and teaching of men? They are shams, snares, traps to extort money. All works are the fruit either of piety or of the flesh; for if you are pious you devote yourself from faith to the things that faith dictates. For whosoever hath faith, God is in him and he in God [cf. I John 4:16]. And let no one say: "This that you ascribe to faith belongs to love"; for we must consider that faith is used variously in the Holy Scriptures: first, for belief; then, for unyielding constancy; then, for confidence in God; and of this last only are we to understand the statement that faith saves [cf. Mk. 16:16]. But those who do not understand that faith, hope, and love are the same thing, namely, this confidence in God, will have to pass by many knotty points in Scripture unexplained. But this will be plain from the Scriptures. "By hope were we saved," Rom. 8:24; and, "To him that believeth, his faith is reckoned for righteousness," Rom. 4:5. If, then, hope saves, and faith saves, faith and hope must be the same thing. And let no one be troubled if sometimes hope and faith are spoken of differently; for then faith is not used to mean confidence in God, but either for some sort of belief, or for unyielding constancy or genuineness. But "God Himself is love; and he that abideth in love, abideth in God, and God in him," I Jn. 4:16. And, Jn. 6:56, "He that eateth my flesh and drinketh my blood, abideth in me, and I in him." That is: Whosoever trusteth in Christ, as having suffered for us, abideth in Christ and Christ in him. Therefore faith and love must be the same thing. And let no one marvel, and fear that I am confounding these three virtues of the theologians. For my part, I have learned from the Holy Scriptures that, unless any one of these virtues is its companion virtue, it is absolutely nothing, much less a virtue. If you have faith in regard to Christ, but do not put your hope in Him nor love Him, it amounts to nothing, James 1. If you say you have hope in God, and do not love Him, you make yourself a liar; for if you have been so taught about God that you see you ought fairly to put your hope in Him, you cannot fail to recognize that He is the supreme good; if you recognize that He is the supreme good, you cannot fail to love Him. If you love Him and do not hope, you are a deceiver; for he cannot love God who does not trust in Him. The union of the human heart with God, therefore, that is, piety, has different names in an ascending scale. We use faith sometimes for belief; this in the order of understanding is followed by hope, and that by love. Furthermore, this whole confidence of the human heart in God is called sometimes faith, sometimes hope and love; yet it is nothing but piety towards God, whether you love, hope, or trust. Hence, since the one thing, piety, embraces these three things, faith is used to mean love and hope to mean faith. The objection that might be raised here from I Cor. 13:13, "But the greatest of these is love," can easily be met; for love, as I have indicated, is but the consummate form of that which is still nothing else than the heart on fire in the Lord.

I come back, however, to the point from which I digressed. He, then, in whom God is, in turn is in God; hence must fruits worthy of God grow, "for without him we can do nothing" [Jn. 15:5]. Since, therefore, good works are the fruit of faith, they are certainly of God, not ours. What, then, shall we claim in return for them, when they are not ours? How much less will those who solemnly came forth boasting of a vision of angels, which they yet had not seen, Col. 2:18, be able to demand for their works, invented and performed according to the rudiments of this world! We must agree, then, that the pious do not put a value upon their own works, and therefore never wrangle about a reward for them. On the other hand, those that put on a value are impious; for the man is not pious who has not renounced self. They that put a value upon their own works have not renounced self; therefore they are impious. Having above,* in considering the law, given a touchstone by which one could find out what part of the law had been abolished and what remained, owing to the stress of my occupations I spoke of that part only which has to do with the second chief commandment, telling, namely, how those things pertaining to love of one's neighbor will last always, and again how the things demanded under pretence of the law of love towards one's neighbor and yet not proceeding from the Law-

**See* above, p. 138.

giver have been abolished. Meantime I forgot to speak of, or perhaps thought I had spoken of, the abolition of the law as far as it has to do with the worship of God. We must consider, therefore, that since Christ said, Matt. 22: 40, "On these two commandments hang all the law and the prophets," whatever laws are tried by them and maintain their integrity are nowhere abolished and never will be abolished. But, when some men say, "Ceremonies, therefore, are by no means to be abolished, since they are governed by the first commandment, 'Thou shalt love the Lord thy God with all thy heart,' etc. [Deut. 6:5], for ceremonies are used from love of God," I answer that ceremonies are no proof that we love God, but the fact that we obey His will. For He says, John 14: 21, "He that hath my commandments, and keepeth them, he it is that loveth me." It is, therefore, an indubitable sign of love of God, if we model ourselves upon His precepts. As to ceremonies, we must constantly bear in mind, "In vain do they worship me, teaching the doctrines and precepts of men," Matt. 15: 9. They say, therefore, again: "In this way it will come to pass that we shall cherish those ceremonies which God under the old law wished performed unto Him, even promulgating directions therefor." I answer, that those ceremonies had been scorned and rejected out of the mouth of God even before Christ, as is clear from Isa. 1: 11-17; Jer. 6: 20; Ezek. 20: 25; Amos 5: 21. As, therefore, Christ said, John 15:8, "Herein is my Father glorified, that ye bear much fruit; and so shall ye be my disciples," so we all surely ought to devote ourselves to the honor of God. But how do we honor Him if we are only disciples of Christ? All who are disciples of Christ will bear much fruit unto the Father, as also Christ did. We must try, therefore, to be disciples of Christ. Now, it is the part of a disciple to become like his master. If, therefore, we are Christ's disciples, we will "walk even as he walked," I John 2: 6. Now, Christ honored the Father by doing good to all and by finally giving Himself for all. So, surely, our ceremonies shall be none other than those that Christ used; for by these is God glorified, that is, when we are zealously devoted to truth and guilelessness, and are more ready to expose ourselves for the brethren than to trample upon them in our own interest. This is to worship the Father in spirit and in truth [cf. Jn. 4: 24].

[25]. PRAYER

It is a most marvelous thing that even prayer has degenerated into a matter of gain. For since those were right who said that prayer is the uplifting of the heart to God, what, pray, more shameless could have been thought of than the prostituting of this union of the heart with God? Hence we cannot help seeing that the prayers we sold for a price were hypocrisy, and not a ὁμιλία [communion] of the heart with God. It is, therefore, necessary for me to speak of prayer also, since the devotion of the heart has dared to sell itself as a work of merit. Prayer has been rightly defined by Augustine* and others as the uplifting of the heart to God. Not that they originated the idea, but they tried to express in clearer words what everyone who was pious felt to be the case. I shall speak, first, therefore, of adoration, that thus it may become clear whence this definition of prayer arose. Adoration is in Hebrew the same as service, for "schahah" [שחה] is a service of genuflexion or bowing down. So also the Latins sometimes take adoration in the sense of looking up to and serving. It is about this kind of adoration that the Hebrews are speaking in Exod. 20: 5. When, therefore, we say, "Thou shalt not adore them, nor serve them," namely idols, it would be better to say, "Thou shalt not serve them nor be a slave to them"; for thus we could have translated the Hebrew literally, so that we should run no risk of understanding by adoration here the devotion of the heart. Adoration is, besides, the devoting of the heart to God, that is, to the Lord who can do all things and to the Father who will. This adoration, this devotion of the heart, was bound to the elements of this world by the Israelites according to the flesh. For they ordered that it be done at Jerusalem, as the woman of Samaria complained to Christ, John 4: 20. This had arisen in this way: The Lord had commanded that three times a year all the children of Israel should assemble at the temple, or tabernacle, that was at Jerusalem [Exod. 23: 14; Deut. 16: 16].

*Augustine *Appendicis sermo 73 de verbo Matth.*, 17 [: 21]: Quid est autem oratio, nisi adscensio animae de terrestribus ad caelestia, inquisitio supernorum, invisibilium desiderium?

This arrangement brought very much gain to the priests. Therefore they began to bind men's consciences to the place by their traditions, so that they should come oftener to Jerusalem; for it was not lawful, according to their interpretation, to appear empty-handed before God [Deut. 16: 17]. And yet the expression, "Thou shalt not appear before the Lord thy God empty," does not according to the real meaning of the Hebrew (to bring out this point also in passing) have this sense, but means, "Thou shalt not appear in vain." The sense is as if He were spurring on sloth and saying: "Be not reluctant to come to me, for ye shall not come in vain." So in Exod. 23: 15 and 34: 20, although (as in Deut. 16: 16, according to our version) the words seem to have the meaning, "Thou shalt not appear before the Lord thy God empty-handed," yet if you consult the Hebrew version they have exactly the meaning that I have given. For it would have smacked of the height of greed not to be allowed to appear without a gift. I am afraid that this native meaning had always been corrupted by the priests of the Jews. The priests, then, bound adoration, in the sense of devotion of the heart, to Jerusalem; and this is what our priests also, or rather those of Antichrist, have hitherto done, inviting us to pray in the temples, where we see and are seen, in order that they may conveniently inculcate the doctrine, "Thou shalt not appear before the Lord thy God empty," though Christ bids us [cf. Mt. 6: 6] go into our inner chamber, that the heart may freely lay its troubles before God. Yet adoration, devotion of the heart, is free, and cannot be confined to any one place. Hence not even by these words of Christ, "Go into thy inner chamber," are we to be so bound as not to be allowed to pray anywhere but in our inner chamber. For Paul desires "that men pray in every place, provided they lift up holy hands" to God, I Tim. 2: 8. It is apparent, therefore, that it is no small part of prayer to lift up holy hands, which is nothing else than to be zealous in guilelessness. Christ, therefore, John 4: 23, took adoration (to come to the point) for the careful guarding of faith and piety towards God, when He said: "But the hour cometh, and now is, when the true worshippers shall worship* the Father in

*Veri adoratores adorabunt.

spirit and truth: for the Father seeketh such to worship him. God is a spirit: and they that worship him must worship in spirit and truth." See how sharp and clear is this exposition of worship or prayer! He says God is a spirit; hence those who are to worship Him cannot do it in any better way, nor ought they to do it in any other way, than by devoting the heart to Him; not by an oath such as the monks once demanded, but by constantly increasing love, so that nothing deceitful remains in it and nothing can come out of it but what is most true and most like unto God. This idea Cato the Elder, or rather God through his mouth, taught the children of the Quirites, saying, "If God is spirit, as the seers tell us, He is to be worshipped especially by purity of heart." They, therefore, who have so given and devoted their hearts to God as to cleave to Him alone and to recognize Him as the one God, certainly worship Him in spirit. And when they have become thus united with Him, it follows that they speak the truth with their neighbor, which is to worship in truth; unless you prefer to understand by "worship in truth" cleaving so truly and faithfully to God that besides Him you recognize no God, that is, no helper and no spouse, so to speak. Prayer, therefore, is the conversation which as a result of faith you have with God as with a father and a most safe and sure helper. Prayer, then, is the uplifting of the heart, not of the breath or voice, to God. We pray, therefore, when the heart draws near to God, when it speaks with Him, when in sincere faith it seeks help of Him alone. Further, who could ever impute it to you as a good work that you often come to Him to ask now for money, now for clothing or food or counsel or aid? Since, then, our praying to God is nothing else than a begging of aid in some matter, why do we impute it to ourselves as a work of merit, seeing that adoration, that is, the confident clinging of the heart, is nothing but the clinging of your own heart? How can you lend that to another? You can, indeed, from faith in God pray for another, but you cannot impart a portion of your faith to anyone; for faith belongs to him only who trusts, and is not a work of merit, though Christ called it a work in a sort of figurative sense, but He did that for the sake of those who still clave to works. And He called it a work in such a way as to mean to say by contrast: "Ye shall be blest by faith, without works" [cf. Rom. 3: 28]. Adoration, then, or prayer, is nothing else than a sure confidence in the mercy of God. The consequence of this is that you come to it in every situation and appeal to it. If, therefore, you have recourse to it on account of your neighbor, it must be from love either of your neighbor or of his goods. If the first, your prayer will be answered, for love of your neighbor is based on love of God. But if your prayer is inspired by eagerness to possess, you make God out impious, as if He were not accessible to all but were a sort of respecter of persons [cf. Deut. 10: 17]. For if He heard your prayer but scorned your neighbor's, would He not be a respecter of persons? Furthermore, you make Him an accomplice of your greed; for if He gave to another only after that other paid you, would that not be collusion? We must admit, therefore, that these mercenary prayers are an insult to God, not an honoring of Him; for what sort of honoring is it to beseech, to importune, to complain? If we are pious, the misfortune of our neighbor hurts us, so that we run to God anxiously in his behalf; if, on the contrary, we have not this love towards our neighbor, we shall pray in vain, even if we do get a thousand bushels of gold for our praying. The Truth knoweth not the prayer that is made for the sake of gain. Now, we pray when we cling to God in spirit, and truly cling, so that when any evil assails us we run to Him alone, and pray that He will alleviate our affliction, but only according to the petition, "Thy will be done" [Mt. 6: 10]. Thus all hired praying, psalms, chants, masses, vigils, fall to the ground, for what we do without love profiteth nothing, I Cor. 13: 3. Now, when a price is received, the deed has proceeded from greed, not from love. Hence, however they snarl: "We take pay only sufficient for our maintenance, that we may pray while others on account of their labors have not time, and we pray from love," I say: "Go ye also, therefore, sometime and till the fields, and let those who have hitherto labored hard while ye were idle refresh themselves in your snug nests. Let us rest and labor in turn, for this is what love demands. But now, since you do not deign even to look at a church or a psalm unless because your belly makes you, and yet at the same time you feign love, it is evident that you are a great hypocrite. For love sympathizes, runs to aid, lifts up; but you do none of these things, but things of no avail. If you wish to pray and sing psalms, pray and sing psalms, but without expecting pay; for the expectation of pay is inconsistent with Christian love. We cannot serve God and Mammon, *i. e.*, riches" [cf. Mt. 6: 24].

I do not want to dwell at tedious length upon this matter, for I think that everybody can easily see from the meaning of religion that hired prayers and psalms are of as little use as if you should agree for a reward to be righteous for somebody else. And even those pray, I think, who when holding the plough-handle feel admiration and reverence for the power of Almighty God in the very soil, and in the seed, and who are grateful for His bounty, even though they never utter a word; for it is the heart that prays. And as to the Christians constantly praying, and praying together, in the early times, it can be done in church today also, only let it be praying and not the wanton tickling of the fancy with chanting. Let us, then, pronounce the collects plainly in the language understood by the congregation,* that all may pray together following the words of him who is leading. Yet, let every church have its own custom; for the same thing is not adapted to all, but everything, as far as its source is concerned, should proceed from the same piety, and what does not proceed therefrom should be quietly abolished. See now what merit amounts to. We owe blamelessness to the Lord, and even if we could offer it (which is impossible), we should still be unprofitable servants [cf. Lk. 17: 10]. We are sons and heirs [cf. Rom. 8: 17], not servants; we do not, therefore, serve for reward.

Purgatory

Holy Scripture knows nothing of the fire of purgatory in the sense used by the theologians, but the mind of man knows it well, for by means of this false notion of the fire of purgatory, such wealth has been heaped up that the riches of Croesus and the Hyperboreans and the gems of India are cheap in comparison. For this is what the mind of man thought up,

*That is, the local language instead of Latin.

as you may see somewhere in Origen: Some men go hence who are not utterly bad; why, then, should they be thrust into everlasting punishment? Others go hence who are not wholly good; why, then, should they be admitted at once into the company of the blessed? This argument has some appearance of soundness and, according to Paul's words, Col. 2:23, some show of wisdom, but in ἐθελοθρησκεία [will-worship], *i. e.,* the religion which is the product of the human will. But if you confront it with the word of God, it will vanish like dust before the face of the wind [cf. Wisdom of Solomon 5:15]. If we do not do this, we shall be abandoned by the Lord just as the people of Israel were once left to their own devices and perished in them, as in Psalm 81:12-13 David indicates, speaking in the character of God: "But my people heard not my voice, and Israel hearkened not to me. So I let them go according to the desires of their heart: they shall walk in their own inventions." But what greater presumption can there be than to declare that in the other world things are just as you have happened to picture them to yourself? We should listen to what the Lord God says within us, not to what presumptuous reason invents within us, which, as soon as it has cunningly produced anything that it hopes will seem probable to everybody, immediately sallies forth to win glory. This state of mind we ought to leave to the Gentiles, as Paul has finely taught, Eph. 4:17, in this fashion: "This I say therefore, and testify in the Lord, that ye henceforth walk not as other Gentiles walk in the vanity of their mind." See how he calls our devices the vanity of the mind. There follows: "Being darkened in their understanding, alienated from the life of God, because of the ignorance that is in them, because of the blindness of their heart," etc. We should not, therefore, walk in the way of our minds and devices.

Since, then, a purgatory (for the custom has long prevailed of so naming this illusory expiation in fire) can nowhere be affirmed from the Word of God, how is it that we are so stupid as to believe in such vapid and suspicious nonsense, when we see, forsooth, that those who affirm a purgatory teach in what ways its fires can be quenched, and in the same breath offer their aid for hire? They bid you give gold, for by this especially is the flame weakened if the man who receives the gold devoutly celebrates mass, prays, and sings psalms; and at the same time he holds out his hand for the gold. Why are we not as shrewd as Lucian's Timon, who in such fine style used his spade upon some philosopher or other who advised him to throw the gold he had found into the sea, but not too far from the shore, since he doubtless had the scheme of gathering it up from there at night and carrying it off? Purgatory is very much like certain quack medicines that are carried about by peddlers. They mount a platform in the midst of the market-place, and tell about some sickness or disease that is committing ravages all about, and say they have themselves suffered from it but by the blessing of the gods have recovered in spite of the malady, thanks to the medicine exhibited before the eyes of all. They add that the disease is not far off; that, in fact, it is already raging in neighboring places. See how, first of all, they produce here expectation and fear of the disease, and then promise a remedy. So those who affirmed a purgatory—what bonds, good God! what snakes, fires, what rivers running fire, sulphur, naphtha, or glowing iron, did they not bellow about! What tales of the poets did they not outdo! And the minds of the stupid were just as much dumfounded by this as when an unexpected and cruel enemy is reported to be before the city walls, firing the farms, killing the farmers, and destroying everything. The blockheads stood thunderstruck at this nonsense, just as if they thought they already felt the woe. But a remedy was at hand, marked at an exorbitant price in the beginning (for that was most necessary), in order to make a raid first upon the pocket-books of the rich. "Do you want to free a soul? You can do it for a piece of gold." But when for the wealthy souls had been set free from their prison-cells, they turned to the paltry souls of the humble, but under a pretence that should prevent the rich from suspecting that they were being made sport of. They pretended that the mercy of God ought not to be denied to anybody; that, consequently, the poor, quite as well as the rich, might free souls from purgatory (that is, their bit of coin from their purse), but on condition that no one should say he was poor, so as to be able to get so great a boon cheaper (for in that way the soul was hurt rather than helped), and that everyone should give as much as he could. And did they not cheat both high and low with this transparent nonsense? Who, pray, is so senseless as not to see that such utter blindness could not have been so widespread unless the Lord had inflicted it upon us because of our unbelief? Since, therefore, we have now recovered our sight, so that we see plainly that those who trust in Christ are the sons of God and come not into judgment [cf. Jn. 5: 24], let us no longer suffer ourselves to be held captive by such foolish lies.

I will show, therefore, certain unequivocal passages by which it will be established that purgatory cannot even exist, much less does exist. And this again from the "Reply to Emser."

[For this quotation from the "Reply to Emser" see below pp. 394-396.]

Thus I spoke on purgatory in answer to Emser, with words few but strong in the Lord. But since several passages have so long been bent to serve their purposes that they think them too fixed for anyone to bend back I will deal with several of them.

Christ, wishing to guard against His followers wrangling with each other in daily quarrels, wished to keep them from quarreling by reasoning of this sort. Because it often happens in courts that the man who had expected to win the case comes off beaten, it is a risky thing to go to law; therefore, if His followers would not refrain from quarreling from other considerations, let them at least allow their differences to be composed from fear of the risk. He therefore says, Matt. 5: 25-26: "Agree with thine adversary as quickly as possible, while thou art still with him in the way; lest in any wise it come to pass that the adversary deliver thee to the judge, and the judge deliver thee to the officer, and thou be cast into prison. Verily I say unto thee, Thou shalt by no means come out thence, till thou hast paid the last farthing." From this passage our sweet friends think they have proved that there is a purgatory, though by these words Christ intended absolutely nothing else than to dissuade from quarreling certain hard, unyielding persons who think that all men have the same feelings and selfish expectations as themselves. To these, then, that sometimes happens which they had prepared for others; they were hoping, namely, to win gain along with the disgrace of their adversary, but the opposite resulted; for they were often cast into prison themselves, and afterwards were compelled to stay there until with poverty, hunger, and all the many other punishments usually inflicted they had made satisfaction for all that was due. That this is the real meaning is proved by Luke, who in 12: 56, thus expresses the same idea: "And as thou are going with thine adversary before the ruler,* on the way give diligence to be quit of him; lest haply he drag thee unto the judge, and the judge deliver thee to the exacter," etc. See how he plainly calls "ruler" him to whom you go with your adversary. St. Ambrose† understood this passage in this sense as far as the language is concerned, for he says, "While thou goest with thine adversary to the magistrate," although he afterwards tries to find a different, allegorical sense, as was the custom of his time. But how can the Holy Scriptures help it, if turning a clear and unadulterated expression into a mystical one you go looking for knots in a bulrush? Chrysostom‡ and Theophylact§ assent to this idea. Hilary** in his Canons comes to the conclusion that the language is to be interpreted according to the drift of the teaching in the passage, and the teaching here is the desirability of pardoning and being reconciled, as is shown with perfect clearness in what immediately precedes. Jerome†† quotes the views of many, and so obscures his own that you come away knowing less than before.

The second passage is Matt. 18: 34-35, where Christ wishes by the parable of the unmerciful servant to teach that unless we forgive we shall not be forgiven. He says, finally, of the wicked servant: "And his lord was wroth, and delivered him to the tormentors, till he should pay all that was due. So shall

*principem: so the Latin Vulgate. Gk. ἀρχοντα.

†*Exposition of the Gospel according to Luke,* bk. VII, ch. 154.

‡*Commentary on Matthew,* Homily 20, ch. 2.

§*Exposition of the Gospel of Matthew* (on Matt. 5: 25f.) and *Exposition of the Gospel of Luke* (on Luke 12: 58).

***Commentary on the Gospel of Matthew,* chap. IV, 19.

††*Translation of the Homilies of Origin on the Gospel of Luke,* Homily 35. Also his *Commentary on the Gospel of Matthew,* bk. I, chap. 5.

also my heavenly Father do unto you, if ye forgive not everyone his brother from your hearts." Here our friends launch out in this fashion: "Christ says here that the heavenly Father will do to us as was done to the wicked servant. He will not, therefore, let us out of the punishment of purgatory until we have paid all that is due." To them I answer, or rather not I, but the Truth itself: This parable is preceded by a discussion about forgiveness, in which to Simon's question about pardoning Christ replies [Mt. 18: 22]: "I say not unto thee, until seven times" (must we pardon our brother, to wit) "but, until seventy times seven." Now follows [Mt. 18: 23], "Therefore is the kingdom of heaven likened unto a certain king, who would make a reckoning with his servants," etc. In saying "Therefore," He made it plain that the parable which He immediately subjoined was intended to encourage forgiveness and to teach justice. This He brought out in the prayer, in Matthew 6: 12, in which God requires that if we wish to be forgiven we ourselves also shall forgive, teaching us to pray, "Forgive us our debts, as we forgive our debtors." By this parable, then, Christ simply wished to teach that, as we continually wish to be forgiven by the heavenly King, whom we offend countless times every day, so we, too, ought always to forgive. For He says, in the character of the king who was wroth against the unmerciful servant [Mt. 18: 32f.]: "Thou wicked servant, I forgave thee all that debt, because thou besoughtest me; shouldst not thou also have had mercy on thy fellow-servant, even as I had mercy on thee?" Here they urge: " 'He was delivered to the tormentors till he should pay all that was due,' and, having paid that according to the laws of the country, he was of course let out. Therefore when those who owe a debt to the justice of God have paid the debt in suffering, they will be let out." I answer: First, you seem to think of a parable just as if it were an actual event, although this is of little consequence, except that you must always let a parable be a parable. In parables there are many details which do not altogether square with the things illustrated by them. For instance [Mt. 10: 24], "A disciple is not above his master"; it does not follow, therefore, no one can ever surpass his master. That is true only in the case of Christ, not of others. And no one should imitate that steward [Lk. 16: 1-18] who provided for his own interests by wronging and cheating his lord, but we must look only to the argument for which Christ employs the parable. He wishes by that parable to teach care and attention as to heavenly things, by reasoning of this sort. If the children of this world, disregarding the punishment of the law, look out for their own maintenance, how much more ought those who are hastening to heaven to use every effort to prevent unjust riches from cheating them out of the salvation they hope for. So, also, in the present parable [sc. Mt. 18: 21-35] we must look simply at the argument. This is: Forgive and you will be forgiven; if you do not forgive, neither will you be forgiven. And as to the objection based on "till" or "until," it brings no support to their argument; but let us grant for the sake of argument that God's forgiveness is restricted by this designation of time. What else follows, pray, than that the man who is thus cast into torments does not come out until the King of Heaven has been satisfied? Who shall say when He has been satisfied? Who shall fix the period? Suppose the punishment be eternal? Then He will be satisfied when you have been tortured forever, not when the Pope of Rome has drained your pocket-book. But, not to give an opening for the disease of verbal contention, it is clear that this word "till" ought not to be twisted into referring to a period of time; and this is clear through Christ Himself, for He was made our righteousness [cf. I Cor. 1: 30], because we could not attain salvation by our own righteousness. We are saved, therefore, by grace, not by our merits, as was said some time back. For if heaven could be scaled by our merits, there would have been no need of Christ's coming down. Likewise, if our sins must be cleansed by the fire of purgatory, of what profit is Christ? Why did He put on the weakness of man [cf. Isa. 53: 4; Mt. 8: 17]? For if we are compelled to endure the fire of purgatory in order to satisfy the righteousness of God, as these people say, the righteousness of Christ will profit us nothing, and all whose aim is to go to the Heavenly Father rely upon Christ in vain, unless they first have been burned in the fire of purgatory. What can be said more foolish or more blasphemous against Christ than this?

They do away with Him who set up a purgatory; nay, if we can go to heaven by means of purgatory also, they make Him a liar when He said that through Him alone is access to the Father possible [cf. Jn. 14: 6]. But εἰς κόρακας [to perdition] with these torturers of souls and executioners of consciences, plotters against pocket-books, who for the sake of their bellies have invented a way to torture the souls of the dead in our hearts rather than in reality, and thereby to squeeze out money in order that it may be well with themselves. While they have inflicted upon the dead weeping, sadness, and torture, though falsely, in doing this they have themselves found most agreeable and pleasant refreshment.

The third passage is Matt. 12: 32: "But whosoever shall speak against the Holy Spirit, it shall not be forgiven him, neither in this world, nor in the world to come." From this passage they argue: "Christ said that the sin against the Holy Ghost is not forgiven in the world to come; therefore certain sins are forgiven in the world to come, for only the sin against the Holy Ghost is not forgiven in the world to come." I answer: It is strange that they either have forgotten their own art or have not learned it properly. For it is no logical sequence this: The sin against the Holy Ghost is not forgiven in this world, and is not forgiven in the world to come; therefore certain sins are forgiven in the world to come. For how can a correct conclusion be drawn from negatives? The proper argument is this: The sin against the Holy Ghost is not forgiven in this world, nor is it forgiven in the world to come; therefore it is never forgiven. It is a case of disjunctive syllogism, as in the Apocalypse 4:8: "And the beasts rested not day and night." The conclusion is not, "Therefore they rested some time," but, "Therefore they never rested." And that by this distinction between this world and the world to come Christ meant to indicate eternity is brought out by Mark, 3: 29, when he says, "hath never* forgiveness," and by Luke, 12: 10, who says, "shall not be forgiven."

The fourth passage is I Cor. 3: 12-15: "Now if any man build upon this foundation gold, silver, precious stones, wood, hay, stubble; every man's work shall be made manifest: for

*in aeternum non.

the day shall declare it, because it is revealed in fire; and the fire shall prove every man's work of what sort it is. If any man's work abides which he hath built thereupon, he shall receive a reward. If any man's work is burned, he shall suffer a loss: but he himself shall be saved; yet so as through fire." This most lucid passage of Paul they have so befouled in the soot of their purgatory, to the support of which they have twisted it, that men otherwise of keenest scent have been unable to smell out its native sense. I shall, therefore, give the sense of this passage, not from my own idea but from that of Paul himself, and of Jerome* on Ezekiel, Ch. 3: 18-19. To build, then, in this passage is to preach. The foundation is Christ. The work which is built is those who have received the word. The fire is the trial or persecution which is inflicted at God's decree: "Thou hast tried me with fire," etc. [cf. I Cor. 3: 13]. The gold, silver, gems, are those who have so thoroughly received Christ that they would die rather than betray Him. The wood, hay, and stubble are those who believe for the moment, or perhaps only pretend to believe, and in the time of trial desert Christ [cf. Mt. 13: 20-21]. Let us now see the argument that Paul makes here, and having seen it let us then measure the whole idea by it, and new light will arise upon us. When Paul learned that certain men at Corinth were setting a high value upon themselves, on the ground that they were more learned or more eloquent than himself, he most courteously warned them not to allow themselves to be drawn away from his simple teaching by any pretence of learning or of eloquence. He was not, he admitted, an extraordinarily clever speaker, though he lacked nothing necessary to the suitable setting forth of the heavenly teaching. There were also other learned men, but how far they excelled him the Corinthians could not easily judge, being still inexperienced when he was teaching in their midst. He was, he said, in the habit of employing every means in order to win as many for Christ as possible. When, therefore, he had been with them before, he had not forthwith disclosed the most abstruse parts of his teaching, because that would have been a vain attempt with persons who were then not capable of

**Commentary on Ezekiel*, Bk. I, ch. 3.

receiving them. Now he was very greatly displeased because some of them had heard him with such dull ears that they could endure to be called followers of Apollos or of Peter or of Paul. These were all, he said, ministers of the word and builders of the house, that is, the church, of God, upon the true foundation, Christ. He was not so covetous of glory as to grieve that others should now be preferred to himself, or so envious as to be unable to endure that the fame of others should increase. Yet, he had always anxiously striven to teach to the best of his ability, and he doubted not that the others also desired to have the same thing thought of them which he, Paul, proclaimed of himself. Therefore he says [cf. I Cor. 3: 9-15]: "We are God's fellow-workers, all of us who teach; ye are God's husbandry, that is, God's building or work. But as for me, I will render an account of my labor. According to the grace of God which was given unto me, after the example of wise master-builders I have laid a solid foundation which cannot be shaken, namely, Christ. Now I see others building thereon, and I send every man to himself in this matter. Let every man take heed how he buildeth thereon. For as far as the foundation that I have laid is concerned, I have no fear that any man can lay other foundation (if only he be minister of Christ) than that which is laid, which is Jesus Christ. And if any one has made some men so strong in Christ that when persecution comes it can have as little effect upon them as fire upon gold and silver and gems, it is certainly evident how faithfully and skilfully he built who administered the word, since his hearers would sooner lose their lives than the word. But if anyone has handled the word so coldly that when persecution comes the hearers disappear as wood and hay and stubble are consumed by fire, the carelessness or faithlessness of the builder, of which until then no one was aware, will become manifest. 'The day reveals all things,' as also heathen writers have said. So, too, this day of the Lord, in which he shall reveal what was hitherto hid, will uncover all things. I am not speaking of the last day, but of the day in which it pleases God to uncover what was for some time concealed and what he has thus far been willing to wink at. On that day, therefore, the teaching of all is proved as by fire. If any man's teaching abide, so that the Lord does not reject it, or those who received it desert, it will appear that he builded gold, silver, precious stones, and according to his building will he receive a reward. But if any man's work is burned up, it was wood and hay and stubble. Although, therefore, the preacher will feel the loss of those whom he had taught, yet he will be saved himself if he takes a brave stand when the fire rages, but only on condition that he walks dauntlessly through the fire, *i. e.*, persecution." In this passage, then, Paul is speaking of the trying of one's teaching, not of the fire of purgatory, as is plainly apparent, if, at least, you half-way open your eyes. All the rest of the things that are now and then adduced to the contrary you will easily quash; as, for instance, the parable of the rich glutton and Lazarus [Lk. 16: 19-31], from which many get flimsy shafts, though it is nothing but a parable—though they refuse to see it—by which Christ wished to teach the same lesson as by that other one about the ten virgins [Mt. 25: 1-13]; namely, that we ought to mend our lives here, while there is time, for after we go hence it will be too late to begin to repent, nay, entirely vain to pray and lament and beseech. Therefore let no one be reluctant to give up this most empty fiction. Rather let us all strive to grow in the knowledge of God and to change our lives for the better every day, whereby our hearts will become so accustomed to trusting in Christ that when death draws nigh we shall rejoice to depart and be with Christ [Phil. 1: 23].

[27]. Magisterial Office

Some deny magisterial office to Christians, declaring persistently that a man who is a Christian cannot possibly administer such an office; but whither their mad theory tends is beginning to be clear.* Having, therefore, observed the saintliness and faith of large numbers of believers who have yet so administered magisterial offices as to glorify God by general peace and righteousness, and having observed also the effrontery and viciousness of bad men who pretend to be Christians but are not truly such, I venture to assert that no man is even capable of administering a magistracy properly

*Reference is to the Anabaptists. Cf. volume 2, pp. 272-273.

unless he is a Christian. How, pray, does the state differ from the church? I mean in regard to the external habits and associations of life; for as far as the heart is concerned, I am well aware that the only church of Christ is that which trusts in Christ, while the state can be content if you show yourself a faithful citizen, even if you do not trust in Christ. The state demands that you serve the commonweal, not your own; that dangers be shared in common, and fortunes also, if necessity arises; that no one exercise a selfish prudence; that no one exalt himself; that no one stir up strife.

See now, alongside of these few things, what the church of Christ requires.

Paul reminds us in many a passage that love is not intent upon her own interest, but upon that of others.

In the second place, he says [II Cor. 11: 29]: "Who is caused to stumble, and I burn not? Who is weak, and I am not weak?" He bids us weep with them that weep, and rejoice with them that rejoice [Rom. 12: 15].

In the third place, the believer demands not from a believer that he share his fortune with him, but the believer puts all his fortune in his girdle to be ready to help whenever occasion requires [cf. Acts 2: 45, 4: 34f.]. I do not wish to treat here as it deserves that ὕπουλον [festering sore] from which those trouble-makers* are suffering, even though they deny it with as much shamelessness as persistence. Their eagerness shows what they have in mind, namely, community of all things, a condition which I with my slender resources could cheerfully endure, but God would not endure that any man should be robbed of his own. For Peter says to Ananias [Acts 5: 4]: "Was it not possible for thee not to sell what thou hast sold" (I paraphrase his words), "and to keep it in thy power? And, on the other hand, after thou hadst sold it, was it not again in thy power?" "If thou wouldest be perfect," says Christ [Mt. 19: 21], "go and sell all that thou hast, and give to the poor." "If thou wouldest," He says; He did not rob, nor bid the poor rob, the rich young man of his own.

In the fourth place, Peter enjoins, I Pet. 4: 10, that every man should minister for the general good the grace he has

*The Anabaptists.

received; for that is becoming to "stewards of the manifold grace of God," etc. Further, Paul bids us pursue humility [Rom. 12:16]. And Christ Himself almost threateningly proclaims that they that exalt themselves shall be humbled [cf. Mt. 23:12]. Finally, factious strife is so generally deprecated that there is not a single one of the other Apostles who does not expressly condemn it.

How, then, as I had begun to say, does the life of the Christian church, as far as those things which we see are concerned, differ from the life of the state? It does not differ at all, for each one demands what the other demands. But as far as the inner man is concerned there is a vast difference. The citizen is compelled by the laws to show himself such and such a man towards his fellow-citizens; but we do in an insincere and rather unfaithful way the things we are compelled to do. The result is that, if you can look out for your own advantage contrary to the law but without being found out, you will not neglect to do it. This is not the case with the Christian state, that is, the church. For they that have the spirit of Christ are His [cf. Rom. 8:9], and they that are Christ's do all things in accordance with His character and will. He so loved us that He gave Himself for us [cf. Eph. 5:25]. We shall, therefore, also do the same, if we have His spirit. Accordingly, we shall love all men as ourselves, and if we love them we shall neglect nothing that concerns the safety of our neighbors. If, therefore, you add love to the character of citizen, fraudulent zeal for individual advantage will disappear. Since, therefore, the spirit of Christ has that which the state particularly needs, nothing more auspicious can come to the state than love; and since the gospel brings this with it, it is evident that the state becomes strong and holy only in case good hearts are united with good laws. No state, therefore, will be happier than that in which also true religion dwells.

What I have said, then, of the state should be understood much more of civil office; for the magistrates are the head of the state, as it were, and if the members should properly have this character, much more should the head itself. Hence I declare, quite differently from what our friends hold, that a magistrate cannot even be just and righteous unless he be a Christian. Take away from the magistrate, who is above the fear of man, the fear of God, and you make him a tyrant. Infuse into the tyrant the fear of God, and of his own accord he will do more freely and faithfully what the law orders than any terror could have caused him to; and out of a tyrant you will make a father on the pattern of Him whom as a result of faith he begins to fear and to serve, namely, God. But here they meet us with this: "The church of Christ ought to be so blameless as to have absolutely no need of magistrates; for Christians do not quarrel but yield. They do not carry their wrongs to court [cf. I Cor. 6: 6], but if smitten upon one cheek turn the other also" [cf. Mt. 5: 39]. I answer: May we, indeed, have such a church! At present, however, when these very persons who demand such blamelessness as is quite justly demanded of us by God but not by those who do nothing that is right—when, I say, these men themselves are so hopelessly far from practicing what they demand so loudly (for no one is so ready at backbiting), what, pray, do they expect of those who do not trust in God? Or do they, perhaps, repudiate the magistracy because they know their own very great propensity for backbiting, and fear that someone may not patiently endure their backbiting but enter complaint before a magistrate, so that they can no longer with impunity indulge in it or without danger scheme to get others' goods under pretence of devotion to Christ? For as this class of men finds great fault with the most blameless for every little thing, so, as soon as you place their malady before their own eyes, they cry out: "Why judgest thou me? To my Lord I stand or fall" [cf. Rom. 14: 4]. See how our friends have no need of tribunals! Of course, if you bear all the wrongs they inflict and do not strike back, and if you suffer them with impunity to make all sorts of trouble over trifles, these persons have indeed no need of tribunals. I say, on the contrary, that just on account of these persons who declare that a Christian cannot administer a magistracy we very greatly need the magistracy; and why should we not have a Christian magistrate to decide between Christians rather than one who is a stranger to Christ?

But now I will confirm the matter with testimony.

In Exodus 18: 21-22, Moses is bidden by the Lord (for I would not ascribe to Jethro himself what the Lord shows through him, as is plainly seen in Deut. 1: 13, where Moses ascribes to the Lord what is here ascribed to the Midianite)—is bidden to "provide and select out of all the people able men, such as fear God, men of truth, hating covetousness." "And place such over them," he says, "to be rulers of thousands, and rulers of hundreds, rulers of fifties, and rulers of tens; and let them judge the people at all seasons." See how Moses plainly sets forth here the qualities which a judge, above all men, must have—ability, fear of God, zeal for truth, hatred of covetousness, as I said a little while ago a good and truly Christian citizen ought. Nor can we fairly deny that this law applies to us. For the more we say it does not apply to us, the more we really need it. For they who under the influence of the Spirit conform themselves to the will of God shrink not from the law; for they by the Spirit bear witness to the law, that it is good, Rom. 7: 7-12. But those who are averse to the law are not spiritual; for the law is good and holy, nay, spiritual. It is plain, therefore, that as soon as these persons snarl at the law they show that they are carnal. Now I mean that law which can never be abolished, namely, that which pertains to love of one's neighbor and is measured, or, as these persons say, regulated, by the second commandment [Lev. 19: 18], "Thou shalt love thy neighbor as thyself." Now see how this kind of men is pierced by "the arrow that flyeth by day and the demon that stalketh at noonday" [cf. Ps. 91: 5-6].

They say they have the foundation for this opinion of theirs in the Holy Scriptures, Matt. 20: 26, "Not so shall it be among you," and Luke 22: 26, "But ye shall not be so." Here they are wrong twice: first, because this law applies to those only who were sent out to teach in place of the Apostles. These, therefore, Christ bids not to exercise dominion. For in regard to such leadership the Apostles had asked who of them should be regarded as superior to the rest. I will not deny, however, that, as far as ambition is concerned, this law applies equally to all of us, in the sense that it is not permissible for any Christian to solicit or to usurp dominion. But when it is offered, the man is not truly pious who refuses to bear this burden which the state imposes upon him. Second, they are wrong in not understanding that Christ is speaking here of a tyranny rather than of a monarchy or an aristocracy conferred by consent of the people or by the calling of God upon one to whom the office of preaching the word has not been committed. I call it tyranny when dominion is assumed on one's own authority. If one man does this, he is a tyrant, and his sway is called a tyranny; if several, not all but some few, arrogate dominion to themselves, the Greeks called it an oligarchy. Tyranny, then, Christ altogether forbids; on the other hand, as even in a flock of sheep there must be some ram that leads the rest, so also there must be some headship in every state. But here care must be taken not to apply to the tyranny of certain Popes what I am saying about civil magistracy. These persons, then, treating the word from the point of view of knowledge rather than of Christian love, fall into the mistake of eliminating all magisterial offices, even the just and lawful ones of which we especially have need for preserving peace and quiet. To their objection that Christians should endure all things and do all things that the Law commands, and therefore have no need of magistrates, I answer: Right indeed. As long, therefore, as we do not all live after this fashion, although we all nevertheless wish to be called Christians, there must be restraint and delay, nay, absolute silence, on the part of Christians in this matter of not administering civil office, lest we abolish a thing that is most necessary before we have secured that for the sake of which we want it abolished. Why continue? These fellows have no other object than to create disorder. Who has ever seen anywhere such universal blamelessness, or where in the world will one ever expect everybody to pursue blamelessness so eagerly, that no one sins? Since, therefore, there have always been those who under the guise of piety indulge in the same reckless course as the impious, we must also always have magistrates, and above all Christian magistrates in a Christian people. Then only must the magistracy be abolished when wrongdoing has been so thoroughly abolished that no man sins either with tongue or in deed. But this will be in the other world; for to this one the enjoyment of such perfect blamelessness has been denied. For God's sake, then, let them, I beg, stop, being wise in these matters, in which it is clearer than day that they are after nothing but to make a disturbance and to get renown in one way or another. Moreover, the insubordination of these brawlers is such that they will obey neither a Christian nor an impious magistrate. If the magistrate is a Christian, as soon as he interferes with them, they say, "We must obey God rather than you," albeit nothing is ordered that does not conduce to the glory of God and the peace of the community. I will give an example. Certain persons recently began to have themselves rebaptized in the Zurich territory.* The authorities, therefore, that is the Council and the Two Hundred, investigated the matter and forbade further rebaptizing. The fellows answered that we must obey God rather than man. When they were told to bring out, then, the law of God by which they taught rebaptism was instituted, they produced what is written in Acts 19: 5 about those who had been better taught by Paul. Though they had not a right understanding of this passage, they yet said that they had been taught by the Holy Spirit, and that they must obey God rather than man. See what a door they are trying to open to all vices under pretence of religion, persisting as they do in these devices of their own invention and daring to defend all their presumption with the assertion, "We must obey God rather than you," even when manifestly they are acting against all love. If they carry their point, this defence of the Apostles will become a laughing-stock, for everybody will find somewhere in Scripture words that he can distort into an excuse for his irregularities, and then say: "God is to be obeyed rather than you." A man will take to polygamy and marry many wives, and say that Jacob did so, and David and Solomon and numberless others, as Scripture tells us; that, therefore, he is answerable to God rather than to the authorities. See what a handle they furnish the Roman Pontiff for dinning into all men's ears, "Look at your teaching. Do you not see how wisely your fathers acted in constituting me the one and only judge of the Holy Scriptures?" And they furnish the same sort of handle

*This was in January, 1525, in the village of Zollicon, six miles from Zurich.

to those that cry for Councils; for when everyone walks according to his own notion, all men again compel the calling of Councils. But that no man may think there is disagreement in that teaching which has to do with the inner man, they confine their raging to these points and similar ones: Are infants to be baptized or not? Are adults to be rebaptized? Also this present knotty problem, whether a Christian can administer a civil office. In regard to these they fight so sharply and so bitterly that, the minute you differ from them, they call you by no gentler names than impious fellow, ἄθεος [atheist], traitor; and they say that this shows an ardent spirit. But who does not see that this is a very temptation of Satan, who always dares to sow tares among the good seed [cf. Mt. 13:25]? I beg all, therefore, as does Paul, Rom. 12:16, to be of the same mind always, and not to cause such great offence to the gospel of Christ for a trifle; not to "mind high things, but to condescend to things that are lowly," not with the feigned humility that is reproved in Col. 2:18; and not to "be wise in their own conceits, etc."

But if the magistrate is not pious (to come back to the second alternative), they think they have a special right not to obey him. Thus does the Evil One transform himself into an angel of light [cf. II Cor. 11:14] that he may be able to drag the conscience back to its primal unhappy state.

I am forced by their contentiousness to say these things about these quarrelsome persons, that others may be able to take measures earlier against such a plague, if it ever appears among them. For the kingdom of God is not meat and drink, and consequently cannot be attained through any of the elements of this world. It is righteousness, peace, and joy in the Holy Spirit [cf. Rom. 14:17]. How base is it, therefore, for those who wish to be looked up to on account of their religion to do combat for the elements of this world as if for the sum and substance of all piety, even if they had a distinct law for their course! For even the word must be dispensed with love as guide.

Now I come back to other testimony, with which to confirm the view that a magistrate among Christians ought by all means to be a Christian. For it is already clear enough that

Christians cannot get along without magistrates.

When Paul is binding together the church as the body of Christ, Rom. 12: 8, he says that all the members are indeed one body, but have separate gifts; and among the gifts and members he reckons προϊστάμενον ἐν σπουδῇ, *i. e.*, the one who rules, holding that he has as a gift of God his zeal for faithfully acting as ruler over others. Hence he ought to devote freely to the whole body that which God gave not for his private use but for the general advantage. Since, therefore, Paul himself, even in writing to Christians, ascribes the right administering of an office to the grace of God, why should we say that a Christian ought not to rule?

Peter, in I Pet. 2: 13-16, absolutely compels obedience to the authorities. Yet they say: "But this was an impious magistrate." I answer: Are you actually going to say that Peter commanded obedience to an impious magistrate, but would have forbidden obedience to one who was a Christian? Or, perhaps, that a Christian magistrate ought rather to give way to an impious man than to undertake the office himself? What greater madness can be imagined? For since commonwealths are governed by the authorities as head, is it not madness to prefer that the ruler should be impious rather than pious, to prefer that an impious tyrant ride the necks of the pious rather than a pious man be a father to the flock of the Lord? For what object has the impious man but to do all things for gain or fame? And what the pious man but from love and fear of God and his neighbor to commit no act that can offend the one or trouble the other? The impious one will heap up riches by means right or wrong, will climb to renown over the dead bodies of his own; the pious will share all things with those over whom he rules, and will prefer the safety and peace of his people to renown. But you say: "It frequently happens on this wise that when we raise even a pious man to a position of authority he degenerates into an impious one." Why do you complain of that? You have thus just what you want—an impious ruler set over you. But away with quibbling! If, then, a pious ruler degenerates into an impious one, remove this impious one and substitute a pious one. But you will say: "He is a king, he is a despot, and he cannot be forced into line by votes." Bear, then, and endure any tyranny which does not interfere with faith; for it happens not in vain that you live under an impious ruler. God is either punishing your sins or testing your patience. But if the ruler attempt to wrest your faith from you, you will snap out even in this unpleasant situation: "One must obey God rather than man" [Acts 5: 29]. At the same time, remember that although the children of Israel were for a long time cruelly afflicted by the despot of Egypt, yet God had regard unto their affliction and brought them out with tremendous disaster to those who had hitherto oppressed them, and that God remains ever the same. If, therefore, He then looked upon, pitied, and rescued His own, neither will He ignore or neglect you.

Paul writes to Timothy, I Tim. 2: 1-2: "I exhort therefore, first of all, that entreaties, prayers, intercessions, supplications, be made for all men; for kings, and for all that are in high place; that we may lead a quiet and tranquil life in all godliness and gravity," etc. Here first consider whether a more quiet and peaceful life can be led under an impious ruler or under a pious one. But if we may pray for a condition of peace, surely we may also pray that God will grant us a pious ruler, in order that peace and concord may better be secured. Since, therefore, it is not unbecoming for God to give us such a ruler, why should it be unbecoming for a pious man to administer that which the Lord offers of Himself? I am speaking all along of the authorities we call lay authorities, not of the tyranny which the Roman Pontiffs have arrogated to themselves. Then, consider this also, that if we may pray that we may lead a life of all godliness and gravity, surely we may also pray that rulers may be inducted into office under whom godliness and honesty and gravity of life may attain the fullest measure possible. And this we shall secure more successfully under pious than under impious rulers.

The Apostles everywhere enjoin upon slaves to obey their masters: I Pet. 2: 18; Paul, I Cor. 7: 21-22; Eph. 6: 5-8; Col. 3: 22; I Tim. 6: 1-2. On the other hand, Paul at the same time enjoins upon masters to govern impartially and to treat their servants kindly. Can that be twisted so as to apply to impious masters? As if, indeed, the impious would have deigned even to look at the writings of the Apostle, much less to listen to and to obey him! He writes, therefore, for believing masters, as is clearly evident from I Tim. 6: 2, where he says: "And servants that have believing masters, let them not despise them, because they are brethren; but let them serve them the rather because they are believing and beloved." But if he could be a Christian who had slaves, much more can a Christian administer a civil office without detriment to piety and the word of God. For it is harder to be a master than a magistrate; and it is nearer cruelty to have slaves than for the sake of the public tranquillity to have citizens obedient to you.

I will now come to examples.

We read in Gen. 14: 14 how large a number Abraham had of slaves born on the estate.

Marvelous, too, was the extent and difficulty of the dominion held by Moses at the bidding of the Lord Himself. And he held it by the method of ordering the most serious cases brought before himself, which could scarcely have failed to arouse suspicion if he had not been so thoroughly faithful in the house of the Lord, Heb. 3: 2.

What shall I say of Joshua and the others, all of whom were put in authority at the word and bidding of God?

We shall never be able to bring up anything to prove that a pious man may not lawfully administer a magisterial office as long as we continue to live in such a way that some men have to be restrained from wrongdoing. Therefore these people say (for they will do any sort of squirming): "It is our own fault, then, that we are compelled to have magistrates, since we do not live according to Christ's directions; for if we did so live, we should have no need at all of magistrates." I answer: Who denies that? Hold the view, therefore, and teach it in all the corners where you conspire together, that Christians ought to lead such a blameless life that they can have no need of magistrates. As it is, therefore, since you see that the life of all men is such that we have need of very stern magistrates, and at the same time you loudly protest again and again that Christians ought not to have magistrates, do you fancy that it is hard to see what you are aiming at? At confusion of all things, forsooth. You keep trying to mix up everything with the idea of climbing to renown in some way. Why do we not all strive to lead a perfectly blameless life, and then the magistrates will not trouble us. If we all in this fashion put on a garment of blamelessness, the magistracy will become a dead letter of itself; for whom shall it smite with the sword when all are perfectly harmless? But, mark you! take heed lest you rather pretend that such blamelessness can be than really expect it, with the view of getting as much reputation for piety out of this clever idea of yours as Plato wished to get for wisdom when he arranged his Republic. Why should I mention David, Solomon, Asa, Josiah, Hezekiah, and others, when our friends are ready with the statement: "Magistrates were necessary under the old law, but these external things do not apply to us"? Right indeed. But this does apply to us: As long as we suffer from the same disease from which they suffered under the law, do we not also need the same remedy? We do. No impious ruler was imposed upon the stiff-necked Jews until they had reached the limit of impiety; and as soon as they forsook their impiety they were delivered from him and installed a ruler of their own nation and religion. Christians also, therefore, recognizing the mercy of God, ought to appoint for themselves a Christian ruler, under whom to live in tranquillity and quiet. For there are among them no fewer who are ready to do wrong than there were once among the Jews, and these must be restrained by punishments. And while they are compelled to endure an impious ruler they ought to recognize their sin and understand that he has been set over them only on account of their impiety. The pious, therefore, may lawfully choose a pious ruler, and a pious man may lawfully administer among the pious the office offered him.

But, as has been said, it is well to support our position with examples from the New Testament also, in order to satisfy these persons.

We read in Rom. 16:23: "Erastus the treasurer of the city saluteth you." If a man is treasurer, is he not a person in authority? Though you deny this flatly, I say that not even a treasurer, be he a person in authority or not, can administer this office without there being a person in authority who has made him treasurer, either by his own power or in accordance with the general suffrage.

Also, in Acts 13:7-13 we read that Paul set sail from Paphos and came to Perga in Pamphilia, leaving Sergius Paulus in the proconsulship. Of Publius, whose father God, through Paul, had healed of dysentery, I will say nothing, since it is not entirely clear that he accepted the faith of our Lord Jesus Christ [cf. Acts 28:7-8]. But why should I not speak of men like Theodosius and Louis, who have governed kingdoms and other dominions most piously? For I do not wish to speak without due consideration about men like Charles the Great, who as far as piety is concerned were masters of ceremonies rather than pious kings. But I make mention of that Theodosius* to whose piety we may find witness not only in the histories of the heathen writers, but also in the writings of most pious men, and of that Louis** who for his marked piety got the name of "the Pious," and of the Louis† who so stoutly resisted the Roman Pontiff that he even congratulated himself upon dying under the ban of his excommunication. Even our Zurichers at the head of affairs at that time were so influenced by his faithfulness that they endured for eighteen years the impious excommunication of the Roman Pontiff.

Since, then, it is plain from both Testaments that a Christian can administer a magisterial office, we will now see what the character of a Christian magistracy is.

We find that there are not, as these persons say, a sacerdotal and a lay magistracy, but only one; for the power of the church by which the shameless sinner is shut out from communion is not that of a magistrate, as the bishops have thus far exercised it; it belongs to the whole church, not to certain persons who have despotically arrogated supreme authority to themselves.

Before I come, therefore, to the magistracy itself, I wish to say something about these guardians of the church, that

*Theodosius the Great, Roman Emperor 379-395 A. D., who employed vigorous measures to suppress paganism.

**Either Louis the Pious, son and successor of Charles the Great; or, more probably, Louis IX (St. Louis), King of France 1226-1270 A. D.

†Louis IV of Bavaria, Emperor of the Holy Roman Empire 1314-1347 A. D.

those who have thus far been in such fear of their words of censure may cease to tremble so at them. Christ, in order that the church, His bride, might be kept guiltless [cf. Eph. 5: 27], commanded, Matt. 18: 15-17: "And if thy brother sin against thee, go and show him his fault between thee and him alone: if he hear thee, thou hast gained thy brother. But if he hear thee not, take with thee one or two more, that at the mouth of two or three witnesses every word may be established. And if he shall refuse to hear them, tell it unto the church; and if he refuse to hear the church, let him be unto thee as the Gentile man and a publican." In the first place, here we see excommunication inflicted for a sin, not for interest and other debts, which are to be collected by the power of the courts when you are unwilling to remit them. Here fall to the ground the bulls, briefs, and diplomas with which the Roman Pontiff (and in naming him I mean the whole Papal hierarchy, *i. e.,* whatever has sworn to obey his laws) has worried the whole church of Christ; for these have chiefly been used because of pecuniary disagreements and differences in regard to property, not because of the offence caused by sin. Second, it is required that you meet the sinner alone and admonish him in a friendly way. Here the Pontifical crowd sin again. For as soon as it pleases them, they summon to their tribunal before the whole congregation some unsuspecting person, very often an innocent one. See what an atrocious exercise of power! No king or presiding officer but first calls the offender before himself; but these fellows cover with shame before the whole congregation an innocent man, or one who has suspected nothing of the sort, and thunder out: "Judge So-and-So admonishes this person to satisfy this other within a fortnight, or he will be excommunicated!" There the eyes of all were instantly turned upon the poor astounded fellow, and he was not allowed to utter a syllable or to plead his case, to protest against the wrong or to defend his innocence; for if so much as even the feeblest sound had escaped him, it would have been all up with the poor wretch. And I am inclined to think that the great king of the Persians dealt with his subjects less roughly and barbarously; whose habit they tell us it was from early times to compel all who approached him first to brush and to kiss the dust with their lips, and then to plead their case. But this poor fellow of ours is more than prostrated to the earth in the sight and hearing of all: with his case unheard, he is forced to depart convicted and condemned in the judgment of all. Or if ever he is permitted to plead his cause, it happens in a corner, not in the public assembly, where he had received the blow. Third, it is required that before you cast off your brother you try speaking to him in the presence of witnesses; so reluctantly does the church of Christ resort to public punishment. On the other hand, pettifoggers of the market place aim at making the greatest possible haste without any regard for mercy, and at causing the greatest amount of loss instead of sparing; for the number of fees increases with the number of summonses and judgments. Finally, the judgment of the whole church is required; not of the Church Universal, for that can never assemble in this world, but of the church in which the accused is a member and communicant. Here the dominion, or rather despotism, of the Roman Pontiff shows itself in its true character. Excommunication is effected only when the church has rejected him who displeases her; but the Pope casts out of the church the very man she herself most desires to be saved to her; nor does he consult the church, but commands her to treat as excommunicated the man whom he himself hates or proposes to ruin. But if we ought to interpret laws by the intention of the lawgiver, as we certainly ought, and not judge that a man has infringed the law who has not infringed it, it follows that those who are excommunicated by the Popes in this fashion are not guilty in the sight of God. For, as far as this form of fixing guilt is concerned, excommunication belongs to the church and to no one else; and unless she excommunicates, the man is not cast off or held guilty in heaven whom the Pope holds guilty [cf. Mt. 16:19]. Hence all the artifices of excommunications and censures must fall to the ground. And we must see to it that the true rod of discipline be restored to the church of Christ, that it may smite the shameless sinner, and when he has changed his heart, admit him into fellowship again. This will keep in the path, even in spite of themselves, some who walk not after the Spirit. But even if it does not profit them, yet those who desire to live honestly and peaceably in this world will profit from not being forced to see sin reaping a harvest unmolested. This power of excommunication, I say, is not that of a magistrate, for it belongs to the whole church; and it belongs to the church so completely that unless she casts out a man he is not cast out. I say this the more willingly, in order that these impostors may no longer be able to shelter themselves by saying: "How, pray, can the dominion of the Roman Pontiff be denied? Did not Christ Himself institute excommunication?" He did not institute it as the Pope uses it. Nay, neither he nor any individual can use it, but only the particular church concerned. For the name itself shows clearly enough what it is, even if we had not so plain an utterance on the subject. For to excommunicate is to remove from the company of those who communicate together. And if you say, "Cannot the Pope cast out of the church?" I say that he cannot, for that belongs to the church alone, and not to the Pope. For Christ never said, "Tell it to the Pope." Hence it came about that persons excommunicated by the Pope did not in like manner seem to the church worthy of such rejection; and so it followed that few shunned those whom he ordered men to abhor. Let them, therefore, fulminate, thunder, storm, and thrust us down to hell with their formulas, but let us not be moved one whit. On the other hand, let us fear exceedingly to tempt the severity of the church by our wantonness. This will be pleasing in the sight of the Most High.

Now we must come back to the real magistrate. He is nowhere more emphatically approved than in Rom. 13:1-7, where Paul discusses with such pains obedience to the authorities that one has a right to suspect that even then there were persons who, just like some in our own time, were trying to turn Christian liberty to the advantage of the flesh [cf. Gal. 5:13]. Not that I approve the unbridled license of power shown by some magistrates or princes, but I would not have those who give themselves out for Christians aim at casting off all authority in the expectation that they are going to live in freedom. This I have always regarded as the height of folly or the height of viciousness. Every company gathered together anywhere must obey some authority; otherwise all combined action would be at an end. Christians, therefore, should not disparage authority, but should do their best to make that under which we live as pious and just as possible. And if this is not in our power, because, for instance, the ruler we are forced to obey was born king or simpleton, we must the more often entreat God to send us at length some Moses to bring us out of servitude into true liberty: not such liberty that every man shall do as he likes (for that is a more baneful tyranny than when one man or a few men exercise such indulgence. For it is more insupportable to have a whole nation running mad than a few individuals), but such that under it truth has free course, justice is administered impartially to all, peace and concord are preserved by common consent. Now, then, let us hear Paul. He says [Rom. 13:1-6]: "Let every soul be in subjection to the higher powers: for there is no power but of God. Therefore the powers that be are ordained of God. Therefore he that resisteth the power, resisteth the ordinance of God: and they that resist shall receive to themselves judgment. For rulers are not a terror to good works, but to the evil. And if thou desirest to have no fear of the power, do that which is good, and thou shalt have praise from the same: for he is a minister of God to thee for good. But if thou do that which is evil, be afraid; for he beareth not the sword in vain: for he is a minister of God, an avenger for wrath to him that doeth evil. Wherefore ye must needs be in subjection, not only because of the wrath, but also for conscience sake. For for this cause pay ye tribute: for they are God's ministers, attending continually upon this very thing." We must now consider Paul's statements separately, in order to get his full meaning. As to his saying "every soul," it is not unusual for "soul" to be used for "man"; so that he said "every soul" for "all men." For this Hebrew expression has somewhat greater vividness than the Latin "omnes homines," "all men."—He said "higher powers" for "rulers," whether they be monarchs or the aristocracy, that is, whether it is a king or the nobles who are high in power.—"For there is no power but of God." What, Paul? Was Pharaoh's power of God? Surely; for on account of our sins God places children and effeminate creatures upon our necks, Isa. 3:4-5. Therefore let them that rule not hold their heads too high when they hear that all power is of God, for they are not thereby justified. For frequently He punishes the bad by means of the very bad. But let them rather, hearing how they have been raised to their position by the providence of God, make it their aim to do nothing that is unbecoming in one who sits in God's place. And let them keep ever before their eyes that from the founding of the world they that have ruled with violence have ever had brief dominion; but that, on the other hand, the posterity of all them that have exercised their power with moderation have retained their ancestral realms as long as might be. A vast and slippery thing is power. Now, nothing tends to fall out of one's hands more quickly than a thing which is at once very large and slippery, especially if you try to hold on to it forcibly. Power is a vast thing of this sort and exceeding slippery; and if you try with all your might to hold on to it, that is, to do everything with violence, it will fall out of your hands. There should be moderation in preserving it, and if you disregard that, it is better not to have it at all. "The powers," then, "are ordained of God." Hence it is evident that "he that resisteth the power, resisteth the ordinance of God." But who would not obey a pious power more willingly than an impious one? I do not mean that you should not obey an impious power (for Paul goes on to say, "they that resist shall receive to themselves judgment"), but that you should not allow yourself to be hurried into the mistake of those who declare that a Christian cannot be a magistrate. For suppose a city so born again in Christ that every one of its citizens lives according to His precepts; it will still require magistrates because of those who come there. Let us, therefore, not talk about abolishing magistrates in general, until blamelessness itself abolishes them. For those that delay to obey the authorities "shall receive to themselves judgment," that is, lay up for themselves a great store of the wrath and vengeance of God.

"For rulers are not a terror to good works, but to the evil." Would that rulers might be as careful to listen to this part of Paul's words as they are to thunder forth those other words: "There is no power but of God; the powers are ordained of God," and, "He that resisteth the power, resisteth the ordinance of God." But we poor mortals are not so constituted that we listen as carefully to what brings us to order as we do to what brings others. It is a rare virtue among rulers, especially as they conduct themselves today, not to be a terror to good works, that is, not to obstruct the truth and not to be hatefully harsh to those who order their lives according to the rule of gospel truth. On the other hand, it is common with some rulers to promote the worst men to places of rank, power, and honor for no other reason than that they may fight fiercely for the Roman Pontiff and treat savagely those who venture to speak out what is true. If anyone says, "I trust in the one and only God and bring my troubles to Him without the intervention of any advocate," he is suddenly hurried off to punishment, because, forsooth, he has refused to desert God for a creature. And those who do this bear witness in official records that their aim is to defend the true and ancient religion of Christ. If to avoid a scandal you, a priest, marry a wife, you are ordered to prison unheard,* while meantime these persons are less horrified to see a whoremonger administering the mass before their eyes than if he were a dog. For sometimes dogs coupling in churches are driven away with a stick, but no one drives away the whoremonger, though he defiles everything we have hitherto considered most holy. If, on the other hand, before the eyes of these rulers (I am speaking of tyrants, well aware that many pious rulers strenuously exert themselves to give us a view in these latter days of pure and simple Christianity)—if, I say, before their eyes you commit the most abominable crime, and yet at least just insult the freshly rising Christ,† you obtain forgiveness. See how everything is turned upside down with them. What pen can leave to posterity a worthy record of this madness? What tongue express its shamelessness, recklessness, monstrousness? What tears bewail these lost ones, rushing with eyes open, such is their madness, into utter destruction? And yet they offer themselves to the simple-minded crowd as champions of righteousness and truth. Ah, if we boast in the name of Christ, ought not His word to have more effect with us than that of any creature? But when

*Cf. Vol. 1, pp. 177-196.
†*i. e.*, the Reformation movement.

you add, "If it is not opposed to the view of the Popes," you are setting the word of man before the word of God. Think not, then, excellent princes, that you can conceal even from the humble folk how far you are from Christ by making formal proclamation that you will defend true religion, while in reality you persecute it more cruelly than any Turks. Practices of that sort last for a while, but they finally bring a disastrous end. You should uphold general righteousness, not persecute the guiltless for the sake of the Roman Pontiff. The wicked man, the murderer, the robber, and all such like pests ought to fear your face, but the pious and blameless ought to rejoice because of it. What am I to say in censure of the boundless lust and luxury of certain princes, upon which they lavish all their substance senselessly, so that it would be better never to have acquired anything than to have squandered it so basely? They stake their money chests at play, for their purses cannot hold such an amount of gold as they stake. They drink, so that it were better the wine had been poured upon the ground than destroy the human body by its use, as if, as Pliny has it, there were no other path through which wine could be poured out and destroyed than the human body. They go awhoring to such an extent that they seem to have a deadly hatred for a pure marriage; and they so defile all things with their lewdness that the man is indeed unfortunate who happens to have a beautiful or clever wife or daughter. And when they have spent everything thus, they not only despoil the wretched people with new exactions and taxes and tribute, but load them with burdens, torment and destroy them, so that they seem to have been born for the general ruin.—"Rulers are not a terror to good works, but to the evil." Those, therefore, who, on the other hand, delight in evil and are a constant menace to the good are not rulers, but tyrants, torturers, butchers.—Then follows: "And if thou desirest to have no fear of the power, do that which is good, and thou shalt have praise from the same." I beg those who disparage magistrates to consider these words carefully. If they hate or fear the power, let them do that which is right. At the same time let rulers reflect that they are not to be a terror to good deeds. Having praise from the power when you have acted rightly is said in reference to the custom prevalent among the Athenians and the Romans of giving rewards or formal thanks to those who served the state well, sometimes before the Senate, sometimes before the general assembly; as we frequently read in Cicero how some were praised in the Senate, others before the assemblage in the Forum.—"He is a minister of God for thy good, or to thee for good." Rulers are set over us for the good of all. Therefore let those who rule to the ill of all see what right they have to boast in the name of Christ, seeing that they not only, like thieves and robbers, plunder the goods of all, but, like plagues, also waste their bodies. But they are ministers of God all the same, just as Satan is a minister of God, who everywhere opposes, deceives, and destroys. "For he beareth not the sword in vain: for he is a minister of God." Swords are carried before certain rulers as an emblem of power, and it is to this custom that Paul is alluding here. He shows that some are so audaciously evil that, unless they be smitten with the sword, the rest cannot have peace. He says, therefore, that the ruler is a minister of God for the guarding of general righteousness and tranquillity. Here I ask those who repudiate the magistracy whether a pious man cannot be a minister of Christ just as well as an impious man. They say it was written among them of old time [cf. Mt. 5: 21f.]: "Thou shalt not kill"; but that we are forbidden to yield to anger, much more to kill. Nice fellows these! They refuse with the very words before them to see what the meaning of God's words is. For when He says that we are not even to yield to anger, it becomes clear that, wishing to block up the fountain-source of killing, He is speaking of that killing which proceeds from ungovernable passion, not of that which is visited by law upon those who have dared to upset the public peace, towards whom we more often feel pity than anger. But, since even in such cases judgment is sometimes too precipitate, is not a pious man more likely to give a right and timely judgment than an impious man?—"For he is a minister of God, an avenger for wrath to him that doeth evil" [Rom. 13: 4]. He says he is a minister of God and an avenger whom He uses for wrath, that is, to assert His justice, against those who do evil. He, therefore, avenges in God's name, not in his own; He smites in God's name, not in his own. "But you are bidden to smite no one." Yes, but God, who kills and makes alive, [cf. Deut. 32: 39], who sends to hell and brings back, has the right to smite; and therefore when He bids a man smite, that man, too, smites without sin. Thus Moses slew, and Phineas, Samuel, Elijah, Jehu, and others; and the slaying is accounted glory to them. But let the magistrate take care not to smite unless the Lord bids him. When the Lord does bid, no man will see the fact better than the pious man, that is, he who knows how often one must forgive, but also knows best when to strike down. For though Peter was bidden to refrain seventy times seven times [cf. Mt. 18: 22], he yet struck down Ananias and Sapphira at once, Acts 5: 1-11, no doubt because the situation demanded it. For not always does there appear one with the aspect or voice of an angel to tell us to strike down, but sometimes the Lord stirs the heart within and instructs it in what cases to pardon and in what not.

"Wherefore we must needs be in subjection to authority, not only because of the vengeance, but also for conscience' sake" [Rom. 13: 5]. He means that we should refrain from evil doing, not so much from fear of punishment as because the conscience is on guard, which we ought to keep so blameless that we in no matter resist the will of God. Since, then, God wills that we should obey the magistrates, we cannot without danger to the conscience neglect to listen to the magistrate. What will those who would abolish the Christian magistracy find to say here? That it is an offence against conscience not to obey an impious ruler, and, on the other hand, is an offence against conscience to obey a pious ruler? What shall I say? I praise knowledge of the things of faith, but contentiousness I do not praise. For that cannot be without lust for glory which is the most indubitable champion of glory. And if lust for glory goads persons on to such violent dissensions, love is certainly very far away; and when love is away, all things are empty and vain.

"For, for this cause pay ye tribute: for they are God's ministers attending continually upon this very thing." Some rulers open their eyes very wide indeed when they hear that the paying of tribute is made a duty by divine pronouncement;

but they do not reflect that Paul says, "for, for this cause." What then, is the cause on account of which the paying of tribute is commanded? This, that the rulers may smite the evil and not the good, maintain the public peace, honor and stablish the good and not the evil. For Paul says they "attend continually upon this very thing," upon taking vengeance in God's stead, and punishing those who do that which is evil [Rom. 13: 4.]. So much from Paul on magisterial office.

It was said, even by the ancient philosophers: "Would you know a man? Give him power." So widely does the desire for wealth and glory corrupt the heart of man, though for a time it may conceal everything perfectly. When, however, the way is once opened, no one can restrain it so that its victims seem to have been moderate in their longings. Consequently there is no other thing that more surely inflames hidden longings than power; for then they think they have found the opportunity to run riot with impunity. Hence it is a very dangerous thing to entrust power to anyone. Saul surpassed all in kindness and simplicity of heart, as much as in stature and splendor of body [I Sam. 9: 2]. Yet how he changed his ways! Who was ever more ungrateful to a benefactor than he to David? Though he had often given the latter occasion, nevertheless he never experienced any ill-treatment at his hands. They say that Pythagoras surpassed all tyrants in cruelty after he obtained the controlling power. A man who had held aloof from so many things, and who had been so persistently taciturn that you would call him a misanthrope rather than a lover of dominion, so intoxicated himself with the unrestrained use of power that, as drunk as a man overloaded with wine, he made onslaught upon the innocent. Who now can safely entrust power to anyone when we see the most single-hearted and the wisest so changed by power? What, pray, are we to hope for from those who born in power yet abhor nothing so much as the knowledge of how to exercise power? When they ought to fulfil the duties, they simply display the outward aspect of a ruler, and leave everything else in the hands of the most greedy men, so that instead of one tyrant those who live under such governments have a thousand. All righteousness flags, greed flourishes, nay, rules, and for no other reason than that nobody learns how to exercise power. They think that if by some means or other the revenues are very large, government is well administered. But why do I complain of these men, when those who wish to be called ecclesiastics—nay, spirituals and monks—bishops, and abbots, are reckoned good and faithful ministers in proportion as they have increased the annual returns? Let us, therefore, not rashly trust supreme power to the indiscreet, to children, stupid and greedy persons, but to those whose probity, faithfulness, discretion, have been proved by long experience (otherwise we shall in vain some day utter the familiar lament, "I did not think"); and may the Father Almighty give us such rulers as look to no other example than His by whose ordinance they are inducted into such offices, that they may conduct themselves after the manner of our Creator, which would make it possible for us to boast of having many fathers instead of being forced to utter the complaint of the Prophet, Mic. 7:1-3: "Woe is me! for I am as one who gathereth in autumn the grape of the vintage: there is no cluster to eat; my soul desired the first-ripe figs. The holy man is perished out of the earth; and there is none upright among men: they all lie in wait for blood; every man hunteth his brother to death. The evil of their hands they call good. The prince asketh, and the judge is for giving; and the great man hath uttered the desire of his soul and they have troubled it," etc. Let the princes, rather, often reflect upon the words of the same prophet in the third chapter, lest overcome with greed they savagely tear the sheep and lend themselves overmuch to false prophets, bishops, monks, and priests of Baal, who, if they cannot turn away from Christ the souls of all, yet by their bribes and devices shake them, and draw them off, if they can. Let the princes look with suspicion upon every hat or mitre, for although their wearers sometimes pretend that they will have access to Christ, it often happens that they bring a heavier load of damage. For they are the very ones who exhaust kingdoms, enjoying so fully the fruits of others' labors that they even trample under foot what would be capable of feeding many thousands. But the words of the prophet are as follows, Mic. 3:1-6: "Hear, ye princes of Jacob, and ye chiefs of the house of Israel: Is it not for you to know judgment? ye who hate the good and love the evil; who violently pluck off their skin from off them, and the flesh from off their bones; who have eaten the flesh of my people, and have flayed their skin off them; and have broken and chopped their bones as for the kettle, and as flesh in the midst of the pot. Then shall they cry unto the Lord, but he will not answer them: yea, he will hide his face from them at that time, according as they have behaved wickedly in their doings. Thus saith the Lord concerning the prophets that make my people to err; that bite with their teeth, and cry, Peace; and if a man put not something into their mouth, they prepare war against him. Therefore night shall be unto you instead of vision; and darkness to you instead of divination; and the sun shall go down upon the prophets, and the day shall be darkened over them," etc. If the rulers would listen every day to this discourse of the prophet, they would show themselves somewhat milder to their sheep than some of them have done hitherto. And as to the second part, they would learn there clearly to recognize the frauds of the Romanists, who, while contumaciously resisting the renascent Christ* at the bidding of their greed, vociferate that they do everything from devotion to peace, in order to win the favor of all. For we wish to seem devoted to peace, even when we hold arms in our hands and live in camp. So grateful a thing is peace to poor mortals, which yet these persons are strongly bent upon disturbing. For, the reason they take such pains to pretend that they are seeking peace is that they may meanwhile devour all things with their teeth. For where peace flourishes, what churches are there, pray, in which they do not make demands like beggars? And if you do not put cakes into their mouths, but refuse, they even hallow a war against you. What princes, pray, for too many years now have refused anything to these Romanists, the bishops and their satellites, that the latter have not declared war upon them? How often have we seen compacts broken by them! How many myriads of souls have they struck down! I say nothing of the havoc done to bodies, property, and estates, of the destruction of cities, the ruin of chastity and faithfulness, the extinction of general righteousness, the barbarizing of men's natures, all of which

*i. e., the Reformation.

war brings with it. Hence it comes that night is unto us instead of vision, that is, that we embrace darkness instead of light. Are we not all blinded to the clear light of truth? And do we not pretend not to see what we really do see? But through whose wiles does this come about? Those of the false prophets, who prophesy for money. Hence it soon follows that the princes also give judgment for bribes. Since, therefore, magistrates ought to strain every nerve to rule rightly, conducting themselves as fathers rather than as masters, and since we yet see them so given over to pleasure and rioting that we can have no hope of our condition being bettered through them, we must supplicate the one and only one who has numbered the hairs of our heads [cf. Mt. 10: 30] to enlighten their minds, made insolent by worldly prosperity, so that they may know God and themselves, and we thereby be able peacefully to abandon this anti-Christian condition due to the Pope. For no other effort is necessary in this matter than abandoning. If we all abandon him, or, even less, if we simply hide our purses so that they cannot discover them, it will be all up with him. Let us pray, I say, that we may all abandon him and follow the banners of God alone, the Lord of all, the Father and Salvation of all. Amen.

[28]. Offence

The Greek word for "offence" [σκάνδαλον, scandal] means not only offence but also insulting treatment, if we are to believe Chrysostom on these words in Matth. 18: 6: "If any one shall offend [scandalizaverit] one of these little ones," etc.* For he takes σκανδαλίζειν for "treat with insult or contempt," doubtless because whoever is treated with contempt or insult is also offended; and, again, whoever inconsiderately offends is treating with contempt. In explaining σκανδαλίζειν as "to treat with contempt" as well as "to offend," Chrysostom, in my

*Chrysostom's comment on these words of Christ is: For, as those who honor these little ones for my sake will gain heaven, . . . so those who dishonor them (for that is to offend them) will suffer the extreme punishment. And if He calls the insult an "offence," do not marvel; for many spiritless persons have been very much offended (scandalized) from being slighted and treated with contempt.—*Homilies on the Gospel according to St. Matthew,* Homily 58: 4.

opinion, shows that he had carefully considered its meaning here. For God wishes His own not to be treated with contempt as well as not to be offended, and He just as little wishes them to be offended as to be treated with contempt. "Offence" [scandalum], therefore, is offence combined with contempt.

I am compelled to speak about this in the last part of this work for the reason that the subject of the book demands it, as well as because certain persons are wrong in regard to both aspects of offence; some, for instance, always wanting special consideration, even when it is impossible for them to receive further offence, since nothing is done to throw contempt upon them; whereas others, as soon as they have beheld the face of liberty, disregarding altogether the question of offence, instead of putting aside things which should be promptly put aside, rudely cast them off with such violent indignation that the noise thereof offends the weak ears of conscientious brethren.

The subject of my book, I say, demands that I speak about offence.

This is because there has been error hitherto not only in teaching (though there it has been most pernicious), but also in ceremonies (and there also it has not been of trifling character, since we have embraced the external elements of this world as things spiritual, vain and empty things as things real and solid). I will speak first of all, therefore, about offence arising from teaching—namely, to what extent we should forbear to teach. We should not forbear to teach. For as soon as you are sent forth, you ought to spread teaching abroad, and not to "confer with flesh and blood," Gal. 1: 16. Yet in teaching there should be special regard to timeliness, as I said above in introducing the discussion of the Eucharist. For Christ praises that, and Paul, I Cor. 3: 2, boasts that in the beginning he fed the Corinthians with milk. Therefore, no one can begin better or more securely than by following the example of John and Christ and the Apostles, thus: "Ye are very evil, ye have turned aside from the way of God thus and so. Therefore, unless ye change your lives, cruel vengeance hangs over you. God is just, and He will not spare to strike when He has once laid the axe to the root of the tree [cf. Mt. 3: 10]. Repent, therefore, of your sins, and loathe them, and ye will straightway find Him a gentle father whom, unless ye mend your ways, ye will discover to be a stern avenger. He is just, but He is also kind, and loveth His own work; and to show His kindness to us He gave His only begotten Son, that through Him we may have life. Thus life will be your portion. I have warned you to cease to be evil and to become good. Since this will throw you into fresh despair—for who was ever so blameless or righteous that he could venture to trust to his own righteousness?—in order that ye may not wholly perish in this despair, I will show who has appeased the divine justice for us, that ye may not be forced to dread it as inexorable: Christ by His own blamelessness has cleansed away the sins of all. If thou trust in Him, thou shalt be saved, but so that thou put off the old man and put on Christ [cf. Col. 3: 9-10], as I have said often and at length already." When you have well taught the knowledge of God, man, and Christ, and the Lord has given the increase [cf. I Cor. 3: 6-7] (which you will easily judge from its fruits), all the abominations and errors that had risen up against God and been received as the true worship of God will fall away. For when everyone has once been taught that he is a Christian who lives blamelessly and trusts in the blameless one, namely, Christ, whom taking up His cross he follows, he will disregard those fallacious hopes which certain persons have told us to place in sacraments, ceremonies, and created things, and will see that all his hopes are placed in God. Therefore they do unwisely who begin by proclaiming very hard and quite paradoxical things, though these seem mild enough to people who have already made some progress. I will give an illustration. If you make Christianity begin, as was mistakenly done for several centuries, with giving up hope in the saints, you will nullify rather than implant your teaching, even though your soul does strongly urge you to such utterance as, "Ye err in worshipping as gods them that are not gods. Cast all your hopes upon the Lord, not upon a creature. They are impious who put the creature in place of the Creator. Those who invoke the creature put it in the place of God. For to every one God is that through which he trusts that he will be delivered from that which oppresses him or be given that of which he has need." Since, therefore, the matter must be begun in such a way that we may bring the most fruit to the Lord, we will never begin with these things that spoil the whole case, but we will set forth faithfully and wisely certain things which are especially necessary, such as the knowledge of God, of man, of the gospel, and will hold back certain things till the favorable occasion.

So much briefly as to looking out for offence in teaching. For Christ says [Lk. 12: 8-9]: "He that shall confess me before men, him will I confess before the angels of God; but he that shall deny me before men, him will I deny before the angels of God." The things, therefore, on which faith hinges should be brought out without delay; but the things that militate against it need to be demolished with skill, lest they do harm in their downfall and bury the little that has been already built up. You can easily persuade an old man to leave his chair if you first put into his hand a staff upon which he can lean, when otherwise he will never listen to you but rather believe that you are trying to entrap him into falling upon the pavement and breaking his head. So the human mind must above all be led to infallible knowledge of God, and when it has duly attained that, it will easily let go false hopes in created things.

Now I pass on to externals, and will show how offence is to be taken into account in the case of these.

Of external things some have to do with eating, some with the regulation of life, and some seem to have to do with salvation, though they really amount to nothing.,

Those that have to do with eating have been made a stumbling-block of offence by the huckster business of the high priest of Rome. For how else am I to name that cunning with which he has forbidden certain foods* simply that we may be forced to buy back for a high price what we cannot do without? Yet Christ says plainly in Mark 7: 18: "There is nothing without a man entering into him that can defile him." Nor is there any reason to say in opposition here that no kinds of food are forbidden, but the use of certain ones is prohibited at particular times. For the word of God is free and does not suffer itself to be confined to particular times. And this very thing

*Cf Zwingli's *Von Erkiesen und Freiheit der Spiesen.* *See*, in this series, vol. 1, pp. 70-112.

that I said, the giving back for money of what had been tyrannically taken from us, shows well enough that no food has been absolutely forbidden by the commandment of God. For if it had been enacted by the word of God that certain foods must be abstained from, there would be no need of a special law to that effect. Hence it is clear that when the Pope promulgates such a law he does it of himself. And when he abrogates it for money received he shows that that which he abrogates is not divine. For who can abrogate a divine law? Paul predicts, I Tim. 4: 1-4, that it will come to pass that some will engage in this sort of traffic, saying: "The Spirit saith expressly, that in later times some shall fall away from the faith, giving heed to seducing spirits, and doctrines of demons that will speak lies in hypocrisy and have their conscience seared with a hot iron; forbidding to marry, and commanding to abstain from meats which God hath created to be received with thanksgiving of them which believe and know the truth. Certainly every creature of God is good, and nothing is worthless, if it be received with thanksgiving," etc. These words of Paul are clear. When, therefore, he says that it is plain to those who know the truth that "every creature of God is good, and nothing is worthless," there will no doubt be persons who will instantly say: "I believe thoroughly that to the pure all things are pure [cf. Tit. 1: 15]; hence I shall have no hesitation in using with thanksgiving anything I please without regard to anybody. For why should my liberty be judged by others' consciences?" Here then we must take offence into account. You must consider your neighbor, whether he be weak, or contumacious, or pious. You should take the weak one to yourself, that is, extend a hand, that he likewise may be able to rise to the measure of your knowledge; and this not by means of marvelously intricate inventions that will tangle him up rather than straighten him out, but with clear sayings like these: "To the pure all things are pure," Tit. 1: 15; "Every creature of God is good, and is created to the end that we may use it with thanksgiving," I Tim. 4: 4; "There is nothing without a man entering into him that can defile him," Mk. 7: 15, Mt. 15: 17; "I know that nothing is in its own nature unclean: but only to him that accounteth anything to be unclean is it unclean," Rom. 14: 14. If he is made stronger by such words, you may then safely eat any kind of food in his presence at any time; if not, you must spare his weakness as long as there is weakness. For so Paul says, Rom. 14: 15: "If because of meat thy brother is grieved, thou walkest no longer in love. Destroy not with thy meat him for whom Christ died"; and, "Overthrow not for meat's sake the work of God" [Rom. 14: 20]. These things Paul here, as always, speaks of by divine inspiration. Again, in I Cor. 8: 13, you have: "If meat offend my brother, I will eat no flesh for evermore, lest I offend my brother." Therefore, as long as your brother is weak and not contumacious, you must spare him. And even if your brother is contumacious, again you must spare him if your meat can cause any turmoil. For you should not "overthrow for meat's sake the work of God"; that is, we should not for the sake of liberty as to foods act so as to render the gospel hateful. But if after sufficient teaching you can eat without offence and turmoil, you may do so. Mortals are not so made that what is nearest right pleases everybody: there will never be lacking persons to object. But we must always look to this, that we pursue the works of peace. Paul circumcised Timothy because the Jews were so insistent about it and he could not withstand them without great turmoil and offence as to the gospel, Acts 16: 3; but he could not be forced to circumcise Titus, Gal. 2: 3, because his teachings had then made such progress that the better and larger number could carry the day without turmoil and offence. So, therefore, we must strive for peace and tranquillity in these things that have to do with food, and spare the weak as long as they are weak; and, indeed, the contumacious as long as we cannot without turmoil freely enjoy that in which we are free. For if we should be obliged forever to spare every contumacious person, we should never be allowed to enjoy anything freely. There are always wanton persons who have the audacity lightly to misinterpret any act or motive whatsoever. If your brethren are pious, there is no offence, no matter what you eat, so long as you observe moderation.

In the things which have to do with the regulation of life we ought all to walk most blamelessly, that by our good conversation unbelievers may be kindled to follow Him whose disciples live so uprightly. We ought, therefore, to cast off at once the license of the Gentiles, for it is enough and more than enough to have lived so long according to the way of the flesh. So Peter teaches, I Pet. 4: 2; and Paul, Rom. 13: 12-14, saying: "Let us therefore cast off the works of darkness, and let us put on the armor of light. Let us walk as in the day; not in revelling and drunkenness, not in chambering and wantonness, not in strife and jealousy. But put ye on the Lord Jesus Christ." In the same manner he says, I Cor. 5:11: "But now I write unto you not to keep company, if any man that is named a brother be a fornicator, or covetous, or an idolator, or a reviler, or a drunkard, or an extortioner; with such a one no not to eat." It is lawful, therefore, to cast off all these things at the first opportunity, for they ought to be as far distant as possible from a Christian, aye, they ought to be so far away that they must be immediately removed from the church. If, therefore, you have hitherto been a fornicator, abandon your mistress; or if continence is denied you, seek a wife, or turn your mistress herself into a wife.* Here, however, very great offence is apt to arise. For if ecclesiastics, as they are called, begin to marry, immediately there rise up persons who pretend to be offended, though they are not in the least offended; but for the sake of their revenues, which they fear will decrease, they make pretence of being offended, as has been said before. Everyone should, therefore, keep as far away from fornication as possible. And every one knows also that fornication is a great sin. You will say, therefore: "Every one ought, then, without any regard to offence to take a wife just as soon as he discovers his want of continence, since nothing forbids or discourages this. For no one can be offended, since there is no one who denies that fornication must be done away with." These are the reasons why for some time I thought that in this matter no attention should be paid to offence. But though I see that these two things, "Fornication ought to be absent from the Christian flock," and, "Everybody knows that fornication is a sin," are strong enough fairly to allow any one to pay no attention to offence in the matter, yet at the same time I see that

*Cf. Zwingli's plea that priests be given permission to marry. *See* vol. 1, pp. 150-165, and 177-196.

Antichrist, that is, the Pope of Rome, has laid an offence upon us, half asleep or rather sound asleep as we are, so that, now that we want to wake up, we give offence. For to whom has he not, against every law of God, forbidden marriage? Since, therefore, for some time much faith has been had in him, it has been absolutely necessary to have regard for offence, but on the same principle as in the case of teaching. As that ought not in any degree to be omitted, but to be imparted in due season, so, too, fornication must be entirely done away with, and to that end a marriage must be brought about if you burn, but at the right time. Hence some brethren among us, to avoid offence, and to quiet the pangs of conscience (for it was torture to be a fornicator), contracted marriage secretly, that the mind might not, being conscious of fornication and suffering from this wound, do everything more listlessly than it ought; and they concealed the fact until teaching on the subject of marriage could be seasonably put forth. When this had once been done, so that all saw plainly that there was no possible reason for hindering any one who wished from taking a wife, new husbands began everywhere to appear. Then certain of the tyrants began to slaughter the innocent, and others to deprive them of their priesthoods and to banish them. This has raised the question, whether those who thus made their marriages public a little too soon ought not to have waited somewhat longer. I answer that there should not have been any further waiting after the teaching had once been well set forth, for impious rulers can never be induced not to indulge in the most savage persecution. Yet there were some indiscreet or false brethren who proceeded to make marriage the foundation of Christianity, and though I do not disapprove their conduct, I do disapprove their conclusion, for it was ill-considered to demonstrate their Christianity by nothing else than their marriage. These men, therefore, seem sometimes rather to have occasioned disturbances than to have prevented them. But, now that the whole matter has been set forth, especially in Germany,* there is no room left for offence; nay, rather it is

*In the writings of Luther, *e. g.*, *De votis monasticis* (1521); *Vom ehelichen Leben* (1522); *Ursach und Antwort, dass Jungfrauen Klöster göttlich verlassen mögen* (1523).

permitted that all who are incontinent contract marriage. And if some tyrants threaten and strike, flee to another country; for it is better with Zeno† to carry away everything, *i. e.,* a heart disburdened of fornication, than to be tortured within amidst the cares of riches, even if no persecutor troubles you without.

In the external things that seem to have to do with salvation, we must have regard to offence in this way. We should set forth how these things that seem to be of some avail for salvation cannot be of any value, and this simply by teaching; but we must do it in such manner as, above all else, to win the approval of Him in whom alone the conscience finds peace. We shall show that these external things are signs with which we do something for our neighbor rather than for ourselves. Such are anointings, sprinklings, benedictions, and such like ceremonies. When everything is already set forth in the word, these signs are to be calmly done away with, having been brought in by device of man, in the same way as forbidden foods. For this is the way we see Paul did with circumcision. Though he knew well that neither circumcision nor uncircumcision is anything, as he taught in I Cor. 7: 19 and Gal. 6: 15, he yet suffered Timothy to be circumcised [Acts 16: 3]. But we must strenuously insist that no hope is to be placed in these external things, for they have no power; and then we must make concession to the weakness of some persons. For the feelings are not lightly persuaded to abandon immediately things that the mind has long since given up. But let no one understand by this that the things I am speaking of are to be tolerated forever, but only for a time. For his armor must be taken away from the enemy, that he may not sometime again equip himself with it for battle. This was what Christ meant in the parable of the strong man armed, Lk. 11: 22: "But when a stronger than he shall come upon him, and overcome him, he taketh from him his whole armor wherein he trusted," etc. See how he approves taking away the armor also, lest, forsooth, if we allow the things that ought to be abolished to remain, they may bring us back sometime to our earlier error. For some are so frail that, like a vine, they cling to the nearest support, and when they have once done so find it hard to let go.

†The saying, "Omnia mea mecum porto," is usually attributed to Bias.

Therefore those things in which there is such great occasion for seduction must be removed; but with due regard to offence. If you now say: "Who, then, will be able to see when those things which must be endured for a time are to be abolished? For who will know when turmoil is likely to follow, and when not?" He whose eye is clear, and single, for his whole body is full of light and has no part in darkness [cf. Mt. 6: 22-23]; that is, he who is faithful to his Lord, does all things for His sake and nothing for his own. For when the glory of God alone is regarded, all things go on well. And if ever the fire, that is, persecution, rages, it will do no more harm than fire does to gold. But when we begin to regard our own interest, we shall be consumed by the fire of persecution, just like wood and hay and stubble [cf. I Cor. 3: 12-13]. But how shall we purge the eye so that we can see plainly when the work should be begun? I answer: We shall purge it with that fire which the Lord wills should burn fiercely [cf. Lk. 12: 49], which is love: this knows all things, sees all things, is ever intent upon building up, not upon tearing down. Knowledge is sometimes so puffed up as even to burst, but knowledge edifieth not; for this is the province of love. I Cor. 8: 1: "Knowledge puffeth up, but love edifieth"; for it desires to extend as widely as possible the domain of him whom it loves. It suffers all things, therefore, for Christ's sake, "beareth all things, believeth all things, hopeth all things, endureth all things, never faileth," that is, is never deceived, never makes a mistake, I Cor. 13: 7-8. For where love is, there is God Himself, as I have said at sufficient length before. But is it at all in our power to love? By no means. But neither is it in our power to have the will or ability to build, though it is in the mouth of all men to boast that they are going to build for the Lord. So bold is hypocrisy. It is to be observed, therefore, that, since "it is God who worketh in us both to will and to work," Phil. 2: 13, surely those who will to build to the glory of God have been taught of the Lord to have this will. Therefore, when you feel that all your plans have as their object the making of the whole world subject to God, when you can both bear and do all things for the sake of God, be sure that the Lord has wrought this in you. Consider yourself, therefore, and be your own judge. No man knows but yourself whether you have any guile hidden in your heart. And when you feel sincerely and truly that you are seeking the glory of Christ, then your will has been led to Him by divine power. For "every one that hath heard from the Father, and hath learned, cometh unto me" [Jn. 6: 45]. You are not for Christ unless the Father has led you to Him [Jn. 6: 44]. Consider now the individual points. If you see that you are so on fire with love for God as to refer all things to His glory, you will wish to raise His building; if your will aims at that, God has wrought this in you. What you build, therefore, will never collapse; for it rests upon a rock that no man can overturn. You will know, too, how you ought to build, for the Lord will give you understanding in all things. You will say: "But who will tell the church whether he who begins to build is minded to build unto God or not? Yet is it most necessary for us to know this; for otherwise the times are such that we shall fall into the greatest dissensions if we know not the mind of the builder. For all men wish to seem to build to the glory of God." I answer: There are many ways in which the individual can judge concerning the builder, and in regard to them I leave each man to be fully assured in his own mind [cf. Rom. 14: 5]. For every man says that from this or that he detects the deceit of a builder. Only let nothing be done in the heat of passion. But there are two ways in particular by which you can infallibly detect the mind of the teacher. One is the way that Christ taught, according to which the teacher is known by his fruits, whether those which he offers or those which he seeks; for it is in this latter sense that Christ says, Matth. 7: 20, "By their fruits," that is, by that which they seek, "ye shall know them." If, therefore, the teacher looks only to being splendidly fed and looked after, no one can fail to see whether he is building for God or for himself. And if he is nothing but a sink of iniquity, even if he is a very brilliant teacher, he is the least in the kingdom of God, that is, he is nothing in the church of God. This judgment, therefore, is derived from the man himself whom you are judging, though in such a way that you alone are not to condemn him before others, but only when the church condemns him. When the church condemns, every one who is a member of the church must also condemn in his heart; although, as I have said, no one ought to pronounce judgment until the church does. For, "judge not, etc." [Mt. 7:1]. I am speaking here of each man's private judgment, by which everyone in the church sees what the mind of a teacher is, even though the church delays to pronounce judgment upon him. That this is so our own time proves, in which all the Christian congregation together, as soon as truth showed itself to the public view, abandoned those whose words savored of greed and domination, and went over to the side of the truth, though in the beginning they had no other *βάσανος* [standard of judgment] than dominion and greed. The other way in which the mind of the builder can be detected, even in spite of himself, whether he is building for the Lord or seeking glory, is this: Paul writes, Rom. 14: 17-18: "For the kingdom of God is not eating and drinking, but righteousness and peace and joy in the Holy Spirit. For he that in these things serveth Christ is well-pleasing to God, and approved of men." When, therefore, a man's efforts are directed towards making public righteousness flourish, so that every man shall above all things be zealous in his own heart for blamelessness; when he is wholly absorbed in keeping peace with all men as far as is in us lies, in bringing men's consciences into the quiet haven of faith and love of God, that they may not be buffeted about by every wind; when his only aim is to banish as far as possible all the sorrows that arise from worldly desires to torment mortals, so that Christian cheerfulness and grace may abide with all—this man surely is building for the Lord. And every man can tell for himself whether the whole force of the teacher breathes God and blamelessness or not. Those, therefore, who for the sake of certain externals, by which the conscience is in no wise helped, disturb Christian peace are seeking nothing but glory, even though they pretend the lowliest humility; for that is just the way hypocrisy goes to work, according to Paul's testimony, Col. 2:15. This is what those do who at this time refuse baptism to infants or give it to adults a second time; for they are so contentious that you never saw anything more harsh and bitter. Where, then, is the humility? For where there is contention and jealousy, there the flesh reigneth, by the testimony of the Apostle, I Cor.

3:3. Their own impudence makes me want to mention certain of them by name, who, simply to carry the point that infants should not be baptized, have dragged into the fiercest discussions whole cities that were beginning to have real knowledge of Christ. What, good God, is insanity, what is madness, what is dementia, if it is not this, namely, thinking that this is your spirit which by its very fruits shows that it cannot be of any one but man's enemy, the Devil? This is the way Satan tempts us: when he sees that he has not succeeded by means of persecution, he tempts us with contentiousness, so that persecution is almost to be chosen in preference to contentiousness; for the one is a peril to the body only, the other to the soul. Some* are like this: When they see that images have been removed at Zurich, both in the city and in the country districts, without the least disturbance wherever they were worshipped, they likewise bend all their efforts to having them removed in their own jurisdictions also, so that they shall not be behind others, though their brethren are still tender and strongly opposed to the change. Let them first teach their hearers to be upright in the things that pertain to God, and they will immediately see all these objectionable things fall away. For where there is trust in God, there we behold "Satan falling as lightning from heaven," Luke 10:18. Let us, therefore, implant blamelessness, peace, and cheerfulness of soul in the Holy Spirit, and we shall drag Satan from heaven, and in all things duly take offence into account; for God aideth His own work.

[29]. Statues and Images

I had determined to say nothing here about statues and images, because I had decided to write a special book† about them in German at the earliest opportunity; but when I was already beginning to shorten sail, some of the brethren would not allow me to make for port until I had explored this bay also. I will, therefore, set down very briefly the essential things in this matter. For who could ever satisfy the contentious spirits?

No one is so stupid as to think that we ought to do away

*The Anabaptists.

†*Eine Antwort Valentin Compar gegeben,* dated April 27, 1525.

with statues, images, and other representations, where no worship is offered them; for who is affected by the flying cherubim on the mercy seat or embroidered on the curtains, whether for their mystic meaning or for decoration, or by the palms, lions, oxen, pomegranates, and such like ornaments cunningly wrought in Solomon's temple [cf. I Kings 6: 1-38]? Again, when they are worshipped, who is so senseless, not to say faithless, as to think they ought to be tolerated? Of course, offence is to be taken into account. But if it had nowhere in the Scriptures been commanded that statues and images if worshipped should be destroyed, love would be enough, which certainly admonishes every faithful heart to convert to the use of the needy that which is spent on the worship of images. For as soon as human reason says, "Thou shalt set up this statue in honor of God or of some Saint," faith certainly contradicts, declaring that all the moneys you expend for the honor of the Lord ought to be converted to the use of the poor. For when Christ in reply to the insulting words of Judas said to all the disciples [Jn. 12: 8], "The poor ye have with you always; but me ye have not always, and ye can do good to them," He turned aside all material service from Himself to the poor. Let us, then, not weary God with any of these marks of honor which He transferred to the poor, but bestow them where He directed. For when He rose from the dead He would not suffer the same Magdalene who had bathed his feet with her tears [Jn. 12: 3] to touch Him [Jn. 20: 17]; for He was on the eve of His ascent to heaven (though He had not yet begun His departure, though everything necessary to it was prepared) where there would be no need of the ministrations which she was preparing to offer. And when some people say that man is taught by the images, and influenced to piety, this is an idea of their own. For Christ nowhere taught this method of teaching, and He certainly would not have omitted it if He had foreseen that it would be profitable. On the contrary, knowing all things that were to come, He saw that it frequently happens that we turn to the things that are evident to sense, and He did not wish images to be made more impressive to us by the influence of teaching. For we do seem to owe something to those who teach us. We ought to be taught by the word of

God externally, and by the Spirit internally, those things that have to do with piety, and not by sculpture wrought by the artist's hand. But I return to the worship. Who has not seen statues publicly worshipped? Has their worship brought to ecclesiastics the smallest part of their wealth? What monks have ever feigned such lowly poverty that they have not begged a donation for the worship of images? Why should I tell of the gold, silver, gems, and pearls of which solid images are made, just as among the heathen, or with which their vestments are so stiff that, if you would command it, they would stand alone? Have we not all thought it a sacred thing to touch these images? Why have we imprinted kisses upon them, why have we bowed the knee, why have we paid a high price merely for a view of them? Such images, I say, the Lord orders removed. But contentiousness again objects that not the images are worshipped, but those whose images they are. I answer that neither were any of the heathen ever so stupid as to worship their images of stone, bronze, and wood for what they were in themselves; they reverenced in these their Joves and Apollos. Hence, although the Holy Scriptures frequently mock at the worship of images, as if the worshippers worshipped wood and stone, yet everybody knew that they did not in the least worship these things, but in them those rather whom they regarded as gods. But since those gods were nothing, unless perhaps evil spirits making sport of poor mortals, it was said in contempt of these who were no gods that they were nothing but stones or wood, gold, bronze, silver, so that worshippers might feel greater abhorrence for them.

When, therefore, it is said that we do not worship images (which is not true, for we do worship them more reverently than any heathen ever worshipped idols; but let us grant this), for all that the conclusion does not follow:

It is, then, permissible to have images; for two reasons:

[1.] First, because we have the worship of idols so expressly forbidden in both the New Testament and the Old. For this is the distinction between the worshippers of the one true God and idolaters, that we worship a God who is invisible and who forbids us to make any visible representation of Him, while they clothe their gods with any shape they please. Therefore, Christians have ever been bound not to fashion an image in representation of Him whom they worshipped, lest they should walk after the manner of the impious, much less in representation of those whom they were in no wise permitted to worship even when still upon earth. The objection that some persons bring up as to Christ is so clumsy that ever since entering upon this subject answering all their nonsense has caused me disgust. For how can they help knowing that, in so far as He is visible and human, Christ is in no wise to be worshipped, but only in so far as He is God? Therefore, when they say that Christ can be visibly represented as God, they are mistaken; for no art can or should represent His divine nature. And if they say that as man He can be represented, I shall ask whether or not it is permisible to worship the image of Him thus represented. They will doubtless say, "No"; for no image whatever is to be worshipped. Then, if we may not worship this, may we worship the pure humanity of Christ? They will again say, "No." What, then, do we understand when we say that Christ is worshipped in the wood of the cross? His divine nature? But that cannot be given shape. His human nature? But that should not be worshipped in this way, much less any image of those who have been redeemed by the blood of Christ. But who can answer in short compass the contentions of all? In that booklet which I promised above I shall, with God's help, clearly shatter these frivolous objections.

[II.] Second, that it is not permissible to have images, even if they are not worshipped, is plain from the fact that the reason which leads them to assert that images can be made use of betrays our vast coldness; first, in that there is no love of God in us, for that is a sufficient spur to right living; second, in that it is not safe to conform to any image but His who wishes not to be represented in visible form. When, therefore, we feel the cooling of the love of God within us, in consequence of which we are lukewarm towards all divine works, no images can kindle our hearts to the love of God. An image can rouse some trifling and fleeting emotion, but it cannot kindle love. An image of wood can kindle a fire and burn the victim, but naught can burn up the brutal affections upon the altar of the heart save the divine Spirit.

I have made these brief controversial remarks only in order to afford a foretaste of the booklet hereafter to be published, that meanwhile those who defend statues and other representations may see that, if the matter is to be settled by reasoning, it will be more evident that no images at all can be kept, than that they are ἀδιάφορα [a matter of indifference] where they cannot fail to have the appearance of evil. Not that my feeling is different from what I said in the beginning, namely, that they ought to be done away with when they are worshipped. Why, then, in this matter, which is set forth with such distinct and clear ordinances all through the Scriptures, do we split hairs, especially as nobody attacks any images but those that are worshipped, and as no image, if set up in the place where we put the things we worship, can fail to be rendered more impressive and august? But the greater and more precious it is in our sight the less is our trust in God. Since there are so many important passages in Scripture on the subject, it is better for me to note them by book and chapter than to give them here in full. Read, therefore, Exodus 20, in which chapter you will find mention of gold and silver statues; Exod. 34: 17, Exod. 19: 1, Lev. 26: 1, Deut. 4: 15-19, Deut. 5: 8, I Sam. 7: 3, Num. 25: 4-5, Deut. 7: 5, Deut. 11: 28, Deut. 13: 6-9, Deut. 27: 15, Josh. 24: 23, Judg. 10: 13, Ps. 96: 5, Ps. 115: 4, Isa. 42: 8, Isa. 44: 9, Jer. 10: 8, Jer. 13: 27, Ezek. 14: 7, Ezek. 6: 6, Mic. 1: 7, Hab. 2: 18f., and II Kings 18: 4, II Kings 10: 27, II Kings 23: 4-15, II Chron. 31:1, I Cor. 5:10, Acts 15:29, I Cor. 5:10, Acts 15:29, I Cor. 8:1-8, I Cor. 10:19, I Cor. 12:2, Gal. 5:20, I Thess. 1:9, I Pet. 4:3, I John 5:21. There are also many besides these, but let him who is not content with these leaf through the whole Bible. Now, when you examine these individual passages, kind reader, you will find in some places strange gods forbidden, in others images, and in others both strange gods and images together. This you are not to understand in the sense that—as the contentious say, but without the authority of the word—strange gods only are prohibited, or that images are considered as gods, or put in their place, although sometimes the passages cited seem verbally to imply this. If God had wished to forbid strange Gods only, it would

be of no use for Him to speak of images; for if, as our friends say, it was permissible to have images, why does He forbid it? Again, if the images and the strange gods are the same thing, images ought certainly as little to be worshipped as strange gods. But if strange gods are forbidden by themselves and images by themselves, why do we not see that there is no further room for argument? No one denies that strange gods ought not to be worshipped, for the reason that they are forbidden by the mouth of the Lord. When, therefore, we admit that images are just as much forbidden as the gods whose images they are, why do we not in the same way admit that we cannot have images at all, any more than strange gods? The reason is that we still have many, or strange, gods. I am sorry to have to say this, for it is a secret disease and those who suffer from it do not acknowledge it. Every man makes a god of that which he hopes can help him when occasion demands. Now let us see whether all the statues and most of the images have not been placed in the churches to remind us of those helpers to whom we are to run in various ills. We set up a wooden Magdalene to remind us of her to whom many sins were forgiven; not because we wish to imitate her by sitting at the feet of the Lord and listening to and following His word, but because we have the hope that this saint, as she once, overcome by the weakness of the flesh, yielded overmuch to her natural desires, so today also will plead before God for those guilty of fornication, nay, will pardon fornication itself. For there have been those who ascribed to the saints what belongs to God alone. We have made this saint a goddess, and no one can truly deny it; and we have worshipped her image for its own sake, as doing a thing acceptable to this goddess of ours. And do we still urge that these images be kept? Do we not all see that men run for help to the places in which images have been placed? To a certain Anna—whether the mother of the Virgin Mother of God was called by that name is not sure from the Holy Scriptures, but let us grant that this was her name—to Saint Anna, I say, prayer has here and there been made, but at the same time statues were everywhere set up, and as soon as they were set up the people prostrated themselves before them, thinking they would be blessed if they were allowed to kiss or touch the wood. See how august an object in our eyes the image has become which the artist, or rather our own madness, has exalted into a god. Since, therefore, the images in the churches are not free from this danger, how comes it that we deem worthy of any advocacy these things that so greatly draw us away from God? It is impossible that those whose only hope is the Lord should not pursue with hatred everything that is even only a reminder of that which draws away from God. Remove this image of Anna, and no one will run to the place where it had stood before. This view is confirmed by the Christian steadfastness of the people of Stammheim, who, seeing the statues of Anna worshipped in their sanctuary in a quite unchristian manner, in conformity with the decree of the Council of Zurich cast them out and burned them, being unwilling to endure longer this abominable worship before the eyes of their Creator and of pious men. After that no one looked there for what certain men falsely declared they had found before. Thus does the evil spirit mock us. This is the view which everyone sees we ought to take of all images in general. And if we did not set great hopes upon those whose images we worship in the churches, we should not take their removal so hard; nay, the greater and more sincere our faith in God was, the greater would be our zeal also to remove from sight everything that calls us away from God. When, therefore, they say, "Images can be kept for teaching purposes," they have already been given a sufficient answer as to the source from which we ought to derive our teachings. But I add this also, that since sure danger of a decrease of faith threatens wherever images stand in the churches, and imminent risk of their adoration and worship, they ought to be abolished in the churches and wherever risk of their worship threatens. So also only those images ought to be abolished which offend piety or diminish faith in God, such as are all those in human shape which are set up before altars or churches, even though they were not at first set up to saints. Length of time makes an image venerable, so that we sometimes see a very bad tyrant and impious man worshipped as a saint for no other reason than that a statue was once set up to him in a church; for, as everything in a church has a certain august character, the simple-minded later on cherished and worshipped the statue, after some centuries had made the image ἀμαυρότερον, *i. e.*, blacker and dingier. Next after these I do not think those images should be disturbed which are put into windows for the sake of decoration, provided they represent nothing base, for no one worships them there. In short, no one who has not experienced it has a right conception of how much the removal of the images aids true piety. At Zurich thankfulness to the Most High, piety, and all zeal for blamelessness began, as if *de novo,* to bloom again with far greater luxuriance after the images were taken away* by order of the Council and People. I am not speaking from personal feeling, for no one is a greater admirer than I of paintings and statuary; but those that offend piety ought not to be tolerated but to be abolished by unyielding command of the authorities. So much here on images and idols, until pressure of affairs allows a fuller treatment. And as far as taking offence into account in abolishing these images is concerned, we must deal with images in the same manner as with those externals that seem to pertain to, or have some power towards, salvation, of which I spoke in the last section. Teaching should come first, and the abolition of the images follow without disturbance; and love will teach all things in all cases.

Epilogue

I want now to gather the substance of all that I have said into a short epilogue, that no one may imagine that the Christian law is so confused and difficult to explain that no one can learn it or explain it in a few words. That I or others have to talk at such length is due to the fault of him† who has dared to corrupt everything, to disturb everything, to defile and to pervert everything, in order to satisfy his own greed, so that there is nothing, or at least very little, in the whole true teaching of the true God that this man of sin [cf. II Thess. 2: 3] has not ventured to destroy. His avarice is so uncontrollable that when he sees himself refused in human things what he needs to satiate himself, he ventures to lay hold of divine things also. When he sees anything holy and undefiled, his first object is

*This was done in June, 1524.

†*i. e.*, the Pope.

to befoul it with his own interpretation; and when he has polluted everything he proceeds to misuse everything in the interest of lust. Hence it has come to pass that we have purchased salvation from the Roman Pontiff as from a peddler, and have got the idea that Christianity is an article of merchandise rather than holiness of life. There is no difference between the life of man and that of beasts if you take away the knowledge of God. For what has man that beasts have not also? Men defend themselves and their children, satisfy their desires, flee from want; so do the beasts. Man founds laws and states. The ἀγελαῖα, *i. e.*, gregarious animals, as cranes, thrushes, starlings, tunnies, deer, cattle, bees, swine, do the same, being governed by fixed laws, dividing the mass now into wedges and now into single lines, now dwelling in one place, now migrating to another, and generally keeping faith better than is done among men. God, therefore, was unwilling to leave man without the knowledge of Himself, and has always taught him in such a way as immediately to call him back when he seemed to have fallen into forgetfulness of God, that he might not in his degeneracy prefer to perish with the beasts rather than to live forever with Him. Hence the anxious inquiry, addressed to fallen man: "Adam, where art thou?" [Gen. 3: 9]. Hence the fire and the flood, in order to keep man to his duty by fear also. Again, the splendid promises and benefits. He promised Abraham offspring that should save the world [cf. Gen. 15: 6-21, 17: 4-9, 22: 17f.]; so to Isaac [Gen. 26: 4-5], Israel [Gen. 28: 13-15], and Jesse's son David. Unwilling to endure longer the affliction of His people, He brought the whole nation under Moses out of the savage tyranny of Pharaoh, and, after punishing the enemy, supported them in the desert, now with bread from heaven, now with the flesh of quail; and where water was wanting He brought it forth abundantly from the hardest rock, or where it was not good sweetened it so that they could enjoy it in ample measure. He hedged them about with laws as with a guard rail, and thus separated them from the rest of the nations, that they might see that they were the peculiar people of God. In this manner He showed Himself a most loving Father to one race; yet He was nowhere lacking to others, that the whole world might recognize that He is the one and the only one who can do all things, by whom all things exist, by whom all things are governed, that miserable man may not go over to the beasts; for He marked them off from the beasts by bringing their passions into line through laws. Yet who would ever have accepted His laws that had not first dedicated his heart to Him, that had not above all the belief that He was the true and only God? Therefore, it is evident that, whenever God manifested Himself to the world, He also so entered the heart that what was heard or seen was recognized as being divine. For the flesh receiveth not what is opposed to it; and whatever the heavenly Spirit does is opposed to the flesh. Therefore man cannot receive God, cannot listen to the law, unless God Himself draw the heart to Himself [cf. Jn. 6: 44], so that it shall recognize that He is its God, and shall receive the law as good. Thus, then, from the foundation of the world God has manifested Himself in various ways to the human race, that we might recognize Him as Father and Dispenser of all things. The first thing, therefore, in piety is that we should firmly believe that He whom we confess as our God is God, the Source and Father of all things; for unless we do so, we shall never obey His laws. The next thing is that we should know ourselves; for when we have not knowledge of ourselves also, we accept no law. For how should one accept a law who thinks nothing lacking to himself? Therefore this Heavenly Householder rises betimes, aye in the night, as the prophet says [cf. Ps. 46: 6], to arrange and prescribe everything early, that we may not begin to labor before the allotted task has been assigned. He hedges the human race about with laws, therefore, that it may begin nothing without regard to law; for He not only compassed the people of Israel about with laws, but also inscribed upon the hearts of the Gentiles the so-called laws of nature; for one of their prophets says: "*γνῶθι σεαυτόν* [know thyself] came down from heaven."* But on knowledge of self rests the law, What you wish done to yourself, do to another [cf. Mt. 7: 12], and its counterpart, What you do not wish done to yourself, do not to another [Tobit 4: 16]. For our own good, therefore, God manifests Himself to us, for whether He enters into our hearts

*Juvenal *Sat.* xi. 27.

—which is the greatest miracle—so that we recognize that He is our God and Father, or whether He accomplishes the same thing by miraculous works, He does it solely with a view to benefiting us. And what is this benefit that He provides with such care for us? It is twofold, verily: namely, to live here blamelessly; and, when the course of this life has been finished, to enjoy eternal bliss with Him. For what need would there have been of knowledge of God, and of laws, if the end of the soul were the same as of the body? Would it not have been better to let man remain a brute, if he had been a brute after this fashion, than to raise him to false hope? God willed, therefore, that amid the numerous and varied progeny of created things the human race should so dwell upon earth as to strive towards the inheritance set for it in heaven. So it pleased the Most High. For what other reason should He manifest Himself to man, and kindle him to love of Him? And knowing that man would wonder exceedingly what sort of an inheritance it was that he should hope for in heaven, He gave him a taste, as it were, of that happiness, but through a mist and a lattice, as the saying is. Man sees all things done with reckless greed and turmoil, but when he hears God say, "Thou shalt not covet" [Exod. 20:17; cf. Rom. 7:7], he infers truly that noxious covetousness must be very far from the place where true happiness dwells, and that the author of such happiness must be still farther removed from all greed. He doubts not, therefore, that it would be a very beautiful thing if, also while we are here, we were far removed from all covetousness. Hence the constant struggle and contest. The soul strives to fashion itself upon the pattern of Him towards whom it is hastening, whose face it desires to see, the face, namely, of its righteous and holy Father, aye, of Him who is righteousness itself, holiness, purity, light, rest, refreshment, joy, and all blessedness together. The body resists, because by its nature it scorns whatever the soul greatly values; it yearns for the things of earth and lets those of heaven go, has no hope at all of seeing God any more than the very earth has from which it sprang. Accordingly, it follows its desires, and if it is ever kept by the power of the soul from attaining them, it proceeds to plot and rage against it. Hence that constant battle between the flesh and the spirit, which ceases not until we have reached our goal. Hence would be born desperation of soul, had not a kind God so manifested Himself to it that it can safely trust to His mercy. For the soul, seeing after all its efforts that the flesh throws itself into all sorts of sin (just as the boy possessed of a demon in Mark [9: 22] cast himself now into the fire and now into the water), could not help being reduced to the uttermost depths of despair by this ungovernableness of the flesh. But when it does not cast away hope nor give up its efforts for blamelessness, it sees that mercy is better than vengeance. And that man might never lose this hope, when it pleased the divine counsel, the heavenly Father sent His only begotten Son, so to strengthen the hopes of all that they should see clearly that nothing can be refused, now that the Son is given for poor mortals; for "how shall he not with him freely give us all things?" [Rom. 8: 32]. He was sent, then, for this purpose, that He might altogether take away this despair of the soul that springs from the ungovernableness of the flesh, as has been said, and that He might also furnish an example of life. For Christ everywhere emphasizes these two things, namely, redemption through Himself, and the obligation of those redeemed through Him to live according to His example. For He says, Jn. 6: 57: "So he that eateth me, he shall live because of me"; and Jn. 15: 8: "Herein is my Father glorified, that ye bear much fruit; and so shall ye be my disciples." We ought, then, to be as eagerly bent upon a change of life as we trust in redemption through Him. A Christian, therefore, is a man who trusts in the one true and only God; who relies upon His mercy through His Son Christ, God of God; who models himself upon His example; who dies daily [cf. I Cor. 15: 31]; who daily renounces self; who is intent upon this one thing, not to do anything that can offend his God. Such watchfulness demands so much diligence and zeal that any one would need many a Theseus to defend his blamelessness, and yet would never come off victorious. The Christian life, then, is a battle, so sharp and full of danger that effort can nowhere be relaxed without loss; again, it is also a lasting victory, for he who fights it wins, if only he remains loyal to Christ the head. Thus has God willed that man be ἀμφίβιος [an amphibian] among the creatures, dwelling sometimes on earth, sometimes in the heavens; and, again, while on the earth sometimes conquering, sometimes yielding; but we are by no means to ask the reasons for His acts. Since, then, God asks of us these things only, faith and blamelessness, no more baneful plague can be imagined than a varied worship of God, the invention of our own industry. This we (being given to magnifying everything of our own) embrace, instead of that true worship of God which consists of faith and blamelessness; and, according to the words of the prophet Jeremiah, 2: 13, "We have committed two evils; we have forsaken God, the fountain of living waters, and hewed us out cisterns, broken cisterns, that can hold no water." We have substituted a vicar for Christ, and in our folly have decreed that he is to be listened to in place of God. When he saw that a way to our purses was open to him through our consciences, what scheme did he not think up? What did he not dare? How many roads to heaven he showed us, but none without a toll! You confessed into the ear of the vicar of Christ; heaven was promised if you counted out so and so much for masses and mumbling. You joined some order, to which the stupid crowd contributed much, and again you attained the heavens; for the greater the accessions to them, the more powerful became our vicar. Run thus through everything that reckless greed has prescribed for us, and you will find that it has removed true religion from men, that is, faith and blamelessness, by which singly and alone God is worshipped; nor does He require any other worship of us; nay, He so scorns other inventions as to say that things which seem high to men are an abomination in His sight. God ought to be worshipped with those things alone in which He delights. For who among men is so crazy as to honor any one with things that are of no avail? Worthless trifles, therefore, are all those things which in our ignorance or presumption we parade as the worship of God. But now why do we ever remain children, when we see that God takes delight in other things than those with which we have hitherto wearied Him? Why do we find it so hard to change from useless trifles to those true and solid things, righteousness, faith, mercy, in which Christ comprehended all religion? We owe faith to Him, righteousness and guilelessness to ourselves and others, mercy to all in need.

So, then, good reader, receive this Commentary, so hurriedly written and printed in three months and a half that, as you see, it stands clumsy indeed, but zealous for the truth and holiness; consider it calmly, and take it in good part.

I doubt not that there are in it many things that will greatly offend certain weaklings, but let these reflect that Paul sometimes spoke as a child [cf. I Cor. 13], and let them consider whether they may not themselves still be perhaps over weak. All that I have said, I have said to the glory of God, and for the benefit of the commonwealth of Christ and the good of the conscience.

Thanks be to God!

II

REPLY TO EMSER

Introduction by
GEORGE WARREN RICHARDS

Reasons for the "Reply"

IN 1523 Zwingli published a Latin tract entitled, *De Canone Missæ Huldrychi Zuinglii Epichiresis,* "An Essay on the Canon of the Mass." He speaks of it as "my confutation of the Canon of the Mass." He wrote it in four days (August 25-29), though not without careful study and serious thought on the subject "for several years" before he began to write.* Emser was sufficiently provoked by it to publish an answer with the title: *Canonis Missæ contra Huldricum Zuinglium Defensio* (1524), "Defense of the Canon of the Mass against Huldreich Zwingli." The author, contrary to custom, did not send a copy of this tract to Zwingli, who accordingly chides him for attacking him treacherously "from the rear" and without giving him "any warning." "You did not, as a Christian especially ought, give any warning; you sent no herald with a demand for satisfaction; and you attacked suddenly, not in front but from the rear, one who suspected no such thing."

Zwingli heard of Emser's *Defense* through his friend George Vadian,† a merchant and "a man of marked piety and culture," who had attended the Leipsic fair. Vadian was not a little amazed to find in Saxony a pamphlet written against a prominent Swiss citizen. He procured a copy‡ of it and sent it to Zwingli, who informs Emser that for "four months" he

*In the explanation of the twentieth of the *Sixty-seven Conclusions,* Zwingli announces his intention to write before long on the "Canon."—Egli-Finsler, II, 213.

†A nephew of Joachim von Watt (Vadian), the Reformer, of St. Gall.

‡A copy of this tract is preserved in the University of Basel.

delayed answering the tract after he had read it, "waiting in the meantime to see whether you would say anything." When he did not hear from Emser, he sent back his "Defense," with a copy† of his own "Reply," which he professes to have written not with the bitterness of spirit of his opponent but "lovingly and benignly." After reading Zwingli's answer one wonders what he meant by these professions of affection. For, as we shall see, Zwingli left little, if anything, unwritten that would detract from the character of Emser.

Emser

The salient facts of Emser's life will throw light on his controversy with Zwingli. Jerome Emser was born in the city of Ulm in Swabia, either in the year 1477 or 1478. His father was of the nobility, and the son proudly exhibited the coat of arms of his family on the title page of his numerous books and pamphlets. Its most prominent feature was the figure of a wild goat with long horns and the inscription "Arma Hieronymi Emser." For this reason his opponents, Luther taking the lead, addressed him as the "Wild Goat Emser" or as the "Goat of Leipsic." Nothing is known of his boyhood. He matriculated in the University of Tübingen, July 19, 1493. For unknown reasons he left Tübingen and entered the University of Basel, matriculating for the winter semester, 1497. In the same year he received the degree of Bachelor of Arts; in 1498, the degree of Master of Arts.

Zwingli charges Emser with having "once spewed out against the Swiss" certain "base charges" on account of which he was "compelled to change suddenly his place of residence." He left Basel in 1502. This accusation is based upon an episode that happened while he was a student in the University. A Swiss fellow-student stirred up Emser's wrath by writing a satirical poem on the Swabians. Emser in retaliation wrote abusive verses in Latin on the Swiss in a notebook of a student who was dozing while both of them were attending a lecture on law.*

†This copy, inscribed in Zwingli's handwriting "Emsero Ibici a Zuinglio," is now in the Prince Stolberg Library, at Wernigerode, in the Harz Mountains.

*The notebook into which Emser wrote the verses belonged to Gregorius Bünzli, one of Zwingli's teachers at Basel.—Introduction to *Adversus Hieronymum, etc.*, Egli-Finsler, III, 231.

The part of the poem that was particularly offensive to the Swiss was as follows:

> Switzer, thou art a tyrant, an enemy of our faith and God,
> Good-for-nothing; nursest thyself with milk, milkest lazily the cow.
> Hereafter the gods can no more tolerate the spoils taken by force,
> Son of the Woods, which thou lovest after the manner of robbers.
> The time is coming, when thou, who hopest for golden booty,
> Wilt flee, when the Gallic prince will send his sharp weapons.

This raillery of students leaked out and the people of Basel felt insulted by the words of the Swabian Emser. He was arrested, imprisoned, and brought before the tribunal for trial, where he proved, to the satisfaction of the court and of the people, that the matter charged against him was a mere student jest. But the Council, inclined to be hostile toward Swabia, turned him out of the city, in spite of the friendly interposition of the Bishop, Christoph von Utenheim. Since Zwingli matriculated for the summer semester of 1502 at Basel and Emser was tried on May 25 of that year, he must have known of Emser's misfortune through personal observation.

Emser served for two years as private secretary and chaplain to the Cardinal Legate Raymund Peraudi, which implies that about this time he was ordained to the priesthood. After he left the service of the Cardinal, he lectured as a Master of the Liberal Arts at Erfurt, 1504. One of his hearers was Martin Luther, who was preparing for his examination for the Master's degree. A few months later, at the beginning of the winter semester, Emser turned up in the University of Leipsic, where he won the degree of Bachelor of Theology. But, contrary to expectations, he did not become a teacher of theology. He was chosen Secretary of Duke George of Saxony, whose court was at Dresden. His "Wanderjahre" were over.

Writings of Emser

Beside the routine work of his office, he was a prolific writer of prose and poetry, and appears to have been a restless, ever-active, controversial spirit with more than ordinary ability. One of the first products of his pen was a Latin dialogue on *The Custom of Drinking Toasts.* A more pretentious work was his *Life of Bishop Benno:* in Latin, 1512; in German, 1517. He read widely in the Latin classics, had knowledge of the Greek, wrote Latin poetry that called forth favorable comment from Erasmus. Luther called him "a versifex" and "a wild poet." He was acquainted with the sources of mediæval history and read the new editions of the Church Fathers, among them Reuchlin's *Athanasius,* Erasmus' *Jerome,* and Faber Stapulensis' *Dionysius the Areopagite.*

Emser and Luther

When Luther turned Protestant and independent reformer, Emser took up the cudgels against him. He opened the controversy (which continued until 1527, when Luther ceased to take further notice of his foe) with a letter, dated August 13, 1519, to the Vicar of the Archbishop of Prague. In this epistle he did not condemn Luther outright, but spoke of him as "a restless head, entangled in many contradictions," and yet "not so obstinate as not to yield to reason."

The letter was brought to Luther's attention, who wrote in reply a tract with the title: *Zusatzbemerkungen Luthers zu dem Emserchen Steinbock,* "Added Observations to the Emseric Wild Goat." Not to be outdone, Emser wrote a pamphlet with the superscription: *An den Stier zu Wittenberg,* "To the Bull at Wittenberg." It does not come within the scope of this introduction to describe in detail the blasts and counter-blasts of these two men from 1521 to 1527. The reader will find a thorough discussion of the controversy between them in *Hieronymus Emser. Ein Lebensbild aus der Reformationsgeschichte,* by Gustav Kawerau. Suffice it to say that when Luther published his *Formula Missæ et Communionis* (1523), Emser issued his "Defense of the Mass of Christians against Luther's Formula of the Mass." In this tract the questions were discussed that were raised also by Zwingli's *Epichiresis,* which Emser answered with his *Defensio.* Through his frequent combats with Luther, Emser sharpened his weapons and became skilled in their use to meet the Swiss Reformer.*

I

Zwingli's "Essay on the Canon of the Mass"

Let us briefly consider Zwingli's *Essay on the Canon of the Mass,* to which Emser wrote a rejoinder, and which, accordingly, prepared the way for the "Reply to Emser."

The service of the Mass in the Roman Catholic Church consists of the Offertory, the Preface, and the Canon. "All this,

*In the discussion of the Mass in his *Defensio,* Emser refers Zwingli to his *Vindication,* written against Luther, 1524.

from Offertory to Communion, forms the Sacrifice, so called." In the form for the Mass of today there is an "introductory service which equals in length the Sacrifice properly so called." This preparatory service consists "of chants, prayers, and lessons or readings from Holy Scripture—the Introit, Kyrie Eleison, Collect, Epistle or Lesson, and the Gospel. On certain days the Gloria in Excelsis and the Nicene Creed are added."* The first part is known as the Mass of the Catechumens; the second part is called the Mass of the Faithful. Zwingli in his *Epichiresis* confined himself to a critical examination and a confutation of the third part of the Mass of the Faithful, namely, the Canon.

In the Preface (August 29, 1523), which is addressed to Diebold of Geroldseck, warden of the chapter at Einsiedlen and friend and patron of Zwingli, the author informs the reader that in this tract he has cast his customary caution to the wind, and that henceforth he will openly and boldly attack the citadel of the mediæval faith and worship, *i. e.,* the Sacrifice of the Mass. "The time has come when it will not do to be concerned about giving offence, but much more to have consideration for those who have accepted Christ's doctrine but are in danger of lapsing again into error, if they do not see those things refuted that are contrary to Christ." At this time, also, Leo Jude, Zwingli's colleague, introduced a baptismal service in the German language, to which he added prayers in German. This was the beginning of the Zurich liturgy.

Notwithstanding his declaration of open warfare, indications are not wanting that Zwingli at this stage was still ready to make concessions in reference to ecclesiastical ceremonies, provided that, at this price, his hope of a reform of the whole Church might be realized. He was willing to tolerate such things as the sign of the cross in praying, the vestments of the priest in the celebration of the Mass, as far as they symbolize the passion of Christ, and choir singing. For the sake of the weaker brethren he would yield at least part use of the Latin language in the service; the Scriptures, however, were to be read in the German. "He who compromises at this point com-

*Cabrol, *The Roman Missal in Latin and English,* Students' edition, "General Introduction," p. iii.

mits sin, for this is the word of life, and whoever casts a shadow upon it takes life away."

About a month after Zwingli finished his *Essay on the Canon of the Mass,* he added an appendix,* probably to guard against misunderstanding of his concessions on ceremonies, for which he was criticised by certain zealots. In this section he insists that anything that leads to superstition is to be abolished. On the other hand, he positively opposes the narrow biblical literalism of those who refuse to use the prayers of the Church and are willing to keep only the Lord's Prayer on the ground that it was revealed of God. "The order of worship," he says, "is left to the choice of the congregation and is not bound to this or that form by the word of God." Again: "We beseech all brethren, that they do not acknowledge our name as having authority, but that they prove everything by the word of God and reject what is contrary to it."

In the *Epichiresis,* the *Letter to Wyttenbach,* June 15, 1523, and the explanation of the eighteenth article of the *Sixty-seven Conclusions* (July 14, 1523), one will find the original material for a study of the early views of Zwingli on the Lord's Supper. In the first part of the "De Canone Missæ" the author criticises the prayers of "oblation," "consecration," and "the elevation"; in the second part he submits an evangelical form for the celebration of the Lord's Supper.

Prayers of the Canon

In quoting passages from the Canon he uses the *Missale Constantiense,* Erhardus Ratold, 1504. He refutes, primarily, the idea of the Mass as a sacrifice to God—the doctrine that is reiterated in the prayers. This conception of the Mass directly contradicts his evangelical idea of salvation, which rests wholly and solely upon the sacrifice of Christ on the cross. From the Gospel it is known "that the Mass is not a sacrifice, but a memorial of the sacrifice and an assurance of the redemption which Christ has shown us." He reminds the reader that Christ did not say: "Go and sacrifice me"; but, "Eat and drink ye."

The following are quotations from some of the prayers which he criticizes and refutes in the first part of the tract:†

**De Canone Missæ Libelli Apologia,* October 9, 1523.

†These prayers were declared by the Council of Trent to have been "brought together without error according to the words of Christ, the traditions of the apostles, and the directions of the popes."

Prayer of oblation for the Church: "Wherefore, O most merciful Father, we humbly pray and beseech thee . . . that thou wouldst vouchsafe to receive and bless these gifts, these offerings, this holy and unblemished sacrifice which in the first place we offer thee for thy holy Catholic Church," etc.

Prayer of consecration and the elevation: "Which oblation do thou, O God, vouchsafe in all things to bless, sanction, approve, ratify, and make acceptable: that it may become for us the body and blood of thy most beloved Son, our Lord Jesus Christ."

The prayer after one of the portions of the Host is put into the chalice: "May this mingling and hallowing of the body and blood of our Lord Jesus Christ avail us that receive it unto life everlasting."*

Zwingli writes with reserve on the belief in the corporal presence of Christ. He does not "reject as god-less" the prayer of consecration, namely, "That it [the oblation] may become for us the body and blood of thy most beloved Son, etc.," but he interprets it in his own way. He concedes that "the bread and wine become the body and blood of Christ to those who partake of them in faith, in which way alone this should be done." He adds, also, that Paul's account of the Supper clearly proves that the whole celebration is nothing more than a remembrance of the suffering of the Lord.†

The Canon, as a whole, he declares to be "full of God-lessness." He says: "One hopes to find in it incitation to god-liness but finds instead a dragon. It contains as much god-less-ness as prayers."

II

"Reply to Emser"

The *Reply to Emser's Defense of the Canon of the Mass* contains an introduction and five sections headed as follows: The Church; Intercession of Saints; Merit; The Mass; Purgatory. He gives his reason for selecting these five subjects for discussion in the following words: "I shall treat these points,

*The English translation of these passages is taken from *The Roman Missal* of Cabrol, pp. liii, lv, lix.

†See Rudolf Stæhelin, *Huldreich Zwingli. Sein Leben und Wirken,* I, 308-315.

which you have passed by, that it may be manifest to all who have the slightest acquaintance with Holy Writ that you skipped them on purpose, either because you could not comprehend them or because you despaired of rebutting them."

Each of these sections, excepting the section on the Mass, was copied by Zwingli into his larger work, *True and False Religion,* which is published in this volume. The autograph copy of this tract is a pamphlet of forty unnumbered pages and is preserved in the city library of Zurich. The author's numerous corrections, of more or less consequence, in the manuscript show the care with which he prepared the text.

The Introduction

In the Introduction Zwingli disposes of Emser himself before he replies to the contents of his *Defense.* He rebukes his opponent by telling him that he will not stoop to the use of the scurrilous language and venomous phrases so viciously hurled at himself. "If I should reply to you in like manner, I certainly should expect nothing but that the pious would stop their ears, and that we both, like mad dogs, would be driven off the stage with hoots and hisses." Yet Zwingli proves conclusively that he is not an amateur in controversy, and that he knows how to cut with a Damascus blade as well as to strike with a sledge-hammer. He can dip his pen into gall and write words that sear and blister. His vocabulary is rich in terms of scorn, sarcasm, irony, and satire. To quote for illustration but a single sentence at random: "Why," asks the author, "speak of the obstinacy, stupidity, ignorance, malicious dissimulation, carelessness, fury, impiousness, and quarrelsomeness, to say nothing of deceit, distortions, and such like artifices?" One could not well say more things adversely about a man in fewer words and shorter space. The reader will find similar sentences bristling in the Introduction.

He begs Emser, whenever he finds Zwingli in error, not to indulge in vain exclamations, such as "O Heaven, O Earth, O Horror!" but "to have recourse to the armory of Holy Writ." The Word of God alone is for him the test of truth. He allows no room for the opinions of the Fathers, however ancient they may be, nor for the reasonings of men at present, however wise they may be: these have value only when they are in agreement with the Word of God. Only once in this tract does he appeal to tradition, when, in opposition to Emser's conception of merit, he says: "Read Augustine's book, *On Free Will and Grace.*"

He concludes the Introduction with a petition: "God grant that wherever I am in error I may be taught better; and God grant that you may know what is error and what is truth. Amen!"

THE CHURCH

The author distinguishes between the visible universal church (multitudo Christianorum), which is "not the spouse of Christ" and is not "mentioned in the Creed," and the holy church that is without spot or wrinkle and "is unknown to men." The former is composed of all persons who outwardly profess faith in Christ, some sincerely and others deceitfully. Both the Old and the New Testaments recognize it. The Greek term "ecclesia" is the equivalent of the Hebrew "kahal" and "edah," and "is used not only for the pious, holy, and faithful, but also for the impious, wicked, and unfaithful, provided only they were of the seed of Abraham according to the flesh and were intermingled with the pious." In the New Testament, also, the word "ecclesia is used for all those who have named the name of Christ and who walk and live within the company of the Christians, even though in reality they were not faithful." This church is not "undefiled"; it has "many blemishes." The latter, that is, "the holy church," is the church "for which Christ gave Himself, to the end that He might sanctify it to Himself"; it is "without any spot or wrinkles." The members of it are "those who believe that Christ so loved us that He gave Himself up for our sanctification." It is spotless because "Christ has washed it with His blood"; it is "the communion of saints which we confess in the creed." The true church "is not some few pontiffs, holy, spotless, pious, though they be, but all who firmly believe themselves redeemed by the blood of Christ."

Someone may object that "such a church can no more exist than does Plato's Republic, because no one lives without fault, because all have sinned." His answer to this argument is that the holiness and purity of the church are not in its members, but in "Christ, Who gave Himself up for it that He might sanctify it," and this we can know only through faith. This church "cannot err." But it has not the infallibility "which the pontiffs arrogate to themselves with as much falseness as impudence." Its inerrancy "rests upon the word of God alone," while "the church of the pontiffs rests upon its own word." He is careful to define what he means by the word of God—"not that word which Emser supposes that I merely look at, which consists of letters and sentences, but that which shines in the heart and recognizes every word by whomsoever spoken, whether it is the Father's and Shepherd's or not."

Congregations

This communion of believers as a whole is divided into "individual churches" (peculiares ecclesiae). These congregations together constitute the church universal (ecclesia universalis, ἐκκλησία καθολική), which, however, is not a gathering merely of all the bishops representing the congregations but a "communion of all the saints."

The Reformers, generally, were compelled to define the rights and powers of the local congregation, which was no longer under the authority and supervision of the priest, bishop, and pope. At this point, Luther,* Zwingli, and the Anabaptists had to face a common issue. Zwingli vested in the congregation the right to discipline disobedient members and the authority to judge the teacher and the doctrine taught in the congregation.

In reference to discipline he says: "The office of these churches is to reject one who is shamelessly delinquent, and to admit him again when he comes to his senses and submits to the rule of Christ." This prerogative has been exercised generally by Protestant congregations, either through the voice of the congregation as a whole or through officers in judicatories appointed by the congregation. What was formerly in the power of the clergy is now the right of all believers. They have authority to admit believers into their fellowship, to exclude the disorderly, and to receive again the penitent who seeks restoration.

In reference to the teacher and his doctrine, the congregation also is the arbiter. He says: "It is theirs to judge of a

*On Easter, 1523, Luther advanced the thesis, "That a Christian assembly or congregation has right and power to judge all doctrines and to call, install, and to depose the teacher: ground and cause taken from the Scriptures."

shepherd and of doctrine." In support of this position he quotes a favorite text of the Anabaptists, who, also, in their way insisted upon the prerogatives of the assembly of believers, namely: "And let the prophets speak by two or three, and let the others discern" (I Cor. 14: 29). Clearly, in the Corinthian congregation, "the people sitting on the benches were permitted to speak in the church concerning the word which the Spirit had revealed." This privilege the members of the congregation could rightfully exercise, not because they were formally counted as believers, but because they had the Spirit of Christ. To use his own words: "However, the faithful judges not by his own judgment, but by that of the Divine Spirit." Or, in Scripture phrase, "only the spiritual judges all things" (I Cor. 2: 15). The objection raised against his idea of the right of a congregation, that "in this way the church, or any church at all, is made the judge of the word," Zwingli meets thus: "Only he who hears the Scripture of the celestial word explained in the church judges that which he hears." He is careful to define the true hearer of the word. Not everyone that hears the word with the ear comprehends it in the heart. "We observe that many both hear and see, yet have not faith." We become "faithful only by that word which the Heavenly Father proclaims in our hearts." Those who are thus illumined by the divine word judge the word that is preached and taught in the congregation.

The neglect of this original prerogative of the believers gave rise to many serious errors in the church at large. "If this custom had never died out, so many errors would not have been introduced into the church of Christ, for there are always persons who through the Heavenly Spirit detect deceitful pretence on the part of one who is teaching, and where this is once exposed the word is freed from violent distortion." The church is usually purified from abuses in doctrine and life not through the common sense of the members, but through the common possession of the spirit of truth by the members. Zwingli had confidence in the Christian people to correct errors even of theologians and officers. The expert and final arbiter of Christian truth is the common man who has the spirit of Christ.

Neither Zwingli nor Luther at this stage of reform (1523-1524) was disturbed by the thought that the Spirit might bear diverse testimonies in the believers. It was assumed that His witness was the same in all the faithful. "Wherever the Heavenly Spirit is, there everybody knows is zeal for unity and peace" (cf. Gal. 5: 22). Confusion in the church is prevented by the presence of God in the midst; and therefore "all who are faithful strive for unity and peace."

Zwingli, however, was disillusioned as to the unity of the Spirit's testimony in the believers and His guidance of the faithful to commonly accepted interpretations of the Scriptures, when the Anabaptists arose and disputed his own and Luther's doctrines. They, too, claimed to have the Spirit of God, and yet their teachings at many points were in direct conflict with those of the more moderate Reformers in Zurich and Wittenberg. It became evident in the light of later controversy that more definite tests and guarantees of truth had to be established.

In Zwingli's theory of the right of the congregation there was involved still another problem, one which he did not consider and which probably he did not think of when he wrote the *Reply to Emser.* It was the relation of the local congregation to the whole multitude of Christians (universa multitudo Christianorum). This question became all the more urgent when the Anabaptists actually established separate conventicles of believers which submitted neither to the authority of the Catholic Church nor to that of the Protestant state churches.

Intercession of Saints

The argument against the necessity of the intercession of saints is based upon the character of God and is summarized in eight paragraphs. The major premise is that "God is good." From Him, therefore, all good is to be derived. The faithful depend upon "the One and Only Good, cling to Him alone, resort to Him alone." The unfaithful, on the contrary, turn from the Creator to creatures, depend upon them and hope for aid from them." The faithful do not even "name any father except the Almighty Father."

In the Old Testament we are assured that "we may flee without hesitation to Him for safety." The New Testament is "a solid confirmation of God's grace." Christ descended from heaven to reveal unto us that there is free access to God. The classic passage against the need of intercessors other than Christ is found in I Timothy 2:5: "There is one mediator between God and men, the man Christ Jesus." The author asks: "If you dignify any other by that name, do you not cast contumely upon God?" If, according to popular belief, there are mediating angels and saints, then Christ died in vain. If God spared not his own Son, will he not freely give us all things?

In view of the clear teaching of the Scriptures, "there is no reason for lack of faith to make for itself this excuse: Of course I know that all my hope rests in God; but yet I have need of advocates to commend me to the Most High God." Such speech does not proceed from faith but from lack of it, and has no warrant in the Word of God. Nothing could be "plainer" and more authoritative than the words of Jesus: "No one cometh unto the Father but by me" (John 14:6).

The "arguments commonly adduced" in favor of intercession of saints "are either frivolous or have been twisted out of shape by the audacity of carnal wisdom." Such frivolous vociferations as Emser presents when he says, "East and West testify that the saints intercede for me," and, "There is no nation under heaven that does not credit its safe condition in great measure to the prayers of the saints, next after God," have no weight before the clear testimony of the Word of God. When he asserts that "many have experienced the aid of St. Nicholas in storms at sea, therefore Nicholas should be invoked as a son of Jupiter and a tutelary God," he does not see that, if he were logical, he ought also to invoke "Castor and Pollux as Jupiter's helping gods, who have saved many more from shipwreck than has any Nicholas." For further light on this subject he refers Emser to his *Conclusions* and his *Confutation of the Canon.*

MERIT PURGATORY

The sections on Merit and Purgatory were transferred verbatim into the *True and False Religion.* An analysis and digest of them is made in the Introduction to that work. See pp. 33, 34-35.

THE MASS

In his discussion of the Mass in the *Defense* against Zwingli's *Epichiresis,* Emser directs Zwingli to his *Vindication* written against Luther (*Missæ Christianorum contra Lutheranam missandi formulam assertio,* 1524). Zwingli says that he does not know the content "of your *Vindication*" for the reason that "your books never reach us." For this reason he will not attempt to answer Emser's arguments for the Mass in detail but presents a series of statements, "drawn from the storehouse of Holy Scripture" and so "unassailable" that "the Roman pontiff with all his adherents would accomplish nothing if he would move up all his engines of knowledge and eloquence."

Following the New Testament, which is "eternal," he lays down the following propositions against the Mass:

"In the first place:

1. "The blood of Christ alone takes away our sins: . . . for he has reconciled all things through his blood (Col. 1:20).
2. "The blood of Christ was offered once only; for it is the eternal blood of God's eternal Son (Heb. 9:12).
3. "The blood of Christ, offered once for all, endures forever to remove the sins of all men.

"In the second place:

1. "Christ is offered only where he suffers, sheds his blood, dies (Heb. 9:25).
2. "Christ can no more die, suffer, shed his blood (Rom. 6:9).
3. "Therefore Christ can no more be offered up, for he cannot die."

Thus, by unanswerable arguments from the New Testament, he denies the doctrine that in the Mass the sacrifice of the body and blood of Christ is repeated and has appeasing value before God.

"I now admonish you," he says to Emser, "not to skip over any one of these propositions, but to examine each carefully. If you do the latter, you will never make the sacrament of the Eucharist into an oblation."

Zwingli concludes the whole discussion with the positive

affirmation that "the Eucharist is spiritual food, by which those who believe that Christ's death is for them a means of life cement, join, unite, themselves together into the one body of Christ" (I Cor. 10: 17).

In his concluding paragraph Zwingli bids adieu to Emser in words that are far from complimentary, and exhorts him: "Transfer your attention from matters of divinity to medicine, that you may at least cure your gout." He offers this advice on the ground that Emser "is naturally less fitted for sacred letters than for anything else."

"Farewell, and may God grant you a good mind."

Lancaster, Pa.
February 17, 1929.

LITERATURE

ZWINGLI, ULRICH. *Sämtliche Werke*, ed. Egli and Finsler (Leipzig).

1. "De Canone Missæ Epichiresis," in vol. 2 (1908), pp. 617-625.
2. "De Canone Missæ Apologia," in vol. 22, pp. 620-625.
3. "Auslegen und Gründe der Schlussreden," in vol. 2, pp. 1-457.
4. "Adversus Hieronymum Emserum Antibolon," in vol. 3, pp. 241-287.
5. "Zwingli an Thomas Wyttenbach," in vol. 8, pp. 84-89.

ZWINGLI, ULRICH. "Die 67 Artikel Zwinglis," *Ulrich Zwingli, Eine Auswahl aus seinen Schriften*, ed. Finsler, Köhler, and Rüegg (Zürich, 1918), pp. 135-142. A translation into modern German by Arnold Rüegg. English translation by Lawrence A. McLouth in Samuel Macauley Jackson, *Selected Works of Huldreich Zwingli* (Philadelphia, 1901), pp. 111-117.

STÆHELIN, RUDOLF. "Zwinglis Schriften . . . über den Masskanon," *Huldreich Zwingli. Sein Leben und Wirken*, vol. 1 (Basel, 1895), pp. 309-314.

JACKSON, SAMUEL MACAULEY. *Huldreich Zwingli, the Reformer of German Switzerland.* New York, 1901.

KAWERAU, GUSTAV. *Hieronymus Emser. Ein Lebensbild aus der Reformationgeschichte.* Halle, 1898.

CABROL, FERNAND, tr. *The Roman Missal in Latin and English. Students' edition.* New York, P. J. Kennedy & Sons [1921].

FORTESCUE, ADRIAN. *The Mass; A Study of the Roman Liturgy.* London, 1917.

REPLY OF HULDREICH ZWINGLI TO JEROME EMSER DEFENDER OF THE CANON OF THE MASS

(August 20, 1524)

[The first edition, printed by Froschauer, has the title: ADVERSVS HIE | RONYMVM EMSERVM CANONIS | missae adsertorem Huldrychi | Zuinglij Antibo- | lon. | Then a woodcut: Christ, standing, with a crown of thorns and halo. | *Venite ad me omnes qui laboratis & onerati estis, &* | *ego requiem uobis praestabo. Matth. 11.* | TIGVRO AEDIBVS CHRISTOPHORI | *Froschouer Anno M.D.XXIIII.* | *Mense Augusto.* | —44 unnumbered quarto pages. Signed at the end of the address to Emser: *Vale ex Tiguro, etc. MDXXIIII. XIII. Kalendas Septembris.* A copy is in the library of Union Theological Seminary, New York.

Printed in *Opera Zwinglii,* tom. I, fol. 192a-201b; Schuler and Schultess ed., vol. III, pp. 121-144; Egli-Finsler ed., vol. III, pp. 241-287.

A German edition, translated by Leo Jud and printed by Froschauer in 1525, has the title: *Ein gegenwurff und widerweer Hulderych Zuinglins, wider Hieronymum Emser des Canons in der Massz beschirmer.* At the end, on p. 66; *Getrucht zu Zürich durch Christophorum Froschouer, im jar M.D.XXV.* 68 unnumbered pages. Another German edition, of which the translator, printer, and place of publication are unknown, has the title: *Huldrichen Zwinglens antwort wider Hieronimum Emser den schutzherren des Canons oder Stillmess . . . M.D.XXV.*

The following English translation was made by George W. Gilmore. It has been revised by the editor.]

NOT far were you, most nimble Emser (for wild goats* should be more nimble than stags), from tearing me away from the very clear light of the celestial word and bringing me over to the side of the Roman Pontiff by that threatening pamphlet of yours† against my confutation of the Canon of the Mass‡ which I thrust forth rather than published. It is so grandiloquent that no one can understand its difficult periods unless he descends into a well; so fortified with things more

*Cf. p. 345.

†Emser's *Canonis missae contra Huldricum Zuinglium defensio.*

‡Zwingli's *De canone missae Huldrychi Zuinglii Epichiresis.*

solid than the Scriptures, namely, legends of the saints and trifles more foolish than old wives' tales, that no one can take it by storm unless he is well equipped with gourds, pumpkins, and rotten cabbage. Besides, the snares which you cleverly spread, because of their unexpectedness, terrify me more than their real importance warrants; for you did not, as a Christian especially ought, give any warning; you sent no herald with a demand for satisfaction; and you attacked suddenly, not in front but from the rear, one who suspected no such thing; nor did you engage at close quarters, so that at least the clash of arms might give notice of an enemy's presence, but you skirmished in quite remote parts. Consequently, not even a rumor of the wrathful ibex who was rashly laying everything waste could have reached me, if it had not by mere chance happened that George Vadian, a man of marked piety and culture, was journeying on certain business in the parts where you were tearing around. While he was at first not a little disturbed by the strangeness of your conduct, yet, having obtained one of your pamphlets—a prisoner, as it were, from your army—he promptly transmitted it to me, and I have treated it a little more kindly than you treated mine. For I did not make a sudden attack upon it, but, though it spoke not courteously, I listened to it courteously, waiting meantime to see whether you would yourself say anything. But now four months have passed without my hearing from you; and so, out of pity for the prisoner I have decided to free it from its long period of distress by sending it back to you, though in a manner far different from that in which I received it; for I send along a companion that will show how well that booklet of yours has been treated by me, and that will do it lovingly and benignly. It will not threaten with scourges or tyrants or crosses, as yours boastfully did; for it is well aware that a disciple of Christ ought to be so equipped as to prefer to experience those things rather than to threaten them, and that this is a battle not of armed men or of lictors, but of truth and piety, which have ever been so hated by the children of this world that they have never put forth their heads without peril to themselves. However, I am using "peril" from your point of view, according to which you think it hurtful if punishment befalls the pious; for unless you thought so you would not threaten it in such a haughty manner. And yet those who not only have not listened to the truth but have busily endeavored to exterminate it with the greatest ignominy may find that they have at length caused themselves damage. Nor, again, will this booklet of mine for any light cause cry out, speak evil, and revile; indeed it will not be able to, since yours has used up all the shades of evil-speaking and refinements of reviling, so that, now that you have left none of these unused, it is forced willy nilly to abstain from them, lest it resemble yours. The one and only benefit I have derived from your booklet is this: that, since you have raved so unseasonably and so tastelessly, I, seeing how little this becomes you, pursue another course. For what, pray, would be the result if to all your revilings I should retort with revilings? Would not the book deserve to be called a rhapsody of revilings? though I could truthfully do it, whereas you do it not truthfully. But why should I rake up the base charges, rather than odes, that you once spewed out against the Swiss?* At the time, you narrowly escaped (for I myself was present then, though hardly more than a boy) being compelled to eat your very shameless words—words that besides were rude, impure, and wicked. Why should I mention the whoredoms and adulteries that not seldom compelled you to change your place of residence? Why should I upbraid you for the vain, frivolous, gross things said so impudently, imprudently, and mendaciously in your pamphlet? Why speak of the obstinacy, stupidity, ignorance, malicious dissimulation, carelessness, fury, impiousness, and quarrelsomeness, to say nothing of the deceit, distortions, and such like artifices? Here are instances of such things: You assume the role of a David and go forth against the uncircumcised one, even though you suffer from gout. Wild goat that you are, you brandish your horns against one who has seen so many of those animals that he does not fear their look at all. You attempt to prove something by the rules of the Chancery†, and you tell a pretty tale about the missals

*See *Introduction*, p. 345-346.

†The papal chancery was the office which prepared and issued bulls and briefs. It adhered to certain formulas, definitions, and rules.

of Ambrose and Gregory§. You call the Roman Pontiffs a Lesbian rule,* although you do this with as much truth as thoughtlessness. You assert that I dignify the forms of bread and wine with the name of the flesh and blood of Christ. You cunningly present in a false light this easy, but to you insoluble, problem, which I resolve thus: since Christ evidently instituted this sacrament only once and with only one rite, it necessarily follows that, since you contend it is a sacrifice, all who ever use it make sacrifice. You bring forward as instances of asyndeton things which have no such form at all as has "These holy, unblemished sacrifices."† You assert that I reject Ambrose's book "On the Sacraments," though I speak of it only in the following manner: "Not to call in question whether this book is or is not Ambrose's," etc. You represent me as boasting that I was the first to confute the Canon, when I was speaking only about order of procedure, as follows: "first,"‡ *i. e.*, before anything else, "I am going to bring the Canon out of the darkness of a cave into the light." You affirm that only to the Apostles was it said, "Drink ye all of this." You call those heretics who cling to the words of Christ alone. You somewhere assert that the true body of Christ is torn with the teeth, but a little later, when defending the Canon, you say: "The Canon calls it spiritual food; and if it is spiritual food, as it certainly is, how is it torn with the teeth?" Why, I say, should

§Emser had told how, in the pontificate of Hadrian I, a liturgical controversy over these two missals had been decided by an appeal to "divine judgment." A sealed copy of each missal was placed on the altar of St. Peter's and left there over night. The next morning the leaves of the missal of St. Gregory were found scattered over the church, while the missal of St. Ambrose was till intact. This was taken as a sign that the former was to be used throughout the whole world, the latter only in the Church of St. Ambrose in Milan.

*The "Lesbian rule" was a leaden scale which conformed to the shape of the object measured (cf. Aristotle *Ethics* V, x, 7). Here it means persons who practice the "accommodation" of law or teaching to the condition or circumstances of those with whom they are dealing.

†The Latin of the Canon is: HAEC SANCTA SACRIFICIA ILLIBATA. From the absence of a connective between the two adjectives Zwingli had argued against the early composition of the Canon, since "no one before the time of Gregory would ever have so spoken."

‡Zwingli had written simply "ante omnia."

I upbraid you for these things when your whole book so abounds in them that if you should take them away it would appear as naked and plumeless as fable says* the jackdaw was after every bird had taken back his own feather. And now consider how it becomes you to assail with so many insulting terms a man quite unknown to you, yet to whom you are very well known. If I were to reply to you in like manner, I certainly should expect nothing but that the pious would stop their ears, and that we both, like mad dogs, would be driven off the stage with stones and hoots and hisses. Or do you hope by this means to draw me over to your side? If I were so stupid as to suppose that you were saying something worthwhile, yet the extraordinary maledictions and furious shouting with which you burst forth even upon no occasion would, by the fear they inspire, deter me from acceding to your way of thinking.

Since, then, you would have it appear that you wrote your booklet to heal my wound, and yet you inflict a thousand others, you make manifest that your determination to write was due either to petulance of tongue instead of a desire to heal, or to hope of filching some reward from pontiffs instead of a purpose to defend the truth (to which you are so blind that, according to the word of God [Deut. 28: 29], you grope at noonday). And when you affirm that for a piece of bread I can be hired to heap insults upon any one at all, though no rewards or honors bestowed either by pontiffs‡ or by the greatest princes have ever been able to lure me from the path of truth, you are doing nothing but seizing upon that charge ahead of me, in order that it may not be uttered against you. For who will be so dull of comprehension that, when he reads your production, he will not at the very beginning see instantly that you are aiming at securing those mitred pontiffs† as spec-

*Phaedrus *Fabulae Aesopiae*, I, 3. Cf. Horace, *Epp.*, i, 3, 19.

‡From 1512 or 1513 until 1520 Zwingli had received an annual pension from the Pope, though in 1517 he came out as a severe critic of the papacy. In a letter (dated August 20, 1521) to the Senate of Zurich, Francis Zink, papal chaplain at Einsiedeln, testified that Zwingli had "never been moved a finger's breadth from the Gospel by the favour of the Pope, emperor, or noble." See S. M. Jackson, *Huldreich Zwingli*, pp. 114-116.

†Emser's *Defensio* began with a dedication to high ecclesiastics.

tators of the fight? And when you leap forward to the battle, you shout more loudly than Stentor, that the eyes of all may be fixed upon you alone; but, because the gout restrains you, you move forward not even a hand's breadth; and when an onset should be made, then you quit, though you never quit shouting. And this is your manner of fighting!

Finally, just as if you had laid at their feet the *spolia opima* taken from me, you make them hopeful of recovering dominion, and you do it so boastfully and vaingloriously that nothing seems to fit your case better than the unctuous remark, "So Pyrrhus, too, was wont to do."* From this it is clear that you strive for the favor of those men in order that you may obtain something from them—a feature assuredly absent from my booklet, as I shall prove to your own satisfaction. As, then, certain friends advise against my undertaking any reply to such great vanity, while others urge me to it, I have decided to do something for both (for who can satisfy all?) in the following manner. Whatever has little pertinence I will pass over with deaf ear; for why should I dispute with you again as to just where or when the Canon arose? For I see that you do not know that in some passages writers use "canon" for the order and rule of any rite whatsoever; but when you read them you thought they were speaking of the Canon of your party. Or why should I apologize for saying certain things too humorously and facetiously, as you think? Everyone knows that he who is refuting an argument employs both jest and earnest in such manner that they avail in effecting conquest. And though you labor greatly over these more trifling matters (for what could you do, seeing that where there was need you could do nothing?), I shall be influenced not at all by them, but shall treat those points which you have passed by, that it may be manifest to all who have the slightest acquaintance with Holy Writ that you skipped them on purpose, either because you could not comprehend them or because you despaired of rebutting them. Such are: The Church, Intercession of the Saints, Merit, Whether the Eucharist is an oblation, Whether or not there is a purgatory. If in these matters I made any

*In Terence *Eunuchus*, 783, Captain Thraso thus justifies posting himself in the rear of his forces.

error, you should have reported and proved it, not by your outcries, but from the celestial fountains of the word. However, I shall treat these subjects rather briefly, in aphoristic style as it were, so that you may the more clearly see through everything. When you see them, do not at once cry out: "O Heaven, O Earth, O Horrors!" (thereby you will show us nothing but an old woman's helplessness); but wherever you find me in error, have recourse to the armory of Holy Writ, and with the sword brought thence expunge whatever mars the most fair order of divine truth, and in its place put that of which there is need. Once you have done that, you will have gained a brother [Mt. 18: 15], and I shall be everlastingly indebted to you; otherwise it is no use for you to write a thousand books, for no matter what amount of human teaching you adduce, you will only be spitting into the sky; for it will all fall back upon you. For "in vain do they worship me" (says He who is above the heavens and beyond the range of these weapons) "teaching the doctrines and precepts of men" [Mt. 15: 9]. I shall not be influenced at all by such things, just as not even now should I have uttered a syllable in reply, had not some, as has been said, thought it worth while not to pass by in silence so unprofitable a booklet.

Therefore surrender your mind as a captive to the obedience of God, not of men or of the Fathers or of the flesh. For the mere antiquity of any saying of the Fathers that you present will find for it some credit among the ignorant. Furthermore, the same reasoning applies to an opinion of theirs as to one of our own times. For what matters it whether today or fifteen hundred years ago you spoke earnestly, but without the authority of the word of God? So approach the Sacred Word that you may there find what you ought to think, not with the purpose of compelling the Sacred Word, even in spite of its protest, to agree with that which you first think in your own heart. If you attain to this, all that pride in disputing will perish, and you will see what ill-furnished minds both the pontiffs and their champions have.

God grant that wherever I am in error I may be taught better; and God grant that you may know what is error and what truth. Amen!

Zurich, August 20, 1524.

The Church: A Reply to Jerome Emser*

The word "ecclesia" is derived from the Greek for "calling together," as everyone well knows. Taken over thence into the Latin, the word is used indifferently in Holy Writ, now for "congregation," now for "assemblage," for "definite multitude," for "people of Israel" both according to the flesh and according to the spirit. In the Old Testament one may see everywhere that when the Hebrew has "kahal" [קהל] or "edah" [עדה] the Septuagint translation has συναγωγή or ἐκκλησία, while the Latin has "coetus, congregatio, multitudo, universus populus Israel," or uses the word "ecclesia" itself. If I were to show this at length I should be diverted from my resolution to be brief. Hence it will be sufficient to exhibit a few definite passages by which to make this manifest.

Exod. 12:3: "Speak to all the multitude of the children of Israel." Here for "multitude" the Hebrew has "edah"; the Greek, συναγωγή. Lev. 8:3: "All the congregation (coetus) of the children of Israel." Here the Hebrew has "haedah hakahal" [עדה הקהל], *i. e.,* "all the congregation of the ecclesia," just as the Greek has συναγωγὴν ἐκκλησίας. Num. 20:4: "the assembly (ecclesia) of the Lord." Here the Hebrew has "kahal"; the Greek, συναγωγή. All these instances have as their one object our seeing that by the word "ecclesia" the whole company, congregation, assemblage, army, multitude, of the people of Israel is meant. Hence it is clear that "ecclesia" is used not only for the pious, holy, and faithful, but also for the impious, wicked, and unfaithful, provided only they were of the seed of Abraham according to the flesh and were intermingled with the pious. How often, indeed, it happened that by their open faithlessness certain ones gave plain proof that, though in body and in the opinion of men they were counted as within the church (ecclesia), yet in fact they were anything but within the church that is without spot and without wrinkle! But of this presently.

In like manner in the New Testament also we see that

*This entire chapter was copied into Zwingli's *True and False Religion.* See p. 178.

"ecclesia" is used for all those who have named the name of Christ and who walk and live within the company of Christians, even though in reality they are not very faithful; as when Paul says that he persecuted the ecclesia of God, I Cor. 15: 9. For he persecuted all who were Christians, *i. e.,* who confessed themselves Christians. But among the Christians there are always evil and unfaithful ones, although we do not recognize such unless they betray themselves by their fruits.

Christ Himself has painted this church in the clearest colors in Mat. 13: 24-30, where, by the parable of one sowing good seed in a field and of an enemy, *i. e.,* the devil, secretly mixing in tares, He means nothing else than that all of us who are called Christians receive the word, or at least wish to appear to have received it, yet none the less we admit the devil's seed also. Yet God allows the crops that grow from both grain and tares to continue until the day of harvest; nay, He even commands us to let both grow, though He keeps account of the noxious, who are destined to rejection, and of the wholesome, for whom favor is meantime in store (about which there is not now room to speak). We are, I say, to let both grow until the day of harvest.

Of the same purport is the parable of the net [Mt. 13: 47-50] spread to catch fish, in which at the same time good and bad are gathered, live, stay, and are mingled together. But finally the angels come and separate the foul from the sound and fresh.

To the same effect is the parable of the ten virgins [Mt. 25].

Here we learn that the whole multitude of Christians that counts itself faithful is called one faithful people, one church, and also is not yet the church undefiled; for it has many blemishes, at some of which it is not foreign to Christ to wink.

You now see that in the Old Testament as well as in the New the church was composed of the faithful and of those who were unfaithful but pretended faith, and therefore was not yet such that neither wrinkle nor spot attached to it. For in time past all either made or worshipped a molten calf [cf. Exod. 32: 2-6]; Judas was with Christ; and with the Apostles were Ananias and Sapphira, and Alexander the coppersmith, and false brethren, and spies who attempted to betray Christian liberty and to join circumcision and Christ. Yet they did not, wherever such persons lived with the Christians, change the name "church," used in this manner.

There is, therefore, a second kind of church, which in Ephesians 5: 25-27 Paul describes thus: "Husbands, love your wives, even as Christ loved the church, and gave himself up for it, that he might sanctify it; which he cleansed by the washing of water through the word, that he might unite it to himself, that it might be a noble church, not having wrinkle or spot." No one denies that in the Song of Solomon [2: 14, 5: 2, 6: 8] the one like a dove is the church; but which church? The one, of course, for which Christ gave Himself up, to the end that He might sanctify it to Himself, and which, believing the saying that Christ gave Himself up for us, having been bathed by the washing of water should thereby be so cleansed as to be a glorious and noble church, the spouse of Christ, without any spot or wrinkle. It follows, therefore, that those who believe that Christ so loved us that He gave Himself up for our sanctification are the church of Christ, and free from every spot or wrinkle; for Christ has cleansed them for this purpose, that He might unite them to Himself. Moreover, those whom the Son has freed are free indeed [Jn. 8: 36]; and what God has cleansed, not even Peter is permitted to call unclean [Acts 10: 15]. Therefore, that one beautiful dove, free from every defect, is not some few pontiffs, holy, pious, spotless though they be, but all who firmly believe themselves redeemed by the blood of Christ and as a beautiful spouse united to Him. For the church refuses to be so narrowly restricted as to contain within it only a few members, and those few arrogating this honor to themselves alone; but, spreading over the whole world, it receives members everywhere; and the vaster and wider it is the more beautiful also is it.

But here certain ones object: "Such a church no more exists than does Plato's Republic, because no one lives without fault, because all have sinned, because we deceive ourselves if we say that we have no sin [I Jn. 1: 8]. How, then, is it possible for there to be anywhere a church that has not spot or wrinkle?" These I satisfy in this way: What is without spot and wrinkle is so not of its own nature but thanks to Christ; for thus Paul says: "He (*i. e.,* Christ) loved the church and gave himself up for it, that he might sanctify it" [Eph. 5: 25-26]. Here you have the source of its holiness, and purity, and freedom from every wrinkle. Christ gave Himself up for it that He might sanctify it. For what are we but a slough of vices? Hence, when we desire to be clean we need some other to purify us, and only Christ can be that other. He is the lamb that taketh away the sin of the world. In His name we shall receive from the Father whatever we have asked. But how shall we implore if we do not believe? Therefore only those who lean on Christ implore and ask of the Father through Christ. But who lean on Christ save those who know that He suffered for us? And how is this known? By faith. It is evident, then, that those who lean on Christ are without spot and wrinkle, for the reason that Christ is without these very things, and He is also ours: for He sanctified us that we might be able to be joined to Him through Himself. And this is what St. John [I Jn. 2: 1-2] teaches: "And if any man sin, we have an advocate with the Father, Jesus Christ the righteous: and he is the propitiation for our sins," etc. And Paul, in Hebrews, 10: 19-23: "Since, then, brethren, we have boldness and sure confidence for entering into the holy place through the blood of Jesus, by the way which he made for us, a new and living way, through the veil, that is to say, his flesh; and since we have a great priest, the same Jesus set over the house of God, let us draw near with a true heart and with absolute faith and a firm conviction that our hearts have been sprinkled, *i. e.,* purified, from an evil conscience, and our body washed with pure water: let us hold fast the confession of our hope that it waver not."

By these testimonies we are clearly taught that through Christ the way to God lies perpetually open, since He who is over the house (*i. e.,* the church of God) has been appointed perpetual priest and propitiation; but only on condition that the confession of faith remain unshaken. They, therefore, are without spot and wrinkle who are in Christ; for only He can remove those defects.

This becomes clearer when we quote the words of Christ

Himself. After He had asked the disciples, Matt. 16: 15, "But who say ye that I am?" and after Peter for them all had replied, "Thou art the Christ, the son of the living God," Christ declared, among other things: "And I say unto thee, that thou art Peter, and upon this rock I will build my church." Not to wrangle at length over the sense of these words (for the view that makes Christ, and not Peter, the rock once prevailed; and, more than that, faith asserts this, and the words of Christ elsewhere clearly show that this is the true view, as when He makes Himself the vine and us the branches, which bear no fruit except they abide in the vine, Jn. 15: 4-5)—not to linger, I say, over this, we here see clearer than day that the church of Christ, His spouse (for He Himself says "my"), has its foundation and strength in the fact that it is His when it confesses that Christ is the Son of the living God. This the truth itself asserts. May they perish who assert the contrary! That this seems to some a very trivial matter proceeds from the fact that they only pretend to believe that Christ is the Son of the living God, instead of really believing it. For if anyone believes that it is the Son of God whom He sees nailed to the cross for him, how can he fail to weigh the immensity of his sin, so vast, indeed, that only the Son of God can expiate it; and, at the same time, our weakness, nay, impotence, which is so great that in no way is it given us by our own efforts to draw near to God? When, therefore, the Son of God has once freed us from the death of sin and we firmly believe this, we cannot help being transformed by a wonderful metamorphosis into other men. That we see this so rarely accomplished is due to the fact that, according to the word of the prophet, all are hypocrites [cf. Isa. 9: 17]. And hence the Apostles labor so earnestly, to the end that we may put off the old man and put on the new, namely, Christ [cf. Col. 3: 9-10].

It is a great work to believe that Christ, nailed to the cross, is the Son of God. That this is the work of God, Christ Himself testified, Jn. 6: 29: "This is the work of God, that ye believe on him whom he hath sent." As many, then, as trust in Christ are built upon a rock, which no blasts of winds can shake, no inundating floods wash away. And as many as are built upon this are the church of Christ, for He Himself said "my." But His church cannot be impure and wrinkled. Therefore it follows that those who trust in Christ are without spot and without wrinkle, for they summon up all their zeal to the end that they may not fall back into sin, in which beforetime they were dead, Rom. 6: 2. But they who do not this utter noble thunderings with their lips, but by their deeds betray Christ, with the result that through them the name of God is in bad repute.

This is the church that cannot err—an attribute which the pontiffs arrogate to themselves with as much falseness as impudence. For this church rests upon the word of God alone, which is so firm and immovable that heaven and earth must pass away sooner than one jot of it [Mt. 5: 18]. On the contrary, the church of the pontiffs rests upon its own word. They run, indeed, as if they had been sent by the Lord, but they speak visions, that is, things pleasing to their own heart [Jer. 23: 16]. Hence they spread nothing but darkness before poor wretches' eyes. For as they have not the light of faith, by which the word is recognized and declared to the brethren, behold how great is the darkness! This Christ has very beautifully suggested, saying, Matt. 6: 23: "If therefore the light that is in thee be darkness, how great is the darkness!" That they have not the light of faith is plain from the fact that they do not preach and defend the word of God alone. For faithful is the mind that looks to God alone; and the mind that does this can hear the word of none but God, its spouse, so far is it from being able to inculcate human absurdities in its preaching to others. All this is made plain by the plain words of Christ in John 10: 2, where He teaches that he who enters the sheepfold some other way than by the door is a thief and a robber; and a little later He shows that He is the door. What, then, is entering the Lord's sheepfold through Christ but putting on Christ [Rom. 13: 14]? What but imparting one thing only, the word of Christ, and setting it before those who hunger? For as the Father had sent Him, so also He sent His disciples. Moreover, Christ very sharply combatted the prescriptions and traditions of the pontiffs, and commanded to hear only the word of God. Therefore those who confidently assert that it is through Him they enter into His fold will do battle against human traditions and will busily engage in declaring the word of God alone; if they do not do this, they are, judged by the word of God, thieves and robbers. And since they are such, how is it possible that they cannot err—they who have become thieves and robbers just because they have turned aside from the true path?

Behold, so far are assemblies of certain pontiffs from being the church, the spouse of Christ, which cannot err, that if you weigh them well in the balance you will pronounce them thieves and robbers rather than aught else.

Yet there must still be a glorious church, having neither spot nor blemish, against which the battlements and gates of hell cannot prevail [Mt. 16: 18]; and which, consequently, cannot lapse or err. Christ pictures it in the beautiful parable of the sheep and the shepherd [Jn. 10: 11-30], teaching there that the sheep hear the voice of the shepherd, if he is a shepherd, and that they follow him; but that a stranger they follow not, because they know not his voice. Is it, then, for the sheep to judge whether he who comes to them is a shepherd or thief, whether the voice is shepherd's or robber's? Whence have the sheep such shrewdness as not to blunder? Because of what immediately follows: "I know my sheep, and mine own know me." And whence have the sheep such discerning knowledge of Christ that they take no one else's voice for His? From the fact that they are known by God [Gal. 4: 9]; from the fact that the Father draws them (for no one comes to Christ save him whom his Father draws [Jn. 6: 44]); from the fact that all are taught of God [Jn. 6: 45]. Therefore it follows that only those sheep do not err who know the voice of their shepherd so well that they receive absolutely no other. Here you have the church that cannot err, the one, namely, which knows only the voice of the shepherd, and not of any shepherd whatsoever, but only of the one who enters in by the door, who brings only that which Christ brings, who comes only in the name of the Father as Christ also came, and (to speak briefly) all because there is only one shepherd, although many are wrongly called shepherds. Finally, only that church cannot lapse and err which hears the voice only of its shepherd, God; for only this voice is from God. He who is of God hears God's word. And again: "Ye hear not, because ye are not of God" [Jn. 8: 47]. Therefore those who hear are God's sheep, are the church of God, and cannot err; for they follow the word only of God, which can in no wise deceive. But if they follow another word, they are not Christ's sheep, nor flock, nor church; for they follow a stranger. For it is characteristic of the sheep not even to hear a stranger. For Christ thus continues: "All that came* (understand, 'in their own name') are thieves and robbers, but the sheep did not hear them" [Jn. 10: 8]. Therefore all who have heard thieves and robbers are not sheep of Christ, for Christ's sheep hear not such. Notice, in passing, that danger threatens the sheep if they hear those who declare their own word.

Now you know what church it is that cannot err: namely, that one alone which rests upon the word of God only—not upon that word which Emser supposes that I merely look at, which consists of letters or sentences, but upon that which shines in the heart and recognizes every word, by whomsoever spoken, whether it is the Father and Shepherd's or not. This light is derived from no other source than the Father of lights [Jas. 1: 17], who through His Spirit so teaches His own all things that they judge all things and themselves are judged of no man [I Cor. 2: 16]; for by no one can they be misled. Though one swells with eloquence and another oppresses all by unjust rule, yet our man stands like an immovable rock, he cannot be moved. He knows what voice is God's, and what is a misleader's. And this is the anointing which I John 2: 20 says teaches us all things. This, I say, cannot err, for none can teach it save only God. Do you see how the frigid subtleties of the pontiffs fail when they contend that the meaning of the clerical word must depend upon the judgment of men? Certainly you do, since from the foregoing it is quite evident that nowhere is there faith in the word unless the Father has drawn [Jn. 6: 44], the Spirit has warned, and anointing has taught; and these are one. I confess here that you must be pardoned, Emser, for not accepting this view of the church, since you do not perceive the power of the word. For you will never know

*The true text has "came before me"; but both the Textus Receptus and the Latin Vulgate omit "before me."

what church it is that cannot lapse unless you recognize the word of God, which has constituted the church, causes it to trust in Him, and defends it from error, not permitting it to hear any other word. Only pious minds have this knowledge; for it does not depend on human judgment, but is most firmly seated in men's minds. It is an experience, for all the pious have experienced it. It is not learning, for we see the most learned men ignorant of this most salutary matter. It is for this reason Christ thanked the Father that He hid these things from the wise and revealed them unto babes [Mt. 11: 25]. In vain, then, are we so anxious for certain persons because they refuse to receive the word; but it will not be in vain that with anxiety we pray God to deign to bestow the grace of His Spirit and to draw to a recognition of His word.

Here you see also, Emser, how perfectly consistent are the things which I wrote concerning the church in my *Confutation,** though you quite uncivilly misrepresent them as very incoherent.

I said that this spouse of Christ, the church, was scattered over the whole world, wherever the faithful are, that Christ's sheep might not, like the ass tied at Jerusalem [Mt. 21: 2], be forever bound so miserably to Rome, or to Alexanders, Juliuses, Leos, Hadrians. That you might not think this a rash statement, I said that it is veiled from men's eyes who or how many are within the church of Christ, to the end that it may be seen that the church is not where a few pontiffs meet together, but where men adhere to the word of God and live for Christ; and this is clear and manifest to God alone. So potent an evil is hypocrisy! It is possible, indeed, that not only those who inveigh against the word are outside this church, Christ's spouse, but also those who assert that they are Christ's and who do many pious works for their neighbor. For these things often proceed from a very wicked mind; for there are some whom vainglory controls. But no one can deceive God; to Him the reins and hearts are open [cf. Ps. 7: 10]. Hence I said that this church is unknown to men, and that it will never come together until the last day, when the Son of God will call all nations to Himself and will contend with them in judg-

**i. e., De canone missae epichiresis.*

ment. There it will be seen of what faith each one has been.

Lastly I spoke of individual churches. From the fact that Christ ordered a diseased sheep to be excluded from the flock, Matt. 18: 17, I made the command apply to them, because the universal church of all the members can never come together here, so that we could tell it what brother refused to come to his senses. And this I said not without example, but I adduced the words, and example as well, of Paul, who commanded the church which was then at Corinth to reject for a while him who was living shamelessly with his stepmother until he should repent of his conduct [I Cor. 5: 1, 13]. So in Acts 13 there were in the church at Antioch Paul and Barnabas, Niger and others. Thus in Holy Writ mention often is made of individual churches. But all those churches are one church, Christ's spouse, which the Greeks call the Catholic and we the Universal. This is not a gathering of all the bishops, but a communion of all the saints, *i. e.*, of all the faithful, as the Fathers added in the creed. For among the ancients the article on the communion of saints was lacking; but subsequently, when those who today still pose as the Catholic Church arrogated this name to themselves, it was added in order to explain the name.

And so it is the office of these churches, as is now clear, to reject one who is shamelessly delinquent; and when he comes to his senses and submits to the rule of Christ, to admit again to favor and communion. It is theirs to judge of a shepherd (as was said above), and of doctrine, as in I Cor. 14: 29-32: "And let the prophets speak by two or three, and let the others discern. But if a revelation be made to another sitting by, let the first keep silence. For ye all can prophesy one by one, that all may learn and receive consolation and exhortation. For the spirits of prophets obey prophets." Here we see clearly that the word of God was once treated in a manner far different from that of today. For not only those who belonged to the order of prophets, but also the people generally, those sitting on the benches, were permitted to speak in the church concerning the word which the Spirit had revealed. If this custom had never died out, so many errors would never have been introduced into the church of Christ, for there are always persons who through the Heavenly Spirit detect deceitful pretence on the part of one who is teaching, and when this has once been exposed the word is freed from violent distortion. But this detriment comes from the fact that the spirits of the prophets have refused to be subject to the prophets. And this makes manifest that the spirits of the prophets who have refused to obey and heed brethren who were prophesying have not been of God; for the spirits of true prophets obey those who prophesy. But gradually it has come to such a pass that any twaddle uttered by the most perverse babbler from the pulpit, *i. e.,* in the prophet's place, is regarded as an oracle; and whoever does not so regard it, but mutters even a syllable against it, is given a most cruel cudgelling.

But at this point someone may object that hereby a church, any church at all, is made the judge of the word, and that I have strenuously denied that any judge may be placed over it. I reply that my opinion is the same as before; for always he that is spiritual judgeth all things [I Cor. 2: 15]. But yet, what or how he judges must be heard. Whoever hears the Scripture of the celestial word explained in church judges that which he hears; yet what is heard is not the very word which causes us to believe, for if we were rendered faithful by that word which is read and heard, evidently all of us should be faithful. For somewhere or other all of us have either read or heard the word, especially in these days in which all things, even woods and fields, re-echo the gospel; but, on the contrary, we observe that many both hear and see, yet have not faith. It is clear, then, that we are rendered faithful only by that word which the Heavenly Father proclaims in our hearts, by which also He illumines us so that we understand, and draws us so that we follow. Of this enough has been said above. Those who are imbued with this word judge the word which in a discourse sounds forth and strikes our ears; nevertheless, the word of faith, which resides in the minds of the faithful, is judged by no man, but itself judges the external word. The latter also God has ordered to be declared in public, although faith is not of the external word. This Christ well explained in the parable of the seed falling on the foot-path, on the rock, amidst thorns, and into good ground [Lk. 8: 5-8]. However, the faithful judges not by his own judgment, but by that of the Divine Spirit. That is why Paul said that the spirits of the prophets are obedient to the prophets. For He is not a God of contention and discord, but of unity and peace [I Cor. 14: 33]. Therefore, wherever there is true faith, there also the Heavenly Spirit is recognized as present; and wherever the Heavenly Spirit is, there everybody knows is zeal for unity and peace [cf. Gal. 5: 22]. And so it is that every faithful prophet, wherever he is ignorant or in error, willingly receives correction and teaching, even from the meanest person. Nor is there danger of confusion arising in the church; for if it is through God that the church has been gathered together, there is He in the midst, and all who are faithful strive for unity and peace. If any persist in contending in an arrogant or hateful manner, the faithful will have a keen sense for detecting who are speaking under the influence of passion, and who under the influence of love and the Spirit of God; and they will restrain the chatterboxes.

That they may do this the more easily, they have the criterion by which St. John has shown how to try the spirits, whether they are of God [I John 4: 2-3]: "Every spirit that confesseth that Jesus Christ is come in the flesh is of God: and every spirit that confesseth not that Jesus Christ is come in the flesh is not of God." But what is it to believe that Jesus Christ is come in the flesh? Has this saving power? By no means, unless we believe that He came for us, and that Jesus Christ, *i. e.,* the Anointed, is a Savior to us, He who is truly King and Savior, Son of God and Son of Man. But if He is Salvation, as He truly is, what does it profit to seek salvation elsewhere? Can this be done without insulting Him who is by nature Savior? That spirit, then, is of God which attributes glory only to Him; on the contrary, that is not of God which attributes to a creature that which is God's [Rom. 1: 25]. But if dispute now arises in the church about the meaning of a word, they who are spiritual at once see which meaning tends most to the glory and will of God, and which the opposite; for he that is of the earth cannot help speaking of the earth [Jn. 3: 31]; and he that is of heaven cannot fail to conquer all things with those who are imbued with the same spirit. An example will make this matter clearer. In these days there has been much discussion about the Keys—how rightly let the pious judge; I will not exhaust that point. Some have adjudged them to the Roman pontiff, others to any so-called priest; and when they have wished to seem especially pious, they have alleged that sins are forgiven by God only, yet so that the priest pronounces them forgiven. To this end they have misrepresented the judgment of the Levites, whose province it was to pronounce upon leprosy; the case of the ten lepers, though one of them, who was a Samaritan, returned to thank the Savior, not the priest; the releasing of Lazarus from the grave-clothes. To them I will now oppose the authority of God's word; but first I will wring from the adherents of the Pope, with the assent of their own writers, an admission that the Keys were not given, but only promised, to Peter on the occasion when Christ said, "And I will give unto thee the keys of the kingdom of heaven" [Mt. 16:19]. Then I will ask of all when they were delivered; for they must be delivered, Christ said, and what He said must have been done. Some reply: "On the occasion when He said [Jn. 20:22], 'Receive ye the Holy Spirit: whose soever sins ye forgive, they are forgiven,'" etc. Others: "When He said, 'Feed my sheep,'" Jn. 21:15. Now see how easily they are caught, both when they depart from the right meaning of "Keys" and when they keep to it. In the latter case they are caught thus: If the Keys were delivered to Peter when it was said, "Feed my sheep," then "to feed" is the function of the Keys. Since, then, no one is so stupid as not to see that "to feed" means "to teach by the word," it follows that their violent contention that the Keys were first given only to Peter amounts to nothing else than that to Peter above all others the ministry of the word was committed. For if "to have the Keys" is "to feed" (as it surely is), they cannot deny that the only thing enjoined upon Peter was the diligent and faithful ministry of the word. As to the additional claim that the first giving of this injunction was to Peter, this is idle talk, for the ministry of the word had been previously committed to all on the very eve of the resurrection.

But others, whose way the Lord wills, say thus: I do not deny that the Keys were delivered on the occasion when Christ said, "Receive ye the Holy Spirit," etc., Jn. 20: 22; but that the Keys are some word of a priest, or anything whatsoever but the word of the gospel, I strenuously deny. For what John expresses in the words, "Receive ye the Holy Spirit: whose soever sins ye forgive, they are forgiven unto them; whose soever sins ye retain, they are retained," Luke told in other words, thus [Lk. 24: 45-48]: "Then opened he their mind that they might understand the scriptures; and he said unto them, Thus it is written, that the Christ should suffer, and rise again from the dead the third day; and that repentance and remission of sins should be preached in his name unto all the nations, beginning from Jerusalem. Ye are witnesses of these things." Where Luke said, "Then he opened their mind," John said, "Receive ye the Holy Spirit"; for He is given for this purpose, to open the mind. Mark puts it this way [Mk. 16: 15-16]: "Go ye into all the world, and preach the gospel to the whole creation. He that believeth and is baptized shall be saved; but he that believeth not shall be condemned." Where Mark said, "Go ye into all the world," John said, "As the Father sent me, so also I send you," and Luke, "Should be preached unto all the nations. Ye are my witnesses." Where Mark said, "Preach the gospel to the whole creation. He who believes" (when the gospel has been preached, of course) "and is baptized shall be saved," John said, "Whose soever sins ye forgive, they are forgiven." For only in this way are sins forgiven, if we firmly believe that Christ suffered for us. And although the forgiveness of sins is attributed to the disciples, yet this is only for the reason that the disciples minister the word; for there is not any other name under the sun wherein we must be saved than the name of Jesus Christ [Acts 4: 12]. So Luke expressed this thought thus: "Repentance and forgiveness of sins should be preached in his name unto all the nations." Where Mark said, "He who believeth not shall be condemned," John gave this: "Whose soever sins ye retain, they are retained." Now, the Apostles retained the sins of the unbelieving when, as they were departing from them, they shook off the dust of their feet, according to the command of the Lord, Lk. 10: 11. And so did Paul, as we read in Acts 18: 6. The Keys are, therefore, "to feed." But "to feed" is to declare the gospel. He who believes on it is saved, is set free; for he knows that he has been liberated through the Son. Contrariwise, he who believeth not is condemned, is bound, is given over to the flesh, so that he cannot attain the things of the Spirit.

That this is the sense of three passages from the Gospels is very evident from the fact that they describe independently the appearance of Christ to the disciples and His discourse with them on the very day of the resurrection. This is easily seen by anyone who gives proper attention to the context of the narrative. I will not dwell longer upon this matter, for in my *Conclusions** I have treated it at length. I will now return to the point from which I digressed. If, I say, dispute arises in the church regarding the Keys, pontiffs claiming them for themselves, and priests for themselves, but the word when weighed in the above manner claiming them for God only, what faithful one in the church will not see clearly that the view here taken is most true and certain, if the Keys are recognized as consisting of the word alone, and of that word only which is believed and resides in the minds of the faithful; and that, consequently, the Apostles do nothing more than carry the Keys, that is, dispense the word? For the two other views smack of the flesh, though the one more than the other. That of the Pope's adherents so smacks of the flesh that it has circumscribed not only the mind but almost the whole being of all the faithful. So, then each church judges of the word that is set before it. But how? By the word of faith, which, having through the Spirit been taught within, is in the minds of the faithful. Therefore this judgment is not granted to individual churches in such a manner as to be granted to them singly, for it belongs to the church which is Christ's spouse. But, inasmuch as this never comes together here, it judges through its parts and members. Thus were they taught in the church at Antioch, at Jerusalem; and Moses was read on each Sabbath, etc. Now you have at considerable length what the Holy Scriptures say about the church, the spouse of Christ, which cannot err. That you may be able to grasp it more correctly and more briefly, I will go back and

**i. e., Auslegen und Gründe der Schlussreden.*

reduce it to certain brief propositions, summarizing, as it were, the preceding discussion.

The church that embraces those also who falsely assume the name of Christ is not the spouse of Christ, and there is no mention of it in the creed.

The church that with firm faith rests upon Christ, the Son of God, is the catholic church, the communion of saints which we confess in the creed, having neither spot nor wrinkle. For Christ has washed it with His blood, that it may be His glorious spouse.

This church—nearly in the words of Peter [I Pet. 4: 3]—walks not for the rest of its life in the way of the Gentiles; for it is on its guard against sin, in which it beforetime lay dead. And since its way is polluted as long as it walks in the flesh, it has need of repentance and of expiation through Christ, its head.

This church is known only to God; for man looks on the outward appearance, but God on the heart [I Sam. 16: 7].

This church cannot err, for it rests upon God's word alone. It is the Lord's flock, the sheep whereof hear no one's voice save its shepherd's.

The church of the pontiffs, which declares its own word, is the church of man's enemy, *i. e.*, the devil, who in the silence of the night sows tares [Mt. 13: 24-30]. And the sheep that hear this church are not sheep of Christ; for Christ's sheep hear not the voice of strangers [Jn. 10: 5]. Behold the infallible judgment of God's word!

The church that is the spouse of Christ judges both the shepherd and His word. Therefore the pontiffs are not the lords or judges of the church, but are its ministers; it belongs entirely to the church to cast them out, together with their word, provided it is their own and not Christ's word that they declare.

Since the church, Christ's spouse, can never come together here, it yet always has need of the word. Consequently, through its parts and members, *i. e.*, individual churches, it judges both shepherd and external word, but only through the word of God written in the minds of the faithful.

The individual church also rejects the shameless, and

receives again into favor the penitent; but only by virtue of the fact that it is a member of Christ's church.

The so-called church triumphant has the character and condition of this of ours. Hence I have considered that nothing need be said about it at present.

These things, most sturdy Ibex (for so you like to be called), you should have refuted, not skipped over. I plead the case by means of the Scriptures, not by means of shoutings. Hence you should have shown where I had misunderstood Scripture or had done it violence, instead of giving reasons why "Communing with"* has the first letter written in red ink, and other trifles of that sort. I had previously discussed such matters with learned men,† and had decided they were only trifles. But now prove even one of the above propositions erroneous and you will have accomplished something. But I hope that when you see the firm and strong foundation of Christ's church you will recede from your former error, become its friend, and join to it all your fortunes.

The Intercession of Saints‡

When you write about the intercession of saints, you are so shallow, not to say foolish, that I am convinced you absolutely failed to understand what I wrote, which is indeed of small compass, because I had pursued the subject at greater length elsewhere,§ but of no small dignity, because it savors only of the pure sense of the word of God. Therefore I will for your benefit reduce it to brief form, but in such a way that what is now given briefly shall throw some light upon the earlier writings, which it is impossible to cut down.

I. God alone is good, Luke 18:19.

II. From this one and only source one must derive whatever good is needed. For every good and perfect gift is from above, coming down from the Father of lights, James 1:17.

*In the *Canon of the Mass* these words begin the prayer in commemoration of the dead.

†A reference to the two Zurich disputations of the year 1523.

‡This entire section was copied into the *True and False Religion.* See p. 268.

§In his *Auslegen und Gründe der Schlussreden.* (Egli-Finsler, II, 157-230) and in his *Epichiresis* (Egli-Finsler, II, 574-587).

III. The faithful are distinguished from the unfaithful by this mark: the faithful depend upon this One and Only Good, cling to Him alone, resort to Him alone, draw from Him alone; on the contrary, the unfaithful turn from the Creator to creatures, depend upon them, and hope for aid from them. Deut. 32:39: "See that I am the only one, and that there is no god except me." Now, to be God is nothing else than to be the Highest Good. To be the Highest Good is nothing else than to be "dai" [די], *i. e.*, the sufficiency of every good. That this Good, then, is Himself, God shows to us by the fact that He is the author of all good, aid, assistance; that only He is the Good, that there is no god, *i. e.*, good, and no fountain of any aid except Him. As testimony to the latter fact you have Jer. 2:13: "For my people have committed two evils: they have left me, the fountain of living water, and hewed them out cisterns, broken cisterns, that can hold no water."

IV. The only faithful ones, then, are those who are so filled with the knowledge that they are God's that they do not even name any father except the Almighty Father, so far are they from having hope in another. For of what avail is it to call God Father, if you are not His son and if you do not hope in Him as Father; especially since the Master forbids us to call any man father on the earth? Matt 23:9. For it is he alone who renders us secure in the hope which we have in him, Ps. 4:8: "For thou, Lord, alone madest me to dwell in hope." "Blessed be the man whose hope is the name of the Lord," Ps. 40:4. And, contrariwise: "Cursed is the man that trusteth in man, and maketh flesh his arm, and whose heart departeth from the Lord," Jer. 17:5. Furthermore, he departs from the Lord who seeks elsewhere than with Him for the good which he needs; unless, indeed, it is not an instance of departing when a son deserts his real father and chooses another to whom he may flee and complain about his troubles, and from whom he may receive help. But the Heavenly Father is our Father because He made us, created us, chose us to be a peculiar people, Deut. 32:6. For is not He your Father who took possession of you and made and created you? They, then, are sons of God who have Him for a Father; and those have Him for a Father who recognize Him alone as Father, depend upon

Him, hear Him only, hope all things from Him only.

V. In the next place, that one may without hesitation flee to Him for safety He has Himself everywhere declared in the plainest terms. In Gen. 15:1 He speaks thus to Abraham: "I am thy shield and thy exceeding great reward." The same sort of thing was said to all who with Abraham were faithful: *e. g.,* Lev. 20:8: "I am the Lord who sanctify you"; Num. 35:34: "I am the Lord who dwell among the children of Israel"; Ps. 35:3: "I am thy salvation"; Isa. 43:25: "I, even I, am he that blotteth out thy transgressions for mine own sake"; Ezek. 18:13-32: "Why will ye die, O house of Israel? For I have no pleasure in the death of him that dieth, saith the Lord God. Turn yourselves and live"; Isa. 44:21-22: "Remember these things, O Jacob and Israel, for thou art my servant," etc. "I have blotted out as a thick cloud thy transgressions, and as a cloud thy sins. Return to me, for I have redeemed thee"; also 55:1: "All ye that thirst, come ye to the waters," etc. Throughout there is nothing but God's free invitation to Himself. And in Lev. 26:40-42 He promises favor even to those who had so greatly offended that they were led away into captivity, if only they cried to Him. These few citations from the Old Testament may suffice. For what is anywhere said but that the people should hasten to the true God, should not separate their hope from Him, nor imagine that they would find safety anywhere but with the Heavenly Father, who so often did great and good things for the fathers. For to everyone God is that which he thinks is sufficient to bestow upon him his heart's desire.

VI. As for the New Testament, what is it but a solid and sure confirmation of God's grace? For how can He refuse anything who spared not His own Son but gave Him up for us all? Or how will He not with Him freely give us all things [Rom. 8:32]? Will He who gave a Son refuse heirship and grace? And such a Son as is Himself our salvation? For Jesus is, that He may be the way, the truth, and the life [Jn. 14:6]. In the days of His flesh He associated with publicans and sinners for the purpose of showing the world that He had come to find the lost sheep [cf. Lk. 15:4-6], and to call sinners to Himself, and to turn none away. For thus He exhibits

Himself to us as He cries: "Come unto me, all ye that labor and are heavy laden, and I will give you rest" [Mt. 11: 28]. He, the Son of God, is an earnest of our salvation [Eph. 1: 14]; for through Him we have access to God [Eph. 2: 18]. For no one comes unto the Father but by Him [Jn. 14: 6].

VII. Hence there is no reason for lack of faith to make for itself this excuse: "Of course, I know that all my hope rests in God; but yet I have need of advocates to commend me to that most high God." From its own words one can easily judge what it is that thus speaks, namely, lack of faith. Since you say, "I know that all my hope rests in God," why do you not in all adversities flee to Him? Are you not a brother of His Son [Rom. 8: 29]? Will the Father who gave His Son for you turn you away? Or the Son, who suffered for you and called you brother [Jn. 20: 17]? Do you want to hear something plainer than, "No one cometh unto the Father but by me" [Jn. 14: 6]? Get an intelligent view of the mass of all creatures and you will be forced to confess that not one of them comes to the Father but by the Son. Nor is there any reason for your giving me the everlasting reply, "I need intercessors with the Son." The fact is, you are not willing to see that He Himself came down for the purpose of making clear how completely the opposite of inaccessible He is. To strengthen through Him our hope in God, could anything clearer than this be said: "Whatever ye shall ask the Father in my name, he will give it you," Jn. 16: 23. "In my name," He says, not "in Abraham's name," etc. "For there is one mediator between God and men, the man Jesus Christ," etc., I Tim. 2: 5. If you dignify any other whomsoever by that name, do you not cast contumely upon the Son of God? For who can be our mediator except Him alone who is Son of God and of man? Is not this trampling upon the Son of God? For if a way of approach to God is open by means of so many different advocates (which is the common pernicious belief), then Christ died in vain; He is not the only mediator, the only way; coming to the Father will be elsewise than by the Son; deceitfully He said: "Come unto me all ye that labor," etc. How blasphemous this is, how impious, ungrateful, and pernicious, no one can adequately describe.

VIII. Again, the things commonly adduced in opposition are either frivolous or have been twisted out of shape by the audacity of carnal wisdom. Frivolous are those which Emser querulously vociferates: "The East as well as the West testifies to this (namely, that the saints intercede for us); there is no nation under heaven that does not credit its safe condition in great measure to the prayers of the saints, next after God." To this I reply: "How about the North and the South, the Troglodytes and the Galactophagists?" I plead by Holy Writ, but he yelps to us about East and West. A little later on he bunches together the tutelary gods (as they are called) of nearly all the German cathedral churches, and in the most wretched fashion fishes for favor for his booklet, saying: "Those churches will never be so ungrateful as to believe that the prayers and suffrages of the saints have no power with God, for from them they have received many great benefits." Here, in the first place, he fails to understand that of God are the benefits which he ascribes to the creature. This Peter and John teach clearly, Acts 3:12, by their indignation at the people's ascribing to them the power that healed the lame man, and by their testimony that the power was Jesus Christ's. And Christ also Himself plainly teaches this, saying [Mk. 16:17]: "In my name shall they cast out demons." He said not "in their name," but "in my name," *i. e.*, "by my power." Secondly, Emser does not see that, if we listen to him when he argues on this wise: "Many have experienced the aid of St. Nicholas in storms at sea, therefore Nicholas should be invoked as a son of Jupiter and a tutelary god"—he does not see, I say, that the logical conclusion is this: Apollo and Aesculapius have restored many to health; Castor and Pollux have saved many more from shipwreck than has any Nicholas, if we believe their worshippers: therefore they are to be invoked as Jupiters and helping gods. After this manner Symmachus* once plaintively cried out in defence of his gods—and far more forcibly and learnedly than this apologist of ours—urging the Romans not to desert the gods whose aid they had experienced

*Quintus Aurelius Symmachus, who in 384 presented to Valentinian II a petition pleading for the restoration of the statue and altar of Victory. See Gibbon, *Decline and Fall of the Roman Empire*, chap. 28.

at home and abroad. To serve this purpose carnal wisdom has dared to torture all the passages of Scripture that contain the word "saint," "intercession," and the like. In my *Conclusions* and my *Confutation of the Canon of the Mass* I have restored a large number of them to freedom; therefore, dismissing these, I will now rescue from the hands of our friend Emser only two, upon which he seems most to rely. "I lifted up mine eyes to the hills," he says, "from whence will come my help" [Ps. 121: 1]; and forthwith he cites the testimony of Cassiodorus† and of Bede,‡ who hold the view that the hills are the saints, etc. But the poor fellow does not look to see what immediately follows: "My help cometh from the Lord, who made heaven and earth." What warrant is there in Holy Writ for the Cassi and Duri§ to make saints out of hills? A half-blind person can see that all the prophet is so firmly intent upon is to make himself acceptable to God, because he expects his help to come from no other source but Him who made heaven and earth. The other passage is: "Remember Abraham, Isaac, and Jacob," etc. [Exod. 23: 13], where at first he did not notice that "O God, remember Abraham, Isaac, and Jacob, to whom thou swarest" and "Abraham, intercede for us" are by no means equivalent, since the former is said to God, that He may deign to bless the children of Israel for the sake of the fathers, whereas the latter would be said to Abraham, though it is found nowhere in Holy Writ. But, since contention always has a defence to present and cannot be silent, he roars out: "Since we see that the people of Israel cried to the Lord in the name of their fathers, surely we also may do the same." To this I will reply briefly in the words of Peter, Acts 4: 12: "And in none other is there salvation" (he is speaking of Christ); "neither is there any other name under heaven given to men wherein we must be saved." And so, Emser, do this: pray to the good and great God to give you a sound mind, wherewith you may learn that, as from the beginning of the world those have been cast out

†In his *Expositio in psalterium.*

‡In his *De psalmorum libro exegesis.*

§Cassi et Duri: a play on the name Cassiodorus: the Vains and the Rudes. The way was prepared for this by using above the plurals "Cassiodoros et Bedas."

among the faithless who sought for help elsewhere than with the one and only God, Rom. 1:25 (for God willed that we should not go limping between the two sides, as He testified through Elijah [I Kings 18:21]), so today also those are deservedly counted among the faithless who call for aid upon others than the one and only God. His name in Greek is from θέειν [to run], because He causes all things to move, and runs to aid all things. For He is a God at hand, not a God afar off [Jer. 23:23]; who, even before thou callest, says: "Lo! here am I." When you have once learned this, you will become as great an influence among God's simple folk—leading them to found all their thought and hope on God, whereby they may become worshippers of the true God—as you have been a public crier, calling them from God to creatures, in which task you have been a real apostate, or more probably an unbeliever. When this has come to pass, I shall at length rejoice that the Lord has enrolled you in the ranks of the faithful. For as long as you cling to creatures, you have not yet laid hold upon that peerless Spouse which in the Song of Solomon [3:4] the soul rejoices to have laid hold on, saying: "I held him and would not let him go." Imitate holy men and saints just as far as they are imitators of Christ, according to Paul's word [cf. I Cor. 11:1]. And meantime firmly believe that where two or three with one accord ask something upon earth from the Lord, they will obtain it [Mt. 18:19]. And when you speak of the prayers of saints, or of their loving care, take care to think of the sainted dead, *i. e.,* of those who are already citizens of heaven, just as you would of those who are still sojourners and exiles here. For anything more consult my *Conclusions* and my *Confutation of the Canon;* and permit me now to take in sail on this subject, that I may shortly come to an end.

MERIT*

When you came to the passage on Merit, you did not touch it even with a finger, but referred to a certain Roffensis,†

*This section was copied into the *True and False Religion.* *See* p. 275.

†*i. e.,* man of Rochester. This was John Fisher, Bishop of Rochester. Emser had cited his *Assertionis Lutheranae confutatio,* published in 1523.

though whether he is a man or perchance some god, I don't know. For if he holds a view of merit different from that of the Holy Scriptures, he must be above that which is and is considered deity; for the holy men of God spoke imbued with the spirit of God [cf. II Pet. 1: 21]. If this Roffensis of yours communicates better and surer things, he undoubtedly is superior to Him who communicated earlier things, which I have followed. But as this cannot be the case, you ought to have exerted yourself to overthrow the things in which I trust; and where I misunderstood God's word you ought to have led me to the true fountains. For, however highly the most excellent men think of Roffensis, yet I should never have referred to him, but to the Holy Scriptures, which Christ Himself commanded us to search [Jn. 5: 39].

To the rich man who with Tantalus was suffering from thirst He said by the mouth of Abraham: "They have Moses and the prophets; let them read them [Lk. 16: 29]. So ought you, I say, to have done, and especially since you could have done it briefly, as I am going to do here.

"No one cometh unto the Father but by me," says the Truth, Jn. 14: 6. For the Truth is the same as the Way and the Life. Therefore we come to God not by our merits, but by Christ only.

Jn. 15: 4-5: "As the branch cannot bear fruit of itself, except it abide in the vine; so neither can ye, except ye abide in me. I am the vine, ye are the branches." So of our strength we can do nothing, but only by the strength of the vine. What, then, do we merit?

"Behold the lamb of God that taketh away the sins of the world," Jn. 1: 29. Our merits, then, do not take away sins; for if they did Christ would have been sent from heaven in vain. Of Him the lamb caught in the thicket and slain by Abraham in his son's stead was a symbol [cf. Gen. 22: 13].

Matt. 19: 26: "With men this," namely, to be saved, "is impossible; but with God all things are possible." Therefore we get ready our own merits in vain, if being saved is not a matter of human power.

Lk. 17: 10: "So ye also, when ye shall have done all the things that are commanded you, say: We are unprofitable servants." If we are unprofitable servants, how is it possible for our merits to be of any use; since a reward for merit can be given only when we have been profitable?

Jn. 15: 5: "Apart from me ye can do nothing." Since, then, we can do nothing, we merit nothing.

Ibid. "Ye did not choose me, but I chose you." Therefore we are not united to God because of our merits, but by the kindness of Christ.

Jn. 9: 1-3: When Jesus was asked by whose sin it was that the man whose sight He a moment afterwards restored was born blind, He replied: "Neither did this man sin, nor his parents; but that the works of God should be made manifest in him." Therefore it is by the free will of God that thus or so we are born, and live, and spend our days. But God manifests His glory according to that same will; and so no one may say: "Why didst thou make me thus" [Rom. 9: 20]? But since the innermost working of divine providence, which we call predestination, here comes into view, and since I must hurry on to other things, I will pass on from Christ's words to Paul's.

Rom. 11: 6: "But if it (*i. e.*, election) be of works, then is it no more grace" or gift. Hence those who rely upon works repudiate grace. Read the whole Epistle to the Romans and the one to the Galatians, and you will see what merit is and what grace is. But if (as seems the case) you are more given to the Fathers than to the one Heavenly Father, read Augustine's book, "On Free Will and Grace."

Rom. 3: 20, Gal. 3: 10: "By the works of the law shall no flesh be justified in his sight." Then why so much about merit?

Rom. 3: 23-24: "All have sinned and fall short of the glory of God, being justified freely by his grace." If, then, we have all so sinned that we have need of the glory of God, and He has manifested His glory by freely justifying us, merit is nothing but a harmful fiction.

I Cor. 15: 22: "As in Adam all die," etc. Therefore in Adam we all are dead. How then shall we work anything living or worthy of life? But "in Christ shall all be made alive"; therefore not by our own merits.

Gal. 2: 16: "Yet knowing that a man is not justified by

the works of the law, but through faith in Jesus Christ." If, then, deeds do not make us blessed, why do we invent merit?

Gal. 2: 21: "For if righteousness is through the law, then Christ died for nought." Therefore if heaven is entered by means of our works, in vain was Christ sent to open it.

Gal. 5: 4: "Ye are severed from Christ, ye who would be justified by the law; ye are fallen away from grace." Therefore they who rely upon works are aliens from Christ. For I suppose you understand well that to be justified by the law is not merely to know the law or to read it, but to try to carry it out so as to be justified. For it would be foolish to think Paul supposed anyone is saved by the tenor or sense of the law.

Philip. 2: 13: "For it is God that worketh in you both to will and to work."

Everything will fail me—paper, pen, time—sooner than the testimonies by which we see clearer than day that blessedness is freely given us only by the grace of God and not because of our merits. And this grace is most richly imparted and made sure through Jesus Christ, so that we all receive of his abundance.

I do not deny that many passages in which merit seems to be asserted might be adduced on the other side; but we must always have recourse to the rule that, whenever the same thing is credited both to God and to us, we are always to follow the view that looks to the glory of God, and, hallowing His name, to refer everything to it, instead of that view which assigns something to us; although God, through loving-kindness, in which He never fails us, sometimes attributes to us as His ministers and sons things that are His alone. For we are His sons only by His own gift, as when He says, Mt. 10: 40: "He that receiveth you receiveth me"; and [Mt. 10: 8]: "Go ye, heal the sick, cleanse the lepers," etc.; and [Jn. 20: 23]: "Whose soever sins ye forgive, they are forgiven unto them." In innumerable other passages, He attributes to us that which cannot possibly be any one's but His. Thus we see that here, too, in the case of merit, to our works is attributed, even by the mouth of God, that which is of His grace, for no other reason than the one just mentioned: namely, because of His loving-kindness; or because among the members of Christ there are always some who still have need of milk [cf. I Cor. 3: 2], who are slow in reaching the stage when they renounce themselves and are wholly drawn to God, when it is no longer they that live but Christ liveth in them [Gal. 2: 20], when they realize that they do not even live save for the reason that God is the life, motion, and activity of all things. But this also I have treated more fully in my *Conclusions* and my *Confutation of the Canon.*

The Mass

A little while ago you referred me to Roffensis; now, when you are discussing the Mass, sometimes you refer to your *Vindication** written against Luther, other times you perpetrate some miserable rubbish. If one may measure the *Vindication* by your cawings (like a lion by its claws), it does Luther as little harm as your present empty chattering does me. I do not know the contents of your *Vindication,* for your books never reach us. So I will offer here only a very few things about the Mass, but those so unassailable that, even if not only you but also the Roman pontiff with all his adherents should move up all your engines of knowledge and eloquence, you would all have to retire without having accomplished a thing. And this solid and immovable strength does not come from myself, but, like everything else that I bring forward against you, is drawn from the storehouse of the Holy Scriptures. So, in the first place:

The New Testament is eternal, as is proved by Isa. 9: 2 and Jer. 31: 31. Therefore the blood also with which the New Testament is sprinkled must be eternal; for it is the blood of the eternal Son of God, I Pet. 1: 19; Heb. 9: 14.

I. The blood of Christ alone takes away our sins; for He is the only one who takes away the sins of the world and who has reconciled all things through His blood, Col. 1: 20. For if sins could have been expiated in any other way, Christ would have died in vain, and those who eat Him would still hunger, those who drink Him would none the less thirst. Far be this from the minds of believers. He Himself, lifted up from the earth, has drawn all things to Himself [cf. Jn. 12: 32]. But

*Emser's *Missae Christianorum contra Lutheranam missandi formulam assertio,* published in 1524.

sin also is not removed without blood, Heb. 9: 22.

II. But the blood of Christ was offered once only; for it is the eternal blood of God's eternal Son, Heb. 9: 12: "Through his own blood he entered in once for all into the holy place."

III. Therefore the blood of Christ, offered once for all, endures forever to remove the sins of all men.

In the second place:

I. Christ is offered only when He suffers, sheds His blood, dies. In fact, these are equivalent. Proof: Paul says, Heb. 9: 25-26: "Nor yet that he should offer himself often, etc., else must he often have suffered since the foundation of the world." Therefore, "to offer Christ" is for Christ to suffer; for Paul proves that the offering of Christ must be the only offering of the kind, from the fact that He was slain only once. Therefore there is offering only when there is death; for offering follows death. For the offering is accomplished only when that which is offered has been slain.

II. Christ can no more die, suffer, shed His blood, Rom. 6: 9-10: "Christ, who rose from the dead, dieth no more; death no more hath dominion over him. For the death that he died, he died unto sin, and that once; but the life that he liveth he liveth unto God."

III. Therefore Christ can no more be offered up; for He cannot die.

I now admonish you not to skip over any one of these propositions, but to examine each carefully. If you do the latter, you will never make the sacrament of the Eucharist into an oblation, though on land and sea you gather all the testimonies of the Fathers. For, no matter how many you bring, they cannot weaken the word of God, except perchance with those who hold the word of man in higher esteem than the word of God, upon whom we have no more effect than upon unbelievers. Grant, then, that the Eucharist is spiritual food, by which those who believe that Christ's death is for them a means of life cement, join, unite, themselves together into the one body of Christ. So Paul, in I Cor. 10: 17 calls all the multitude which proclaims, in the way explained, the Lord's death, one body and one bread; for by that means of grace we all partake of the one bread and the one cup. That will be far the most salutary use of this sacrament. For, since Christians ought to live as one body, the members cannot be cemented together more faithfully, closely, and strongly than with that cement which made both one, namely, Christ [cf. Rom. 12: 4-5]. Therefore all who claim to be Christ's will prove that this is really the case by regarding a brother as a member—eye, hand, or foot; if they do not exhibit this, they who come to this table eat and drink judgment to themselves [cf. I Cor. 11: 29]. For it is set for this purpose: that, eating together the same bread, *i. e.,* through the faith that is in Christ Jesus, and coalescing into one body, we may by this holy sacramental initiation, as it were, be united into the one army and peculiar people of God.

Purgatory*

You were as much surprised as if you had found a horseshoe (if one may use a native proverb in a foreign language) that I rejected purgatory because of these words of Christ: "He that believeth and is baptized shall be saved" [Mk. 16: 16]. Yet nothing more effective could be employed for exposing the mercenary fictions about purgatory of those who think that godliness is gain [cf. I Tim. 6: 5]. For by these words above all is revealed by what way salvation comes to the wretched, namely, by faith; and if by faith, then not by works. Just see, now, how purgatory has all at once vanished; for it had been cooked up to patch the holes left by our works; yet not by them does one come to God, but by faith.

Hence it follows that:

"He that believeth and is baptized shall be saved"; not, he that is roasted in a purifying fire. For it must be that all who die depart hence either in the faith of Christ or without that faith. If they go hence in faith, they are saved; for He says: "He that believeth shall be saved." If in disbelief, they are condemned; for on the other side He says: "He that disbelieveth shall be condemned" [Mk. 16: 16].

Jn. 3: 16-18: "God so loved the world, that he gave his only begotten Son, that whosoever believeth on him should not perish, but have eternal life. For God sent not his Son into the world to judge the world, but that the world should be

*This section was copied into *True and False Religion.* *See* p. 286.

saved through him. He that believeth on him is not judged; but he that believeth not hath been judged already, because he hath not believed on the name of the only begotten Son of God."

You see, in the first place, that the Son was given that he who believeth on Him should have eternal life. Next, you see that eternal life is to follow. But that would not be eternal which would during a long period of time endure grievous suffering in a purgatory fire. In the third place, you see that the world is saved through Christ. In the fourth place, that he who believeth on Him is not judged; yet, He who would be thrust into purgatory certainly would be judged. For, after weighing men's offences, the Roman pontiffs, like Minos and Rhadamanthus, cast them into Cocytus or send them off to the Fortunate Islands. In the fifth place, he that believeth not has been condemned already, because he has not relied upon the grace and strength of Christ. This, therefore, is assured, that we depart hence either faithful or unfaithful, etc.

Yet, lest someone suspect danger in delay (as the saying is), let us hear what Truth again says, Jn. 5: 24: "Verily, verily" (notice the asseveration), "I say unto you, He that heareth my word, and believeth him that sent me, hath eternal life; and he cometh not into judgment, but hath passed out of death into life." But what, pray, is judging, if to sentence to the fire of purgatory is not to judge? Therefore, those who trust in Christ pass, nay, have passed, out of death into life, not life that lasts but for a time, but eternal life.

And the rich man of the parable, who sees Lazarus in Abraham's bosom, is driven to despair by these words: "Between us and you there is a great gulf, so that neither can go across to the others," etc. [Lk. 16: 26]. But here the discourse is about those released from the body, and it posits only two regions, one represented by the person of Lazarus, the other by that of the rich man. Hence those who depart hence either are carried by angels into heavenly mansions and cannot descend to those who are in another place; or else they are thrust into the lower world and will never be allowed to ascend.

Why, then, do we wrangle so fiercely, when Truth says that the latter cannot ascend and the former cannot descend?

Is it our business to manufacture in another world penitentiaries, prisons, fetters, fires, cold, hunger, and other torments? Why, then, do we mislead wretched consciences with these fictions?

Rom. 8: 1: Paul asserts that no condemnation awaits those who are in Christ Jesus. Therefore, if we continue firm and immovable in Christ Jesus unto the end, we shall be saved, Mt. 24: 13.

On the very same day on which he shared Christ's punishment, the robber was a participant of His joy and glory [Lk. 23: 43]. Where did he endure scourgings and the other evils? Or is God unjust, that He should not match His words with deeds? Not so, for we see that in the case of the robber He exactly fulfilled the saying, "He hath not come into judgment, but hath passed out of death into life" [Jn. 5: 24].

Paul forbids us to be anxious concerning them that fall asleep, I Thess. 4: 13, as if we had no hope of a future life, just as the heathen have no hope. But if there were a purgatory, undoubtedly he would have taught us to sorrow for those who we knew were being sadly afflicted with torments. Therefore, since he had occasion to mention the dead, and, more than that, to discuss the anxiety of the living in regard to them, and yet gave not the slightest hint of purgatory, it is quite evident that Paul knew nothing about purgatory. He realized that it was sufficient for him to know Christ and Him crucified [I Cor. 2: 2].

But what need of many words, when we see that purgatory has the support only of human fiction and not of God's word? For all the passages of Holy Scripture used in its defence have been violently twisted to serve that purpose.

Therefore, Emser, henceforth consider not how readily you can rise to heights of insult or of eloquence, but how truly and justly you can speak. Do you think that what you are after in your writings is not clear even to a blind man? Yet all you prove by them is that you are a blatherskite, and that for your belly's sake you are furnishing the Romanists a feeble defence. Their domination is so little able to last that, though it were defended by all the arms of all the princes, nevertheless its patrons will perish along with its vassals sooner than it be restored. Wherefore, since you are a German, you ought loyally to befriend your race, even though Christ is of little concern to you. For you see how all are embracing Christ returned from Egypt,* are listening solely to His word, and cannot be torn from Him even by death; wherefrom there would arise nothing but peace, joy, righteousness, holiness, and innocence, were there not certain illy employed idle fellows like yourself, enemies of all tranquillity, who so persistently disturb the common safety as to have no regard for evils, seditions, and wars, that they may supply an abundance of everything to the belly, their God [Phil. 3: 19], for its gluttonous use. Indeed, I do not hesitate to say that they would make a soup of the whole world, did we but connive at it. Do you, then, favor the work already begun; do not live for the ruin of Germany; do not suppose that they act wrongly who rescue the celestial word from an iniquitous tyranny. But if you cannot have a mind so fair, transfer your attention from matters of divinity to medicine, that you may at least cure your gout, either with ox-dung, or with rape elixir, or with hot vinegar. For you are naturally less fitted for sacred letters than for anything else.

Farewell, and may God grant you a good mind!

**i. e.*, the Reformation.

Index

Scriptural Citations

Thurs
26 May

BRS - 6.20 → CPH - 11.05

Sat
28 May

CPH 16.25 → BRS - 21.15